TALLAHASSEE
LIBRARY
COMMUNITY COLLEGE

D1595800

Captives in Gray

Captives in Gray

The Civil War Prisons of the Union

Roger Pickenpaugh

THE UNIVERSITY OF ALABAMA PRESS
Tuscaloosa

Manufactured in the United States of America

Typeface: AGaramond

∞

The paper on which this book is printed meets the minimum requirements of American National Standard for Information Sciences-Permanence of Paper for Printed Library Materials, ANSI Z39.48-1984.

Library of Congress Cataloging-in-Publication Data

Pickenpaugh, Roger.
Captives in gray : the Civil War prisons of the Union / Roger Pickenpaugh.
p. cm.
Includes bibliographical references and index.
ISBN 978-0-8173-1652-5 (cloth : alk. paper) 1. United States—History—Civil War, 1861–1865—Prisoners and prisons. 2. United States. Army—Prisons—History—19th century. 3. Military prisons—United States—History—19th century. I. Title.
E615.P53 2009
973.7'71—dc22

2008043153

To Parker Dianne Brooks

Contents

List of Illustrations ix

Acknowledgments xi

1. "Arrangements should be at once made": Plans and Prisoners, 1861 1

2. "I fear they will prove an elephant": The First Wave of Prisoners, 1862 19

3. "All seem rejoiced at the idea of going": Prisoner Exchange, 1862–63 43

4. "In view of the awful vortex": The Collapse of the Cartel and the Second Wave of Prisoners 62

5. "The first time I ever desired to be in a penitentiary": Capture and Transport 80

6. "Nothing to do & nothing to do it with": The Constant Battle with Boredom 94

7. "i had rather bee hear then to bee a marching": Keepers in Blue 118

8. "Don't be so hasty and you may get out": The Possibility of Escape 160

9. "Almost starving in a land of plenty": Rations and Retaliation 180

10. "Inevitable death awaited its victims": The Health of the Prisoners 202

11. "Our honor could in no way be compromised": The Road to Release 220

Notes 239

Bibliography 269

Index 279

Illustrations

Following page 144

1. The Old Capitol Prison in Washington, DC 145
2. The parade ground at Fort Warren in Boston Harbor 145
3. Camp Morton, a training camp at the Indiana State Fairgrounds 146
4. Another view of Camp Morton, showing the stream that ran through the middle of the camp 146
5. Confederate prisoners at Camp Douglas in Chicago in 1864 147
6. Prisoners at Camp Chase Prison No. 3 147
7. Barracks at Camp Chase for Union recruits 148
8. Johnson's Island 149
9. A portion of the Hoffman Battalion 150
10. Handbill for a performance by the Rebel Thespians at Johnson's Island 151
11. Fort Delaware, located on Pea Patch Island in the Delaware River 152
12. Fort Delaware prisoner barracks 153
13. Point Lookout prison, established to accommodate captives taken at Gettysburg 154
14. The busy wharf at Point Lookout 154
15. Roll call at the Rock Island prison 155
16. "Riding the mule" was a common punishment at Union prisons 156
17. Guards from the 108th United States Colored Troops, Rock Island 157
18. At Elmira tents initially housed prisoners 157

19. Eventually barracks were built for the Elmira prisoners 158
20. Col. William Hoffman 158
21. Gen. Henry W. Wessells 159
22. Belle Plain, Virginia, served as a holding camp 159

Acknowledgments

Of all the debts incurred in writing this book—and they are many—the greatest is to my wife, Marion. Whether as a tireless (and skillful) researcher, a thorough indexer, or a patient listener, she was there from first to last. In addition, she understands how these books have a tendency to take over my life, and her support has been a blessing.

My mother, Fern Pickenpaugh, also served as a keen proofreader and an eager supporter. From an early age she drilled grammar into my head, and if my writing sometimes falls short, it does so despite her best efforts.

I was also lucky to have family strategically placed for research purposes. Stepdaughters Anya Crum and Jocelyn Brooks, son-in-law Patrick Brooks, granddaughter Parker Dianne Brooks, and grandson Patrick Harrison Brooks live close enough to the Washington, DC, subway system to make work at the National Archives easy. More important, their company gives me much to look forward to after a day spent sifting through old prison records.

My sister and brother-in-law, Jill and Gene Stuckey, live in Atlanta and Plains, Georgia. They, too, offered support along with a base of operations. As work begins on *Captives in Blue,* I expect to see much more of them.

Locally I had a number of strong supporters. Ken Williams, Gary S. Williams, and Mary Lou Podlasiak of the Noble County Authors' Guild offered proofreading skills and empathy. Retired colleague Dave Arbenz kept alive his record of proofreading everything I have churned out. My fellow teachers at the Shenandoah Elementary School were extremely supportive, as were principals Mike Romick and Sandy Goff. A gifted former student, Emily Murphy, also helped with proofreading.

Dr. Rick Nelson of the Ohio State University Hospitals shared his considerable expertise when questions arose concerning the health of the prisoners.

In visiting prison sites throughout the North, I encountered numerous local residents who were eager to offer assistance. Pat Broderick took me on a very interesting and informative tour of Rock Island. Professor David Bush was a gracious and informative host when I visited the archeological dig he has been conducting at Johnson's Island. Public library staffs in Sandusky, Ohio, and Elmira, New York, helped me secure many valuable materials. Paul Clay and Lois Neff of the Hilltop Historical Society in Columbus were key allies in locating Camp Chase materials. R. Hugh Simmons and Martha Bennett of the Fort Delaware Society guided me through the society's impressive collections. I also received valuable information from Daniel Citron of Fort Delaware State Park.

Innumerable archivists at institutions around the country made the task of research easy and enjoyable. Among those providing key assistance were Jill Abraham and DeAnne Blanton (National Archives); Edward Gaynor (University of Virginia); Janie Morris (Duke University); Alanna J. Patrick (Mississippi Department of Archives and History); Naomi Nelson (Emory University); Jennifer Ford (University of Mississippi); Ed Frank (University of Memphis); Laura Clark Brown (University of North Carolina); Gregory Stoner and Lee Shepard (Virginia Historical Society); Jim Holmberg and Rebecca Rice (Filson Historical Society); Michael Ridderbusch (West Virginia University); Amy Shaffer (Virginia Tech); Jeffrey Flannery (Library of Congress); Dale Couch (Georgia Department of Archives and History); and Marylin Hughes (Tennessee State Library and Archives). Mary Williams, Kate Wenger, and Zelda Patterson of the Muskingum College Library handled numerous interlibrary loan requests pleasantly and efficiently.

The staff of the University of Alabama Press went above and beyond to make the daunting process of producing a book as painless as possible. All of my questions, no matter how inane, received prompt and cheerful responses.

Captives in Gray

I

"Arrangements should be at once made"

Plans and Prisoners, 1861

In the summer of 1861 the American psyche reflected a combination of patriotism and impatience. The former had been fueled on April 12 when Confederate guns fired on the American flag at Fort Sumter in the harbor of Charleston, South Carolina. The result had been an outpouring of volunteer soldiers that would reach 640,000 men before the year was over. The latter had grown over the following weeks as the Northern people began to wonder why the soldiers they had sent away with such enthusiasm had not yet been given the opportunity to win the war. "On to Richmond!" was the cry of a public that expected—and was beginning to demand—a quick and easy victory. This feeling was not limited to exuberant citizens. Newspaper editorialists and members of Congress had begun to ask the same question as July arrived.[1]

Among the few realists that summer was Montgomery Meigs. A career officer, fifth in the 1836 graduating class at West Point, Meigs had been named quartermaster general of the Union army on June 16, 1861. With the assignment came the rank of brigadier general and responsibility for overseeing military spending that would eventually exceed $1 billion. The problems that Meigs confronted in the weeks following his appointment were daunting. First the quartermaster general had to secure arms, uniforms, and equipment for the troops pouring in from the states, as well as horses and wagons to enable those troops to move. Beyond that he had to organize a department and a contract system that would guarantee that the army would continue to be supplied as the war continued.

Unlike other Union officials, Meigs realized the conflict would continue for some time. He also realized early on that his boss, Secretary of War Simon Cameron, "was an utter babe-in-the-woods so far as administering an army was concerned." For example, only five days after his appointment, Meigs found it necessary to urge Cameron to see to it that all factories capable of manufacturing rifle muskets begin doing so at maximum capacity.[2]

On July 12 Meigs turned his attention to another topic. Writing to Cameron, he predicted that in "the conflict now commenced it is likely to be expected that the United States will have to take care of large numbers of prisoners of war." Up to that point, Meigs noted, "persons arrested on suspicion of disloyalty" had been housed in "the common jail of Washington." The quartermaster general was already searching for "some building here more suitable for their temporary safe-keeping." As military campaigns commenced, many more captives would begin to arrive. "Arrangements should be at once made for their accommodation," Meigs insisted, "to avoid great embarrassment when they begin to come in." Toward that end, Meigs made two recommendations. One was the appointment of a commissary general of prisoners. This officer would be "charged with the care of prisoners now in our hands and preparations for those likely to fall into our possession." The other was the selection of a "depot and place of confinement for prisoners of war." Meigs suggested one of "the Put-in-Bay Islands of Lake Erie," located near the community of Sandusky, as the best spot to establish a permanent Union prison.[3]

After receiving Cameron's approval of his plans, Meigs, on October 3, recommended Lt. Col. William Hoffman for the post of commissary general of prisoners. Four days later Hoffman received orders from the quartermaster general to head for Lake Erie. He was to visit four islands, North Bass, Middle Bass, South Bass, and Kelley's Island, and "examine them with reference to the lease of the ground upon some of them for a depot for prisoners of war." He was also authorized to visit other islands he found to be "better fitted for the purpose." Meigs placed only one restriction on the mission. "The locality selected," he ordered, "should not be in a higher latitude than that of the west end of Lake Erie in order to avoid too rigorous a climate."[4]

In naming Hoffman commissary general of prisoners, Meigs selected a man who had spent his entire life with the military. The son of a career officer, he had grown up at a succession of posts. Hoffman then made the army his career, graduating from West Point in 1829. By the time the guns sounded at Fort Sumter, Hoffman had three decades of military experience behind him. Along the way he had shown many of the traits that would characterize his Civil War service. "Although never brilliant," his biographer notes, "he was an able and efficient officer, earning the commendations of his superiors." Hoffman was also "a stern disciplinarian, who seemed to have memorized the army regulations."[5]

The new commissary general of prisoners brought a wealth of practical experience to his position that would aid him in overseeing the construction of the Union's Lake Erie prison. His frontier duties had included the erection of Fort Bridger and the rebuilding of Fort Laramie. Life on the post–Mexican War frontier had also led Hoffman to develop "a habitual preoccupation, bordering on an obsession, for thrift." This attitude was born of necessity as the War Department slashed funds for western outposts. Quartermasters were ordered to erect only the "cheapest kind" of barracks, and post commanders were urged to have their men provision themselves by raising their own crops. Like many other officers, Hoffman had established a "post fund" by reselling surplus rations to the commissary. While commanding at Newport Barracks, Kentucky, in the 1850s, this fund had allowed him to build an icehouse and a "ten pin alley" and purchase such items as curtains and vegetables for his men. It was a concept that Hoffman would continue as he settled into his role as commissary general of prisoners.[6]

Hoffman also brought a brief experience as a military captive to his new position. The secession crisis of 1861 found Hoffman in Texas commanding the Eighth United States Infantry. Perhaps he should have become suspicious when his command was stationed at the Alamo. In any event, he and his men were soon surrendered to a Texas home guard by Hoffman's superior, Gen. David Twiggs. Twiggs joined the Confederate army, and Hoffman and other Unionist soldiers found themselves on their way north. They carried with them paroles pledging that they would not "take up arms or serve in the field against the Government of the Confederate States of America" until exchanged. This limited Hoffman's options severely and made him available for the role Meigs had in mind. Hoffman did not desire the position. He attempted to arrange a special exchange that would free him for active service, going as far as to write an appeal to Cameron. All was in vain, and like the good soldier he was, Hoffman assumed the duties of what would prove to be a thankless post.[7]

Those duties first took him to Lake Erie to determine the best site for the military prison that Meigs desired. Arriving in early October 1861, Hoffman was thorough in his island-hopping expedition. He quickly ruled out North, Middle, and South Bass Islands. Each offered a variety of problems. North Bass was far too close to Canadian islands, making escape or rescue realistic dangers. Besides that, the residents of the island, farmers and fishermen, were not willing to give up their land "for any reasonable rent if at all as they make their homes there." Middle Bass posed the same problem. It also did not have any cleared land. South Bass was largely occupied by vineyards, and Hoffman feared that the few residents living there could not resist "the depredations of lawless men," a blunt reference to the soldiers who would occupy the post. In addition to those problems, none of the three islands was close enough to Sandusky to transport construction materials easily. Hoffman also visited Kelley's Island, located nearby. He found it to be a likely site except for one problem. The island contained a "wine and brandy establishment," Hoffman noted, "which I fear would be too great a temptation to the guard to be overcome by any sense of right or fear of punishment."[8]

After studying and rejecting the first four islands, Hoffman reported, he next visited Johnson's Island. Located in Sandusky Bay, the three-hundred-acre island was two and three-quarter miles from Sandusky. It offered forty acres of cleared land, fallen timber that could be utilized as fuel, and a reasonable lease price of $500 a year. Hoffman informed Meigs that Sandusky was "a cheap and abundant market for lumber." The commissary general of prisoners had "consulted with an experienced builder there," who said he could have seventeen buildings up at the site by December 10. Hoffman proposed erecting four two-story barracks for the enlisted prisoners, each capable of holding 270, plus a separate barracks for Confederate officers. Quarters for guards and officers, a hospital, and a storehouse would also be required. "I would suggest a substantial plank fence to inclose the ground on three sides," Hoffman wrote in his report, "[and] a high open picketing closing the fourth toward the water for security in winter time." He also called for a blockhouse "sufficiently large for the guard" and a smaller blockhouse "at the angle near the water to guard that front." Hoffman estimated that all of this, plus stoves and other needed equipment, would cost $26,266.[9]

Meigs gave his approval to the proposal and on October 26 dispatched Hoffman to Sandusky Bay to establish the depot. "In all that is done," Meigs insisted, "the strictest economy consistent with security and proper welfare of the prisoners must be observed." This comported with Hoffman's inclinations, and for the next four years he would take these instructions literally and follow them rigidly. His near-obsessive insistence upon the cheapest materials and the most economical methods has often led historians to dismiss Hoffman as an unfeeling penny-pincher. However, while adopting Meigs's insistence upon "the strictest economy," the commissary general tempered his orders by also remembering his responsibility for "the proper welfare of the prisoners."[10]

This latter concern was reflected in Hoffman's November 15, 1861, report to Meigs. In sending the lease and construction contract to his superior, Hoffman explained that he had allowed the contractors an extra $1,500. This amount, "which seems to me only reasonable," Hoffman wrote, was added to make the buildings "more suitable for this winter climate." The project was already under way, he reported, and the work was "progressing rapidly." Although he had originally hoped to have the facility completed by the end of the year, Hoffman had given the contractors a deadline of February 1. "Circumstances," such as bad weather, he feared, "might render it beyond their power to fulfill the contract in less time." Prisoners' quarters were to be in two rows. Although the depot would be large by the standards of the antebellum army, Hoffman included in his plans space for a third row of barracks "if more room may be required." At the time neither Hoffman nor Meigs had any idea how prescient that decision would prove to be.[11]

Meanwhile, Hoffman's superiors were making plans to staff the facility. On October 29 Cameron called upon Ohio governor William Dennison to raise "a select company of volunteers" to serve as guards at Johnson's Island. Dennison replied that he would "cheerfully comply" with the request. He also agreed to consult with Hoffman regarding the selection of officers. The governor went so far as to name the companies being formed the "Hoffman Battalion," a designation they would hold until the outfit was increased to regimental strength later in the war. On January 1, 1862, the *Sandusky Register* announced that men enlisting for service in the battalion would receive a bounty of $100. "Men enlisted to garrison [the] Government section on Johnson's Island," the *Register* continued, "receive the above bounty in addition to good pay, excellent quarters and abundant rations." Volunteers were required to "be of good height, and between the ages of twenty and forty."[12]

On December 28 Hoffman named William S. Pierson commander of the depot. A former mayor of Sandusky, the thirty-seven-year-old Pierson brought no military experience to the post. Hoffman insisted that the newly minted major was "very industrious and attentive," a man of the "strictest integrity," and an "experienced man of business." It would appear, however, that the main factor recommending Pierson for the job was his availability. As Hoffman would quickly discover as he attempted to staff a number of Union prisons, the best military men were all serving at the front. In April 1862 he expressed regret to David Tod, who had succeeded Dennison as governor, that another, more experienced officer had recently turned down the post. "The commander must have some military experience," Hoffman pointed out, "the more the better, and he should be a little advanced in life, as years will give weight to his authority which a young man could not command." Hoffman indicated that Pierson concurred in this assessment. "He appreciates his deficiencies," Hoffman wrote, "and is very willing to resign his place into more able hands if such are within my reach." Unfortunately such hands were beyond the reach of the commissary general of prisoners. Pierson would retain command of Johnson's Island until January 1864.[13]

With no replacement in sight, Hoffman offered all the advice to Pierson that he could. Despite the fact that he was known in military circles as "Old Huffy" for his often-prickly disposition, Hoffman's instructions to his young commandant were couched in understanding, almost fatherly, terms. He urged him to avoid consulting members of his command before issuing orders. "The more silent the Commanding Officer is about his measures the better the effect," Hoffman counseled. "What he requires to be done should be announced in orders without any preliminary discussion." Also important, Hoffman advised, was attention to details. "The neglect of trifles leads to other neglects, and step by step discipline is undermined," he wrote.[14]

Hoffman was able to devote virtually his full attention during 1861 to establishing the prison on Johnson's Island because of the Union army's lack of success elsewhere. During the spring and summer of 1861, the resounding cry of "On to Richmond!" had proven irresistible. The resulting political pressure led the Lincoln administration to send Gen. Irvin McDowell's army into the field prematurely. On July 21, 1861, that army was soundly defeated at the battle of First Manassas. Meanwhile, in the West, Gen. John Fremont managed only to demoralize border-state loyalists with a premature order declaring slaves in Missouri to be free. Few victories in the field meant few prisoners with whom to deal. If the Union's lack of success in 1861 accomplished nothing else, it gave Hoffman time to prepare for the waves of prisoners that would arrive in early 1862.

Many of the Union's captives in those early days of the war were civilians. Termed "citizen prisoners" or, even more honestly, "political prisoners," they generally came from the border regions of Maryland, western Virginia, Kentucky, and Missouri. They represented a wide variety of social classes, ranging from the illiterate to some of the most prominent figures in Maryland politics. The threat they posed to the Union ranged from significant to none at all. What they had in common was being caught in a rather wide net cast by an administration facing an unprecedented challenge to the nation's existence.[15]

Many of the early Union prisoners ended up in Washington, DC, at the Old Capitol Prison. Finished in 1816, the Old Capitol had been built with funds raised by volunteer subscribers after British forces burned the U.S. Capitol during the War of 1812. It served as the home of Congress for three years. After that it functioned successively as a school, a hotel, and a boardinghouse favored by politicians. The Old Capitol had been abandoned for ten years when Union officials pressed the structure into service as a prison. It functioned in that capacity for the duration of the war, housing prisoners as late as October 1865. The number of captives generally ranged from a few hundred to twelve hundred. They represented, notes historian James I. Robertson Jr., an "indescribable heterogeneity" of individuals. Prisoners of war usually composed the majority of the inmates. Old Capitol's prison population also included Union soldiers facing various charges, political prisoners of all social classes, and "contraband" blacks captured with their masters. Two Old Capitol inmates, Rose O'Neal Greenhow and Belle Boyd, arrived after achieving celebrity status as Confederate spies.[16]

There were three levels to the building. The ground floor included guard quarters, the mess hall, and receiving rooms for new prisoners. Political prisoners and Union soldiers under arrest occupied the second floor, as well as the attic above it. "The rooms were exceedingly small and low-ceilinged," Robertson writes of the attic. "Ventilation was poor; mold, must and heat were oppressive."[17]

A more blunt assessment was offered by George Henry Clay Rowe. Arriving in August 1862, he wrote, "This structure, both in the outward and inner appearance, very closely resembles the Negro jails of Richmond." Rowe was among a group of nineteen of the "oldest and most esteemed" citizens of Fredericksburg, Virginia, arrested by Union officials in late July. Ostensibly held as hostages for seven men arrested by Confederate authorities, they included the mayor and the pastor of the Fredericksburg Baptist Church. The Fredericksburg captives found themselves incarcerated with "about [350] prisoners of every rank, condition and degree." Included among them, Rowe recorded, were "statesmen, lawyers, bankers, doctors, editors, merchants, soldiers, deserters, and vagabonds." He quickly added that the "great majority" were "dirty, lousy, half clad soldiers." Rowe was so alarmed by the "danger of the vermin which swarmed on all sides . . . that I retreated with a friend into a corner."[18]

The nineteen Fredericksburg citizens remained in the Old Capitol for only six weeks before they were exchanged for Union captives and released. During that time they experienced treatment typical of that which most Union prisoners received during the early months of the war. For example, there were virtually no restrictions on the foodstuffs supplied to them by their friends on the outside. "As an instance of the liberality of these donations," Rowe recorded on September 8, "on one day three barrels of [the] best bottled ale and porter, fifty pounds of cut loaf sugar, thirty pounds of Java coffee, ten pounds [of the] best tea, and a large quantity of bacon, hams, pineapple, cheeses, nuts and fruits [arrived]." The prisoners could also make purchases to supplement their meager rations. "Our room now begins to wear some appearance of comfort," Rowe noted on August 20. "We have purchased cooking utensils, sheets, pillows, and provisions." A few days later Rowe and his friends "got hold of some excellent wine, together with some choice eatables, and we set up nearly the whole night enjoying ourselves royally."[19]

This is not to suggest that, even in the early and relatively innocent days of the war, the prisoner experience was an enjoyable one. Spotting holes in the floor, Rowe assumed that they had been drilled to drain away water when the rooms were cleaned. A friend told him "to my great surprise that they were bullet holes," pointing out in the ceiling "a corresponding opening where the charge had passed out." The friend then called his attention to "several points where prisoners had been shot for such trifling reasons as placing their hands outside the window bars or making manly answers to the brutal charges of sentinels." There is no evidence in existing prison records either to support or refute the claims of the man, but Rowe's experiences appear to offer some confirmation. On one occasion, Rowe recorded, a guard threatened to shoot him for standing by the window and taunting the sentinels. He did not, however, include in his diary a single instance of any shootings occurring during his time at Old Capitol. Although less dramatic than shootings, crowding likely posed a greater threat to the survival of the prisoners. On September 10 Rowe complained of the arrival of "a large number of dirty Yankee deserters." As a result, "The building, and even the yard, was crowded almost to suffocation," and he concluded, "A breath of air is an impossible luxury." Rowe did not record the deaths of any prisoners, but another Old Capitol diarist did. Two months before the arrival of the Fredericksburg captives, George L. P. Wren, who was captured at Port Republic, Virginia, wrote on both June 20 and 21, 1862, "An other death among the prisoners."[20]

Not many miles to the north, another historic structure, Baltimore's Fort McHenry, was also transformed into a prison for captured Confederates. Although nearly seven thousand prisoners would pass through en route to other facilities in the wake of the battle of Gettysburg, it was never a major depot, generally housing only a few hundred Confederates. Like Old Capitol, Fort McHenry's inmates included a mix of military and political prisoners and Union soldiers under arrest. Its first recorded use as a military prison came in July 1861, when Gen. George B. McClellan won a victory at Rich Mountain in western Virginia. The venerable Winfield Scott, then serving as the Union's general in chief, ordered most of McClellan's prisoners released on parole. He excepted any prisoners who had recently served as officers in the U.S. military who "left with the intent of bearing arms against the United States." They were to be shipped to Fort McHenry, where they remained briefly before being sent on to Fort Lafayette in New York Harbor.[21]

Located in "the Narrows" between Staten Island and Long Island, Fort Lafayette had been built after the War of 1812 as a part of the defenses of New York. As a Civil War prison the tiny fortification was a minor facility. According to official reports, its inmate population never exceeded 135, although published prison narratives claim that it held nearly 200 military and civilian prisoners at one point. In any event, it often far exceeded its recommended capacity of 50.[22]

A more important prisoner of war depot in the New York area was Governor's Island, located below the southern tip of Manhattan, where the East River opens into New York's Upper Bay. On September 4, 1861, a group of Confederate prisoners, taken in one of the Union's rare victories that summer, arrived on the island. They had been captured at Hatteras Inlet, North Carolina, on August 29. Flag Officer Silas H. Stringham and Gen. Benjamin Butler led the Union expedition to take the inlet, which had proven a valuable haven for Confederate blockade-runners. On September 2 Stringham informed Lt. Col. Martin Burke, commanding Fort Lafayette, that he had 678 prisoners aboard the *Minnesota,* his flagship. "Will you please inform me," Stringham requested, "at what point I shall land them and deliver them into your charge for further safe-keeping?" Burke's response is not recorded, but two days later, Col. Gustavus Loomis, commanding Fort Columbus on Governor's Island, announced, "I have received the whole of the prisoners of war upon this island."[23]

Among the terms of the surrender was Stringham and Butler's guarantee that the Confederate officers and men would "receive the treatment due prisoners of war." According to Capt. Thomas Sparrow, his Union captors were true to their word, particularly as it applied to the captured officers. The officers of the *Minnesota,* he wrote, treated the Southerners "with uniform kindness." During the daylight hours Sparrow and his fellow officers had the freedom of the ship. The chief engineer allowed Sparrow the use of his stateroom and provided him with pen, ink, and paper so he could inform his wife that he was well. "The voyage at sea was thought delightful as could be," Sparrow wrote. The ocean was calm, the temperature mild. "A fine band of music assembled at sun set every afternoon on the poop deck," he noted, "& performed fine pieces of music, even to Dixie, as a special compliment I suppose to us."[24]

At this time Hoffman's appointment as commissary general of prisoners was not well known. This would later be a sore point with him, but in late 1861, preoccupied with the construction of Johnson's Island, he did not have time to worry about protocol. Prison commanders, therefore, were largely on their own in formulating policies and regulations. On September 10 Loomis wrote to Col. Edward D. Townsend, assistant adjutant general in the War Department, proposing certain rules for the prison. First he wished to "issue such articles of clothing to the prisoners of war as will make them comfortable." He also recommended that they be allowed to receive supplemental items from friends, subject to inspection, and to make purchases from the post sutler or merchants in the city. Loomis wished to allow the prisoners to send and receive letters, also subject to inspection, with the condition that any found to "contain objectionable matter are to be rejected." Perhaps the most significant of Loomis's proposals was his desire to segregate the men and the officers. While this in itself posed no particular hardships, the men clearly got the worse end of the bargain when it came to quarters. The officers were housed in Fort Columbus, located at the northern end of the island. The men were confined in Castle Williams, at the island's southern tip. Neither facility was particularly healthy, but with the men far outnumbering the officers, crowding was a much more severe problem at the Castle. The officers received paroles that gave them ample time and room to exercise. The men were allowed outside twice daily, for an hour at a time, and their sphere of movement was much more restricted.[25]

Soon Sparrow was recording accounts of sickness among the men in the Castle. On September 20 he wrote, "The Camp Measles have broken out among the men at Castle William[s], and there are now some twenty five cases there." Ten days later Sparrow reported that 115 of 615 men in the Castle were sick. Two casemates used exclusively as sick wards were filled, and ill prisoners could be found in the other casemates as well. By then Sparrow was noting the deaths of the men. On October 7 he recorded the seventh and the eighth, and the captain, whose diary is remarkably free of complaints, lashed out at his captors. "Unless something be done to add to their comforts," he wrote, "the sad list will be greatly enlarged." The men in the lower casemates were "destitute of almost every comfort. They are crowded in the corners to avoid the cool winds, with a straw sack & one blanket covered with dirt and not a change of garments. It is a disgrace to humanity," Sparrow concluded. "Their brutal keepers will be guilty in the eyes of God." When two more died the next day, he reflected, "What shells did not do, confinement and want of comforts are surely doing for our enemy."[26]

On September 29 Loomis informed Townsend of the unhealthy condition of Castle Williams and asked that something be done about it. "They [the prisoners] should be removed before cold weather comes on," he wrote, "or prepared for it by some means of warming the portion occupied as quarters." The post surgeon, William J. Sloan, agreed. On September 30 he reported that "the condition of the Fort Hatteras prisoners is such as to require the immediate attention of the Government. They are crowded into an ill-ventilated building," he added, "which has always been an unhealthy one when occupied by large bodies of men." Sloan placed some of the responsibility on the prisoners, saying they were "not disposed to use the means prescribed by me for the prevention of disease unless compelled to do so." He concluded, "Every building upon the island being crowded with troops, with a large number in tents, I know not how the condition of these prisoners can be improved except by a change in location to some other place for all or a portion of them."[27]

Meanwhile, most of the officers at Fort Columbus, as Sparrow noted on September 25, had "begun to live quite well." The prisoners were issued "common army rations" of "fat pork, Irish potatoes, rice, & occasionally beef." Thanks to friends in New York, they were able to supplement their diets with crackers, cheeses, hams, molasses, and numerous other items. They also received "an almost daily supply of lager" from an unnamed source, as well as wine. On October 19 Sparrow received a shipment of smoking tobacco and "two boxes of very superior cigars." Despite all the supplemental items that were available to them, the North Carolina officers were determined that they receive their fair quantity of rations. In an entry that future prisoners would have found painfully ironic, Sparrow complained on October 26 that the Yankees had cheated his mess. He and a fellow captive had measured their coffee ration and found it to be short by one quart. The pair complained, and "the result was good strong coffee for supper."[28]

The Hatteras officers also saw to the needs of their less fortunate men. Sparrow visited the Castle daily and did all he could to ensure the comfort of the enlisted soldiers of his company. On October 9 he noted that he had delivered clothing, combs, and toothbrushes to his men, and grapes, peaches, and wine to the sick. The next day he returned with more clothing. Two days after that he distributed various foodstuffs, including vegetables, butter, and cheese. "It has in this respect been to all of them an agreeable day," Sparrow noted, "and they have seemed cheerful." He added, "Large amounts of clothing from our friends in N. York have also come in, and this had contributed largely to their improved spirits."[29]

Visits to the enlisted men quickly became part of the daily routine of the officers confined in Fort Columbus. "There is much sameness in our life," Sparrow wrote on September 24, "but nevertheless we manage to keep occupied, so that time does not hang heavily upon our hands." The officers generally ate breakfast at 7:00. Many followed their morning meal with walks. One of the officers had an opera glass, and the prisoners spent much time "spying the vessels & various objects of interest in the Narrows, the Bay, & the Harbor, all of which are in full view." The morning newspapers arrived at 9:00. Sparrow received three, the *Tribune,* the *Herald,* and the *Times,* which he passed around to his comrades. Visiting hours for the Castle were from 9:00 to 10:00 in the morning and 4:00 to 5:00 in the afternoon. Sparrow proudly noted that he "never fail[ed] to make two visits each day." Reading and napping occupied the afternoon hours for some. Others engaged in such games as chess, backgammon, draughts, dominoes, and whist.[30]

Supper came at about 5:00, followed by walking or a discussion of "the political topics of the day." The officers often congregated near a grove of poplars on the west side of the island. "Here, or on the lawn," Sparrow observed, "the younger officers exercise themselves with throwing heavy stones over their heads backwards and at jumping at leap frog." He noted, "The latter at times becomes not only amusing but ludicrous," prompting laughter even from the Union officers. Later in the evening the Confederate officers took tea before reading, writing, conversing, or engaging in games. Prison regulations called for lights-out at 10:00 p.m. "At this hour," Sparrow noted, "a sentinel is apt to refresh our memories as to the time if we transgress."[31]

This all changed on October 28 when the Governor's Island prisoners received word that they and their counterparts at Fort Lafayette would soon be departing for Boston aboard the Union vessel *State of Maine.* Their destination was Fort Warren. A relatively new facility, completed in 1845, Fort Warren sat upon an island at the entrance to Boston Harbor. Like many other Union prisons, it had begun its Civil War service as a training camp. It proved too small for that purpose, and following the exchange of the North Carolina prisoners, it would never house more than four hundred captives.[32]

When the Tar Heel soldiers arrived at about dusk on October 31, they discovered that they had not been expected and that all was not in readiness to receive them. The commander of the fort, Col. Justin Dimick, had been assigned to the post only twelve days earlier. Told to expect about 150 captives, he was shocked to discover that the *State of Maine* had brought over 600 prisoners of war plus 155 political prisoners. Thomas Sparrow appreciated the irony of the situation. "Although we had received notice three days before that we were to come to this place, Col. Dimick, in command here, had received no notice of it." Sparrow and his fellow prisoners were less amused with the result of the bureaucratic bungling. For most of them it meant another night aboard the *State of Maine.* Four companies were allowed to come ashore after the commander of the vessel convinced Dimick that conditions on the ship were such that one more night could lead to sickness.[33]

It was not the last time that Dimick would base his actions on the welfare of the prisoners. When he was assigned to the command of Fort Warren, Dimick received a series of "general instructions" from the War Department concerning the treatment of prisoners. They were based largely on the regulations Loomis had proposed to Townsend when the prisoners first arrived at Governor's Island. The prisoners could send and receive unsealed letters and make purchases to supplement their clothing and rations. Visitors were prohibited without "express permission from proper authority in Washington." Although the prisoners were to be "securely held," they were also to receive "every privilege consistent with this end," and were to be "treated with all kindness."[34]

This Dimick took to heart, as did most members of his command. The prisoners quickly noticed. "We find the officers here from Colonel Dimick down to the Captains & Lieutenants, & from them to the sentinels & sergeants disposed to be polite and obliging," Sparrow noted the day of his arrival. This contrasted with Governor's Island, where he found the officers to be "stiff & insolent & pretentious" and the enlisted men "rude." Indeed, Sparrow believed that the kindness of the guards threatened to breach military etiquette. "The sentinels on the island are polite," he wrote, "and disposed to be familiar if we would permit it." Thomas W. Hall, a Baltimore political prisoner who had been at Fort Lafayette, also found his new keepers to be an improvement. In a letter to his mother, Hall wrote that he was pleased to have left behind sentinels eager to "sink the soldier." Those at Fort Warren, by contrast, had "manifested every disposition to make us comfortable." Dimick and his officers joined the prisoners at Sunday services, and the commandant paid occasional social visits to the Confederate officers' quarters. The colonel had served in North Carolina before the war, and he discussed his time there as well as the various war rumors circulating around the fort. On at least one occasion he shared a glass of "whiskey punch" with the Southern officers.[35]

The prisoners also found the fort itself to be an improvement over the New York prisons. "The work is a splendid one of solid granite," wrote Sparrow, "elegantly finished & one of the best on the continent." It remained unfinished, and over a hundred workmen were engaged in completing the facility. Despite the improved quarters, Sparrow regretted that his new home lacked the lawns and trees that the officers had enjoyed at Fort Columbus. The rations, too, were of a poorer quality. This was in part due to the suddenness of the prisoners' arrival. After three days in the fort, the situation was so bad that the famished enlisted men threatened to "die in an attempt to take the place or have food." A group of their officers appealed to Dimick, "and soon the matter was remedied."[36]

The officers having the means to do so were quickly able to improve both their quarters and their diets. On November 7 Sparrow and his messmates replaced their tin plates and cups with stoneware. They also secured soft bread and butter, an improvement over the military hard crackers. "[We] have begun to live like white people," Sparrow enthused. In the days that followed iron bedsteads and bedding arrived from Boston, along with folding stools, apples, and a barrel of ale. On Christmas Eve, eggs, sugar, brandy, and crackers reached the island, contributing to a holiday dinner that also included turkey and cranberry sauce.[37]

Sparrow continued to do what he could for indigent prisoners. Finding one in need of underclothes, he gave him drawers and socks from a supply he had received from a Philadelphia merchant. The captain told the man to let him know if there were others in need. His beneficiary soon returned with seven or eight men, whom Sparrow also supplied. More and more showed up, and soon Sparrow had exhausted his supply. In addition to the socks and underclothing, he gave out a dozen pairs of shoes and slippers. "These men have been here and have been overlooked," Sparrow lamented, determining to secure more items for them.[38]

Most of the men he assisted were political prisoners from Maryland. Like the prisoners of war, these captives represented every social class. While some depended upon the charity of others for underclothing, others shared messes with the highest-ranking military prisoners. Among the latter group was George William Brown, mayor of Baltimore. Arrested at 2:00 a.m. on September 13, 1861, by order of Secretary of State William Henry Seward, he had been held at Fort McHenry, Fortress Monroe, and Fort Lafayette before his tour of Union military outposts took him to Fort Warren. He suffered little from the experience, informing his brother-in-law in January 1862 that his weight was fifteen pounds above average. "We have procured servants from Boston and are well served," he wrote. "We have a French cook and the waiter who attends our room is an Italian named Antonio. Our meals are now good in every respect."[39]

Brown was not alone among prominent Maryland residents in Fort Warren. Most had been arrested in the latter half of September. Many were members of the state legislature. They included E. G. Kilbourn, speaker of the House of Delegates, said to be a "dangerous secessionist." Dr. Charles Macgill of Hagerstown had allegedly said that he would "give aid to the rebel cause to the extent of every dollar he could spare." A large number of the legislators arrested were "known to be conspiring to pass an act of secession." Others, such as L. G. Quinlan, were simply charged with being "a disloyal member of the Maryland Legislature."[40]

On November 20 Col. Dimick informed the officers of Sparrow's mess that they would have to "make room for either Mr. Mason or Mr. Slidell, our captured ministers. He had no difficulty in effecting such an arrangement," the captain wrote, "as we shall be glad to have such distinguished company." The prisoners had access to Boston newspapers, and they were quite familiar with the names of James Mason and John Slidell. The two men had been named Confederate ministers, Mason to Great Britain and Slidell to France. They were bound for Europe aboard the British mail ship *Trent* on November 7, when Capt. Charles Wilkes, commanding the Union warship *San Jacinto,* forcibly removed them. The unauthorized action threatened to lead to war between the United States and Great

Britain before Seward skillfully defused the crisis. The pair created a sensation among the prisoners at Fort Warren, and many sought out the detained diplomats to learn their thoughts on various topics. Mason seemed to have the greater storehouse of opinions. He predicted, incorrectly as it turned out, that both England and France would withdraw their ministers to Washington and that recognition of the Confederacy would follow. Lincoln he dismissed as "a baboon, only fit to engage in coarse anecdote. Seward," he added, was "a man of smartness, but of no practical sense." Slidell, meanwhile, appeared to be more reticent. He did, however, join his fellow prisoners in a game of "foot ball."[41]

Far to the west, the nature of another Union training camp was beginning to change as a mixture of military and political prisoners arrived. Camp Chase was located four miles west of Columbus, Ohio. It had received its name from Gen. William S. Rosecrans, who commanded there temporarily and chose to bestow a questionable honor on Treasury Secretary Salmon P. Chase, a former Ohio governor. Although none of its prisoners approached the level of celebrity enjoyed by Mason and Slidell, prominence lay ahead for three of the camp's trainees, Rutherford B. Hayes, James Garfield, and William McKinley.[42]

Prisoners began to trickle into Camp Chase in July 1861. They continued to arrive throughout the summer and fall, reaching 278 by mid-November. For a time they shared quarters with Union soldiers who had been placed under arrest. A representative of a nearby newspaper who visited the camp said the prisoners enjoyed comfortable surroundings at the camp. "Being mostly Western Virginia 'snake hunters,'" the reporter wrote of the captives, "aside from the loss of liberty, they lose little by imprisonment." Pvt. John Smith, a Union trainee, was even less charitable. "They dont look like human to me," Smith observed. Another recruit, Mungo Murray, noted that many of the captives were over sixty years old, some perhaps past seventy. Mixed with them was "a youth of probably 15." The boy appeared to be "very weak and faint," and was eventually unable to walk. "He made a soldier feel [pity] all over," Murray wrote to his family.[43]

For Governor Dennison the amalgam of military and civilian prisoners posed a problem. Unsure of what to do with them, or whether he even had the authority to do anything with them, he sought advice from Secretary Cameron. For example, the governor wondered if prisoners charged with such serious crimes as rape and murder should be held at Camp Chase or returned to their home states to face trial. Some were accused of committing specific acts of treason. Others had done nothing more than express an "opinion in favor of the rebels." Dennison apparently got little help from Cameron, because his successor faced the same dilemma when he assumed office in January 1862. Governor Tod wrote to Secretary of State Seward, "Please define and point out my several duties and I will most cheerfully perform the trust."[44]

Tod finally got satisfaction from Edwin M. Stanton, who replaced Cameron as secretary of war in January 1862. In August Stanton named Samuel Galloway, a former member of the U.S. House of Representatives, as a special commissioner to examine individually the cases of Camp Chase's political prisoners. Between November 1862 and May 1865, Galloway considered the cases of 2,090 political prisoners and Confederate soldiers who claimed they had been impressed into the service. Some arrived with specific charges, such as being a "rebel mail carrier" or a "rebel horse thief." Others were accused only of "being a rebel." A farmer from western Virginia was arrested because he had two sons in the Confederate army. In many such cases Galloway recommended release if the prisoner would take an oath of allegiance to the Union. Often he concluded that the charges were "not sustained by proof." Sometimes Galloway simply decided that the detainees were not dangerous individuals. One he deemed "an ignorant man entirely unacquainted with the questions at issue." Another he termed "simple minded."[45]

Although most of the Union's prison camps were training facilities or established fortifications converted for the purpose, St. Louis proved an exception. There, in early examples of eminent domain, two pieces of confiscated Rebel property became pens for military and political prisoners. One was the former slave market of Bernard Lynch, a secessionist who fled south during the early days of the war. In September 1861, twenty-seven prisoners arrived at the brick structure, located at the corner of Myrtle and Fifth streets. Because of its location, the facility became known as the Myrtle Street Prison. Three months later Union officials seized the McDowell Medical College. Like Mr. Lynch, Dr. Joseph McDowell had departed for the Confederacy, leaving behind his imposing Gratiot Street building. Soon McDowell's classrooms became cells and the dissecting room became a mess hall.[46]

At the time, Maj. Gen. Henry W. Halleck was the commander of the Department of the West. Known as "Old Brains," Halleck was a desk operator who showed much more interest in regulating prisons than he did in capturing actual prisoners. Soon after the Gratiot Street facility was occupied, Halleck placed Col. James M. Tuttle of the Second Iowa Volunteers in command of the prison. On January 9, 1862, he sent Tuttle detailed instructions for its management, all the way down to "requisitions for the necessary implements such as brooms." If clothing was issued to the prisoners, a board of surgeons would decide what was needed. Friends could also furnish clothing to the prisoners, but all such items were to be inspected so as to exclude "articles of luxury or ornament." To ensure their good health, the prisoners were to be given the opportunity to wash themselves. A place was also to be set aside in front of the prison for exercise. "In regard to the sick," Halleck ordered, "every proper facility will be afforded to the surgeon in charge in the matter of sending for necessary supplies &c." They were to be issued the same rations that ill Federal soldiers received. The surgeon would have the authority to send the "dangerously ill" to "the nearest general hospital designated by the medical director."[47]

As department commanders and officers at individual camps wrestled with the problems posed by influxes of Confederate captives, the commissary general of prisoners was busy finishing his Lake Erie depot. On January 27, 1862, Hoffman reported to Meigs that all the buildings had been completed at Johnson's Island. The only work remaining for the contractors was to finish the furniture for the prisoners' barracks. "I was in hopes to have had the bunks and benches made by carpenters from the [guard] company," the cost-conscious administrator explained, "but I found it impossible to do this." He went on to explain to his equally frugal superior, "Though made in the simplest manner, there being a great many of them, the bill will be pretty large." With ice blocking Sandusky Bay for several days, the workers had not been able to get machinery to the island. This forced much of the work to be done by hand, adding even more to the cost. Hoffman also had to admit that the price of the fence was double his previous estimate. The inability of the unorganized guard battalion to do the work was a factor. So, too, was Hoffman's decision to increase the height of the fence from nine to eleven feet while ensuring that it had enough stability to resist high winds on the lake.[48]

The contractors had met Hoffman's February 1 deadline for construction of the prison buildings, but the depot was not yet ready to house captured Confederates. On February 24 Hoffman informed Meigs that the guard force had not received the revolvers he had ordered, "nor is it sufficiently instructed to take charge of a large number of prisoners." Two days later he added that lanterns needed to illuminate the compound as a security measure were not yet on hand. In addition, the guard quarters had proven to be too small for the number of men recruited for the Hoffman Battalion. Plans were already being made for the erection of additional facilities. Even if everything had been in readiness on Johnson's Island, no prisoners could be transported because of the breaking ice on the lake. Once it cleared, Hoffman reported, the prison would be ready to receive "a limited number of prisoners, say 500 to 600."[49]

By the time this message was sent, circumstances had made the Union's new prison inadequate, at least in terms of capacity. In 1861 the lack of success of Federal forces had given Hoffman the time he needed to complete his Lake Erie depot. As the 1862 campaigns in the West got under way, a reversal in fortunes brought the Union sudden success. With that success came an overwhelming number of prisoners. Johnson's Island could house only a small percentage of them. As a result, Hoffman and other Union officials would soon be scrambling to find facilities for thousands of captives in gray.

2
"I fear they will prove an elephant"
The First Wave of Prisoners, 1862

"No terms except unconditional and immediate surrender can be accepted. I propose to move immediately upon your works."

When Brig. Gen. Ulysses S. Grant sent this message, demanding the surrender of Fort Donelson, to Brig. Gen. Simon B. Buckner, who was commanding the Tennessee fort, on February 16, 1862, many things changed. The Northern people had an immediate hero, much needed in a period in which the Union had received more bad news than good. Grant had a fort and an open path to Nashville along the Cumberland River. He also had problems. His men were in need of blankets and overcoats to replace those lost on the battlefield; and Grant suddenly found himself in possession of fifteen thousand prisoners. "I am now forwarding prisoners of war to your care and I shall be truly glad to get clear of them," Grant reported in a February 17 message to Gen. George W. Cullum, chief of staff for Grant's boss, Gen. Halleck. He added, "It is a much less job to take than to keep them." The logistical problems of handling such a number of captives proved vexing to the victorious commander. Grant wrote to Cullum, "I would suggest the policy of paroling all prisoners hereafter," and then exchanging them. As the captives departed for St. Louis, he warned Cullum, "Seeing the trouble I have had myself, I began to pity you the moment the first cargo started." Grant concluded, "I fear they will prove an elephant."[1]

This was the type of administrative challenge Halleck was suited to handle. He ordered Grant to send sick and wounded prisoners to Cincinnati, "our own men and the enemy to be treated precisely the same." Meanwhile, he sent a flurry of messages to the governors of Illinois, Indiana, and Ohio asking how many prisoners could be housed in their states. As these telegrams went out, the captives were on their way to Cairo, where Cullum was stationed. Halleck instructed his chief of staff to send them on to St. Louis. "Give them everything necessary for their comfort," Halleck ordered. He again stressed, "Treat them the same as our own soldiers."[2]

At least one of the Confederate prisoners noted that his captors followed Halleck's instructions. "We were treated with respect and kindness by the Federal Troops," wrote James E. Paton of the Second Kentucky Infantry. Recalling the surrender five months later, Paton also recorded fond memories of his commanding general. "As we passed by the headquarters of Genl. Buckner," Paton wrote, "the gallant hero came out with his hat in hand and as the men passed along he would take their hands, tell them goodbye, bid them be of good cheer, to hope for a better day and that he would be with them again." Paton and his comrades then boarded a steamer bound for St. Louis via Cairo. There, too, the Union officer in charge "did all in his power to make us comfortable."[3]

Other Donelson prisoners recorded less positive accounts of the trip to St. Louis. "The boat is very much crowded and very disagreeable to me," wrote Col. Randal W. McGavock of the Fiftieth Tennessee on February 19. Andrew Jackson Campbell of the Forty-eighth Tennessee blamed exposure, poor rations, and foul water for much of the sickness on the boat transporting him up the Mississippi. "At night," he wrote, "we had to pile up like hogs, scarcely room enough for all on the floor, which was covered over with mud, slop, and tobacco spittle, well tramped up through the day." At two points along the river, Campbell added, Federal troops along the shore fired at the boat, wounding several prisoners. According to another captive, James Calvin Cook, somebody threw rocks at the boat he was aboard as it passed Cape Girardeau.[4]

The officers' situation did not improve when they reached St. Louis. Halleck had made quick arrangements to forward the enlisted men to various camps in the Midwest, and their layover in the Missouri city was generally brief. He ordered that the officers be "placed on a boat and anchored in the stream where no communication can be had with them." McGavock wrote of the parting, "It was a sad sight to see [the] men marched away from their officers." He added, "It seems to be the policy of the [Union] Government to separate the officers from the men, in order to break all the ties existing between them, and to prevent any future organization." Whatever the motivation, it was a policy that Northern authorities would pursue for the duration of the war.[5]

Both Campbell and Cook ended up aboard the steamer *Hiawatha.* Cook wrote that the *Hiawatha* and the two or three other boats containing the officers were "verry much crowded." According to Campbell, the prisoners received rations of "loaf bread, half-cooked beef and pickled pork—raw." Hearing that the captives were "suffering much" from a lack of rations, Halleck ordered commissary officers in St. Louis to see that they were supplied. Federal officials were less approving of local citizens who attempted to provision the prisoners. The arrival of the boats transporting the Confederates prompted an outpouring of Southern sympathizers. Campbell reported that a boat loaded with them came alongside the craft on which he arrived. "They made a great to-do over us," he wrote, "somewhat surprising us at seeing such a strong Southern sentiment there." They supplied the prisoners with apples, cakes, and tobacco and exchanged Federal money for Confederate currency at face value. Even after the boats holding the Southern soldiers were towed out to the middle of the river, the citizens rode out in ferryboats. Some were arrested for their efforts, and many more were threatened with arrest. Campbell saw two young boys taken into custody for throwing apples toward his boat "and a Federal officer shake his fist in a lady's face for the same offense." With apparent satisfaction, Cook wrote, "That dont stop them when ever the ladies can by any means get the name of an officer on bord they are shure to send them some thing that they supose they kneed."[6]

The field officers were eventually taken to Fort Warren. Included among them were Buckner and Brig. Gen. Lloyd Tilghman, who had been captured on February 7 with his staff and about sixty men at Fort Henry. The pair arrived at Boston on March 3. Secretary of War Stanton ordered the two officers "kept confined in separate apartments and allowed no intercourse with anyone except by his special permission." Although there is no official record of the order being changed, George William Brown later reported that it had been. "Gens Buckner & Tilghman have been released from solitary confinement," the Marylander wrote on July 29, "and last night took tea in our room." He added, "Buckner is a very superior man and wields great influence with the young men."[7]

For the majority of the prisoners, life at Fort Warren remained quite tolerable. On February 10 Thomas W. Hall informed his mother that most of his fellow prisoners had organized messes and hired "cooks and attendants from Boston." Brown described his confinement almost as if it were a vacation. "The harbor is fine," he informed his niece, "and the view of the water, the picturesque island, the main land with its villages & towns, and the many passing sails is always pleasing." Afternoons invariably brought football games. Brown wrote, "Old and young, tall and short, soldiers and civilians join in the melee and tumble each other & themselves about on the grass in the most unceremonious manner."[8]

Col. McGavock, who found himself at Fort Warren on March 6, also experienced a life that later Confederate prisoners could have only envied. The day of his arrival he wrote, "Very comfortable rooms were furnished us and iron cots, with mattresses and blankets—which with the fervid heat from an anthracite fire rendered our condition very comfortable." The next day he and eight other officers, eventually including Gen. Tilghman, joined a mess that included several Baltimore political prisoners. "We have French cooks and waiters," he noted, "and as well served tables as can be found at any first class hotel in the country." Friends sent boxes of provisions that contained such luxuries as whiskey, brandy, cigars, cheese, ham, and sardines. Like the prisoners who had arrived there before him, McGavock credited Justin Dimick for the kind treatment the prisoners enjoyed. On the night of July 4 the elderly colonel allowed the Southerners to go out on the parapets to enjoy Boston's Independence Day fireworks. "Altho not a citizen of the U.S. now," McGavock appreciated the gesture. He also supported Dimick's order barring liquor from the fort. Some of the prisoners, he conceded, had "abused his kindness by getting drunk in an unbecoming manner." When Dimick's son, who had served on the commandant's staff, left to join Gen. McClellan's army, McGavock was among a group of prisoners who sent him off with a letter. The missive praised both father and son for their courtesy and asked that "the same treatment [be] extended to him in the event he should be captured."[9]

Although the field officers ended up in Boston Harbor, the other officers and men captured at Fort Donelson were sent to a variety of western prisons. Most had started as training camps for Union recruits. An exception was the former state penitentiary at Alton, Illinois. Constructed in 1830, the facility had been abandoned by the time the war began. On Christmas Day 1861 Gen. Halleck sought permission from the War Department to press the facility into service as the prisons in St. Louis became crowded. The next day he ordered Quartermaster Robert Allen to prepare the site for use. Among his suggestions was to build fires in the stoves "for a day or two" to dry out the prison, which flooded frequently. Halleck named Lt. Col. Sidney Burbank commander. "Every measure will be adopted by you to insure [the prisoners'] safe custody," Halleck ordered. "At the same time you will exercise toward them every dictate which enlightened humanity prompts and the laws of war permit." As at other camps, the limits of "enlightened humanity" depended upon the rank of the prisoners. Officers were to be given the freedom of the city during daylight hours or, at Burbank's discretion, allowed to live in Alton.[10]

On April 3 Col. Richard Cutts, Halleck's aide-de-camp, inspected the prison. There were 791 prisoners held there, including 58 officers. None were housed in the cells. About 300 were in "wide passage-ways running around the three different tiers of cells." The rest were lodged in various outbuildings. Cutts found the quarters to be "excellent, certainly equal if not superior to those at Camps Butler, Douglas, and Morton." The prisoners received two meals a day, prepared by cooks taken from their ranks. Cutts noted that the rations were the same as those received by Federal soldiers. Fresh beef was issued daily. Confederate surgeons were in charge of the hospital, which contained about seventy-five patients. Virtually all were suffering with pneumonia and diarrhea, which Cutts insisted were brought on "generally by exposure previous to their arrival at Alton."[11]

Not far away, a second Illinois prison opened despite protests from prominent state officials. As Halleck struggled to find housing for the thousands of prisoners taken at Fort Donelson, he received an urgent message from several Illinois political leaders. Governor Richard Yates was among a group that implored him, "We think it unsafe to send prisoners to Springfield," explaining, "there are so many secessionists at that place." Despite the governor's concern, Halleck replied that he would "probably be obliged" to send about three thousand to the Illinois capital. In a separate message he added, "In the confusion of sending off so many prisoners it is quite probable that proper guards may not be sent with them."[12]

The men ended up at Camp Butler. Located six miles east of Springfield, the camp had been established the previous August as a training facility. It was named for state treasurer William Butler and was "considered an ideal place for a military camp." A spring-fed lake provided good drinking water, and the trees that surrounded the lake offered a source of fuel. During the summer and fall of 1861, twenty Illinois regiments received their training at the facility.[13]

With the arrival of approximately two thousand Fort Donelson prisoners on February 22, 1862, Camp Butler's role suddenly changed. Although there were no reported problems with secessionists, the *Illinois State Register* reported that "streams of visitors poured in" to witness the arrival of the Confederate captives. Another newspaper, the Republican *Illinois State Journal,* was unimpressed with the enemy soldiers. "The common soldiers are clothed with a variety of many colored garments," the *Journal* observed. "Their appearance is decidedly grotesque. Their yellow, brown, gray and white blankets, with here and there fragments of parti-hued carpeting, cause a most unfavorable idea of the resources of the Quartermaster's department of the Southern Confederacy."[14]

The majority of the Camp Butler prisoners were housed in the fifteen barracks already in place when they arrived. The remainder stayed in tents. According to Hoffman, who inspected the camp in early March, the quarters were adequate for the number of prisoners confined. This was, however, the only positive thing he could say about the facility. "The hospitals are crowded and are in a deplorable condition," he informed Meigs on March 10, "and the sick could not well be more uncomfortable." One young doctor was in charge of the entire camp, assisted by two company physicians who had "not energy to be of much service." The commissary general of prisoners appealed to Halleck for "an active, energetic medical officer" for the camp. Hoffman had attempted to secure the services of Springfield physicians but had been only partially successful. "One went this morning," he reported, "but I don't know if he will go again." Hoffman concluded, "Something should be done immediately to relieve the sick from their sad condition." Statistics bear out Hoffman's concerns. During March there were 112 deaths at the camp. All were blamed on pneumonia. Deaths became so prevalent that the camp's commander, Col. Pitcairn Morrison, employed a carpenter to build coffins at the site.[15]

At the same time Col. Morrison was facing other challenges. Foremost among them was the lack of a fence around the camp. Hoffman informed Meigs that "the detention of the prisoners thus depends more on their willingness to remain than on any restraint upon them by the guard." Complicating the situation was the fact that the guard force in question was composed of raw recruits. It would cost $1,500 to enclose the prison, but Hoffman recommended a higher expenditure to double its capacity. The suggestion was a wise one, because on April 13 over one thousand additional prisoners, taken in fighting at Island No. 10 in the Mississippi River, arrived at the camp.[16]

As summer arrived, conditions at Camp Butler began to improve. On June 22 Maj. John G. Fonda of the Twelfth Illinois Cavalry succeeded Morrison. Fonda allowed the men to go to the nearby Sangamon River to wash themselves and their clothes. He joined Dr. J. Cooper McKee, the camp's surgeon, in an extensive program to improve the health of the prisoners. Under it, the camp was policed daily, drainage was improved, and cooking facilities were removed from the barracks to separate sheds. This, McKee reported, avoided "much filth" and went "very far in doing away with an active cause of disease." McKee concluded, "I am well satisfied with the marked improvement in the health and appearance of my sick. The deaths have greatly decreased in number." Statistics bear out the doctor's optimistic claims. Camp records show that the number of deaths was forty-one in July, twenty-five in August, and just five in September. In all those months Camp Butler's prison population was just over two thousand.[17]

To the north a Chicago training camp was also pressed into service as an impromptu prison. Camp Douglas was named for Senator Stephen Douglas, the Unionist Democrat who died in June 1861. A portion of the camp actually rested upon land that Douglas had owned. By November 1861 Camp Douglas occupied about three hundred acres of land and housed some forty-two hundred recruits. They occupied one-story barracks that, as Confederate prisoners would soon come to realize, afforded little protection against the Windy City's bitter winters. Like Johnson's Island, Camp Douglas was initially commanded by a businessman with no prior military experience. Governor Yates had selected Col. Joseph Tucker of the Sixtieth Illinois to build the camp. He left the veteran banker in command once the post was completed. The assignment proved temporary. By the time the Tennessee prisoners began to arrive, Col. James A. Mulligan, himself an exchanged prisoner, commanded the camp.[18]

On February 18, 1862, Allen Fuller, adjutant general of Illinois, advised Halleck that the site could handle seven thousand prisoners and asked if the general wanted the camp prepared for that purpose. Halleck replied in the affirmative. "Guards will be sent with the prisoners of war," he promised Fuller, adding, "Can't say when they will reach you." Fuller was in Springfield when the first trainloads began passing through. He noticed that, despite Halleck's promise, there were not enough guards. The adjutant general telegraphed Chicago and asked that a sufficient guard be raised there. It was critical that enough men be found because the fence around Camp Douglas was not even six feet tall. The situation greatly concerned Chicago mayor Julian S. Rumsey. On February 24 he informed Halleck that the guard at the camp was dangerously inadequate. "I have seen two men guarding 300 feet with no arms other than a stick," Rumsey wrote. Police had been pressed into service, the mayor complained, to escort prisoners from the trains to the camp. He feared for his city's safety, concluding, "Its destruction would surely do away with the glorious victory at Donelson."[19]

Halleck's reply was less than encouraging. He instructed Rumsey to detain the guard that accompanied the prisoners, send the Confederate officers to Camp Chase, and raise a special police force if he had to. "I have taken these Confederates in arms behind their intrenchments; it is a great pity if Chicago cannot guard them unarmed for a few days," the general whined. "No troops can be spared from here for that purpose at present." Halleck's claim was pure hyperbole. He had been in St. Louis when Fort Donelson fell, and he had approved of Grant's assault only reluctantly. His outburst, however, was understandable. As Grant had predicted, his captives were proving to be "an elephant." Halleck was a talented military administrator, but the deluge of prisoners was taxing his abilities, his resources, and apparently his patience.[20]

Hoffman arrived to inspect Camp Douglas in early March and reported to Meigs on the 7th. There were over five thousand prisoners at the camp. The commissary general found them "very well quartered and the sick comfortably provided for in well-arranged hospitals." Although he was not specific, Hoffman reported that few prisoners had died. Approximately four hundred were in the hospital. Hoffman informed Mulligan that he found the "prisoners of war in your charge well provided for in every way." He made only two suggestions to the camp commander. One was that no visitors be admitted. The other was the suggestion that a portion of the prisoners' rations be withheld. "The regular ration is larger than is necessary for men living quietly in camp," he wrote, "and by judiciously withholding some part of it to be sold to the commissary a fund may be created with which articles may be purchased and thus save expense to the Government." Based on similar funds Hoffman had established at frontier posts, the idea would become a central feature of his administration of Union prisons.[21]

If Mulligan reduced the prisoners' rations, the fact did not bother Willie Micajah Barrow. Captured at the battle of Shiloh, the Confederate private arrived at Camp Douglas on about April 17. "We are well fixed off for prisoners," he wrote on the 27th. "Our quarters are plenty large enough and we are permitted to go out and walk in the inclosure." As for food, he recorded the next day, "They treat us as if we were their own soldiers give us the same rations and everything that is necessary." The men of the mess took turns serving as cook. On May 1 Barrow served beans, fried beef, and Irish potatoes for dinner and coffee and bread for supper. The bill of fare for May 14 was beefsteak and mashed Irish potatoes. Barrow's mess apparently had some money available, because they supplemented what was issued with "a bread-pudding with a nice sauce."[22]

Barrow's mood changed when he made a shocking discovery on June 4. "This morning," he wrote, "the first thing I caught was a body louse, Ugh!" The realization made sense of a restless night largely spent scratching what Barrow had assumed was a rash. It also prompted the private to change into a clean undershirt. Removing the old one, he found it "filled with lice, horrid! The whole mess profiting by my discovery," Barrow continued, "we soon had a tub full of the varmints." The next day, following dinner, his mess "had a very exciting Louse hunt."[23]

Although Barrow remained at Camp Douglas until September, his diary ends on July 13. Other than his battle with lice, he apparently remained satisfied with the treatment he received. Union officials, however, were less pleased with the way the camp was being run. One problem was a lack of consistency in command. In June Col. Mulligan led his command off to war again. Col. Tucker, the businessman that Mulligan had replaced, reassumed command of the camp. Hoffman returned in late June to investigate reports that guards or the camp sutler was assisting prisoners in escaping. "There has been the greatest carelessness and willful neglect in the management of the affairs of the camp," Hoffman informed the War Department, "and everything was left by Colonel Mulligan in a shameful state of confusion." The policing of the camp he found "in a most deplorable condition." Record keeping had been virtually nonexistent. Hoffman doubted that he could determine what prisoners had even been at the camp, never mind the identities of any who might have escaped.[24]

As the commissary general arrived in Chicago, he was greeted by a report from the U.S. Sanitary Commission that raised even more concerns about the camp. Henry W. Bellows, president of the commission, reported that the depot was "as desperately circumstanced as any camp ever was." He explained, "The amount of standing water, of unpoliced grounds, of foul sinks, of unventilated and crowded barracks, of general disorder, of soil reeking with miasmatic accretions, of rotten bones and the emptyings of camp kettles is enough to drive a sanitarian to despair." As possible solutions to this long list of problems he recommended either a relocation of the camp or a fire. Although less dramatic, Brockholst McVickar, Camp Douglas's post surgeon, concurred in the need for improvements. On June 30 he reported that there were 326 patients in the hospital. He expected the number to go up if changes were not made before the weather became warmer. Residue from privies, kitchens, and quarters was saturating the ground, and McVickar called for a drainage system to remove it. Hoffman concurred with the recommendation and went even farther. Despite his subsequent reputation for cheapness, the commissary general urged upon Meigs the construction of new barracks and a new sewer system. Altogether the project would cost at least $10,000. This was too much for the quartermaster general. "Ten thousand men should certainly be able to keep this camp clean," he brusquely replied, "and the United States has other uses for its money than to build water-works to save them the labor necessary to their health."[25]

To the east, yet another training facility changed roles as Camp Morton, located just north of Indianapolis, prepared for the arrival of some three thousand Fort Donelson prisoners. The city had purchased the thirty-six-acre tract of land in 1859 as the site of the state fairgrounds. When the war began it seemed a logical place to train Indiana's eager volunteers. The land was well drained, trees provided shade, and a stream supplied water for the recruits. Barns and other buildings converted easily into quarters. By May 1861 nearly seven thousand Hoosiers were training at the camp, which was named for Governor Oliver P. Morton.[26]

On February 17, 1862, Governor Morton informed Halleck that the camp could handle three thousand prisoners. He then departed with several surgeons and nurses for Fort Donelson, leaving Adj. Gen. Lazarus Noble to see to the arrangements. On February 22 Noble reported to Halleck that five trainloads of captives had reached Indianapolis safely and were "comfortably quartered." Apparently Camp Morton was unable to accommodate all the prisoners sent to Indiana because a sixth train had been stopped at Terre Haute. According to J. K. Farris, one of the Donelson prisoners, portions of at least two regiments were sent from Cairo to Lafayette, Indiana.[27]

Farris kept his diary only sporadically while at Camp Morton. Most entries were largely devoted to the daily menu enjoyed by Farris and his mess. Cornbread, mutton, bacon, and coffee were among the rations. They were supplemented by items that the prisoners were able to buy. On one occasion Farris and a fellow captive made pudding using eggs, flour, ginger, baker's bread, butter, and sugar they had purchased. He also noted that the men's spiritual needs were served by a variety of preachers, "both soldiers of our own army & Citizens of Indianapolis."[28]

The commanding officer at Camp Morton was Col. Richard Owen of the Sixtieth Indiana. Apparently on his own, Owen devised a set of rules governing the camp, which largely made the prisoners responsible for their own discipline. The regulations divided the captives into thirty divisions. Each division selected a chief, who was "responsible for the general appearance, police and welfare of their division." Chiefs were expected to report prisoners who forged signatures of camp officials, refused to share in their duties, sold items issued to them to the camp sutler, stole, insulted sentinels, or made "improper use of premises." Together the chiefs composed boards to hear the prisoners' grievances, subject to Owen's approval. The commandant agreed to provide space for exercise and facilities for the prisoners to wash their clothes. Sentinels received orders to fire upon any prisoner who climbed the fences or trees "after three positive and distinct orders to desist." After dark, offending prisoners would get only a single warning. Owen also instituted a prison fund, likely at Hoffman's insistence. Its proceeds were to be used for "the purchase of tobacco, stationery, stamps and such other articles as the chiefs of divisions may report." Owen concluded, "Every endeavor will be made by the commandant to give each and every prisoner as much liberty and comfort as is consistent with orders received and with an equal distribution of the means at disposal, provided such indulgence never leads to any abuse of the privilege."[29]

Visiting Camp Morton on March 5, Hoffman found the prisoners to be "as well cared for as could be expected under the circumstances." Many of them were sick, but the commissary general blamed that on exposure that occurred before their capture and during their transport to Indiana. Expecting the situation to be temporary, Hoffman rented a variety of buildings in and around Indianapolis to accommodate them. He recommended making an addition to the city hospital rather than constructing a new facility at the camp. City officials, Hoffman informed Meigs, had agreed to the plan. He also proposed the addition of a bake house as a cost-saving measure, suggesting that the baker employed at the time was less than efficient. The quartermaster general approved both recommendations. Hoffman also ordered Capt. James Ekin, Indiana's assistant quartermaster, to add windows to the prisoners' barracks and try to find some means to make those barracks less crowded. These measures, he believed, would reduce sickness.[30]

The commissary general of prisoners was more concerned with the situation at Lafayette. There some seven hundred prisoners were "very uncomfortably quartered in a pork house," Hoffman informed Meigs on March 7. He believed they should not be kept there more than a week or two longer. Were it not for the uncertainty of ice in the bay, Hoffman noted, he would have ordered them immediately to Johnson's Island. The guard at Lafayette consisted of a regiment of volunteers that had been organizing there when the prisoners arrived. Hoffman also considered the surgeon in charge, Thomas Chesnut, to be incompetent. Complicating the matter was the fact that Governor Morton had appointed Chesnut to the post. On March 6 Hoffman wrote to the governor, "I regret to say that Dr. Chesnut does not seem exactly to be fitted to have charge of a large hospital." Four days later Hoffman sent Morton a clipping from a Lafayette newspaper claiming that the surgeon was hindered by "red tape" in carrying out his duties. "The tenor of it satisfied me that Doctor Chesnut is at the bottom of it," Hoffman wrote. As further ammunition he told Morton that female volunteers attending the sick had a low opinion of the surgeon. "The ladies say that the sick have no confidence in him and refuse to take his prescriptions," Hoffman claimed. Lafayette did not serve long as a prison depot. Dr. Chesnut's fate is not known. However, on April 3 he wrote to Hoffman to complain that his pay was not high enough for the amount of work his job required.[31]

On February 19 Halleck's search for locations to house Grant's prisoners led him to Camp Chase. The Columbus camp was already home to a mix of political and military captives taken mostly in Kentucky and western Virginia. Halleck wired Governor Tod, asking how many the depot could handle. "We now have accommodation for 300," Tod replied the next day. "Can make ready for 1,000 in three days." Small numbers trickled in over the next few days before a contingent of 720 arrived at the Ohio capital on March 1. The train hauling the captives had been scheduled to reach Columbus during the early morning hours. It ended up being delayed, as a local reporter wrote, "till our good people had taken breakfast and were ready for a sensation." The scribe was less than impressed with the prisoners. "Their clothing," he informed his readers, "was without uniformity; some brown, some gray, some blue in color, of varying texture, and by no means to be coveted by the Union soldiers in guard over them."[32]

On the same day that the 720 Donelson prisoners arrived in Columbus, Col. Granville Moody, a Methodist minister, assumed command of Camp Chase. In doing so he became the latest in a continuing parade of officers to hold the post. Like his predecessors, Moody appeared to earn the job because his regiment, the Seventy-fourth Ohio, was training there at the time. He would remain in command until June 29, when he departed with his unit for the front. Although Moody was the commandant, Tod attempted to call the shots at Camp Chase. Signing his correspondence as "Governor and Commander-in-Chief," the governor issued a set of special orders on March 2 to deal with "the recent large additions of prisoners." They called for descriptive rolls of the captives, a strict limit on visitors, and comfortable hospitals for sick prisoners. The prisoners were to be divided into "conveniently sized messes," with officers and men segregated. They were also to receive the same rations as Federal troops. Not one to miss any details, even obvious ones, Tod insisted, "A strong guard will at all hours be maintained."[33]

Col. Moody added his own instructions. Although Tod's orders permitted visitors, Moody insisted that the visits be brief. He added, "If any language disrespectful to the government of the United States is used, the interview will be immediately terminated." He also restricted the prisoners' letters to two pages. As at all other camps, all incoming and outgoing correspondence was subject to inspection. Any prisoner "committing a nuisance away from the sinks" would be punished. Any approaching closer than ten feet to the fence could be shot. This became the "dead line" that all prisoners, Union and Confederate, quickly came to respect. The orders required the prisoners to be "respectful in their language and deportment" toward their guards. They also informed Union soldiers that they were "strictly forbidden to use any insulting or ungentlemanly language towards any prisoner."[34]

Also inserting himself into the Camp Chase command structure was Col. Hoffman. On February 28 he wrote to Tod, "In virtue of my office of commissary-general of prisoners I am invested with the supervision of all prisoners of war." He added, "In the performance of these duties it will afford me much pleasure to consult with you in relation to those at Camp Chase and have the advantage of your advice." Hoffman went on to describe a number of actions that he had already taken at the camp without consulting the governor. He had ordered a fence to enclose the section of the camp where the prisoners would be located. He had also made arrangements with Capt. Frederick Myers, assistant quartermaster, to furnish "such clothing, bedding and cooking utensils as may be absolutely requisite." Hoffman confessed that no funds had been appropriated to pay for any of this. He asked Tod if the state could make the payments, promising future reimbursement from the Quartermaster Department. It must have come as a relief to Hoffman when the governor replied, "I will most cheerfully comply with your request, governed by your general direction."[35]

Among the prisoners destined for Camp Chase were Andrew Jackson Campbell and James Calvin Cook. Both men had been among the Confederates confined aboard the *Hiawatha* opposite St. Louis; and both were among the contingent that arrived in Columbus on March 1. Neither was particularly impressed with his new home. "We found no accommodations but cloth tents," Cook wrote in his diary, "with straw for beding." Despite the conditions, Cook slept well his first night at Camp Chase, having gotten no sleep the two previous nights. He added, "Waking up the next morning one could fully realize that we were prisoners of war." Provisions were plentiful, Cook wrote, but wood with which to cook them was scarce. The weather was cold, and water in the prisoners' tents "render[ed] it very uncomfortable." Camp officials provided planking to floor the tents, and Cook concluded that his captors "show every sign of having our welfare in view."[36]

Campbell's first impressions of Camp Chase were similar. He realized immediately that there were not enough barracks available for the flood of arriving prisoners. "Tents were stretched in the mud for those to pile up in who could not get into the shanties," he wrote. "Our clothing was all left outside to be examined and we were tramping around like a herd of swine, so thick we could hardly turn around." Like Cook, Campbell complained of the lack of wood. He also bemoaned the dirty camp kettles, which, combined with poor-quality soap and a lack of dishrags, produced meals that were "not fit for a dog to eat." The situation improved for Campbell and several other prisoners on March 8, when they were transferred to the portion of the camp previously occupied by Union trainees. This area, christened Prison 3, was the largest of three prisons within the compound. It had taken some time for camp officials to get it ready for prisoners, but when it was occupied tents were no longer necessary. Reflecting on the situation a few weeks later, one prisoner recalled, "We had a rather rough time [at first], but as soon as quarters could be provided we had them assigned us & had a comfortable time."[37]

In late April, Campbell and other Confederate officers at Camp Chase were transferred to Johnson's Island. The order came directly from the secretary of war, who had instructed Hoffman on the 13th to make the Sandusky depot "a prison for officers alone." On June 21 Hoffman also ordered all officers at Camp Douglas to Johnson's Island. By the time Stanton's order arrived, Hoffman was scrambling to enlarge the Lake Erie facility, which Grant's success had rendered woefully inadequate. On March 17 he informed Meigs that land had been cleared for ten more barracks that would accommodate a total of three thousand additional prisoners easily. "They are well ventilated," the commissary general added, "and by crowding [they] will quarter near 4,000 men." Meigs replied nine days later, giving his approval and assuring Hoffman that the entire matter "is intrusted to your discretion and judgment."[38]

Among the prisoners heading north from Camp Chase was Capt. John Henry Guy of the Goochland, Virginia, Light Artillery Battery. Guy considered the change as being for the better. "At Camp Chase," he wrote, "our grounds were little more than a fourth as extensive as they are here & were little better in rainy weather than a mudhole, or in dry weather than a dust bowl. Here we have prison grounds covered with fine grass. There the water was horrid, here it is good. There we were likely to suffer from heat & doubtless sickness. Here we are comparatively secure from both. There we saw nothing but the plank walls around us, the cabins within & the tops of a few of the nearest trees. Here we look on a beautiful lake, its water reaching to the east farther than the eye can follow." Guy's assessment might have been different if he had remained for a Lake Erie winter. Nevertheless it suggests the advantages of a camp that was carefully selected and designed as a prison facility. The news for Guy was not all good. He had been one of the last of the Camp Chase prisoners to arrive at Johnson's Island. As a result, the best quarters were already occupied, and Guy and several others found themselves in "undesirable buildings." Even in this important area, he was willing to give his keepers the benefit of the doubt. Hoffman's construction project was under way, and "as matters are all in confusion yet, we hope to fall upon an arrangement which may better our condition."[39]

The officers confined at Johnson's Island included a number of diarists. Their accounts of the prison's early days reflect elements of life that would become familiar to captives in every Northern prison camp. Among them was the development of a prison economy. For much of the war prisoners were allowed to purchase items they desired to supplement their rations. Many arrived with money. Others had friends or relatives in the North who were willing to send them funds to make purchases. Either way they were required to turn all their money over to Maj. Pierson. "Anything we buy," prisoner Edward William Drummond noted, "we [draw a] check on [Pierson] for he is a regular Bank and has checks printed for the purpose." Drummond arrived on June 21. An enlisted clerk, his position as a member of the headquarters staff at Fort Pulaski, where he was captured, most likely explains his presence at Johnson's Island. At first he and his messmates had enough money to hire three Confederate lieutenants as cooks at 25¢ apiece per week. By July 5, however, Drummond wrote, "If we stay here much longer we shall have to come down to Government Rations, as all our funds are getting rather low."[40]

Prisoners in Drummond's situation, those who enjoyed neither funds nor friends, had to resort to skill or ingenuity to secure the needed proceeds. This group included Richard L. Gray of the Thirty-first Virginia Infantry, who enjoyed a monopoly in his craft. "I am the only cigar maker here," he recorded on July 13, 1862, "and have been employed near 2 months at work and suppose by fair estimate have sold nearly $50.00 worth [of] cigars." Other entrepreneurs, Gray noted, included tailors, bakers, and a dentist. Several prisoners made boots and shoes. Others ran "washing establishments" for clothes. The largest, Gray reported, was operated by three Virginians, who handled up to 160 pieces on a good day. An engineer officer turned out "drawings and plats" of the island and its buildings, which he sold for $1. The most common vocation was the manufacture of jewelry and knick-knacks. Men following this craft, Gray noted, began early in the morning and worked throughout the day. William Henry Asbury Speer of the Twenty-eighth North Carolina observed, "Many thousands of these wrings, breast pins, Shirt buttons, Bracelets & watch fobs are made. Some of the prisoners pass their time in makeing canes of peculior Stripe and kinde various pieces & kindes of furniture, notions etc." More than anything else, the prisoners turned out gutta-percha rings. Some were able to decorate them with bits of gold or silver. Most took advantage of the opportunity allowed them to bathe in the lake, gathering shells as they did.[41]

Drummond arrived at Johnson's Island from Governor's Island. Although disease had led Union officials to transfer the Hatteras prisoners away from the facility during the fall of 1861, they pressed it into service again a few months later. The return of prisoners to the unhealthy site was one of many instances during the war in which practical considerations trumped humanitarian concerns in the formulation of Union prison policy. In this case the considerations grew out of a pair of minor Union victories in the East. On March 14 Gen. Ambrose Burnside captured New Berne, North Carolina. Four weeks later, on April 12, he started some 160 prisoners north to New York. One day earlier Capt. Quincy A. Gilmore had forced the surrender of Fort Pulaski, a Georgia coastal fortification, with a withering artillery barrage. Some 380 Confederates were captured. The last of them arrived at Governor's Island on April 18.[42]

Since prison officials assumed that he was an officer, Drummond ended up in Fort Columbus. The accommodations there pleased the Confederate clerk. "We could not have chosen a better place for imprisonment if we had made our own selection," he wrote on April 24, his second day on the island. The rations were good, and, he noted, "We have made arrangements for getting extras over from New York." In addition to foodstuffs, those extras included cooks and washwomen. Drummond reported that he and his messmates were "fixed very comfortably at about $3 per week." The prisoners even managed to secure bats and balls from the city, allowing them to organize a "Base Ball Club." On May 9 Drummond wrote, "We have been playing considerable today and I feel quite fine in consequence." The next day he conceded, "All hands went in to strong yesterday and what a sore lot of bones there has been today."[43]

As had been the case the previous autumn, the enlisted men at Castle Williams did not fare nearly as well. "We Get Soup now only Every Second Day, the intervening Day Bread and a Little Boiled Beef," George Bell wrote. While the officers used money from their friends to supplement their rations, Bell picked wild onions during the men's brief exercise period. The enlisted prisoners also had to cook their own meals. The men chosen as cooks were so inept, Bell claimed, that it took them over four hours to make coffee. "Particular Hell Kicked up," he noted in one entry, as a result of their incompetence. Bob Lewis, selected as the head cook, resigned his position following a brief ten-day tenure "after Burning the Bottom out of the Boiler." Bell's situation was not universal among the enlisted men at Governor's Island. J. C. Bruyn, who was also captured at Fort Pulaski, wrote that a man in New York City accepted Georgia money at par value. As a result, "All of our Boys are getting pretty well supplied with what they want."[44]

In mid-July the officers confined at Fort Columbus were transferred to Johnson's Island. The men at the Castle were sent away as well. Some went to Fort Warren, but most, including George Bell and J. C. Bruyn, went to Fort Delaware. The facility that, in the words of historian Nancy Travis Keen, was destined to become "dreaded above all other Federal prisons," Fort Delaware was located on Pea Patch Island in the Delaware River. The island had housed a small number of political and military prisoners since the summer of 1861. On April 22, 1862, Meigs ordered the deputy quartermaster general at Philadelphia to prepare shanties for two thousand prisoners of war "on the island outside the fort but under its guns." Hoffman arrived in mid-June. The shanties Meigs had ordered were in place and housing six hundred prisoners. "The island is a very suitable place for the confinement of prisoners of war," the commissary general reported, an assessment that time would prove questionable. Hoffman ordered barracks for an additional three thousand and informed Stanton that there was room for more.[45]

The first impressions of the Fort Delaware prisoners did not match those of their chief captor. Despite the fact that barracks had been constructed, both Bell and Bruyn found themselves housed in tents. "We are all Camped in a piece of Swampy Ground with Ditches & Canals Cut all through," Bell wrote after arriving on July 12. "I don't Know but they Mean to Let the water in Some Night and Drown us all out." As it was, some of his comrades were forced to retreat when they found about four inches of water where they lay. Two weeks later Bell reported that sickness among the prisoners was on the increase. The water was very bad, and "Bowl Complaint and Scurvy" were commonly reported. Bruyn's situation was similar. "It is pretty close quarters," he wrote of his crowded tent, "but would not mind that in particular if when the Tide rises it did not make the ground under us so wet. Some of the men have to get up in the night & stand up to keep out of the water." As for the rations the prisoners received, Bruyn wrote that the bread was sour and the meat spoiled. "Many are getting Sick Every day & not a few dying," he wrote on July 27. By July 12, according to A. F. Williams, who had also been transferred from Governor's Island, there were nearly three thousand prisoners on the island. He agreed with Bell and Bruyn that conditions were not good. "Four of us have two yankee overcoats one blanket, and an old india rubber overcoat to lye upon and cover with," he wrote. "Most of the boys have nothing at all to cover with or lye upon."[46]

Despite the complaints of Bell, Bruyn, and many other Southern prisoners in 1862, a main concern of Northern citizens and government officials was that prisoners were being treated far too leniently. The most common objection was the alleged "license" allowed Confederate officers. The notion of a "gentlemen's war" was still strong at the time of the Fort Donelson surrender. That attitude, combined with the suddenness of the capture and the overwhelming number of prisoners, led to confusion. Compounding the problem was the fact that Hoffman had devoted virtually all his time to the construction of the Johnson's Island prison. As a result, no policy was in place for dealing with the flood of captives heading north. On February 21 Adj. Gen. Fuller of Illinois asked Gen. Halleck, "What character of discipline shall be enforced upon prisoners in our camps so I may instruct commandants at camps?" Fuller wrote that there was "much indignation that the rebel officers [at Camp Douglas] have been feasted at the principal [Chicago] hotels." The problem was not limited to Chicago. Reports of paroled Confederate prisoners walking about freely, sometimes in uniform, also emanated from St. Louis and Washington, DC. In April the *Indianapolis Journal* reported that Camp Morton prisoners had been spotted at saloons in the city. They arrived, the newspaper claimed, with unarmed escorts.[47]

Critics of lenient treatment of "traitors" reserved their greatest indignation for Camp Chase. It began with the arrival of the Fort Donelson prisoners. Many reached Columbus still carrying their ceremonial swords. Some arrived attended by their slaves. One newspaper reported, "Indignant remarks were made by many prominent citizens against the mistaken generosity which treats rebels as if they were honored belligerants." Soon reports were circulating that Confederate officers had been paroled to the city, registering at Columbus hotels and adding the initials "C.S.A." to their signatures. One account had several of them attending the theater and hissing a line calling upon people to stand by the American flag. In a letter to his wife, Kentucky prisoner Charles Barrington Simrall wrote that he had gone target shooting with a group of local residents. He proudly informed her, "I was the most successful and so sustained the honor of Dixie."[48]

Soon politicians at both the state and the national level were involved in the controversy. In March a committee of the state senate visited Camp Chase. It discovered seventy-four black prisoners, about two-thirds of whom were slaves. Committee members reported, "The relation of master and slave [was] being as vigorously maintained by the master[s], and as fully recognized by the negroes and the other inmates of the prison, as ever it was in Tennessee." Such a situation, the legislators concluded, made the Ohio Constitution's ban on slavery "a nullity." The committee carefully avoided placing any blame for the situation on Governor Tod. Instead it faulted "federal authorities" for policies that were beyond the control of state officials. The general assembly passed a resolution of protest, which it forwarded to the state's congressional delegation and to Secretary of War Stanton.[49]

Meanwhile, reports from other quarters were arriving at Stanton's office. "We are greatly annoyed by the laxity prevailing at Columbus, Ohio, in guarding rebels," Adj. Gen. Noble of Indiana wrote on March 30. Word had reached the Hoosier State of Confederates walking around Columbus, wearing sidearms and "talking secesh on the streets." The same day Stanton fired off a message to Halleck, demanding that the officer in command of Camp Chase be removed. In a somewhat more restrained tone, he also informed Governor Tod that he had received complaints about "license permitted the rebel officers at Camp Chase." With his message to Halleck in mind, Stanton added, "By general regulation the commander of the department has charge of prisoners."[50]

An angry Tod responded the next day. "There is no just cause for complaint of treatment of rebel prisoners at Camp Chase," he wrote. The commander of the camp, Col. Moody, he termed "a strong anti-slavery Republican" who performed his duty "faithfully and discreetly." Despite Tod's assurances, Stanton dispatched Maj. Roger Jones, an assistant inspector general, to Columbus to find out exactly what was going on. He arrived in early April and discovered a still-peeved governor who informed Jones that his boss was "ignorant of the state of matters." Jones's report tended to exonerate Tod. Copies of orders the governor had issued showed that he had paroled only prisoners who were in ill health. Any other Confederates at large appeared to be those who had been paroled by department commanders such as Halleck. Indeed, the general's own words tended to bear out the notion that he was more responsible than Ohio officials were for the situation. On February 19 Halleck had reported that he planned to "send all officers to Columbus on parole." Citing Union sentiment in Kentucky and Tennessee, he had suggested to McClellan that such a policy would "have an excellent effect."[51]

Jones noted that there were about one hundred black prisoners at Camp Chase. This appears to have been the only portion of his report upon which officials acted. On April 21 Hoffman asked Tod to have the black captives released. The governor so ordered Moody the next day. They were to be sent away at a rate of three or four a day "that they may not be in each other's way in providing for themselves." They also received three days' rations but apparently no further assistance as they entered a strange city far from home.[52]

The black prisoners left no account of their release, but if the Confederates they left behind can be believed, the parting at Camp Chase and other depots was a sad one. On April 1 Andrew Jackson Campbell wrote that Col. Moody removed the black prisoners from the compound. Then, Campbell continued, "he proceeded to speak soothing words to his favorite race, telling them that they had been wronged by the wicked men of the South and that they were now free by the laws of Ohio." Campbell delighted in recording that at least one, the slave of a Mississippi captain, replied "that he did not want to be free, but that he wanted to go to Dixie." Randal McGavock described what he considered "quite an effecting scene" when he and his fellow field officers left Camp Chase for Fort Warren. Two free blacks, McGavock wrote, attempted to follow but were summoned back by Col. Moody. "They replied that they wished to go with their Cols and share their fate," McGavock continued, but to no avail. Edward William Drummond wrote that "a dark cloud" hung over the Governor's Island prisoners when the War Department ordered "all of our Negro Boys to be sent to New York and turned loose in the city. We all feel that it is hard and unmerciful," he added. "All the boys are in trouble, some crying and some begging to be [allowed to] stay with us." A different aspect of the issue was expressed by John Henry Guy. When the Camp Chase officers were transferred to Johnson's Island, their servants were left behind. "Some of us feel greatly the loss of them," he wrote, adding, "There are luckily some of the prisoners who are willing to cook & wash for pay."[53]

Missing from most of the correspondence regarding the "license" allowed Confederate captives was the name of the commissary general of prisoners. Still working to complete the Johnson's Island prison at the time Fort Donelson surrendered, he had to scramble to demonstrate that events had not rendered him as marginal as the Lake Erie facility. Out of necessity other officers had to deal with the logistical challenges that would have been his had a Union prison policy been firmly in place. Halleck became chief among them. More an administrator than a fighter, he brought a high level of competence to the challenge, leaving Hoffman on the sidelines as the prisoners headed north toward their makeshift prisons.[54]

Complicating the situation for the commissary general was the lack of official authority for his office. This bothered the prickly career officer, and he struggled to make for himself a definite position within the chain of command. This might have been easier under Cameron, but things changed when Stanton assumed control of the War Department on January 15, 1862. The new secretary combined a brusque and irritable personality with an uncompromising devotion to the Union cause. As a result, many aspects of the Union war effort were soon under the immediate control of the War Department and its indefatigable secretary. Policies for dealing with contractors, lax at best under Cameron, were quickly reformed. The military telegraph was transferred from army headquarters to the War Department. Stanton also moved to take control of the prison system. Previously, Secretary of State William Henry Seward had largely handled this duty. This was in part because, in the early days of the war, foreign blockade-runners had more often ended up in Union prisons than had military captives. It also reflected Lincoln's lack of trust in Cameron. Over time the shift to the War Department may have occurred anyway. Stanton's elevation guaranteed that it would. It also guaranteed that Hoffman would have a careful and constant eye looking over his shoulder.[55]

As early as December 7, 1861, Hoffman had complained to Adj. Gen. Lorenzo Thomas, "The office and duties of commissary-general of prisoners are not familiar to the service." He requested that an announcement of his appointment be made to all officers in charge of prisoners. He repeated the request, this time to Meigs, on February 26 and again on March 19. "General Halleck," Hoffman complained, "has given orders in relation to the prisoners taken at Fort Donelson, even when they were beyond the limits of his department." The only way the commissary general received information about the movements of prisoners was from "newspapers or other chance sources." Meigs forwarded Hoffman's latest plea to the War Department and added the suggestion that "some orders in regard to this important matter should be given."[56]

Two sets of orders from the War Department soon followed. The first, issued April 2, fell short of giving Hoffman the authority he desired. General Orders No. 32 formally established the post of commissary general of prisoners but announced that his "general duties will be those of an inspector." The strangest section of the orders—already rendered unworkable by the capture of Fort Donelson—was the call for "a general depot for prisoners," which the secretary of war would designate. The commissary general would command the camp, making his headquarters there. These regulations, which confused the situation more than they clarified it, were superseded on June 17 by the publication of General Orders No. 67. "The supervision of prisoners of war sent by generals commanding in the field to posts or camps prepared for their reception," the orders clearly stated, "is placed entirely under Col. William Hoffman . . . who is subject only to the orders of the War Department. All matters in relation to prisoners will pass through him." Those matters included regulations for issuing clothing, the establishment of new prison camps, and the management of prison savings funds. By previous orders, Hoffman's headquarters were in Detroit, although they would be moved to Washington in October. He had also received some assistance in performing his duties. On June 13 Capt. Henry M. Lazelle was assigned to Hoffman's office. The following day Capt. Henry W. Freedley joined the staff.[57]

Hoffman put both officers to good use, sending them on an inspection tour of the western prisons. Freedley first ventured to Camp Butler, where he arrived on July 3. Maj. Fonda remained in command of the camp. The captain "found affairs there in some confusion." Portions of two regiments still being formed composed the guard force. The majority of the sentinels, as a result, had been at the camp only a few days. There was an inadequate supply of water. The prisoners were "sadly in want of clothing." Hoffman's orders for the establishment of a prison fund had been ignored. Freedley reported that the prisoners were housed in fifteen frame barracks and approximately two hundred tents. The barracks, he noted, were poorly ventilated and improperly policed, so much so that the prisoners in the tents were more comfortable. The rations Freedley termed "good and wholesome." He also considered the health of the prisoners to be "good under the circumstances." The hospitals were policed better than the barracks, and "every care has been taken by the enforcement of cleanliness to render these hospitals comfortable and pleasant." Freedley concluded, "The sick are treated with utmost kindness." Before departing, Freedley secured a promise from Governor Yates to assign a permanent guard regiment to the camp. The captain also "endeavored to impress upon the commanding officer as well as the prisoners themselves the vast importance of cleanliness of camp and quarters."[58]

In November Hoffman dispatched Freedley to Alton. There he found affairs more confused than they had been at Camp Butler. Freedley unequivocally placed the blame on the camp commander, Col. Jesse Hildebrand, and his staff. "There has been a complete want of system, method, and organization in everything that relates to prison affairs," Freedley informed Hoffman. "None of the officers fully understand their duties and obligations." One night during his visit, the prisoners set fire to one of the buildings, allowing four of their number to escape in the confusion. If he had held the proper rank, an exasperated Freedley wrote, he would have assumed temporary command. As at Camp Butler, many of the prisoners were "sadly destitute of clothing." The police of the prison was also "not as satisfactory as could be expected." Freedley, however, placed the blame for this on the prisoners. They received ample water and cleaning supplies, "but many of them are so excessively indolent that they will live in filth, and force must be employed to cause them to keep themselves in a condition to meet the sanitary regulations of the prison." This did not explain the other problems, and Hoffman responded to his subordinate's report by ordering Hildebrand removed from command.[59]

Lazelle spent much of his summer at Camp Chase. There he found the command structure much like that described by his comrade at Alton. The problems started at the top. Col. Charles W. B. Allison commanded the Eighty-fifth Ohio Volunteers, a three-month regiment. Lazelle concluded that Allison was "not in any degree a soldier." The captain explained, "He is utterly ignorant of the most common requirements of the Army Regulations, but [he is] a 'good lawyer' or he is said to be." Allison was also the son-in-law of the lieutenant governor. Either that or the fact that his term of enlistment would be brief explains why Hoffman did not order his dismissal.[60]

Lazelle found the spaces between the barracks "heaped with the vilest accumulations of filth which has remained there for months, breeding sickness and pestilence." Streets, drains, and gutters were no better. The inspector considered the prisoners' rations to be "very inferior." The beef, bread, beans, peas, rice, sugar, molasses, potatoes, and coffee issued were all included in this assessment. Lazelle even criticized the salt, which he termed "coarsely ground." He blamed the situation on Allison, who signed requisitions without question. Lazelle left a lengthy list of suggestions for improvement before leaving. When he returned in late July he reported that most had been acted upon. "As a consequence, a marked change is observed in the health, cleanliness, police and comfort of the prisoners and decidedly for the better."[61]

The commissary general of prisoners did not merely remain in his office and await the reports of his subordinates. He frequently inspected prisons in person and performed other duties in the field. In May Hoffman made a reconnaissance trip through Wisconsin, Minnesota, and Iowa. His main purpose was to scout potential locations for future prisons. Hoffman also made it a point to visit Camp Randall, near Madison, Wisconsin, a training camp to which Halleck had shipped about twelve hundred Fort Donelson prisoners. The commissary general had received an alarming report about the camp from Assistant Quartermaster Joseph A. Potter. An untrained regiment had been pressed into service as guards, Potter informed Hoffman on May 1. Their arms were in poor condition, which mattered little as the ammunition on hand was of the wrong caliber. "But this is not the worst feature," Potter ominously reported. "I fear there is an utter want of discipline." The sentries, he claimed, had torn down barracks to erect cookhouses. Cots, sheets, and pillowcases sent for use in the hospital had also apparently been appropriated by Union soldiers. "I find prisoners helplessly sick lying on the bare floor," Potter wrote, "and many are dying I believe for want of proper care and attention."[62]

Hoffman's inspection largely confirmed Potter's dire observations. "Lumber, straw, and fuel sent to the camp by the quartermaster have been seized upon by the officers and used without authority," he informed Stanton. As Potter had reported, Union troops had torn down buildings and used the materials in any way they desired "without any interference of the commanding officer." A six-month supply of medicines had been sent to the camp from Chicago. Included were 168 pint bottles of liquor. Five days later they were empty. Hoffman took quick and decisive action to remedy the situation. He placed Maj. R. S. Smith, a regular army officer, in charge of the camp. He ordered Smith to clean up the facility, to see to it that the sick had clean sheets and clothing, and to make sure that "strict orders" were issued in regard to camp property. On May 23 Smith informed Hoffman that conditions at Camp Randall were improving, although there remained "an extraordinary delay in fulfilling promises to execute orders." By then Hoffman had apparently decided that the camp was more trouble than it was worth. On August 22 Smith reported that only four prisoners remained. Camp Randall's days as a military prison were over.[63]

At the time the decision to close the depot seemed an easy one. Indeed, it appeared that all prison camps on both sides of the Mason-Dixon Line might soon be permanently out of business. One month earlier Union and Confederate officials had agreed to a cartel for the exchange of prisoners. Its signing represented the culmination of complicated and contentious negotiations between the two sides. It also represented a victory for public pressure over the desires of the Lincoln administration to avoid any appearance of recognizing the Confederate government. Most important, to thousands of captives in both blue and gray, it represented the prospect of freedom. These men would be heading home as the Civil War prisoner experience entered an exciting—but temporary—phase.

3
“All seem rejoiced at the idea of going”
Prisoner Exchange, 1862–63

Although not the official policy of either the Union or the Confederate governments, the release of prisoners of war on parole actually predated the opening shots of the conflict. Hoffman and his fellow soldiers serving in Texas were surrendered and paroled before the guns sounded at Fort Sumter. When those guns did sound, Maj. Robert Anderson and his Union garrison were not only permitted to depart for the North but were supplied with transportation home. The Confederates even allowed the fort's defenders to hold a ceremony to salute the flag and to retain their arms and other possessions.[1]

As contending forces headed into the field in the summer of 1861, military commanders began to negotiate exchange agreements with their opposite numbers. One of the first took place in Missouri. The Confederates made the first move. On August 28 Gen. Gideon Pillow sent a message to Col. W. H. L. Wallace, offering to exchange prisoners. Wallace's response presaged many of the concerns that would trouble his and Pillow's superiors when negotiations for a general exchange got under way a few months later. The colonel pointed out that the "contending parties" had not agreed to an exchange. He further insisted that any exchange to which he agreed should not be interpreted as a precedent. When Pillow, believing Wallace held the greater number of prisoners, proposed that Federals held in Richmond be included in the swap, Wallace declined. He also balked at Pillow's suggestion to exchange civilian prisoners as well as military captives. Wallace's superior, Gen. John C. Fremont, added yet another stipulation to the proposal. Only regular soldiers would be accepted, no home guards. By the time all the restrictions had been put in place, each side received only three prisoners when they met on September 3. Still, despite Wallace's insistence that the arrangement not be construed as precedent setting, a pattern for future exchanges had been established.[2]

Two days earlier, Col. M. Jeff Thompson had proposed to Gen. Grant an exchange of prisoners as their forces sparred in the vicinity of Cairo, Illinois. Realizing that many of his captives had expressed a desire to swear allegiance to the Union, Grant declined. When Gen. Leonidas Polk made a similar offer on October 14, Grant offered another reason for rejecting the proposal. "I recognize no Southern Confederacy myself," Grant informed Polk. Although he held to the latter point, the ever-practical Grant decided seven days later to return three Confederate prisoners through the lines. Col. Napoleon Buford, who conducted the captives aboard a flag-of-truce steamer, received specific orders to "avoid all discussions upon the rights of belligerents." Polk responded to Grant's unilateral move by returning sixteen captured Union soldiers. Although Grant would later become a determined foe of prisoner exchange, he pursued the policy for the next several weeks. He avoided any possible recognition of the Confederacy by simply returning captives, implicitly counting upon his rival commander to do the same. Eventually the two generals met face-to-face to expedite the exchange of 238 wounded prisoners. Grant, however, was careful to limit the scope of the talks to his little corner of the war.[3]

Similar limited exchanges took place in the eastern theater as well. On October 12, 1861, after the "States in rebellion" released fifty-seven prisoners, the Union responded by releasing an equal number. In December at least two pairs of rival generals agreed to individual exchanges. One occurred between Maj. Gen. John E. Wool, commanding the Union Department of Virginia, and Maj. Gen. Benjamin Huger of the Confederate Department of Norfolk. Capt. John W. Sprague of the Seventh Ohio was exchanged for Capt. Lucius Johnson of the Seventeenth North Carolina. Senator John Sherman of Ohio pressured the administration to effect the exchange, boasting, "Captain Sprague is a gallant officer and is worth any ten traitors in our possession." In an even more unusual transaction, Col. John W. Geary, commanding the Twenty-eighth Pennsylvania, made arrangements with Judah P. Benjamin, the Confederate secretary of war, that eventually resulted in the exchange of ten prisoners. It is unlikely that a regimental commander would have been allowed to negotiate at such a level under normal circumstances. Geary, however, was no ordinary colonel. A prominent politician, he had served as governor of the Kansas Territory before the war, which likely explains the administration's willingness to allow him to freelance as an exchange agent.[4]

The greatest number of early exchanges in the East took place between Huger and Maj. Gen. John E. Wool, the Union commander at Fortress Monroe, Virginia. Flag Officer Louis M. Goldsborough, commanding the Atlantic Blockading Squadron, started the process with Huger in October 1861. At first the two officers agreed to a number of exchanges, usually involving only a few prisoners at a time. All exchanges between Goldsborough and Huger involved members of the navy and Marine Corps. When Wool became involved in the process, exchanging army prisoners, the numbers increased, but still seldom reached a hundred at a time. The two commanders also arranged for clothing to be shipped to prisoners held by both sides. This was the only deviation Wool made from individual exchanges. He never allowed discussions to expand to a general exchange of prisoners held by both sides.[5]

On December 29, 1861, Wool sent Fort Warren prisoner Thomas B. Griffin south to Norfolk. Released on parole, Griffin was to obtain the release of a Union soldier of equivalent rank, thereby securing his own exchange. Griffin was one of the Hatteras prisoners, and he followed 249 of his fellow North Carolina captives who had been sent south for the same purpose on December 13. In orders approved by Secretary Cameron, Col. Dimick was instructed to select "the most feeble and infirm and . . . those who have families dependent upon them for support." The Confederates were meanwhile playing the same game. Capt. George C. Gibbs, commanding Confederate prisons in Richmond, recommended for exchange a list of prisoners who "from my personal knowledge of all the prisoners I think . . . are those least likely to be efficient for harm to the Confederacy in the event, not probable, that they again enter the service of the United States." Self-arranged exchanges went on for about six months. They ceased when the parolees began ignoring the terms of their release and instead simply headed for home.[6]

Individual exchanges continued, but for the first year of the war the Lincoln administration adamantly refused to consider the idea of an exchange cartel with the Confederacy. The reason for this policy was the government's almost obsessive fear of doing anything that would in any way imply a recognition of the Southern government. As a purely philosophical question, Lincoln's policy was consistent with his often-expressed view that secession was illegal under the Constitution. In his inaugural address the president had asserted that the Union was perpetual both "in contemplation of universal law, and of the Constitution." As for secession, he continued, "Resolves and ordinances to the effect are legally void." Finally, he promised to "take care, as the Constitution itself expressly enjoins upon me that the laws of the Union be faithfully executed in all the states."[7]

The war that followed soon raised practical considerations that rendered philosophical concerns moot. The president found this out when his administration pursued a policy of treating Southern privateers as pirates rather than belligerents. Confederate president Jefferson Davis, learning of the policy and of the capture on June 5, 1861 of the schooner *Savannah* and its crew, at first made a proposal for the exchange of the prisoners. When the offer was rebuffed, Davis threatened retaliation if the crew members were not treated as prisoners of war. The situation escalated with the capture of another Confederate privateer, the *Jeff Davis.* After its crew was convicted of piracy and sentenced to death, the Confederate commander in chief sent word through the lines that an equal number of Union captives had been selected for like punishment. Putting philosophy aside, Lincoln backed down from what threatened to be a senseless bloodbath.[8]

It took a different type of pressure to advance a reluctant Lincoln toward an acceptance of a general exchange of prisoners. An adroit politician, the president was sensitive to the rumblings of public and political opinion that began to be heard late in 1861. Among the loudest of them was a joint resolution of the Senate and the House of Representatives on December 11. The legislators pointed out that exchange had already been "practiced indirectly." The expansion of such a policy, they added, "would not only increase the enlistment and vigor of our army but subserve the highest interests of humanity." The resolution concluded by calling upon the president to "inaugurate systematic measures for the exchange of prisoners in the present rebellion." On January 8, 1862, the House followed up with a resolution requesting the president to "communicate what if any steps the Executive Department has taken for the systematic exchange of prisoners." Two weeks later the Michigan legislature added its voice to the issue. The Wolverine lawmakers were particularly concerned about Col. Orlando B. Willcox of the First Michigan Infantry, who had been wounded and captured at the battle of First Manassas. Willcox was being held in close confinement in Richmond as a hostage for Confederate privateers. The resolution specifically asked that Willcox's exchange be secured. With the colonel's uncertain fate in mind, the legislators also called for captured privateers to be treated as prisoners of war.[9]

By this time Stanton had assumed control of the War Department. Fully supporting Lincoln's desire to avoid any recognition of the Confederacy, Stanton deflected calls for prisoner exchange. Instead he addressed humanitarian concerns with an attempt to send food, clothing, and other needed supplies to Federal prisoners held in the South. On January 20 the new secretary named Methodist bishop Edward Ames and New York congressman Hamilton Fish to run the operation. He ordered Wool to secure passes for the pair to visit the Confederacy to determine what was needed. As an incentive for cooperation, Stanton further directed Wool to deliver unconditionally any prisoners held at Fortress Monroe.

Confederate officials had a different idea in mind. They seized upon the appointment of the Northern commissioners to achieve their goal of securing an exchange agreement. Rather than grant a pass to Ames and Fish, Secretary Benjamin instead sent two Southern negotiators, James A. Seddon and Charles M. Conrad, to Fortress Monroe. They were to meet the Union representatives "with the view of acceding at once to the proposition of exchange and of release of prisoners of war on equal terms, thus sparing those gentlemen the necessity of further travel in the accomplishment of their humane purpose." Fish and Ames realized immediately that Benjamin's motives went well beyond saving them a trip, but they were uncertain as to how to proceed. Stanton, whom they asked for guidance, was not. "Leave to pass through opposing lines having been denied you," he wrote on February 11, "you will consider your mission terminated and you will return at your convenience to this city."[10]

Lincoln and Stanton realized the failure of the Ames-Fish mission would not end the public outcry for exchange. Indeed, it was clear to the president and the secretary of war that there were no further options available for deflecting it. Yielding to the pressure, Stanton, on the day he ordered Ames and Fish home, sent a remarkable message to Wool. Seeming to imply that exchange had always been the policy of the North, he wrote, "You will inform General Huger that you alone are clothed with full powers for the purpose of arranging for the exchange of prisoners." He then specifically authorized the general to "arrange for the restoration of all the prisoners to their homes on fair terms of exchange." On February 23 Wool and Gen. Howell Cobb, who had succeeded Huger, attempted to do just that. They apparently came close, but one item of phrasing in his counterpart's proposal troubled the Union negotiator. Cobb proposed, Wool informed Stanton, "that prisoners be discharged or paroled within ten days after their capture, and . . . be delivered on the frontier of their own country free of expense to the prisoners and at the expense of the capturing party." Wool reported that he objected to the word "frontier," although the phrase "their own country" would appear to have been equally troublesome. Stanton either agreed or saw the phrasing as an excuse to scuttle the agreement. Whatever the motivation, he replied, "The proposition is obnoxious in its terms and import and wholly inadmissible, and as the terms you were authorized to offer have not been accepted you will make no arrangement at present except for actual [individual] exchanges."[11]

The decision proved temporary. On June 23 the Senate adopted yet another resolution. The Upper House requested that Stanton supply any information he had regarding prisoner exchange or negotiations upon the subject. That same day the *New York Times*, a paper generally friendly toward the Lincoln administration, editorialized, "Our government must change its policy, our prisoners must be exchanged!" On July 11 Gen. McClellan added his voice to the debate. Calling for exchange in a message to Stanton, he wrote, "I deem it a duty to our soldiers who are suffering in captivity and whose condition tortures the heart of the nation." Three days later McClellan was thinking in more practical terms. "I am very anxious to have my old regiments filled up," he wrote to the president, "rather than have new ones formed." McClellan's stock in Washington was not particularly high at the time. His campaign to capture Richmond had failed miserably, and his whining, inaccurate claims that he was outnumbered had endeared him to neither Lincoln nor Stanton. He remained a prominent figure, however, and his endorsement of exchange added even more pressure to the administration.[12]

By the time of McClellan's second message, the president and the secretary of war had again relented to the demand for a general exchange. This time two different representatives met in an attempt to reach an agreement. On July 12 Stanton informed Gen. John A. Dix, Wool's successor at Fort Monroe, that the president had authorized him to negotiate an exchange cartel. "You will take immediate measures for that purpose," Stanton ordered, "observing proper caution against any recognition of the rebel Government and confining the negotiation to the subject of exchange." Two days later Gen. Robert E. Lee assigned Gen. Daniel Harvey Hill as the Confederate negotiator. Hill's orders were simple, stating, "He is authorized to conclude any arrangement which provides for the exchange of prisoners upon terms of perfect equality." Following a series of meetings at Haxall's Landing on the James River, the two generals reached an agreement on July 22. Patterned upon a similar arrangement used by the Americans and the British during the War of 1812, the cartel established a sliding scale to calculate the relative values of officers and enlisted personnel. It also called for each side to appoint an agent of exchange to oversee the process. The final article, which was ultimately ignored, promised that exchanges would continue even if misunderstandings arose between the parties. Such disputes were to be "made the subject of friendly explanations in order that the object of this agreement may neither be defeated nor postponed."[13]

Weeks before Dix and Hill reached agreement on the cartel, rumors of an expected exchange started spreading through Northern prison camps. On June 11 Camp Butler prisoner Josephus C. Moore wrote, "There has been various letters and papers received here which all go to prove that there is a fair prospect of a general exchange of prisoners." Moore had been contemplating an escape attempt, and the news served to "delay my exit for a few days at least." At Johnson's Island exchange rumors at first produced skepticism. "We have had some news about an immediate exchange," Edward William Drummond noted on June 24, "but put no confidence in anything." In the days that followed, the Johnson's Island officers had their hopes raised and dashed by repeated rumors. Three days after his initial entry on the subject, Drummond heard that a telegram from the War Department had announced an immediate exchange. The next day he reported that "the Exchange Business had all been knocked in the head." As time wore on at the Lake Erie depot, Drummond and his comrades grasped at any hopeful sign. A July newspaper report that all captives in New York prisons were to be shipped to Delaware Bay was viewed as a first step toward exchange. So was the rumor that commissary officials at Johnson's Island had been ordered to make no additional purchases of supplies. Eventually the rumors came true for Drummond, but it was not until September that he began his journey home.[14]

A pair of Fort Delaware prisoners also found positive indications of an impending exchange. "Every thing looks toward an Exchange soon," J. C. Bruyn wrote on July 29. "The Feds all say that we will go home soon." The same day Bruyn's fellow prisoner George L. P. Wren recorded, "Three vessels now lie at anchor in the bay for the purpose of carrying us, the prisoners, to the land of Dixie all seem rejoiced at the idea of going." Within four days both men had begun their journey.[15]

Not all prisoners were "rejoiced" at the prospect of a return trip to the South. One week after signing the cartel, Dix informed Stanton that there were "several insurgent prisoners" at Fortress Monroe who were "very unwilling to return." Some had offered to take an oath of allegiance to the Union. Others preferred to give their parole of honor to remain in the North and not serve the Confederacy. Over the next three days similar reports from three Union prisons arrived at the War Department. Col. Tucker wrote that a number of Camp Douglas prisoners preferred not to be exchanged. Many claimed to have been forced into the Southern service, while some "professed to be tired of the rebellion." Governor Tod claimed that a large number of Camp Chase prisoners had begged him "to protect them against unconditional exchange." Assistant Quartermaster James Ekin of Indiana reported that between a thousand and twelve hundred captives at Camp Morton, mostly Tennesseans, felt the same way.[16]

Although the Tennessee soldiers likely made up their own minds, several of their fellow citizens had been working hard to help them arrive at the correct decision. Beginning in early 1862, a parade of colorful politicians visited the various Northern camps, urging men from the Volunteer State to reaffirm their allegiance to the Union. Among the busiest was William G. "Parson" Brownlow. A minister, former Whig, and future Reconstruction governor, his *Knoxville Whig* had been the last pro-Union newspaper in the Confederacy when driven out of business in 1861. His Northern speaking tour included at least three prison camps. At Camp Douglas, according to the postwar memoirs of prisoner "Spot" Terrell, the minister of the gospel called for the hanging of Confederate leaders. He also asserted that "the stares and stripes must and should wave all over Tennissee over evrey town and hill." Terming Brownlow an "old blackhearted scoundrel," Terrell concluded, "We did not thank him for his pitaful talk." Joseph W. Westbrook of the Fourth Mississippi was at Camp Chase when Brownlow arrived. "I remember one word only that he said," Westbrook later wrote, "and that was that the Confederacy was about out of soap." In May the parson arrived at Fort Warren. There, accompanied by Governor John Andrew of Massachusetts, he reviewed the garrison. According to Randal McGavock, Brownlow also offered paroles to three east Tennesseans. "I did not see him to-day," McGavock recorded in his diary, "and I am glad that all of the prisoners showed the disposition to give him the go-by."[17]

On August 15 William B. Campbell, a former Whig governor, spoke to the Tennessee prisoners at Camp Morton, telling them they had all been "given over to Andy Johnson." The implication, prisoner J. K. Farris wrote, was that they would be held as hostages if they refused to take the oath of allegiance. Farris reported that some 150 did before the process was suddenly and mysteriously stopped. Johnson himself made at least two visits to Camp Chase. Mississippi prisoner Timothy McNamara was present when the war governor and future president arrived on March 31. He wrote that "his mightiness" had "kindly notified us that he will in private hear our application for pardon." To this, McNamara added, "Bah." Nearly a year later Johnson returned, and according to Lt. J. K. Ferguson of the Nineteenth Arkansas, his reception was less than positive. "Governor Johnson and several great nabobs of the same stripe as him self came in to prison to see the rebels," Ferguson wrote on March 4, 1863, "and to hold out inducements to [the Tennessee prisoners]." One of the would-be beneficiaries, Gen. Thomas Churchill, refused to meet with the governor. Johnson departed, Ferguson happily recorded, to cheers for "Jeff Davis and the secesh. The honored jentelman left in a rage of disgust," he added.[18]

The results of these visits are difficult to measure. Diary accounts of the prisoners suggest that the number of oath takers varied from one camp to another. According to Terrell's recollections of Camp Douglas, several hundred Chicago prisoners returned to the Union fold. Among them were forty-three from his regiment, the Forty-ninth Tennessee. Farris wrote in his diary that some three hundred Camp Morton prisoners took the oath when given the choice in August 1862, a few days before exchange commenced. A large majority, he noted, were from Tennessee. Camp Butler prisoner Josephus Moore wrote on September 1 that ex-Governor Campbell had administered the oath to about three hundred Tennessee prisoners that day. Among them was Moore himself, making him a rarity among Civil War diarists. Three days earlier he had written, "I have the matter under consideration now as to the best course to pursue with a decided tendency toward [accepting the oath]." He explained, "My time for which I enlisted is out and two or three months over so I am not bound to report myself to Jeff Davis or anyone else." He had pledged himself to the state of Tennessee for twelve months, Moore rationalized, and he had honored that pledge. He concluded, "Now whether I take the oath of allegiance or not I intend to follow no man. If I cannot form an opinion of my own I will keep silent until I can." The day after he signed his oath, Moore was released.[19]

At Johnson's Island, where only officers were confined, the oath was much less popular. When a Tennessee soldier took it on July 9, prisoner William Drummond wrote, "I wish we had his name. He should be recollected." On August 10 Drummond and his fellow Confederates were "all startled by a continued yell and all hands were anxiously looking for the cause." The cause proved to be a large painted sign announcing, "Prisoners who prefer taking the Oath of Allegiance to going South to join the Southern Army will apply to Maj. Pierson immediately." The sign, Drummond reported the next day, netted only one or two oath takers. "The Yankees seemed surprised," he proudly wrote, "that their flaming announcement is not more fully appreciated." According to Andrew Jackson Campbell, Drummond's fellow Johnson's Island captive, several handbills bearing the same offer also went up on August 10. "Of course we deem the act an insult to the prison," he wrote, noting that the prisoners quickly tore them down. Undeterred, "Old Person [Maj. Pierson] immediately sent in and had the bills posted around the walls so the sentinels could keep them from being torn down." Virginian John Guy gave the Yankees at Johnson's Island only slightly more credit in obtaining oath takers. In an August 27 diary entry he wrote that five prisoners had agreed. One, he added, was of foreign birth, and three others were natives of the North.[20]

A. F. Williams had a similar opinion of the oath takers at Fort Delaware. According to Williams, a group of Yankee sergeants visited all the barracks on July 30 to get the names of the prisoners wishing to take the oath of allegiance. "I am very sorry to say that a great many of them have given their names," he wrote. "They are principally of foreign birth and all rascals." Their fellow prisoners "gave them a groan as they passed out," ending up in the prison dungeon as a result. There were more groans and a few comments that evening when the oath takers returned to gather their personal effects. All stopped, however, when a guard fired his carbine.[21]

Regardless of the camp, the overwhelming majority of Confederate prisoners preferred exchange to taking the oath of allegiance. The result was a logistical challenge for the Union officials charged with arranging for the return of captives to the South. The Confederates appointed Robert Ould, a private citizen who had formerly served as district attorney in Washington, DC, as agent of exchange. Adj. Gen. Lorenzo Thomas served as the Union agent until October 23, when Lt. Col. William H. Ludlow, a member of Dix's staff, succeeded him. Eastern prisoners were to be delivered to these officials at Aiken's Landing on the James River. Vicksburg was designated as the destination for exchanged prisoners from camps in the West. Thomas dispatched Capt. Lazelle of Hoffman's staff to the Mississippi city to oversee operations there. Maj. N. G. Watts was his Confederate counterpart.[22]

Hoffman also headed west, traveling from prison to prison as the exchange process got under way. Since the western camps held the vast majority of the Confederate captives, the commissary general of prisoners started them toward Vicksburg from one camp at a time. The colonel began at Camp Morton. On August 22 he gave detailed instructions to Col. D. Garland Rose, who was then commanding the facility. Over the next twelve days he repeated them, with minor alterations, at Camp Chase, Johnson's Island, Camp Douglas, Camp Butler, and Alton. The prisoners were to be shipped in detachments of about one thousand, each guarded by a company of soldiers. Except for the Alton prisoners, the guard would be responsible for getting them by rail to Cairo, Illinois. Alton's captives would go to Cairo by boat. From there all of the exchanged prisoners were to travel by river to Vicksburg. Ever the conscientious administrator, Hoffman warned that the guard must be vigilant to prevent escapes en route. He also instructed camp commanders to return any money belonging to the prisoners. Those wishing to take the oath of allegiance could be released after the exchanged prisoners had departed.

As the first detachments of prisoners reached Cairo, Lazelle gave equally detailed instructions to the captain in charge of the transport that was to carry them south to Vicksburg. He ordered that sentinels be placed on "those parts of the vessel the most advantageous to constantly control the prisoners." Their weapons were to be loaded but not capped. Nobody but officers could burn lights. Smoking was allowed only on the upper deck and was forbidden there after 8:00 p.m. Lazelle instructed the captain to detail a sufficient number of cooks for both prisoners and guards and to monitor cook fires carefully. "You will take the most vigilant measures," Lazelle concluded, "to guard against fire and all casualties of whatever nature which proper precaution will prevent."[23]

On September 10 Lazelle delivered his first contingent of thirty-nine hundred prisoners to Confederate authorities. They disembarked at Young's Point, twelve miles above Vicksburg, the place Confederate officials selected for the transfer. The trip from Cairo had taken twelve days. Some twenty prisoners had escaped at Memphis while the boats were taking on coal. However, since the boats were traveling under a flag of truce, the Union still received credit for the missing men under the terms of the cartel. Otherwise the voyage was without incident. Capt. Freedley, whom Hoffman had sent to Camp Morton to help oversee the departure of prisoners, reported that between eight and ten guerrillas had managed to leave with the exchanged soldiers by answering for dead men when the rolls were called. Union officials reported no other serious problems as the process of prisoner exchange got under way.[24]

The administrative details that most concerned the prisoners, of course, were those affecting their ability to get back to Dixie as quickly as possible. Such was the case for J. K. Farris and several other Camp Morton prisoners. The delay came at Cairo, where they had to wait ten days for arrivals from the other western camps. "We are all very ancious to leave here for Vicksburg," he wrote on September 6, "where we hope to live better, as it is hard liveing here." Farris and his comrades were crowded into five steamers anchored in the middle of the Ohio River. Farris was aboard the *Fanny Bullitt,* subsisting on bacon, hard crackers, and coffee. Since there was only one stove on the boat, the meat was generally eaten raw and hot coffee was seldom available. On the 7th Farris was transferred to the *J. H. Dove,* which had been designated as the hospital boat for the fleet. "Have a good deal to do," he recorded on September 8. "I have entire charge of every thing & [am] responsible for the treatment of the sick, & their general welfare." Farris had one assistant, a steward, and eighteen nurses to assist him in caring for 150 patients. With the position came the freedom to visit the shore to procure supplies.[25]

On September 5 a contingent of prisoners from Johnson's Island arrived at Cairo. They had left Sandusky four days earlier. It took most of the day for Union officials to get them across the bay before they were put on passenger cars at the Sandusky depot. Their route took them through Bellefontaine, Ohio, Indianapolis, and Terre Haute before they reached Cairo. "We were treated with great civility in Sandusky and in fact all the way through," Edward Drummond wrote. Richard Gray noted that there were several delays along the way as the prisoners waited on sidings for higher-priority trains to pass. Occasionally the men were allowed to get off the cars and visit local stores as they waited. Gray was pleased to report that the Confederates discovered "much S[outhern] feeling from Indianapolis along the route to Cairo." He was less pleased with the transportation. From Sandusky to Indianapolis the men had ridden in passenger cars, but at the Indiana capital they were transferred to boxcars and cattle cars.[26]

Reaching Cairo on the 5th, the Johnson's Island prisoners were immediately placed on the waiting steamers and towed out into the river. They were no more impressed with their living conditions than Farris was. "Our rations and feeding, rather rough," Gray wrote on the day of their arrival. "Our water from River warm and very unpalatable." His only consolation came from the scenery. "The view at night of Cairo in the moon light with the numerous steamers at wharf and anchored in stream with their lights is to me grand and beautiful." Drummond, who was aboard the *Universe,* wrote, "Over twelve hundred of us have been crowded together and every conceivable place that a man can crawl into is occupied. The whole Boat, four decks, is full and when we lay down at night it is snug work for all to get room." Even after the guards removed four hundred men to another vessel, the *Universe* remained uncomfortably packed. Like Farris, Drummond complained of rations that had to be eaten raw because of a lack of cooking facilities on board.[27]

On September 8 the flotilla started down the Mississippi. It consisted of ten steamers, including one gunboat and the hospital boat aboard which Farris served. Now military tourists, the passengers observed the wreckage of boats and encampments of Federal soldiers. The veterans of eastern campaigns pointed out locations where various engagements of the still-young war had occurred. As the boats passed into Tennessee waters, Gray recorded what he termed "the most interesting and affecting incident of our Trip." Passing the home of one of the prisoners, they saw the man's wife on the bank. Somehow the couple made contact, and as the boats continued downriver, the woman mounted "a swift footed Animal" and followed at a gallop. Along the way she managed to shout over that "all was well and doing well." The prisoners lost sight of her at a large bend in the river. She reappeared a short time later, having ridden six miles across the neck of land formed by the bend. "The cheers which greeted her," Gray noted, "[were] hushed to give her and her husband a chance to speak to each other. In her were evidenced the beautiful Virtues of womanly devotion, constancy and Patriotism. . . . Never did Lady have more earnest cheers and heartier greetings given her by thousands of Sons of the South than she."[28]

Another highlight for the prisoners was the layover in Memphis, where the boats stopped to take on coal. Despite a broiling sun, Gray noted, "the ladies of Memphis came out in great numbers giving every demonstration of pleasure & hearty welcome to us." Many were friends and acquaintances of the prisoners, which may help explain the escapes that took place at the Tennessee city. "Multitudes of wimmin crouded around and hallowed for Jeff Davis and the South," wrote "Spot" Terrell, who was returning home from Camp Douglas. "Tha give meny Gifts of tobaco apples and peaches candy and all sorts of grappess. The boys gave them rings in return which was verry acceptable with the Tenn Girles." While at Memphis, Farris received permission to leave the boat "to procure some stimulants for the sick." The welcome he received was overwhelming. "The ladys every where met me with smiling faces and all ancious to shake me by the hand & say to me God bless you." He returned with whiskey, brandy, and wine, plus pickles, preserves, and money to purchase anything else his patients required.[29]

The hospital boat left Memphis ahead of the others, using the extra time gained to bury a patient who had died. Farris himself soon fell ill, adding misery to what had already become a frustrating job. "Dr. Moorehead of Louisiana my assistant & companion has done all in his power," Farris wrote from his sickbed, "but with the scant supply of medicine, inefficient nurses & great amount of labor he has not been able to do what he might have done under favorable circumstances. Consequently several have died." Farris reported on September 15, two days before reaching Vicksburg, that twelve men had died aboard the hospital boat. "Several have died on other boats," he added, "but how many I do not know." It was a problem that would continue to haunt the exchange process. In a letter to his sister, Roland K. Chatham, who was exchanged in early November 1862, reported that nearly one hundred of six hundred men on the boats had died "by neglect." It was not just prisoners who complained of poor medical care aboard the exchange boats. In March 1863 Hoffman reported that the Union doctor sent from Camp Chase to accompany Lazelle and a shipment of exchanged prisoners was "of no service to him at all." The physician, Hoffman continued, "was listless and apathetic and very indifferent to the wants of the sick." His assistant, a Confederate prisoner, ended up caring for his comrades.[30]

One prisoner who was well satisfied with the medical treatment he received was John Henry Guy. The Virginia captain became ill on the last leg of the voyage. "The doctors had no medicine," he noted in his diary, "but by their advice I took heavy drinks of brandy from the bar every hour or two and found it the very thing." Otherwise he felt the latter days of the trip were uninteresting. "The river was low & the passage difficult on account of sandbars & the seeming inexperience of the pilots," he wrote. The boats dropped anchor every night. On September 18 they reached the spot designated for exchange. The prisoners were transferred to Confederate steamers and taken on to Vicksburg. "The boys were nearly worn out," Farris reported, "but very glad that they are alive." Farris was relieved to be "out from under the bayonet," but he was less than pleased with the prices of articles in Vicksburg. He met a friend with a new pair of boots that had cost him $30. A "very common worsted shirt" was $7.50, apples were 10¢ apiece, potatoes $4 per bushel. Despite the inflation, Gray noted that the citizens of Vicksburg had made "extensive preparation for eating & lodging." The Virginia soldier found Vicksburg to be "a romantic & beautiful place." He also discovered a fact of which Union officials had become well aware. "It is a remarkably naturally fortified place in a military point of view," Gray concluded.[31]

Meanwhile, prisoners in the eastern camps had, in many cases, made their way back to the South. Fort Warren's captives departed on July 31. To the last moment the Massachusetts fortification maintained its reputation as an unusually friendly prison. Confederate colonel McGavock described the parting with Col. Dimick, the fort's commander, as "very effecting. This being accomplished, we bid a final adieu to Ft Warren amid the sweet strains from the band—and the waving of handkerchiefs from the ladies, and even the federal soldiers." Three days later the single steamer bearing McGavock and his comrades reached Fortress Monroe. There they started up the James River, passing the Union ironclad *Monitor* as they went. "We were badly fed on these transports," the colonel complained, "having nothing to eat but hard sea crackers and concentrated coffee." He added, "Four or five men died on the boats for want of proper nourishment and attention." Reaching Aiken's Landing, the point of exchange, on August 5, McGavock was little more impressed with the efficiency of Confederate authorities. "Our government officials are very culpable for not having any transportation for the prisoners to Richmond or any one to receive us," he wrote. While most walked the fifteen miles to Richmond, McGavock hitched a ride on an ambulance. Despite the inconvenience, he noted, "Nearly every man as he stepped off the boat—seemed to draw a long breath—and evidently looked like he felt better and happier."[32]

The attitudes of the Fort Delaware prisoners upon leaving were quite different from those of the Fort Warren captives, at least according to George L. P. Wren. "We left silently," Wren wrote on August 2, the day of the departure, "not a tear was shed all bid it farewell hoping never to see it again." Writing from a camp of exchanged prisoners at Richmond, J. C. Bruyn exclaimed, "I really do believe that I am the happiest man on the face of the earth." Still, he was finding old habits hard to break. "I have to ask the guards if I can go there & there, or if I can do so & so," he explained, "at which they laugh at me & Say go where you please and do as you please." Bruyn complained that water had been scarce on the voyage to Aiken's Landing. Rations consisted of only "3 Hard tack & a thin slice of raw salt meat which was realy too tough to Eat." Some of the men supplemented their fare by stealing a ham that the captain of the boat had put away. Five died during the short voyage, and twenty arrived "very sick." For Wren the journey was not nearly as bad as the news that greeted him upon his arrival at Richmond. Eight members of his company had been killed in the fighting around Richmond, and "several others of my best friends [had been] wounded and had died. All this had happened during the two months that I was a prisoner," Wren continued. "I don't know when I had met with such a shock."[33]

In 1863 Gen. Grant's campaign for Vicksburg ruled out the river city as a point of exchange. Indeed, a group of nearly eight hundred captives sent from Alton in January were returned to the Illinois prison. As a result, prisoners from western camps found themselves making a circuitous journey through Virginia to rejoin their outfits. One of them was J. K. Ferguson. The Arkansas lieutenant was among a group of exchanged prisoners that left Camp Chase on April 10. Upon departing, the men were searched, and, according to Ferguson, relieved of many of their personal possessions. They then marched the four miles to the Columbus depot to begin their journey back to Dixie. The trains delivered them to Philadelphia via Pittsburgh. Ferguson and comrades then boarded steamers for Fort Delaware, where they remained from April 12 to April 29. The next leg of the trip was aboard the steamer *State of Maine,* which carried them to City Point, Virginia, which had become the location for exchange. They arrived on May 2.[34]

Two days later, still waiting aboard the steamer, Ferguson noted the arrival of Ludlow and Ould, along with a boat carrying 250 Confederate prisoners. Late that evening the exchange process was completed. "We were glad to be set at liberty once more," Ferguson related, "and to set our feet on our own native soil." As Bruyn had discovered, there was a slight readjustment that went along with the return to freedom. Ferguson noted, "I felt very strange after being in confinement almost four long months among a frowning enemy." He found it pleasantly unusual "to be here set at liberty to roam without asking the permission of a sentinell and to be enthusiastically received by Ladies who come in the cars to meet us." Ferguson took a train that night to Petersburg, where news of the battle of Chancellorsville and the mortal wounding of Gen. "Stonewall" Jackson was beginning to filter in. He left the next evening, May 5, for Richmond, where he secured pay for himself and some men of his regiment who were serving as pickets along a road north of town.[35]

Ferguson left Richmond on May 11. His expected destination was Vicksburg, where he planned to rejoin his brigade. The route was through Lynchburg, Bristol, and Knoxville. Along the way Ferguson marveled at the mountain scenery through which the train passed. "Our rout has been through a beautifull and wild region of country," he wrote on the 14th. "We past over a portion of ranges of the Allegheny mountains beautiful valleys the high clifts of the noted blew ridge." Although the returning Confederates were cheered as they went through Virginia, the lieutenant found the residents of east Tennessee to be "some what tainted with abolition principles." On May 17 Ferguson arrived in Tullahoma, Tennessee. Here he was reunited with his division. The news, however, was not all good. Instead of returning to the trans-Mississippi forces with which he had served before his capture, Ferguson's division was assigned to Gen. Braxton Bragg's Army of Tennessee. Making the news even more bitter was the fact that about four hundred men from Ferguson's regiment remained in Arkansas. "Our consolidation may be but temporary and we may be sent to them again," he wrote hopefully. He immediately added, "But I fear that we will be kept on this side of the river."[36]

On April 1, 1863, a contingent of about 850 prisoners left Alton prison to begin the long journey back to the Confederacy. Among them was Missouri Confederate Henry Martyn Cheavens. A member of Gen. Sterling Price's Missouri State Guard, Cheavens had been wounded in July 1861 at the battle of Carthage. After recovering, he joined a band of guerrillas in August 1862. He was attempting to rejoin Price when he was captured in November. Cheavens was first sent to Gratiot Street Prison before being transferred to Alton in February 1863. Traveling by rail, the exchanged prisoners passed through Terre Haute, Columbus, and Harpers Ferry before arriving at Baltimore on the morning of the 5th. They spent the night there, "packed in masse into a large warehouse." A steamer was waiting the next morning to deliver the prisoners to City Point. Like the men who had ventured down the Mississippi, the Alton prisoners observed already historic scenes of the war in which they were engaged. "We saw the turret ship Monitor at the mouth [of the James] looking like a big turtle," Cheavens noted.[37]

On April 8, his thirty-third birthday, Cheavens boarded the train at City Point for Petersburg. Over the next few days several more trains arrived bearing exchanged prisoners from Camp Douglas and St. Louis. The great majority, Cheavens wrote, were being sent to Bragg's army. He was not, departing instead on April 13 with a group of 125 that was sent to Alexandria, Louisiana, to report to Gen. Edmund Kirby Smith. They never made it. At Meridian, Mississippi, the soldiers were pressed into service to guard the city against Union cavalry that was reported to be in the area. Once the danger there had blown over, the men were sent to Jackson, where they helped guard Union prisoners. On May 4 Cheavens and his comrades were sent to Vicksburg to help defend the river city against Grant's advancing force.[38]

The assignment proved ironic. On July 4 Gen. John Pemberton surrendered the city and its defenders to Grant. Cheavens was once again a prisoner. This time that status proved temporary. Not wishing to deal with twenty thousand sick and starving prisoners, Grant paroled the entire lot. Halleck, who was by then serving as general in chief of all Union armies, grumbled for a while about the action, complaining that since the men had not been delivered to "a proper agent" they were eligible to reenter the Confederate service. It was not Halleck who had just won one of the most important victories of the war, however, and Grant's decision stood.[39]

Cheavens would have agreed that the action had been correct, and not just because he had avoided a second trip to a Union prison. The lengthy siege of Vicksburg had left the soldiers in a pitiable condition. "Our men were like skeletons, and many came out but to die." He joined them on their march to Raymond, Mississippi, just west of Jackson. "We went on till we were tired," Cheavens wrote. Other stops were made to care for the sick and bury the dead. Upon reaching Raymond, Cheavens became ward master at a house that was pressed into service as a hospital. "Soon the house was crowded and I had my hands full," he wrote. The women of Raymond came out to assist and were "very attentive to the sick." Local residents brought what supplies they could, and one of the doctors journeyed to Big Black, Mississippi, to locate more. Although not a physician, Cheavens mixed up several prescriptions and assisted with a number of operations. "Since being here I have studied a good deal of medicine and practiced more," he concluded.[40]

On September 8, with only four wounded men remaining at the makeshift hospital, Cheavens and two other members of the staff started out in a spring wagon for Demopolis, Alabama. From there he would eventually go on to participate in more campaigns in Tennessee and Georgia, followed by a career in medicine that continued until his death in 1920. First he spent some seven weeks at the South's parole camp in the Alabama community. Grant's decision to parole the Vicksburg prisoners had transferred a logistical nightmare from his forces to the Confederates. The result was the parole camp at Demopolis. Cheavens apparently enjoyed his time there. He discovered about twenty members of his company camping just north of the town, "with a splendid spring of water and everything pleasant." A religious revival was going on, he reported, with several men coming forward to join the church.[41]

Confederate officials viewed the Demopolis camp in a different light. On June 3, weeks before the Vicksburg prisoners began to arrive, camp commander Henry C. Davis reported that parolees arriving there were "in a destitute condition, having no clothes or money." With the arrival of the Vicksburg men at Demopolis, other problems arose. Many of the men believed the terms of their parole prohibited them from bearing arms, even for purposes of drilling. Others believed that they were exempt from all military service, including remaining at a parole camp until exchanged. "The men are coming in, but will not stay in paroled camps at Demopolis," Pemberton informed Secretary of War James Seddon on August 24. "Unless there is prospect of immediate exchange, I recommend that each regiment be ordered to rendezvous at given points in its own State, and a brigade camp should also be established in the State where the command may be ordered armed and disciplined." On September 9 Gen. William M. Gardner, then commanding at Demopolis, made his own appeal to the War Department. "Up to this time there has been very little disposition evinced on the part [of] the paroled men to return to this point," he quaintly reported. In somewhat more blunt terms, Gardner continued, "I do not think they will come in in any large numbers unless some strong measures are adopted." Specifically, he called for the publication of "an order from an authoritative source."[42]

Gardner had a personal stake in making his appeal to the War Department. Many of the men who should have been reporting to Demopolis had been serving under his command when he was forced to surrender Port Hudson after the fall of Vicksburg. Nevertheless, the order that he called for would not appear until January. In the meantime Lt. Gen. William J. Hardee was placed in command of all Vicksburg and Port Hudson parolees. Hardee moved their rendezvous from Demopolis to Enterprise and attempted to appeal to their patriotism. "Soldiers," he declared on August 27, "look at your country! The earth ravaged, property carried away or disappearing in flames and ashes, the people murdered, negroes arrayed against whites, cruel indignities inflicted upon women and children. . . . He who falters in this hour of his country's peril is a wretch who would compound for the mere boon of life robbed of all that makes life tolerable." He appealed to the men, "Come to your colors and stand beside your comrades, who with heroic constancy are confronting the enemy." If his appeal shamed any of the parolees into reporting to Enterprise, it mattered little. There were not enough officers present at the camp, he reported on September 17, to organize the paroled prisoners into regiments.[43]

In November Lt. Gen. Leonidas Polk, a corps commander in the Army of Tennessee who had refused to serve any longer under Gen. Bragg, replaced Hardee. Hardee, who also had problems with Bragg, returned to the Army of Tennessee. Polk, a bishop of the Episcopal Church, tried his own patriotic appeal. "It is hoped," he announced on November 20, "that the gallant men who, by their courage and heroic sacrifices, have made Vicksburg and Port Hudson immortal, will need no new appeals to induce them to make their future military history as glorious as their past." Perhaps the men did not see Vicksburg and Port Hudson in the same glorious terms that Polk did. Perhaps they sincerely believed that their paroles released them from military duty until exchanged. Maybe they were simply tired. Whatever the reason, Polk experienced the same problems the commanders before him had encountered. "It is contended by many of them that they are forbidden by that [parole] instrument from assembling in military camps at all, or performing any military duty whatever," he informed the War Department, "and holding that construction they refuse to come into camp or attempt to leave at their pleasure." Many had crossed the Mississippi and gotten beyond his authority. Like Gardner before him, Polk called for "a direct expression of the opinion and decision of the Department."[44]

By the time that "direct expression" came, exchange had become a virtual dead letter. Each side blamed the other for the collapse of the cartel, but it was likely doomed from the start. The issues were debated at the time by the contending sides, and contending historians have debated them since. What is beyond debate is that, while it lasted, the exchange cartel brought home thousands of fortunate captives in both blue and gray. Whatever problems were associated with the cartel, those men and their families would have certainly considered them a small price to pay.

4
"In view of the awful vortex"
The Collapse of the Cartel and the Second Wave of Prisoners

On July 23, 1862, one day after the Dix-Hill exchange cartel was signed, Gen. John Pope issued General Orders No. 11. The date would prove to be ironic, and the orders themselves would prove to be one of many examples of Gen. Pope's poor sense of timing.

The previous month Pope had been named commander of the Army of Virginia, an amalgam of forces serving in western Virginia. Pope had earned the position based on successes he had enjoyed as a commander in the western theater, including the capture of Island No. 10. His new command had a less sterling record, and in a tactless message issued on July 14, he reminded them of that fact. "I have come to you from the West," he boasted, "where we have always seen the backs of the enemy." If his message had been less than endearing to his new command, General Orders No. 11 were outrageous to the Confederates. Unit commanders were ordered to "arrest disloyal male citizens within their lines or within their reach in rear of their respective stations." Those willing to take the oath of allegiance would be allowed to remain. Those unwilling were to be conducted beyond Union lines. If they returned they would be "considered spies and subjected to the extreme rigor of military law." Anyone deemed guilty of violating his oath would be shot and his property seized. The Confederate response was equally sharp. Acting upon the orders of President Davis, Gen. Robert E. Lee proclaimed Pope and his officers to be "robbers and murderers, not . . . public enemies entitled if captured to be treated as prisoners of war." General Orders No. 54, issued by the Confederate War Department on August 1, made Lee's response official. Lee soon made the question moot by defeating Pope at the battle of Second Manassas, leading to Pope's dismissal. His orders were rescinded, and soon after so were the

Confederate general orders issued in response. This crisis had been defused, but it showed from the outset the difficulties of maintaining an exchange agreement in the midst of a bitter civil war.[1]

Other disagreements quickly surfaced. On October 5 Robert Ould summarized many of them. In a letter to his Union counterpart, the Confederate agent of exchange enumerated nine grievances. Some were minor. For example, Ould complained of the small number of exchanged prisoners arriving on flag-of-truce boats. One, he contended, had delivered but four men. "It puts the authorities here to great and unnecessary trouble," he complained. Most of his points concerned individuals or small groups of either citizens or irregular troops allegedly held in close confinement. Many cases, he asserted, involved "peaceable, non-combatant citizens of the Confederate States, taken in some instances with almost every possible indignity from their homes and thrown into military prisons." Ould's response to this was ominous for the future of the cartel. "I do not utter it in the way of a threat," he wrote, "but candor demands that I should say that if this course is persisted in the Confederate Government will be compelled by a sense of duty to its own citizens to resort to retaliatory measures." It was, of course, a threat, and it would not be the last uttered by either side.[2]

The next one, again issued by Ould, came on November 29. As the previous one had, it began with a list of grievances. Prominent among them was a demand for information about the hanging of William Mumford on the orders of Gen. Benjamin F. Butler. Butler had been named military governor of Louisiana following the Union occupation of New Orleans in May 1862. He had proceeded to earn the especial enmity of the South—and the nickname "Beast"—after issuing orders declaring that women insulting Federal soldiers were to be "regarded and held liable to be treated as [women] of the town plying [their] avocation." Mumford's execution came after the New Orleans citizen took down an American flag flying above the Crescent City. Confederate officials had sought details about the hanging in July. Ould now demanded them. If the Confederacy did not receive a response within fifteen days, Ould warned, "they will consider that an answer is declined and will retain all commissioned officers of the United States who may fall into their hands."[3]

When no response was forthcoming, Davis made good on the Confederacy's threat. In a Christmas Eve proclamation, the president declared that Butler was "a felon deserving of capital punishment" and his officers were "robbers and criminals deserving death." All who were captured were to be executed. Davis further proclaimed that "no commissioned officer of the United States taken captive shall be on parole before exchange until the said Butler shall have met with due punishment for his crimes." The Union response soon followed. Four days later, Stanton ordered Ludlow to exchange no officers until he received further instructions.[4]

Stanton's response was clear. Less clear was the portion of the proclamation to which he was responding. Davis positioned his charges against Butler and the suspension of officer exchange early in the proclamation. He then moved on to address twin issues that had recently come to trouble the Southern government and populace. One was Lincoln's announced intention to enforce his Emancipation Proclamation on January 1, 1863. The other was the Union's decision, sanctioned by Congress in July 1862, to employ black troops. The last two sections of the Davis proclamation declared:

3. That all negro slaves captured in arms be at once delivered over to the executive authorities of the respective States to which they belong to be dealt with according to the laws of said States.
4. That the like orders be executed in all cases with respect to all commissioned officers of the United States when found serving in company with armed slaves in insurrection against the different States of this Confederacy.[5]

Although the fate of black soldiers and their officers would eventually doom the cartel, Ludlow at first confined his concerns to the Confederate government's refusal to exchange officers. "I desire to know whether in compliance with the terms of the cartel the commissioned U.S. officers now in your hands are to be released," he wrote Ould on January 14. Ould's response, sent three days later, was only somewhat reassuring. After reasserting a number of Confederate grievances, including the execution of Mumford, he affirmed the terms of the Davis proclamation. Union officers held as prisoners would not be generally paroled for purposes of exchange. However, individual exchanges might still be made. In addition, Ould wrote, "We are ready at any time to release on parole and deliver to you your non-commissioned officers and privates." A personal interview with Ould the following month was apparently more positive. Ludlow, who appears to have been sincere in his desire to see the cartel succeed, hastened to deliver the good news to his superiors. In a message to Lincoln, Stanton, Halleck, and Gen. Ethan Allen Hitchcock, who had been named commissioner of exchange, Ludlow announced, "It is now quite certain that the Confederate Congress will overrule Mr. Jefferson Davis in his retaliatory proclamation . . . and exchanges will go on as heretofore under the cartel."[6]

This proved to be only partly true. The Confederate Congress blocked the plan to deliver captured Union officers to the states but otherwise supported the policy of the Davis administration. Ludlow was nevertheless undeterred. On March 25 he virtually pleaded with Hitchcock. "It is very necessary to get our officers out of prison," the agent of exchange wrote. "They are suffering. If not authorized to deliver all Confederate officers and have the difference arranged by [those] captured hereafter cannot authority be given to deliver an equal number or equivalent to ours and get the latter out of prison?" Two days later Stanton, however grudgingly, agreed to "exchanges of officers man for man without reference to the cartel."[7]

Exchange was back, albeit in a much more constrained form; and the problems that had plagued it still remained. After special exchanges of officers were resumed, Ludlow informed Ould on April 8, "The best mode of arranging all questions relating to exchange of officers is to revoke formally or informally the offensive proclamation relating to our officers." Ould responded by asserting that the Union had allowed Confederate officers "to languish and suffer in prison for months before we were compelled by that and other reasons to issue the retaliatory order of which you complain." As spring wore on, other issues entered the mix. On April 22 Ould complained about a "large number" of arrests of citizens by Union authorities. "You know how earnestly I have protested against this arrest of non-combatants," the Confederate agent wrote, adding ominously, "You also know to what it must ultimately lead." In May Ould learned of the execution at Johnson's Island of two Confederate captains convicted as spies and for recruiting within Union lines. He informed Ludlow that two Union captains had been "selected for execution in retaliation for this gross brutality." Learning that other Confederates had been condemned to death, he added, "In view of the awful vortex into which things are plunging I give you notice that in the event of the execution of these persons retaliation to an equal extent at least will be visited upon your officers, and if that is found ineffectual the number will be increased."[8]

Throughout this time the question of black Union soldiers captured by the Confederates was never raised. The issue had lain dormant following the refusal of Confederate legislators to sustain Davis in his plan to turn officers leading black troops over to the states. This changed after the Confederate Congress adopted a joint resolution on May 1 that again brought the issue to the forefront. The rationale for the action was the assertion by the Congress that the Emancipation Proclamation and the Union policy of sending black soldiers against the Confederacy would "bring on a servile war [and] would if successful produce atrocious consequences." As a result, the Congress declared that officers leading black troops would be "deemed as inciting servile insurrection, and shall if captured be put to death or otherwise punished at the discretion of the court." The soldiers serving under them would be turned over to the states and presumably returned to slavery.[9]

Ludlow's response was vociferous. He termed the resolution "a gross and inexcusable breach of the cartel in both letter and spirit." Reminding Ould that color was never mentioned in the cartel agreement, he wrote, "You have not a foot of ground to stand upon in making the proposed discrimination among our captured officers and men." Writing in a less noble manner, he also asserted, "You had Indians and half-breed negroes . . . organized in arms under Albert Pike, in Arkansas." The legislature of Tennessee, he added, had recently passed a measure conscripting male blacks. He concluded, "I now give you formal notice that the United States will throw its protection around all its officers and men without regard to color and will promptly retaliate for all cases violating the cartel or the laws and usages of war."[10]

Meanwhile, Ludlow's superiors were making his threats into formal Union policy. On May 25 Halleck informed all department commanders that no Confederate officers were to be paroled or exchanged. The same day Hoffman instructed Ludlow to send Confederate officers at Fort Monroe to the prison at Fort Delaware. On July 13 Stanton upped the ante considerably, ordering that no more prisoners be delivered to City Point. Ludlow believed the war secretary's order went too far, and he protested to Hoffman. Five days later Ludlow was relieved and replaced by Brig. Gen. Sullivan Meredith. Stanton was clearly exerting control over Union prison policy. Meredith firmly grasped the obvious, taking a hard line in his negotiations with Ould.[11]

For several decades historians have pondered and debated the true motives of the secretary of war. There is nothing in the documentary evidence to suggest that Stanton was motivated by anything other than a genuine concern for the fate of black Union soldiers and their officers. On August 25, 1863, in reply to Ould's proposal to resume exchanges, Meredith declined unless those blacks were included. To this the Southern agent of exchange responded that the Confederates would "die in the last ditch" before conceding the point. In his annual report, submitted November 15, Halleck cited the issue of black soldiers as the point that led to the end of exchanges. The matter was also prominent in Stanton's annual report to the president, although he complained as well of the Confederate policy of releasing men from paroles in what, Stanton alleged, was a violation of the cartel. These reports, of course, were matters of public record. As such, they fall far short of proving conclusively that concern for black soldiers and their officers was Stanton's sole concern. Victories at Vicksburg and Gettysburg had left the Union in a much stronger position militarily. They also left the North with an advantage in the number of prisoners held, strengthening its hand in exchange negotiations. As a result, there is no conclusive answer to the question of the government's motivation.[12]

There is one other aspect of the question that must be considered. That is the Union's frustrating experience with paroled soldiers. It was a problem that did not seriously plague the Confederacy until the parole of the Vicksburg prisoners in July 1863. For the Union troubles arose almost as soon as the exchange cartel was signed. As news of the agreement spread from camp to camp, soldiers realized that capture would no longer result in months of confinement in dreary prisons. Rather, it would offer the opportunity for a trip home following parole and what one termed a "little rest from soldiering." Among the first officers to address the issue was Gen. Don Carlos Buell, commanding the Army of the Ohio. On August 8, 1862, Buell issued orders asserting, "The system of paroles as practiced has run into intolerable abuse." All future paroles, Buell ordered, had to receive his consent. Those that did not would "not be recognized and the person giving it will be required to perform military duty and take the risks prescribed by the laws of war." The order violated the terms of the cartel, and when Gen. Sam Jones, Buell's Confederate counterpart, pointed out that fact, Buell rescinded it. A few weeks later Governor Tod of Ohio added his voice to the issue. Following the surrender of four thousand Union soldiers at Richmond, Kentucky, the governor complained to Stanton. "The freedom in giving paroles by our troops in Kentucky is very prejudicial to the service and should be stopped," Tod wrote. "Had our forces at Richmond, Ky., refused to give their parole it would have taken all of [Confederate general Edmund] Kirby Smith's army to guard them."[13]

Tod's appeal was especially urgent because thousands of parolees were ending up in Columbus, creating a logistical problem for both state and federal officials. On June 28, nearly a month before the cartel was signed, the War Department had issued General Orders No. 72. Designed to make parole less of an incentive, the orders declared that no furloughs would be granted to paroled prisoners. Instead, they were to report to one of three parole camps. Those from the East were ordered to a camp near Annapolis, soon rechristened Camp Parole. Western troops were sent to Benton Barracks in Missouri. Camp Chase was designated for parolees from midwestern states. Commanders at those camps were ordered to organize the paroled soldiers into companies and battalions, "keeping those from the same regiment and of the same State as much together as possible." Beyond that the orders offered no guidance.[14]

The men soon began arriving at the camps. They showed up unorganized and upset that, after many months of service to their country, they were not to be furloughed to their homes. In replying to Tod's message, Stanton informed the governor that he had ordered fifteen hundred men to Camp Chase. The secretary "wish[ed] to have them kept in close quarters and drilled diligently every day, with no leave of absence." That was not what Tod wanted to hear. "It is with great difficulty we can preserve order among them at Camp Chase," he replied. The governor had a better idea, suggesting that the men be shipped off to Minnesota to quell an uprising of the Sioux Indians. Stanton pronounced the suggestion "excellent" and promised that it would be "immediately acted upon."[15]

The secretary was true to his word. On September 17 he dispatched Gen. Lew Wallace to Columbus. In forwarding the orders to Wallace, Halleck hinted at the problems ahead when he informed Wallace, "Officers will be sent to you as soon as possible." Recalling his arrival, Wallace later wrote that the quarters he found the men inhabiting at Camp Chase were in a horrible condition. "They were stained a rusty black; the windows were stuffed with old hats and caps," he wrote in his autobiography. "The roofs were of plank, and in places planks were gone, leaving gaping crevices to skylight the dismal interior." Reporting to Adj. Gen. Thomas, he wrote that only two thousand of the five thousand men who were supposed to be there were present, "and if they have deserted they should not be blamed." Scores had neither shoes nor socks, and many lacked breeches. "I assembled them on the parade ground and rode amongst them," Wallace continued, "and the smell from their ragged clothes was worse than in an ill-conducted slaughterhouse." The future novelist concluded that the men were no better off than they would have been in a Confederate prison.[16]

Wallace attempted to make effective regiments of the demoralized troops, but the odds were against him. Stanton demanded results but offered little support. He refused to provide needed tents and arms for the parolees and only grudgingly agreed to supply them with back pay. The men themselves were no more cooperative. Wallace established a new camp, Camp Lew Wallace, northwest of Columbus. His plan was to march the men from Camp Chase to Columbus for pay and then send them on to the new camp. This, he believed, would separate "the willing from the unwilling." It did not work out that way. Several men from one company, after receiving their pay, fled down the streets of Columbus. Others deserted from Camp Lew Wallace, leaving their weapons resting against trees. The desperate Wallace virtually begged the War Department not to send any more parolees. "Whoever gets into Camp Chase or comes into contact with its inmates," he explained to Thomas, "is instantly seized with the mutinous spirit I have described."[17]

The "inmates," of course, were Union soldiers, and the treatment they received at the hands of their government was little better than that endured by Confederate prisoners. The Union was in a fight for its survival. Officials such as Stanton were waging that fight with a single-minded determination. Conditions at Union parole camps suggest that this left virtually no room for concern about the plight of captives—whether they were clad in gray or blue. Certainly the parolees at Camp Chase and Camp Lew Wallace felt that way. "We are becoming very much demoralized here [at Camp Chase]," Ohio soldier William L. Curry wrote in his diary on October 30, adding, "Prize fights and black eyes are all 'the go' now." On November 4 he reported, "Boys have been playing the Devil generally. Burn the guard house. Whip all the officers who show their heads." Another Ohioan, Abner Royce, expressed a similar view. "There is great dissatisfaction among the paroled men," Royce wrote his parents on October 3. "General Wallace requires them to perform camp duty, when their parole positively says they must not perform such duty until exchanged." What was perhaps the most telling remark about the condition of paroled soldiers at Columbus was made unwittingly. In a letter to his wife, Benjamin Franklin Heuston of the Second Wisconsin wrote that he was pleased with conditions at the camp hospital, where he was a patient. "We are well used here," he asserted, "have plenty to eat, a library to get books from, and the medicine I take is not bad." Then, with no apparent sense of irony, he added, "There is not quite one funeral a day."[18]

Camp Chase was not alone in problems involving paroled soldiers. Iowa parolees at Benton Barracks complained to Governor Samuel J. Kirkwood that they had been provided neither equipment for cooking nor utensils for eating. The men of one company informed the governor that they had not been paid for eight months, and virtually every petitioner protested the requirement that they perform guard duty. Many had refused, one of the men wrote. As a result, "About 100 of these brave boys are now in irons for this cause." The situation was even more serious at Camp Parole. In November 1862 two reports reached Washington complaining of lawlessness at the Maryland camp. "Drunkenness, fighting, burglary, robbery, gambling, &c., are witnessed by us daily," a New York soldier wrote Stanton, "and even murder is not of infrequent occurrence." Governor Edward Salomon of Wisconsin forwarded a petition he had received from Badger State troops making the same complaint to Hoffman. The commissary general of prisoners demanded a report from camp commander George Sangster but did little further to address the concerns.[19]

As serious as the problems at Benton Barracks and Camp Parole were, they were destined to pass when the cartel collapsed and the facilities were no longer needed to house paroled soldiers. The situation was different at Camp Chase. The facility suffered as a result of its service as a parole camp. Some of the destruction was senseless. Some of it resulted from the desperate circumstances of the Union soldiers confined there. The latter was reflected in a circular issued on January 21, 1863, that complained of the "unnecessary destruction and damage to the public buildings at this camp." The men were informed that "it will be no excuse that soldiers have not received their allowance of wood."[20]

Things were even worse at Camp Douglas, where some eight thousand parolees arrived in late September 1862. The men had been surrendered at Harpers Ferry after Stonewall Jackson took possession of the heights surrounding the garrison. They arrived upset that their officers had surrendered them and even more upset that their government planned to ship them on to Minnesota to fight the Sioux. "This caused much hard feeling against our government and our field officers," wrote Cpl. Charles E. Smith of the Thirty-second Ohio, "for we were sworn to go home to our state and attend to our private business until we were duly exchanged man for man." If this were not bad enough, the parolees arrived at Chicago to find the camp filled with recruits. Instead of barracks, they ended up in tents and stables. Gen. Daniel Tyler, a sixty-three-year-old West Point graduate, was put in command over the unruly parolees. As he labored to whip his reluctant command into shape, the *Chicago Tribune* complicated his job by publishing the terms of the Dix-Hill cartel. The paroled men interpreted these as not requiring them to drill, let alone fight Indians, and many of their officers agreed.[21]

The result was a series of riots at Camp Douglas that caused wholesale damage to the camp. According to Cpl. Smith, it began on October 1 with "a number of the boys climbing over the prison fence; the guards were not close enough to keep them in and they broke through and over wherever they pleased." When the officer of the guard tried to stop the outbreak, the men greeted him with volleys of rocks. They also drove away a carpenter sent to repair the damage to the fence. The following day, Smith wrote, "The first thing on the list was to charge on the fence." When Tyler sent the 125th Vermont against the mutinous troops, their weapons proved defective. On the evening of October 3, Smith attended a prayer meeting. It was interrupted by the sound of another section of fence coming down and the subsequent cheers of the parolees engaged in the work. The greatest destruction came on the 16th when a fire, rumored to have been started by members of the Sixty-fifth Illinois, consumed eleven barracks and a dining hall. "There was a strong breeze and the roofs being covered with pasteboard and pitch burned finely," Smith wrote. News that the Sioux uprising in Minnesota had been quelled and no parolees need be sent eventually eased tensions somewhat. In the meantime, Camp Douglas had sustained $7,600 worth of damage. It was never a pleasant, sanitary facility; now the paroled men had made it much worse for the horde of Confederate prisoners that would soon be headed there.[22]

When the Southerners did begin to return to Camp Douglas and other depots the numbers increased quickly. On June 30, 1863, monthly returns from Union prisons showed that there were 380 prisoners at Camp Chase, 49 at Camp Douglas, 111 at Camp Morton, and 806 at Johnson's Island. Fort Delaware housed 3,673 Confederate captives, but that camp was being used as a temporary holding facility for prisoners bound for exchange. Three months later the numbers were 2,073 at Camp Chase, 5,112 at Camp Douglas, 1,487 at Camp Morton, 2,155 at Johnson's Island, and 6,490 at Fort Delaware. In addition the Point Lookout prison in Maryland, which had not even existed on June 30, held 3,909 prisoners. By the end of the year that number would reach nearly 9,000.[23]

The collapse of the cartel alone did not account for the dramatic increase in the Union prison population. The summer of 1863 was the first generally successful one for Northern arms. Like Grant's success in the late winter of 1862, the victories of 1863 resulted in a dramatic increase in the number of captives held by the Union. Foremost among them was the battle of Gettysburg. When three days of fighting in and around the Pennsylvania village ended on July 3, the Union held 13,621 prisoners, nearly as many as Grant had captured at Fort Donelson. Of those, 6,739 were wounded, including nearly 3,000 who were still unable to be moved as late as the 22nd. Gen. Lee, commanding the Confederate Army of Northern Virginia, proposed the morning after the fighting ended that "an exchange be made at once." Gen. George Gordon Meade, the commander of the Army of the Potomac, refused, claiming that it was "not in my power to accede to the proposed arrangement."[24]

Because of Meade's obstinacy, several thousand Confederates were soon destined for Point Lookout, Maryland. Located at the tip of the peninsula between the Potomac River and Chesapeake Bay, the former resort area had become a military installation early in the war. Among its many buildings was the Hammond General Hospital, a fourteen-hundred-bed facility that Stanton believed would be a good place to send the wounded prisoners. When the hospital proved too small for that purpose, the War Department decided on a new use for the location. On July 20 Meigs informed Gen. Daniel H. Rucker, the army's chief quartermaster, that a prison was to be established at the site. Although wooden kitchens and storehouses were to be constructed, the prisoners would occupy tents, making Point Lookout unique among Northern prison camps. Three days later St. Mary's County, Maryland, was detached from the Middle Department and made into a separate military district. Brig. Gen. Gilman Marston became the commander. His first assignment was to travel to Meade's army to secure a guard force. He also relieved Meade of a small number of prisoners, whom he set to work helping to construct the camp.[25]

By the end of August there were 1,800 Confederate prisoners at Point Lookout, as well as 800 sick and wounded Union soldiers at the hospital. On October 8 Marston reported to Hoffman that there were 810 tents at the camp capable of accommodating 5,046 prisoners. Of this total, 720 were what he termed "common tents." The remainder included Sibley, wall, and hospital tents. Five mess houses with kitchens attached had gone up, and the fence, enclosing about forty acres, was completed. Marston strongly urged that barracks be erected for the prisoners. "The ground on which the camp is located, being low and flat, will be very soft and wet in the rainy season," he explained. In what was perhaps an attempt to convince his economy-minded superior, Marston pointed out that the savings in fuel would be "immense." The prisoners, he added, were willing to do the work, and the cost of materials could easily be covered by the prison fund. Hoffman dutifully forwarded the request to Stanton, who promptly denied it. "It will, therefore, be necessary," Hoffman informed Marston, "to have on hand a supply of tents to meet any unexpected arrival of prisoners." The commissary general of prisoners instructed the camp commander to requisition enough to accommodate a total of 10,000 prisoners.[26]

The camp quickly filled. In addition to the Gettysburg prisoners, Hoffman ordered all enlisted prisoners at Old Capitol to the new camp in August. By the end of November Point Lookout's prison population was over nine thousand. This made for a vast tent city and uncomfortable lodgings for the prisoners confined there. Among the later arrivals was Sgt. J. B. Stamp of the Third Alabama, who was captured on May 5, 1864, at the battle of the Wilderness. He wrote in a postwar memoir, "Prisoners who had preceded us there were quartered in what was apparently old army tents, of many shapes and sizes." Another former Point Lookout prisoner, B. T. Holliday, recalled, "We were put in 'Sibley tents,' which was a round tent with a pole extending from the top to an iron tripod, the pole fitting in the top of the tripod." One hundred men, he added, were housed in six of those tents. "These tents had been used by the army and had seen so much service that they would leak and we spent a very uncomfortable time." They slept like the spokes of a wheel, their heads at the edge of the tent and their feet against the tripod. Holliday noted, "We were packed like sardines in a box. When we wanted to turn over in the night, the signal was given to turn, and all made the turn from necessity."[27]

According to prisoner William H. Haigh, conditions at Point Lookout did not improve with the passage of time. As he awaited release in May 1865, Haigh began recording his memories of the four months he spent at the prison. "We were put into that old rickety tent," he wrote of his January 22 arrival, "without fire or fuel to pass the night on the damp ground, with no covering but a blanket & nothing to protect us from the ground." By May 27 Haigh's memoirs had become a diary. Despite the season the day had been "blustering, stormy, and cold." The wind had blown down several tents, and even those who had not lost their homes were uncomfortable. "The soil here is nearly all crawfish clay intertwined with gravel," he explained. "It retains water, becomes slushy and slippery and almost at all times [is] damp inside the tents." James A. Low, a Union soldier who helped guard a group of prisoners taken to Point Lookout in August 1864, noted that the conditions were little better in dry weather. He informed his brother, "The Pt. is very sandy, which is deep & hard getting along, & when the wind blows is bad. Should not like to be stationed there," he added.[28]

In addition to being uncomfortable, the tents were vulnerable to thieves. During the night men would cut through the canvas and remove knapsacks, boots, clothing, and sometimes money. "A thief cut into our tent last night and abstracted three haversacks," Charles Warren Hutt of the Fortieth Virginia wrote on February 10, 1864. George Quintus Peyton of the Thirteenth Virginia noted that the thieves would often drop by, innocently so it seemed, to see if there was anything of value near the edge of the tent. On November 16, 1864, someone stole a wagon from his tent. The prisoners used it to wash themselves and to soak fish when they caught them in the bay. Peyton solved the problem by stealing a wagon the next night, pointing out, "It may be the one that they stole from us." When his mess again became victims the following month, Peyton wrote, "Someone stole our waggin last night so I reckon we will have to steal another one." Even in the rough-and-tumble world of Civil War prisons, crime did not always pay. On April 10, 1864, Joseph Kern, another member of the Thirteenth Virginia, observed two prisoners being paraded around the grounds wearing barrels that bore signs reading "Tent Cutters." Adding to the severity of the punishment was the fact that they were "on their 'forced march' with a negro [sentinel] and his bayonet at their backs." This was, Kern concluded, "a just punishment."[29]

Although the means of Civil War prisoners were severely limited, their ingenuity was not; and in the precardboard days of the 1860s the wooden boxes in which supplies arrived allowed Point Lookout prisoners to better their living conditions. "We have to raise our tents on cracker boxes which greatly adds to our comfort," wrote Charles Hutt on January 1, 1864. Soon Hutt and his messmates carried the process a step farther. On May 2 they began constructing a cabin out of cracker boxes. They finished their wooden home, "which presents quite a good appearance," Hutt boasted, three days later. The finishing touch was a sign that said, "Here We Rest." By June, Kern observed, "Many of the men have procured cracker boxes and put up quite comfortable houses." Kern mentioned Hutt's makeshift home in his diary as well as abodes bearing signs reading "Home Again," "In for the War," and "Star of Dixie." The cracker box house that Bartlett Yancey Malone and five fellow prisoners erected in January 1865 cost $8.80 for materials. They then spent another $8 to purchase a stove from the camp sutler.[30]

Thirteen days before Hoffman gave orders to establish the prison at Point Lookout, Meigs sent Capt. Charles A. Reynolds, an assistant quartermaster, to Rock Island, Illinois. The Mississippi River island, three miles long and one-half mile wide, had long been the property of the United States government. Meigs ordered Reynolds to "take charge of the construction of a depot for prisoners of war to be established there." In doing so, the quartermaster general counseled, "You will be governed by the strictest economy consistent with the completion of the depot at the earliest practicable period." Following up a month later, Meigs was still concerned with economy and speed. On August 12 he instructed Reynolds, "The barracks for prisoners at Rock Island should be put up in the roughest and cheapest manner—mere shanties, with no fine work about them, and the work should, if possible, be done by contract and in the shortest possible time." On the 22nd Reynolds submitted plans to his impatient boss. Meigs approved them on September 11, and by the end of the month the barracks were under roof.[31]

Meigs's desire for speed proved prescient. Just as Gettysburg had necessitated the establishment of the prison at Point Lookout, another Union victory soon resulted in a flood of prisoners bound for Rock Island. On November 25 the forces of Gens. Ulysses S. Grant and George H. Thomas drove Gen. Braxton Bragg's Army of Tennessee from its position on Missionary Ridge overlooking Chattanooga. In addition to relieving a Federal army under siege in the Tennessee city, the victory resulted in 6,142 Confederate prisoners. On December 1 Hoffman announced that 5,000 of them were on their way to Rock Island.[32]

They were bound for a camp not yet prepared to receive them. At least that was the opinion of Col. Richard H. Rush, who had assumed command of the post on October 24. On November 24, one day before the fight at Missionary Ridge, Rush informed Hoffman, "There is not now at this post nor can I obtain a single record book, blanks, or paper of any kind." The guard force numbered only 380 and most of them were needed to clear the ground of trees for the compound. The next day Rush complained that the post was "entirely destitute" of clothing and camp and garrison equipment for the men stationed there. On the 26th Rush wrote to Meigs, saying he had neither fuel nor a quartermaster to procure it. He also informed Col. James Fry, the United States provost marshal general, that the men assigned to Rock Island as guards were "obedient & willing," but also "entirely without instruction or discipline." He had found only one private who could write well enough to serve as a clerk. After Hoffman informed him of the impending shipment of prisoners, Rush replied on November 30 that he would "do what I can for the 5,000 prisoners expected." He added, "No water yet in prison yard, except one well at west end. Steam forcing engines not ready yet. Weather extremely cold. No rebel clothing [or] blankets on hand."[33]

The war could not be delayed over such details, and on the night of December 3, the first trainload of 468 prisoners reached Rock Island. In reporting their arrival to Hoffman, Rush added, "I require more officers and men for Guard duty." Over the next several days, according to local press accounts, prisoners arrived in lots ranging from 830 to 1,300. By January 9, 1864, a total of 6,158 Confederates had reached the Illinois prison. By then they were no longer the responsibility of Col. Rush. On December 5 he turned command over to Col. Adolphus J. Johnson, who had been the commander of the guard at the post.[34]

Among the prisoners arriving at Rock Island from Missionary Ridge was A. C. Kean. Writing some forty years after the war, Kean recalled "intensely cold" weather as he and his comrades rode in boxcars across Indiana and Illinois. "We were packed so closely together in the cars," he added, "that we did not suffer." His morale did suffer, however, as he viewed the potential soldiers waiting to replenish the Union armies. "I could see our cause was hopeless for the depots were all crowded with young men who had never been to war, while the South was exhausted as far as recruits were concerned." Upon reaching the depot, the prisoners were marched about one-fourth mile through snow that was two feet deep. At the prison they entered barracks, each holding 120 men. The barracks contained three tiers of bunks, the arrangement at most Northern prisons. The Southerners were happy to discover stoves and "plenty of coal to burn."[35]

Ironically, two contemporary diarists at Rock Island recorded less positive impressions of the early days of the prison. William H. Davis of the Ninth Tennessee was captured on November 27 as his rearguard forces attempted to retreat south from Missionary Ridge. Although he claimed the snow was only six inches deep on the march to Rock Island, Davis did not agree with Kean's implication that the barracks were warm. "They are very open and cold," he wrote on December 15, his first full day at the depot. In future entries he wrote that six men had frozen to death. Several hundred, he added, were barefoot. As late as December 29, Davis wrote that the prisoners had received neither clothing nor blankets. Mississippi soldier Lafayette Rogan confirmed much of what Davis had to say. "Many fellows have no blankets yet and are very thinly clad," Rogan wrote on January 3. "Such men suffer greatly." Rogan secured better quarters by accepting a job "making up the record of the prisoners." In doing so he suffered less from the elements but more from a troubled conscience. "The new Qrs are vastly more comfortable than the old," he noted, but added, "It is however a streach of conscience for me to think it right to work for 'Uncle Sam.'"[36]

The third major Union prison camp to open after the collapse of the cartel was destined to become one of the war's most notorious. As early as June 1862, the draft rendezvous at Elmira, New York, had been on Hoffman's mind as a potential site for a prison camp. On the 12th of that month he ordered Lazelle to visit the camp, as well as facilities at Albany, Utica, Rochester, and Buffalo. The meticulous commissary general of prisoners called for "a ground plan of each camp and . . . the dimensions of all the buildings with the number of men they will accommodate." His thorough subordinate provided detailed reports on every facility, including four camps located at Elmira. The signing of the cartel rendered Lazelle's report unnecessary, and it was filed away for the next two years. Hoffman was reminded of it on May 14, 1864, when Asst. Adj. Gen. Edward D. Townsend passed along a bit of news. "I am today informed," Townsend wrote, "that there are quite a number of barracks at Elmira, N.Y., which are not occupied, and are fit to hold rebel prisoners."[37]

From there things moved quickly. On May 19 Hoffman informed Stanton that there would soon be fifteen thousand prisoners at Point Lookout. It would not be advisable, he counseled, to exceed that number. Barracks were available at Elmira, Hoffman continued. The budget-conscious commissary general noted that for only $2,000 a fence could be erected, instantly turning the training camp into a prison. It did not take Stanton long to act upon Hoffman's suggestion. Before the day was over, both Hoffman and Townsend had notified Lt. Col. Seth Eastman, the commander at Elmira, that his camp was about to become the newest Union prison. Hoffman added his expectation that the facility would hold between eight and ten thousand Confederates. "I am unable to say how soon the barracks will be required," Hoffman blithely continued, "but possibly within ten days."[38]

If the suddenness of Hoffman's message did not shock Eastman, the commissary general's math certainly did. As had Col. Rush at Rock Island, Eastman passed along his concerns to his new superior officer. On May 23 he advised Hoffman that the barracks at the proposed site were "in excellent condition and well ventilated." However, they were built to accommodate only three thousand soldiers. Eastman believed that four thousand prisoners could be crowded into them. Tents on the grounds could hold another thousand. The kitchen, he added, was capable of providing meals for five thousand men daily. In addition there was no hospital, although one was under construction. Finally, Eastman explained that there were only two hundred men available for guard duty. "I would recommend that no prisoners be sent here until I report that the barracks are ready to receive them," Eastman concluded.[39]

If Hoffman was sympathetic to Eastman's concerns, there is no record of him saying so. Instead, on June 22, the commissary general instructed the Elmira commander to prepare the camp to receive prisoners. Hoffman ordered Eastman, "if practicable," to enclose enough ground to hold ten thousand prisoners, whether in barracks or tents. Eight days later Eastman reported that the camp was ready to receive prisoners. The same day Hoffman ordered two thousand sent from Point Lookout. The first detachment arrived at the New York & Erie Railroad depot at 6:00 a.m. on July 6. "They were a fine looking body of men physically, taller than the average," the *Elmira Daily Advertiser* conceded. The paper quickly added, "They did not exhibit a high degree of intelligence, but looked to be men that would go where they were told, let what might happen." The Confederates arrived in "all sorts of nondescript uniforms," the *Advertiser* reported, adding, "Some had nothing on but drawers and shirts." Over the next month the local paper chronicled the arrival of detachments ranging from about five hundred to just over eight hundred. Their presence provided an opportunity for local residents to view real live Rebels, and several sought out cracks and knotholes in the fence to get a look. "People from the country are hardly willing to go home after their shopping is done without a peep at the varmints," the *Advertiser* reported on July 11.[40]

As for the "varmints" themselves, the views of at least two concerning their new quarters were generally positive. "The prison here is a very fine one and the fare tolerably good for prisoners," wrote Henri Mugler of the Fourteenth Virginia, who arrived from Old Capitol Prison on July 24. Mugler added that the prisoners transferred from Point Lookout were "much better satisfied here" than they had been in Maryland. Mugler improved his situation by agreeing to head a drum corps composed of prisoners. The members of the organization enjoyed separate quarters, and Mugler and the other officers of the corps received extra rations and tobacco. Another prisoner who gained special treatment by working for the Yankees was Wilbur Gramling of the Fifth Florida. Arriving on July 24, he secured a job two days later as a waiter. The position involved much work but gained for him "plenty to eat." As time wore on Gramling became disenchanted with the position. "Have to wait on three tables, each 135 men," he later complained, "& don't get any more than they do after washing all the dishes & everything."[41]

Although the early observations of the prisoners were generally positive, Union officials spotted signs of problems that would soon plague the camp. On July 14 Charles T. Alexander, an army surgeon dispatched by Hoffman to inspect the camp, reported, "I found the sick, fortunately but few, in no way suitably provided for except as for shelter." Rations were not sufficient, and there was a shortage of bed sacks and blankets. The surgeon in charge of troops at Elmira delegated much of the work at the prison to a young assistant. Alexander concluded that the youthful physician was "not a suitable person to organize or control a hospital such as will be needed."[42]

On August 17 Eastman raised an even more serious concern. He informed Hoffman that "the pond inside of the prisoners' camp . . . has become very offensive and may occasion sickness unless the evil is remedied very shortly." He was referring to Foster's Pond, and time would demonstrate that Eastman's concerns were vastly understated. The camp sat on land leased from William Foster, a local farmer. Once the Union converted the site into a prison, Mr. Foster's pond became a receptacle for the sinks of the camp. Eastman recommended that a drainage ditch be dug from the pond to the Chemung River. He had already ordered a survey for the mile-long ditch. Eastman supported his contentions with a detailed report from Eugene F. Sanger, the surgeon in charge of the camp, who reported that seven thousand prisoners would produce 2,600 gallons of urine daily. Much of this, he added, would seep into the stagnant pond. "Unless the laws of hygiene are carefully studied and observed in crowded camps," Sanger warned, "disease is the inevitable consequence." Despite this and subsequent warnings from Eastman and his successor, Col. Benjamin F. Tracy, Hoffman was reluctant to approve the project. Cost was a factor, as was the commissary general's hopes that autumn rains would remove the problem. As he dragged his feet, sickness and death at the camp increased dramatically.[43]

Foster's Pond was but one symptom of a larger problem facing Hoffman and other Union prison officials. During the period of the cartel, it had been assumed that most Union prisons would be abandoned. Indeed, in August 1862 Hoffman had predicted that Johnson's Island would soon accommodate all prisoners held in the West. The same month he informed Joseph Darr, the provost marshal at Wheeling, Virginia, "Camp Chase will probably be abandoned as a military prison." On September 11 he ordered that guards at Camp Butler, Camp Douglas, and Camp Chase be mustered out when their terms of service expired "or when no longer necessary." Thinking the cartel would solve the government's prison crisis, officials did nothing to address maintenance needs at the depots. As a result, when the cartel collapsed the government was little better prepared to receive the flood of prisoners that arrived in 1863 than it had been to accommodate Grant's 1862 captives. Indeed, thanks to the parolees that had been stationed at Camp Chase and Camp Douglas, those camps bore scars that had not been there a year earlier. At the same time the success of Union arms at Gettysburg and Chattanooga created a sudden need for additional prison space. This left little time for planning as camps such as Point Lookout and Rock Island were established. The same was true at Elmira, set up as Grant's Virginia campaign of 1864 was getting under way. Meanwhile, reports of allegedly ghastly conditions in Confederate prisons were reaching the North, greatly lessening the desire of Union officials to treat prisoners humanely. It was a convergence of factors that did not bode well for the thousands of Confederate captives that would soon be headed north.[44]

5
"The first time I ever desired to be in a penitentiary"
Capture and Transport

D. C. Thomas was among a group of prisoners captured on October 22, 1863, by the Seventh Illinois Cavalry. Recalling the event thirty-five years later, Thomas did not make clear his place of capture, writing only that he was taken in "North Mississippi." He indicated that he was part of a large group of prisoners and that his fellow captives included a friend who was a paroled Vicksburg prisoner. The Union soldiers, Thomas wrote, refused to recognize his friend's parole papers. Thomas recalled with gratitude a Yankee sergeant who "rode up to me and assured me that I should not be mistreated, not even insulted, and told me to report any ill usage to him." The sergeant allowed Thomas and his friend to remain together and ordered a corporal to see to it that the prisoner was well treated. The contingent was taken to Collierville, which Thomas described as "a town of tents, as we had burned the place about a week before." The corporal invited Thomas to share supper with him, apologizing for the "short meal," and gave his captive a cigar for dessert. That evening the prisoners boarded a train for Memphis, where they joined about a hundred fellow captives in the "Irving Block." Thomas wrote, "We were searched and robbed" before being sent to their quarters. Once inside, he continued, "Two filthy negroes, each with a tin bucket, came in. One handed each of us a cracker, and the other would gig up a small piece of fat meat with a sharp stick and push it off to us with his thumb." The prisoners remained in Memphis for about two weeks before starting up the Mississippi on "the boiler-deck of an old steamboat." Alton prison ended up being his destination.[1]

Although differing in details, Thomas's experiences between capture and arrival at a Northern prison were representative of those of most Confederate captives. The majority recorded generally kind treatment from their original captors in the field. As they traveled farther from the front lines, the prisoners encountered guards who were much less compassionate. The captives attributed the change to the fact that the men at the front respected their enemies and could sympathize with their situation. "I had no reason to complain of the treatment received from our captors," former Camp Chase and Fort Delaware prisoner George H. Moffett later recalled. "They were veteran soldiers who had seen a great deal of service. Consequently they were respectful in their behavior, and shared their scanty rations with us." Moffett continued, "Our hardships on that march were merely incident to the conditions of war. It was not until we got away from them and into prison pens that the regime of inhumanity began."[2]

Another common theme was suffering en route to the prison camps. As Moffett indicated, whether their captors were benevolent or not, the prisoners were military freight. As such they posed a challenge that Northern officials viewed as more logistical than humanitarian. Rations often failed to catch up with them for several days. Many fell into Union hands already ill from disease or exposure, a condition that transport north only exacerbated. In January 1863 Northern forces captured Fort Hindman at Arkansas Post, fifty miles above where the Arkansas River empties into the Mississippi. They netted some 4,700 prisoners in the process. Isaac Marsh was among the Union soldiers detailed to guard the captives as they started up the Mississippi toward St. Louis. A few miles above Memphis, Marsh wrote in a letter to his wife, they "landed to fix our Rudder and Burry some dead Butternuts." He added, "There is a number of them sick and they are dieing every day." A few days later Marsh went ashore to guard a Confederate burial party. "There was 3 to be buried that died last night," he wrote. "They dug a hole 2 1/2 feet deep in the sand and put all 3 in the same hole 2 heads one way and one the other wrapped up in their dirty Blankets and then threw dirt rite on them like as thou they were hogs." The procedure disgusted Marsh, who wrote, "I looked on and thought of the wives and children and fond parents and loving brothers and sisters that they no doubt have at home."[3]

On July 9, 1863, five days after the fall of Vicksburg, the Confederate forces at Port Hudson, Louisiana, surrendered. Among those captured was Capt. Thomas Jones Taylor of the Forty-ninth Alabama. On July 16 Taylor boarded the steamer *Planet,* destined for Johnson's Island. The boat reached Vicksburg three days later, and the scenes Taylor beheld there saddened the Confederate officer. "The streets were full of soldiers, negroes in the uniform of the Federals were to be seen on all sides, all gave unmistakable evidence of a conquered and ruined people," he wrote. Continuing up the river, Taylor noted the lack of livestock, farmhouses either abandoned or burned, and "all vestiges of life actually obliterated." Meanwhile, the Mississippi was crowded with boats as the Union took advantage of its latest military prize. Taylor spoke little of guards aboard the *Planet* other than to note, "On our voyage we found the Federals jubilant over their success and prophesying as usual on every gleam of success the speedy termination of the war." Reaching Cairo on the 25th, the prisoners transferred to railroad passenger cars for the journey to Johnson's Island. "The soldiers composing our guard [on the trains], though very strict, were very civil," Taylor wrote, "and though a couple of pompous young lieutenants made rather an offensive display occasionally of their authority, yet upon the whole the trip was as agreeable as could be expected." At Indianapolis the men received "a passable supper" and "poor cigars" at the Soldiers' Home, as well as a song from a group of local female singers. They also received an unwelcome transfer from passenger to freight cars at the Indiana capital.[4]

Had Grant not decided to parole his Vicksburg prisoners, Capt. Taylor's route north would have been a very crowded one. As things turned out his was among the last large groups of prisoners to travel up the Mississippi. With the river opened to Union traffic, the war in the West shifted eastward. Chattanooga became the focal point, to be succeeded by Atlanta. For Confederate prisoners this meant the route to captivity would frequently pass through Nashville and Louisville.

Such was the case with Pvt. W. C. Dodson of the Fifty-first Alabama Cavalry. Dodson was captured on September 9, 1863, at McLemore's Cove, a skirmish that was a prelude to the battle of Chickamauga. Writing thirty-seven years later, Dodson recalled that he politely declined the offer of a Union officer to claim that he had been conscripted against his will into the Confederate service. He then returned to his captors' rearguard headquarters, where he remained for several days "and could have not been treated with more courteous consideration." The Union soldiers apologized for the skimpy rations offered, explaining that they "would have waited supper" had they known Dodson was coming. A teamster offered him a blanket, and all of his captors respected Dodson's refusal to associate with a fellow captive who claimed to have deserted from a Georgia regiment.[5]

Dodson's experience was not unique. Mississippian William H. Young was captured on December 16, 1864, near Nashville. "They treated me very kindly," Young wrote of his captors. "Spoke to me as if we had been friends of long Standing." Despite that, the rations that the Yankees promised that evening did not arrive. After being taken prisoner in September 1863, Capt. Richard Henry Adams of the Fifth Alabama found himself guarded by the Fourteenth Michigan. The members of the outfit "treated us like gentlemen," Adams wrote. Their major "treated us with the greatest kindness and courtesy," going so far as to parole them to the limits of Columbia, Tennessee, for a few days. Pvt. James W. Anderson also received generally kind treatment at the hands of his original captors. A member of the Sixth Tennessee Infantry, Anderson was at home on furlough in March 1864 when Federal troops arrived at his house and arrested him. Although one of the Union men robbed Anderson of his boots, he otherwise "had respects shown me personally." He had a lengthy conversation, punctuated by a "warm debate," with a Tennessee Unionist who was a member of the guard force. In the end, Anderson noted, "we parted friendly."[6]

Anderson followed a circuitous route to captivity. Along the way former neighbors who were serving in the Confederate army joined him. For the first four nights they camped at the estates of prominent Tennesseans. According to Anderson, who tended to avoid hyperbole, the Union soldiers looted them brutally. Of one victim he wrote, "Thousands of dollars of the wealth this man had laid up for the Saturday evening of his life and to aid his children to embark on the ocean of life with their heads above the wave . . . passed away in 12 short hours." On March 13 the party of prisoners reached the Tennessee River. They marched along its banks to Fort Henry, where they spent the night. There the prisoners received ample rations but suffered from a lack of fuel. The next evening they boarded a boat and started down the river, escorted by gunboats. The captives followed the river to Paducah, Kentucky, where thirty of them endured three nights in a poorly ventilated basement. From there they went a short distance up the Ohio then up the Cumberland to Nashville.[7]

The Tennessee capital was a common but brief stopping point for Confederates captured in the West. They were generally housed in the east wing of the penitentiary. Their numbers usually ranged from 400 to 2,000, although there were 7,460 Confederates confined there during December 1864. Of that total, however, 6,229 were soon transferred to other facilities. The prisoners' observations of the prison were almost universally negative, and at least one Union official agreed with them. On March 13, 1864, Dr. Augustus M. Clark, Hoffman's primary medical inspector, submitted a report on the penitentiary and the two hospitals that treated sick prisoners. Although he found the prison "in a very fair condition of police," Clark was disgusted by the sinks. There were far too few of them, he wrote, and those that were there were not cleaned nearly as often as necessary. "I found them full to overflowing and exceedingly offensive," Clark wrote. The inspector found the prison hospital adequate and the care good, although he suggested that the military prisoners be segregated from the general prison population at the hospital. He was less impressed with the hospital outside the prison.

"This hospital," Clark observed, "is located on the public square and consists of two large warehouses not at all well adapted to this purpose." He added that the prisoners "bear evidence of being well cared for."[8]

Pvt. Anderson spent forty-eight hours at the penitentiary. "The filth, dirt, and vermin with which this place abounded is more than I will attempt to describe," he wrote, "simply because I could not do it justice." Twice a day Anderson and his fellow prisoners received "a handful of dry crackers" and "a piece of fat pork or beef." Those with a cup also got some weak coffee. They slept on a brick floor covered with sawdust "which was almost alive with lice." The noise of the convicts kept the military prisoners awake, and they found it necessary to assign at least one man to picket duty to prevent "a charge on our blankets." During waking hours the Confederates remained in groups "to protect ourselves against the inmates who often mugged new comers."[9]

For Young, incarceration in the penitentiary came as a relief. Following an eight-mile march, he and his fellow prisoners were kept in a rock quarry for five days and nights "in rain & snow with hardly any thing to eat & no fire of consequence." Several of the prisoners froze to death. William H. Davis, who was captured at the battle of Chattanooga, endured the same ordeal for three nights in December 1863. "To day is my birthday," he wrote on the 7th, "and I am enjoying it finely Standing out in the Rain with out Shelter or fire on Rock yard half froze to Death." Conditions improved when he was taken to a local hotel the next day, but the company did not. Speaking of his fellow Confederate prisoners, Davis wrote, "I was never in such a mixed [crowd] in my life gamblers, Deserters Rouges, and all the mean in [Gen. Braxton] Braggs armey are confined in this place."[10]

Samuel Beckett Boyd arrived at Nashville already suffering from exposure. A lieutenant in the Confederate Ordinance Department, Boyd was captured at Bristol, Tennessee, in December 1864. After being taken to Chattanooga via Knoxville, he started toward Nashville in a boxcar. His car derailed nine hours into the journey, and he found himself atop another freight car for the last sixty miles "through a cold drenching rain." The train reached Nashville at 9:00 p.m., but the men were kept outside for the next two nights in mud and snow without a fire. Observing the adjacent prison, Boyd wrote that it was "the first time I ever desired to be in a penitentiary."[11]

Crowding in the prison is the only possible explanation—although not a justification—for the conditions Young, Davis, and Boyd endured. The experience of Virgil S. Murphey, who was captured on November 30, 1864, at the battle of Franklin, suggests that overcrowding was a problem at the Nashville facility. Murphey wrote that sixty-eight officers were packed into a fifteen-by-eighteen-foot cell. There were twenty-one plank bunks and one bucket of water. "It was a long wretched night," Murphey wrote a few weeks later, "the most miserable of my life and will remain in memory as a monument to Yankee hardness of heart." On three occasions guards arrived promising rations that never arrived. Early in the morning of December 2, Murphey received a slice of ham and some bread, his first meal since his capture.[12]

For A. C. Kean, captured at the battle of Chattanooga, the Tennessee convicts were a greater problem than the lack of rations. Writing forty-two years after the incident, Kean recalled that the felons "subjected us to such indignaties" that the weary military prisoners flew into a rage. The Confederates, Kean readily admitted, held all the advantages. They numbered about four hundred, the convicts closer to one hundred. The soldiers had access to a pile of stove wood. Their tormentors "had nothing but their fists." Kean recalled, "We turned loose on them and beat their brains out, broke their heads, arms, legs, and threw many of them over the railing to the hard floor below which was the height of . . . thirty feet, killing many of them." The guards heard the ruckus, Kean added, observed what was going on, and promptly left.[13]

After forty-eight hours at Nashville, Kean found himself on a boxcar bound for Louisville. Upon reaching the Ohio River city, "We were placed in barracks which were good and warm with plenty of nice warm straw to sleep on, a luxury that we didn't know anything about, plenty to eat and lots of comfort." Kean added that the facility was "very lousy," but he noted, "We didn't mind that as we already had a good stock ourselves." Kean's was apparently a majority view. "Louisville Prison more comfortable and better fare," Samuel Boyd jotted in his diary after arriving from Nashville. He found the guards, members of the Twentieth Kentucky, to be "kind and obliging." James Anderson also contrasted his Louisville lodgings with those at Nashville. "This prison was not so crowded and its inmates were not all thieves," he reflected. "So we could sleep, and have some rest, and right glad we was too that we could do so." Anderson was less impressed with the arrangements for eating. Three times a day their guards marched the prisoners into a dining hall, where they stood at tall tables with neither plates nor utensils. "At appropriate distances," he wrote, "was laid on the table a piece of bakers bread, a piece of fat mess pork or beef on it." His greatest complaint was the prevalence of chimneys in the neighborhood, spewing forth smoke from coal fires. The Southerner noted that it was enough "to almost stifle those not accustomed to it in the presence of pure air."[14]

Virgil Murphey also found Louisville an improvement over Nashville, but he did not enjoy his trip to the Kentucky city. The 173rd Ohio guarded Murphey's contingent of prisoners. He claimed that the Buckeye outfit had abandoned its position at Franklin "and now applied a salve to their wounded vanity by wreaking vengeance upon their defenseless opponents. They were the most blasphemous vulgar and disgusting ruffians I ever met," Murphey wrote. At Louisville "a federal soldier dressed like a cabin boy" demanded that the prisoners turn over their pocketknives, an indignity that Murphey also resented. Things quickly improved when he met three fellow prisoners. The unusual trio included an English physician who had formerly lived in Macon, Georgia, a Union major, and "a youth from Kentucky." The doctor had been a Union contractor before being charged with fraud. The major, who had served as a paymaster, faced charges of malfeasance and embezzlement. Murphey did not record the offense with which the young man was charged. The doctor and the major were apparently well connected with prison officials. "Through their influence with the prison commandant I was enabled to procure a heavy blanket," Murphey wrote. He also received hot coffee, rolls and butter, and two bottles of ale. As Murphey departed the doctor "filled my pockets with sandwiches to deliver to my unfortunate comrades."[15]

Murphey's friends represented a blend of prisoners that was not uncommon at Louisville. Reporting on December 6, 1862, Capt. Freedley informed Hoffman that 2,417 military prisoners had been sent south for exchange the previous month. A total of 190 Confederate deserters, natives of England, Ireland, and Scotland, were released during the same period, as were 186 deserters and 50 political prisoners. Another 30 political prisoners had been transferred to Camp Chase. "The prison quarters," Freedley wrote, "are temporary frame buildings, conveniently arranged, entirely separated from the quarters of the troops and inclosed by a high fence, which includes sufficient grounds for exercise." He pronounced the rations, police, and health of the prison good. Dr. Clark, a more difficult inspector to please, agreed. On October 28, 1863, he pronounced the quarters "sweet and clean." He noted, "The prison is merely a receiving depot, the prisoners constantly changing, and unless sick or under sentence being rarely retained more than twenty-four hours. Notwithstanding this constant change," Clark continued, "the general condition of the prison is admirable." When the doctor returned three months later, he was somewhat less impressed. Discipline, the policing of the camp, and the condition of the sinks all left much to be desired, although he placed some of the blame on harsh winter weather.[16]

For prisoners captured in the East, the pattern of treatment was much the same. Officials in the eastern theater received their most daunting challenge in dealing with prisoners following the battle of Gettysburg. In addition to nearly 14,000

Confederate prisoners, 6,739 of whom were wounded, the Union also had to care for 13,603 of their own wounded. Although medical inspector John Cuyler reported, "Every effort was made to alleviate the sufferings" of the Confederate prisoners, he conceded that the care did not come quickly enough. "For some days after the battle," Cuyler wrote, "many of the rebel wounded were in a most deplorable condition, being without shelter of any sort, and with an insufficient number of medical officers and nurses of their own army."[17]

Among the many wounded Confederates was Lt. William Peel of the Eleventh Mississippi, who suffered a minor leg wound shortly before his capture on July 3, 1863. The first thing Peel noticed after being taken was the crowd of soldiers that formed, all eager to escort the prisoners to the rear. "It is a mighty good thing to get to take prisoners to the rear, especially when the front is as well heated up as that of Gettysburg was," the lieutenant concluded. The volunteer sentries urged their captives quickly ahead. Peel and a wounded comrade were unable to keep up, and they were finally left behind in charge of a single Union soldier. "We at length reached the point of concentration for our part of the line," Peel wrote. Here he discovered about a thousand fellow Confederate captives. Later contingents of prisoners, large and small, increased the number to approximately eighteen hundred by nightfall. "Meantime there were several surgeons going round to see after the wounded, & each in his turn, was as well cared for as could, under the circumstances have been expected." Peel's doctor informed him that his wound was "of no material consequence, being only a flesh cut & not very deep." He applied a bandage and cautioned Peel against "unnecessary walking." The lieutenant ended up at Johnson's Island, where he would remain until his death in February 1865.[18]

John Dooley, a captain in the First Virginia, was also wounded during the third day's fighting at Gettysburg. Shot through both thighs, he went down about thirty yards from the Union guns as he advanced as part of Gen. George Pickett's ill-fated charge. Like Peel, Dooley spent the night in an open field. A light rain, he wrote, proved "extremely refreshing and grateful to thousands of fevered brains and burning wounds." Late on July 4 Dooley was placed in an ambulance with a wounded Union soldier. By the time he reached the "field hospital," it was pouring rain. The hospital proved to be nothing more than an open field with "some kind of medical attention and rations of crackers and substitute coffee." Union officials attempted to separate Northern and Southern soldiers, but they were not always successful. "The whole ground for miles around," Dooley observed, "is covered with the wounded, the dying and the dead."[19]

There Dooley remained for five days. On the 9th he was placed in a tent with five other prisoners, and for the first time his wounds were washed and bandaged. Three days later Dooley and several fellow prisoners boarded a train for Baltimore. Their destination was Fort McHenry, which Dooley described as "this noisome place [with] filth and vermin in profusion." Even the wounded were forced to sleep on the floor without blankets. Dooley did receive attention for his wound from a Union doctor. On July 17 he removed four maggots, and seven days later he extracted several pieces of fabric that had entered the wound from Dooley's trousers. That and the opportunity to purchase a pitcher of beer daily for 50¢ were about the only positive aspects of prison life at Fort McHenry. Dooley's stay there proved to be relatively brief. On August 22 he departed for Johnson's Island.[20]

Edmund DeWitt Patterson of the Ninth Alabama was captured on July 2, along with some sixty other soldiers from his regiment. Patterson was not wounded, and the next day he joined some six hundred fellow captives on a thirty-mile march to Westminster, Maryland. The prisoners suffered from hunger and heat. Patterson wrote, "We were fortunate in having a very gentlemanly sort of fellow in command, who endeavored to make us as comfortable as the circumstances would permit." Indeed, the Confederates received kind treatment from everybody except a single Union officer who swore at them and said if it was up to him, he would shoot them all down in the street. That evening they received a day's ration of hardtack and pork. The prisoners spent the night in a stock pen.[21]

The next morning they were packed tightly into boxcars for the trip to Baltimore and Fort McHenry. Two days later, on July 6, Patterson and his comrades boarded a steamship for Fort Delaware. "A respectable hog would have turned up his nose in disgust at it," he wrote of the depot. Patterson's luck was with him, and his stay proved brief. On the 16th the officers learned that they would soon depart for Johnson's Island. "This is glorious news to us," he wrote, "for we are anxious to go anywhere (except to Hell and some even said they would prefer the aforementioned place for the same length of time) in preference to remaining here."[22]

Following Gettysburg the burgeoning Union prison system enjoyed a respite, at least in the eastern theater. This changed with the launch of the spring campaign of 1864. Grant had been promoted to general in chief and had decided to travel with the Army of the Potomac. Now it was Grant vs. Lee. The result would be fighting that was constant and casualty figures that were appalling. Combined with the collapse of the cartel, this struggle also meant that thousands of new prisoners would soon be heading to already-crowded Union prisons.

On May 12, twelve days into the campaign, Stanton sent Hoffman to Belle Plain, on the Potomac River near Fredericksburg. The commissary general was to make arrangements to forward prisoners north. (In perhaps his only assignment of the war not associated with prisoners, he also received orders to arrange for a line of communications to and from Grant's headquarters.) He found transportation already in place. Some guards were on hand, and more were on their way from Washington. On the 13th Hoffman sent a group of Confederate officers to Fort Delaware on a steamer and made arrangements to forward the enlisted men. He advised Gen. John Abercrombie to send up to fifteen thousand enlisted men to Point Lookout. As many as six hundred officers and two thousand men could be shipped to Fort Delaware.[23]

J. B. Stamp of the Third Alabama fell into Union hands on May 5, 1863, the first day of fighting in the battle of the Wilderness. A Union soldier hustled him to the rear. As they headed for the "bull pen," Stamp and his escort passed a number of wounded soldiers on their way to the hospital. The pen was close to Grant's headquarters, and Stamp watched with interest the bustle of activity as troops and artillery headed toward the front. As the day wore on, over two hundred of Stamp's comrades joined him. As was so often the case in the West, promised rations never appeared. "The guards were kind to us," Stamp later wrote, "and as it was prudent, divided their rations with us."[24]

After spending eleven days with the Union army, Stamp and his fellow prisoners began their march to Belle Plain. Along the way they passed a contingent of black troops. News of the massacre of several hundred black soldiers at Fort Pillow in Tennessee had recently arrived. As Stamp recalled, "We were greeted with cries of 'remember Fort Pillow,' and this was followed by a tirade of the most obscene and insulting epithets, that their vulgar and depraved minds could conceive." Stamp waited three days at Belle Plain for transportation to Point Lookout. The prisoners finally received rations there, three-quarters of a pound of pork and twelve crackers. Some of the men had not eaten for five days, and many consumed the entire issue immediately, not even bothering to cook the pork.[25]

From the Wilderness, Lee and Grant raced southeast toward Spotsylvania Court House. There the fighting resumed on May 8. Four days later George Washington Hall of the Fourteenth Georgia became a prisoner, along with about thirty other men from his regiment. Hall was at the "Bloody Angle," where he spent "nearly two hours under the most terrable fire I ever saw." As the prisoners were escorted to the rear, the skies opened up with a torrent of rain. "Shells from our Batteries begin to fall & burst near us," Hall wrote in his diary, "we are carried on farther to the rear halt again the rain chills us to the bone." After separating the wounded prisoners from the rest, the eager captors hurried the Confederates another two or three miles. There they remained until it was nearly dark, when the procession moved out behind a wagon train. It was a slow march through mud and water that was sometimes knee deep. Shortly before daybreak on the 13th, the prisoners were halted on a plank road near Chancellorsville. "[I] lie down exhausted in the mud and rain," Hall recorded, "and soon I am unconscious of my ill-fated position. So ends the most eventful day of my life and what I have sketched is only a faint outline."[26]

Late in the afternoon of the 13th, the contingent marched toward Fredericksburg, halting some three miles short of the community. As they moved out the next day to the sound of cannons, Hall wrote, "I would give any thing I possess in this world to be with my company and know the casualties of our regts & Brig." The marches of the next two days were obviously slow because Hall did not reach Fredericksburg until May 15. There he observed "an immence number of the enemys wounded" and a city "deserted & laid waist." The next morning the prisoners crossed the Rappahannock on pontoon bridges and started toward Belle Plain. Hall observed, "There is six or eight thousand Rebel prisoners here at present on an area of 40 or 50 achers, principally in a small valley surrounded by high hills, verry well adapted to the purpose." Supplementing the natural security of the pen was artillery well positioned atop the hills.[27]

Wilbur Fisk Davis was another Confederate who fell into the hands of the Union on May 12. Recalling the event in 1902, Davis wrote that he and his fellow captives were taken back about three miles and crowded together in the rain and the mud. He claimed to have reached Belle Plain the next day, but being an enlisted man, he had to wait there for transportation. When the transportation arrived it turned out to be a steam freighter bound for Fort Delaware. The trip took two and one-half days, with between five and seven hundred Confederates "crowded on the lower deck—with not room enough for us to lie down." Davis sought out a position next to a "large open gangway," which afforded him a view during the daytime and constant fresh air. Hardtack and brown sugar composed the rations for the voyage. From his relatively comfortable position, Davis stood the trip well. He recalled that a comrade, who had been in the stern section, arrived at the prison pale and weak. A few days later the man was taken to the hospital, and that was the last time Davis ever saw him.[28]

Hall's experiences aboard the transport ship, a steam frigate in his case, were similar. He wrote in his diary, "We had to remain crowded together so thick we could scarcely sit down with our feet & legs doubled up under us without any air being able to reach us only what came down through the hatchway, for 2 nights & nearly 3 days." Several men fainted before the guards permitted them to go up on the deck for air. The conditions were such that Hall considered it "a great relief" to reach Fort Delaware "out of the foul air of the hold of that old frigate." That opinion proved temporary. Just three days later Hall wrote, "I hope & pray, night & day, for us soon to be delivered out of here."[29]

For Wilbur Wightman Gramling of the Fifth Florida the voyage to a Union prison included a lengthy layover in a Washington, DC, hospital. Gramling suffered a wound to his right arm on May 6 at the battle of the Wilderness. Several members of his regiment were among the six hundred prisoners taken with him. They were sent to the rear, where the ball was removed from Gramling's arm and the wound dressed. The Union guards tried over the next two days to get their prisoners to Fredericksburg, but Confederate cavalry commander John S. Mosby blocked their way. On the 9th they made it to Fredericksburg, where a hospital had been established in a Presbyterian church. There he remained until May 20, when he was able to walk to Belle Plain.

Following an overnight trip aboard a steamer, Gramling arrived at the Union capital, where he was "very comfortably situated" in a hospital on the north side of the city. Despite that positive assessment, he noted a few days later, "Some die here nearly every day." The sights of Washington interested Gramling. One day he got a brief look at President and Mrs. Lincoln. On another he saw an artillery battery pass by. He also wrote, "Sometimes a negro man and a white woman [can be seen] riding together in a carriage with a negro driver—frequently see them walking together." On May 27 Gramling was moved to Lincoln Hospital. "Met a very cold reception," he wrote. "Had to sit a long time before I got a bed. All very sullen. Nasty out of the way place." Gramling remained there until July 12, when he was transferred to Old Capitol Prison. He departed Washington eleven days later for Elmira.[30]

Although thousands of prisoners passed through Belle Plain on their way to Northern prisons, the scope of the Civil War precluded a single route to captivity. Writing thirty years later, Capt. W. Gart Johnson recalled his capture during a September 4, 1864, skirmish at Berryville, Virginia, near Harpers Ferry. Johnson was one of about seventy-five prisoners taken to Harpers Ferry and placed in a three-story factory building. He and his fellow prisoners occupied the middle floor, along with various other military and political prisoners. Below them were their guards. Above them was "the meanest, motliest crew imaginable. They were a mixed lot of bounty jumpers, thieves, deserters from the Federal army, roughs, and toughs from Northern cities," Johnson recalled. The captain remained there for two weeks before being transferred to Baltimore. His stay there proved brief. After separating the officers and the men, Union officials sent the former to Johnson's Island and the latter to Camp Chase. Several former colleagues greeted Johnson upon his arrival at the Lake Erie depot. Following the handshakes they escorted him to the washhouse, where both he and his clothes were scrubbed free of the lice that had accumulated during the previous two weeks.[31]

On July 10, 1864, Henri Mugler, formerly of the Thirteenth Virginia, surrendered himself, for reasons never made clear, to Union pickets near Annandale, Virginia. The men at the picket post were suspicious of their voluntary captive until Mugler convinced them that he had been a regular soldier and "no Bush whacker." After that, he observed in his diary, "they treated me very kindly and gave me a very good breakfast, a large tin cup of genuine coffee, sweetines and cream in it, beef steak, & loaf bread & butter." Although he was placed in the guardhouse, Mugler received rations "in abundance" and enjoyed access to a New York newspaper. On or before July 19 Mugler arrived at the Old Capitol Prison. Four days later he boarded a train for Baltimore. There were 740 prisoners in the group. "Saw a great deal of Southern simpathy expressed by the ladys of Baltimore," Mugler observed. "Good many of them kissed their hands to the prisoners and there was any quantity of smiles for the Rebs." A number of Baltimore residents showed up at the depot to bid the Confederates farewell as they departed for Elmira.[32]

Ten days before Mugler's capture, a detachment of Union cavalry surprised E. L. Cox near Norfolk. Explaining the circumstances in his diary, Cox wrote that he was "somewhat wearied with long marching & sat down to rest." As did most prisoners, Cox wrote that he was "kindly received" by his captors. A lieutenant gave up his tent for the prisoner and offered him some "contraband whiskey." Another apologized for the scanty rations they had to offer. "Books and papers were offered me in order that time might go off more smoothly," Cox noted. The next day he found himself at the Norfolk guardhouse, which Cox considered "the filthiest place that I had seen." On the 4th he was transferred to the city jail. "I found it to be a very nice place compared with the guard house which I had just left," Cox wrote. He remained eleven days, and was questioned three times during that period by the provost marshal. On the 16th Cox left for Old Capitol Prison. By then that facility had become little more than a holding pen. Cox remained only a week before departing for Fort Delaware.[33]

Although George Washington Hall was at first relieved to reach Fort Delaware, Cox's experience was different. For one thing his journey to the facility was by rail rather than ship. The guards, Cox wrote, were "very kind. They would bring any articles we desired from the stores at a very small price." Upon reaching the fort, Cox and his contingent of captives heard "strange and horid stories" about the "fare and treatment of prisoners." They included tales of shootings and the news that an outbreak of smallpox had struck the camp.[34]

The prisoners had entered a strange new world. As some noted, at least they now had bunks, stoves to provide heat, and steady if not bountiful rations. For most this initial relief soon gave way to frustration and despair as the reality of their situation became obvious. Months or even years of hunger and loneliness lay ahead; and the prisoners quickly realized that survival meant battling both.

6
"Nothing to do & nothing to do it with"
The Constant Battle with Boredom

With the collapse of the cartel, Confederate captives arriving at Union prisons knew their stay in the North was likely to be a long one. Realizing this, they often carefully recorded their first impressions of their new quarters in their diaries. The details varied a great deal. The negative tone of the prisoners' early observations, following their initial relief at finally having shelter, did not. For Camp Chase prisoners, arriving in Columbus tired, hungry, and often ill, the march to the prison itself provided a harsh initiation to life as a captive. The facility was located four miles west of the city and its railroad depot. This made necessary a four-mile forced march in all sorts of weather. Thomas A. Sharpe, a citizen prisoner from Georgia, arrived at Columbus on April 10, 1864 "in cold wet weather [and] walked from R. R. out to the prison through mud and water." Tennessee prisoner James W. Anderson, who had reached Camp Chase ten days earlier, noted that he walked "through the middle of the muddiest road I ever saw." The train bearing Lt. James Taswell Mackey of the Forty-eighth Tennessee pulled into the Columbus depot at 4:00 a.m. on January 18, 1864. A cold march through a snowstorm followed.[1]

Upon reaching the camp, Mackey and his fellow prisoners had to remain in the elements as guards searched them and took all their money and valuables. "Receipts are given for greenbacks," Mackey wrote, "none for Confederate [money]." Anderson endured the same procedure, noting that his patience eased the ordeal somewhat. "We passed in five or six at a time and were examined closely in general," he noted. "I was proud however that I was not subject to so close an inspection as most of those who seemed to murmur at this as a hardship, while common sense ought to have taught them that it was but reasonable to expect under the circumstances." He watched with amusement as his fellow prisoners attempted to conceal pocketknives and other items rumored—falsely, as it turned out—to be contraband.[2]

Pvt. Curtis Burke of the Fourteenth Kentucky Cavalry made a similar attempt when he arrived at Camp Morton on July 24, 1863. "The Yanks commenced taking the prisoners in small squads through a building and taking everything from them," he noted in his diary. "The rest of us soon found out what was going on and we went to work hiding our money and destroying other things." The guards saw them, and the prisoners soon received a lecture from the camp adjutant. They could keep their Confederate money, he reassured them, and they would receive sutler checks for Union funds. Less reassuring was the information that the guards had orders to shoot any prisoner caught hiding or destroying anything. Burke found that the adjutant's promise was only partly true. "Some of the sergeants kept account of the money that they took and the men's names that they took it from," he wrote, "but others did not thus pocketing the money for their own benefit as fast as they took it."[3]

Inclement weather made the lengthy search procedure even more annoying. Virgil S. Murphey, who was captured on November 30, 1864, at the battle of Franklin, found himself entering the gates of Johnson's Island seven days later. "The night was bitter and intensely cold and the fierce north wind penetrated through our thin garments as we were halted at the office of the prison commandant for examination," he wrote. The roll was called alphabetically, forcing Murphey to wait some time in the cold before the guard shouted out his name. Meanwhile, "My feet became thoroughly feeling less and almost failed to perform their accustomed functions." A thorough search followed. Murphey wrote that a "detective" forced him to undress to be certain that he was sneaking nothing contraband into the compound. Another Johnson's Island prisoner, John Dooley, complained that he had to wait for several hours in a drizzling rain before his turn came to be searched.[4]

Pvt. C. W. Jones of the Twenty-fourth Virginia Cavalry, who arrived at Point Lookout in December 1863, received a stark introduction to prison life. "The first . . . scene presented to our view," he wrote after the war, "was a pile of coffins for dead rebels." When Curtis Burke was transferred with a group of prisoners from Camp Morton to Camp Douglas in August 1863, he and his comrades immediately sought ways to ameliorate their condition. They found that the barracks included one large room that would accommodate some eighty men as well as smaller rooms that would house anywhere from two to ten prisoners. "There was a general stampede of our boys to secure the little rooms," he wrote. Burke and six comrades ended up in one of the coveted apartments. It had two windows, which they quickly threw open to get some fresh air.[5]

Soon after settling in, Confederate prisoners learned that they had entered compounds that were at once bustling and boring. "It's all bustle and confusion," wrote Joseph E. Purvis of the Nineteenth Virginia after spending three days at Fort Delaware. Another Fort Delaware prisoner, John Alexander Gibson, complained, "The inside of the barracks is a continual confusion almost everything is carried on there are shoemakers & carvers all the time at work those that do not work are engaged in talking playing cards chess & drafts." Even mealtime, Gibson continued, was disrupted by men "continually hollering" over who had a place at the table. If this were not enough, he concluded, "We have a fight or two occasionally." When a rainy day limited the options available to Rock Island prisoner Lafayette Rogan to indoor pursuits, he bemoaned his fate. "No means of out-door amusements can be adopted on such days & such a continual clatter of toungs—whistling, singing, speech-making, dancing, hollowing &c &c renders it impossible to read with any degree of pleasure."[6]

The confusion was especially annoying to many of the officers confined at Johnson's Island. Edmund D. Patterson of the Ninth Alabama observed, "Perhaps one of the worst features of prison life at this place . . . is that it is so public, that is, it is impossible for one to get away from the crowd, the bustle, and confusion." James Mayo complained of the "perfect babel of voices" at the Lake Erie depot. "In the room here all are talking at once," he wrote on January 10, 1864. One was complaining of being sick. Another was singing "Bonnie Blue Star." A Capt. Burwell was "standing in the middle of the room and looking as if he wanted something to do." The distractions were not limited to talking and singing. Mayo continued, "Lt. Mills coughs, so do several others, while several others spit and blow their noses." The personal habits of his fellow prisoners were especially annoying to Patterson. "Would I could go some place where they did not chew and smoke tobacco," he wrote on another occasion. "The habit is disgusting." Virgil Murphey wrote that he could "neither study nor reflect" because of "the immense crowding and congregating of the officers together." It was a situation that he also considered unhealthy. "Such a shocking crowding of men together in a narrow contracted space," he theorized, "breeds disease [and] debilitates the system from the constant asperation of the same air, filth accumulates to add its baleful influence and finally results in a heavy bill of mortality."[7]

In the midst of all this activity, many prisoners complained of the boredom and inactivity of prison life. Reflecting on life at Fort Delaware, George Washington

Hall wrote, "Nothing of interest transpires here one day more than another the dull monotony that seems to hang over us like some terrable & dense fog is never dispersed." In a letter to his brother, Johnson's Island prisoner Thomas Gibbes Morgan complained of "this horrid life of inactivity and uselessness." On October 23, 1864, John Joyes, a member of John Hunt Morgan's division of cavalry, summed up his opinion of Johnson's Island succinctly: "Nothing to do & nothing to do it with." With little prospect of exchange, Confederate prisoners—as well as their Union counterparts in Dixie compounds—faced months or years of such inactivity. It was not a pleasing prospect, and to some the lack of anything to do was high on the list of things that made prison life unbearable. Writing to his wife from Johnson's Island, Daniel Printup said his rations and treatment were generally good. With the money he and his comrades had to supplement their fare, Printup added, "We can live very well." He concluded, "With the exception of the confinement and inactive life, I might say I could be comfortable." Camp Chase prisoner Thomas A. Sharpe expressed the same sentiments in his diary, writing, "Imprisonment is hard to bear—however mild the treatment might be." For Wilbur Gramling, his job as a waiter at Elmira provided the only respite from the monotony of prison life. On October 31, 1864, he wrote, "The way I spend my time. 1st. Set the table and then clean up afterwards, the 2nd, read and knock about until 3 o'clock and 3rd, it is dinner, which I have to take an active part in, working after the rest."[8]

For men confined far from home, loneliness was a twin evil to boredom. As it did with inactivity, the likelihood of a lengthy stay following the collapse of the cartel only made a bad situation worse. It was a gloom that constantly hung over the prisoners, a melancholy that was enhanced by a variety of causes. It struck Curtis Burke as he climbed a Camp Douglas barracks to do some repair work. Observing a crowd at a nearby racetrack and "people walking about as if there was no war going on," he wrote, "I could not help envying them their liberty, yet I try to be contented." Johnson's Island prisoner Edward Drummond was engaged in a baseball game when his wife's picture fell out of a locket he was wearing. "I would not have lost it for anything," he wrote, "but found it gone and there was no trace to be found. I have worn it over Four years and shall miss it very much." For devout Confederates the approach of the Sabbath was often all that was necessary to remind the men of happier times with loved ones. "Tomorrow is Sunday and Oh! I wish I was at home. I know I would be the happiest being in the world," Joseph Purvis wrote at Fort Delaware. The fear that his parents believed him killed at Gettysburg only added to his anxiety. At Elmira Wilbur Gramling wrote bluntly on a Sunday evening, "I am homesick. Get the blues or something else. This evening seems very much like Sabbath evenings at home. Makes me want a stalk of cane to chew and some potatoes. Oh! me."[9]

About the only thing that could ease the depression and anxiety of the prisoners was mail from home. In facilities where news and rumors traveled quickly, the most exciting announcement was that a "Dixie mail" had arrived via flag-of-truce boat. "One finds but little enjoyment except in these silent messengers that come from home & friends," wrote William G. Woods in a return letter from Johnson's Island. "When the mail comes while some are rejoicing over letters from home and friends, others are downcast," he added. "Almost the only events that prison life can boast are the reception of letters," Francis A. Boyle of the Thirty-second North Carolina noted in his Fort Delaware diary.[10]

Officials at all prison camps limited the length of letters to a single page. The stated rationale for this policy was that all correspondence was subject to inspection. Reading the mail of thousands of prisoners took time, and limiting letters to one page also limited the amount of time spent in the inspection process. Occasionally at some camps prisoners could send longer letters by bribing the inspectors. "Have been writing some 'dime letters,' or in other words, letters of four pages," Edmund Patterson wrote at Johnson's Island on November 24, 1863. "The examining clerks will read a letter of any length provided they find money enclosed in the letter to pay for it at the rate of two and a half cents per page, and although this seems to be a very small matter, they make several dollars a day at it." According to Patterson, the same fee schedule applied to incoming mail. Another Johnson's Island prisoner, A. M. Bedford, informed his wife that Meriwether Jeff Thompson had secured this arrangement with the inspectors and that it "suits us first rate." Thompson, who led both regular and irregular Confederate troops during a colorful Civil War career, later wrote that the censors readily agreed to his proposal provided it remained a secret. "But at last," Thompson added, "some mean 'cuss' who had to pay ten cents for a four page letter, wrote the commanding officer that he was taxed ten cents, and the matter was inquired into, and the long letter mail was suddenly stopped." In a letter to a friend, T. J. Pitchford wrote that the same system was in place at Fort Delaware. Explaining that longer letters could pass "for a consideration," he added, "And this is proper enough because it is an additional trouble to the person whose business it is to examine them."[11]

Johnson's Island prisoner Robert Bingham found himself in trouble with the examiners when he placed an extra personal message to his wife under the stamp of a letter he sent home. According to Bingham, others used the same method to inform friends that they had added secret communications in "chemical ink" that could be read if the letter was placed close to a fire. Although Bingham had not engaged in that practice, he found his mail suspended. Further, Col. Pierson threatened to halt all communications. For Bingham and many other prisoners this was a double threat. Not only would they be deprived of welcome letters from home, they would also not receive the money that the letters often contained. Bingham sent a note to Pierson, explaining that he had "nothing to do with the chemical ink." After a day of suspense, Pierson wrote back to inform a relieved Bingham that his mail would continue. "The tone of his note was kind and courteous," Bingham recorded.[12]

Because of censorship, letters written by Civil War prisoners shed little direct light on conditions in the camps where they were confined. Indeed, the men tended to write much more about life back home than about life in their compounds. "I suppose you have gathered your crops &c.," James R. Ervin wrote in a September 21, 1864, letter to his father from Johnson's Island. Writing to his brother, Otis Johnson, a Camp Chase prisoner, observed, "I had heard from different sources that father had contemplated leaving Bloomsburg and though feeling sad at the prospect at first have since concluded it was best for all." B. E. Priest, who was confined at Camp Douglas, asked his sister, "Tell father not to kill himself at work for that is nonsense but to enjoy what he has." In a letter written on December 3, 1863, Daniel Printup asked his wife if his brother had sold Printup's tobacco crop yet. "Say to him not to be in a hurry," Printup wrote. "Tobacco crop in northern states was destroyed by frosts very badly which will increase its price very much." A strong poignancy laces many of the letters. "Your intention to have father's remains transferred to mother's tomb meets with my full approbation; it is a more fitting place," William Lambert Campbell wrote from Elmira in a letter to his sister. "Please tell my sweetheart she may get married as soon as she likes," Johnson's Island prisoner James A. Riddick asked his cousin. "Release her from all obligations and hold her to the promise no longer as I expect never to get away from prison."[13]

Often the men reminded family members of how important it was to them to hear from home. "I must express approval of your determination to write me weekly," James A. Thomas wrote his sister from Camp Morton, "for were it not for letters I cannot imagine how I could endure prison life. As it is they afford me the greatest relief." Point Lookout prisoner Henry E. Parberry complained to his sister when he failed to receive word from home. "I have been waiting for some time expecting to receive a letter from you," he wrote on May 18, 1864, "but you either have not received my letters or yours have been lost. I have received no letter from you or from [home] since the 10th of Apr." It was a common sentiment in Civil War prison correspondence. Even worse was the prospect of not receiving a letter that had arrived at the camp. On one occasion Johnson's Island prisoner E. John Ellis received an empty envelope marked "letter contraband in length." He appealed to a camp official, who turned the letter over to him. "It was from my sister," he wrote in his diary. "What a sweet tender letter it is . . . I would not swap it for Maximilian's scepter and the patronage of Napoleon thrown in to boot." As for the captain who secured the letter for him, Ellis determined that "if I ever catch him down South, I'll take care to remember that one 'Yankee' at least did me an act of kindness."[14]

Usually a great deal of time elapsed between letters, meaning the prisoners had to find diversions within the walls of their compounds. These were rare but not nonexistent. Henry Massie Bullitt, a cavalry trooper under John Hunt Morgan's command, later recalled that he and his fellow prisoners "greatly enjoyed" the afternoon concerts of the Camp Chase band. "I go every evening to the Suttler's shop to sit on the platform to hear the band perform," James Mayo wrote from Johnson's Island. "It plays 'Coming Through the Rye' (much rye goes through to them) and one or two others that are quite pretty, but they have not a great variety of tunes." Elmira prisoner Henri Mugler, himself a musician, recorded in his diary in August 1864 that the guards had formed a regimental band. "I had a severe spell of the blues until I heard the band play," he wrote, "but no longer. Music truly hath great powers."[15]

Depots near bodies of water offered scenery that helped reduce the monotony of prison life. "We have a nice view of the [Delaware] river and bay," Joseph Purvis wrote from Fort Delaware. "There is always ten or twelve vessels in sight." Edward Drummond enjoyed watching the start of New York's annual yacht regatta from Governor's Island. "They looked very beautiful as they passed down by with their white sails," he wrote. "All had a fine start and a good breeze added greatly to the excitement." After being transferred to Johnson's Island, Drummond noted that excursion boats were common sights. On one occasion the band on board played "Dixie," "and such a tremendous shout never went up as went from this pen." William Speer was less thrilled when a boat of black passengers passed the island. "O! how the black Bucks & wentches laugh at us," he noted. William Peel found Johnson's Island to be an excellent place for bird watching. "Our black-birds are building all around," he wrote on May 5, 1864. "Our wood-pecker has been reinforced to double his original strength; & today a mocking-bird sang to us for a short time quite cheerfully." The winter scenery of Lake Erie impressed Virgil Murphey. "To the Southerner reared in a mild genial climate of almost perpetual summer, it is a grand view to look upon the lake," he observed. "As far as the eye can extend, it is one unbroken sea of ice so brilliantly white when the sun is shining as to be painful to the naked eye."[16]

When they could not depend upon the scenery for a diversion, the prisoners depended upon one another. Within the limits imposed by officials, the captives often spent much of their day visiting. Many collected autographs from their fellow prisoners, filling several pages with the signatures. Otherwise, socializing was a common method of passing the time. "Part of my time I spend in walking up & down & visiting various parts of the prison barracks & conversing with several pious brethren I have formed the acquaintance of since I have been here," George Washington Hall wrote from Fort Delaware. "The mess frequently gets into animated discussions some times on interesting subjects," observed Camp Chase prisoner Thomas Sharpe. "We have three lawyers among us, and they are generally ready for disputation for instance whether the moon has any influence on animal or vegetable life." On September 17, 1864, the discussion turned to the question of exchanging black prisoners. "Some are not willing that our Govt. should ever back down from its present position," Sharpe wrote. "Others are willing that if this C.S. Govt. find it necessary, positively, then do that or almost anything for independence." Describing the scene inside his Fort Delaware barracks, William Jonathan Davis wrote, "Some few are in an animated strain relating adventures by 'flood and field,' and some are pleasing their small audiences with anecdotes—funny and well told many of them, but others, I am sorry to say, broad and coarse."[17]

An example of the former was a story related by a Johnson's Island prisoner concerning Gen. John Bankhead Magruder. As John Dooley recorded it, Magruder had surprised a sentinel who was cleaning his musket. "What are you, sir?" asked the general. The man replied, "Well you see, sir, I'm what they call sort of a sentinel; and I'd like to know what are you, sir." To this Magruder replied, "I'm, you see, a sort of a General." Without flinching the man said, "All right, General, if you'll just hold on a piece until I get this here musket together I'll give you a sort of salute." Dooley concluded, "The General sent him, I believe, to a sort of a guard house."[18]

The most common topic of conversation among the prisoners, at least if their diaries are to be believed, was the war. Known as "grape" among the captives, rumors spread quickly through the camps. "I play chess a great deal and loaf around to hear the latest 'grape' the rest of the time," noted Francis Boyle of his routine at Fort Delaware. He added, "This is the general occupation." Often the items of news the prisoners spread were accurate and surprisingly timely. A Johnson's Island prisoner reported the capture of Vicksburg on July 7, 1863, three days after the city fell to Union forces. "The discouraging news of the capture of Savannah by [Gen. William T.] Sherman reached us today," Camp Douglas prisoner Thomas R. Beadles wrote on December 28, 1864, just six days after the Union general took the Georgia city. Fort Delaware prisoners had learned of Sherman's triumph two days earlier. "Many of the prisoners are greatly depressed in spirits," wrote E. L. Cox of the news.[19]

Many prison camp rumors were not nearly so accurate. Five days before Sherman captured Savannah, Elmira prisoner H. H. Wiseman wrote, "We have news that Sherman has been badly whiped neare Savanah." Writing in August 1864, Thomas Sharpe reported a Union loss at a second battle of Antietam and the news that Sherman had been forced to retire from Atlanta. Not only was Sherman defeated, according to the rumor spreading around Camp Chase, but he had suffered twenty thousand casualties and lost his artillery and horses. "It is rumored among the Rebs that General [John Bell] Hood still holds Atlanta & that Gen. Sherman has been defeated before Atlanta by Hood," Henri Mugler wrote from Elmira on September 5, 1864. Sherman had actually entered the city three days earlier. This news the prisoners termed "a 'big Yankee lie' gotten up for some purpose." On May 22, 1864, word reached the prisoners at Rock Island that it was "a certainty" that the Confederacy had retaken Vicksburg. A rumor at Point Lookout had Gen. Benjamin Butler installed as secretary of war for the Union. A later version placed Gen. Nathaniel Banks in the post. The most common—and the most cruel—prison camp rumor was the one that announced that the exchange process was about to resume. "For the 189th time we are all exchanged and will leave for Dixie," John Dooley wrote from Johnson's Island. The latest report of an impending exchange, he added, had left the prison "in an uproar."[20]

The prisoners followed with great interest the Union presidential election of 1864. Indeed, Elmira diarist Mugler wrote that the prisoners followed the political events of 1864 more closely than did their guards. The contest pitted President Lincoln, seeking reelection, against George B. McClellan, the general Lincoln had dismissed shortly after the battle of Antietam. Lincoln was a known quantity to the prisoners, and his renomination by the Republicans seemed a certainty. As a result, the captives showed more interest in the Democratic Convention. "The Chicago Convention now attracts our whole attention," Rock Island prisoner Lafayette Rogan wrote in his diary. The first report to reach Camp Chase had Representative Fernando Wood, the former mayor of New York City, as the nominee. News of McClellan's nomination followed the same day. "We are generally in favor of McClellan," a Johnson's Island prisoner wrote, "thinking his election will, at least, bring about an exchange of prisoners, & probably give us peace." A prisoner at Elmira reported that his comrades were less enthusiastic, feeling the party platform did not go as far as they would have wished in its call for peace. "There is not enough of recognition [of the Confederacy] about it for them," Mugler wrote of his fellow prisoners.[21]

When the returns arrived, most prisoners who mentioned the election results did so with little comment. Typical was Wilbur Gramling's entry in his Elmira diary, "Seems to be no doubt but Abe is reelected." The results were depressing for Johnson's Island prisoner John Philip Thompson, who believed they meant "the utter hopelessness of our release from prison." Another Johnson's Island captive, Capt. Thomas J. Taylor, felt the "black republican triumph" meant little. "It is utter folly in the south," he wrote, "to base their hopes of political independence in anything short of the strong right hand." Fort Delaware prisoner William H. S. Burgwyn offered a different point of view. "Election returns show that Lincoln was elected," he noted on November 11, "and I don't know but that it is better for us."[22]

The thirst for news among the prisoners made "fresh fish," newly arrived captives, very popular people. Prisoners descended upon them, hoping to secure accurate, recent information from the outside world. "About sixty officers come in to day," Cox wrote from Fort Delaware on October 23, 1864. "They have no late nuse from the front though we have been able to here from many of our friends threw them." Several shipments of prisoners arrived at Johnson's Island during the spring of 1864. Unfortunately, William Peel wrote, most were transferred from other camps and had little information to share. The shouts of several prisoners directed Peel's attention to one such arrival. "The men called loudly for news," he noted. They forced one of the "fresh fish" to mount an open-ended barrel and report all he knew while three prisoners held him up so he would not fall. Before the new arrival could share any information a sentinel broke up the gathering. "I was literally besieged with questions," Virgil Murphey wrote of his arrival at Johnson's Island. "I sat there and answered inquiries until 3 oclock [a.m.] notwithstanding my weariness and desire for repose." Murphey was pleased that he brought "no message of grief and woe" about comrades and that his reassurances about friends "cheered many disponding hearts."[23]

The desire for information also made newspapers precious commodities among the prisoners. Their availability varied according to the whims of the officials at the various camps. On March 19, 1864, Camp Douglas prisoner Thomas Beadles wrote that prisoners could "again" subscribe. At Point Lookout, Charles Hutt noted the same change of policy three months later. Even when they allowed prisoners access to newspapers, the officers in charge of most Union prisons were careful to limit what papers the Confederates received. Those advocating, depending upon one's point of view, Peace Democrat or "Copperhead" political views were generally kept out. An exception was Johnson's Island, where prison officials rescinded an order banning such sheets in May 1864. Even where the papers were officially kept out, prisoners managed to smuggle them into the compounds. This was done "at some risk," according to Camp Douglas prisoner Curtis Burke. Joseph Kern wrote that his fellow Point Lookout prisoners were "well pleased" with the news received from smuggled newspapers, "though it is so meager."[24]

News from within the camp could be found on prison bulletin boards. Often their messages were unpopular. These included announcements of new, more restrictive rules and offers for prisoners to take the oath of allegiance to the Union. They also served as a lost and found or a way of announcing items wanted or for sale. Often the notices informed prisoners that they had letters waiting for them or boxes of food or clothing sent by loved ones. Some announcements brought even better news. While strolling across the Point Lookout compound, C. W. Jones noticed an announcement declaring that a group of prisoners was to be paroled. "After reading that notice," he wrote in a postwar memoir, "I had forgotten where I had started, and ran back to my tent to inform the boys of the good news."[25]

Those who could read found solace in books. "He who was so fortunate as to get a book or paper was very much envied," a Camp Chase prisoner later recalled. There is no way of determining the literacy rate of Confederate prisoners, but as they came from a region where there were no public schools, it was likely much higher among officers. Cox hinted at this when he noted of Fort Delaware, "There is a library of good and useful books here for the benefit of the officers here confined." At Johnson's Island the prisoners received books from outside friends. Writing that a friend had sent him a book of Shakespeare's works and a French reader, John M. Porter boasted, "Our supply of books is now very respectable. Historical, Religious, Dramatic and Poetical." Not included in the collection were texts on the subject of warfare, which the prisoners were not allowed.[26]

Shipments of books allowed Union captives the opportunity to expand their horizons. With time in abundance, many took advantage of the opportunity. Elmira prisoner Arthur H. Edey informed a benefactor, "The box of school books will enable me to start a school with 200 scholars and ten teachers." It may have been the "Primer School" that Wilbur Gramling mentioned in his diary a few weeks later. At Point Lookout a Professor Morgan, who had reportedly taught at the College of William and Mary, opened a school in the spring of 1864. He conducted classes in a vacant cookhouse. According to Joseph Kern, there were nearly twelve hundred students attending by July. One of the prisoners who studied under Professor Morgan later recalled that there was no tuition fee to attend the "first class high school." The student boasted, "I was entered in the most advanced class. I found this was quite profitable," he added.[27]

The student-captives could even specialize in certain areas of study. Cox noted that a group of officers at Fort Delaware offered instruction in "mathematics the languages and danceing." Individual prisoners, he wrote, also studied Greek, Latin, French, medicine, and law. As the spring of 1864 arrived, William Peel noticed that "the Officers seem to have become, in a great measure, 'boys again.' Some of them," Peel explained, "have resumed the study of the languages, while many may be seen diligently employed with their slates, pencils, & Arithmetics or Algebries, & others are brooding over their Grammars." Peel concluded, "Indeed a stranger slipping into the Block at nearly any hour of the day would almost imagine he had gotten into a country school." Prisoners could also attend lectures covering a variety of subjects. A series of lectures at Point Lookout addressed the issue of "moral progress." An individual talk concerned the "Influence of Woman." Lectures delivered at Fort Delaware covered such topics as astronomy and "the necessity of education and the good and bad influence which every man has or may have in society."[28]

Debates were also popular among prisoners seeking mental stimulation. Point Lookout's Mess 22 took up the question one winter evening of whether monarchy or republicanism was the better form of government. At Johnson's Island the "Island Prison Debating Society" addressed a number of topics during the late summer of 1863. One was whether the reopening of the African slave trade by an independent Confederacy would be beneficial or injurious. Other issues considered included whether education should be a precondition for suffrage and whether the North's banishment of pro–Southern Democratic politician Clement Vallandigham had helped or hurt the Confederate cause. On one occasion they debated "whether our imprisonment is beneficial or injurious to us," a matter that diarist James Mayo considered "hardly a debatable question."[29]

When the topics became too political, prison guards sometimes called a halt to the proceedings. A Johnson's Island prisoner noted that this happened on one occasion when the sentinel heard "some expressions that sounded treasonable to father Abraham's regime." Writing perhaps about the same incident, another noted, "The officer of the day said that we should not have a meeting in which treason was talked while he was officer of the day—and so broke it up." Soon afterward camp officials informed the prisoners that they could not debate any question touching upon the war or the idea of an independent Confederacy.[30]

The issue came to a head on February 22, 1864. It was Washington's birthday, and Mayo noted that the Yankees began celebrating early with the firing of guns and "some flameing speeches." To the Confederates, Washington was, as John Dooley pointed out, "the Father of Rebels." Determined not to be outdone, the prisoners quickly organized their own ceremony outside Block 5. A Capt. Fellows, originally from New York but more recently a resident of Arkansas, was the main speaker. According to William Peel, who was in attendance, the captain spoke briefly and apparently quite innocently. Other speeches and numbers from a prisoners' band followed. Then Fellows gained his second wind—and a good deal more nerve. He related a story of a girl who was caught by her mother as she allowed her boyfriend to kiss her. "'I know it is wrong, mother,' said the girl, 'but it is awfully soothing,'" was how the story ended. To this Fellows added, "I know it is not right for me to abuse Yankees, but, God bless you, it's mighty soothing." At that point the officer of the day, with a sergeant in tow, approached the gathering. He arrived as Fellows opened a sentence with "While the stars and stripes exultingly wave in the land of the thief & the home of knaves." The Union officer made several attempts to interrupt Fellows, but the excited Rebel continued undaunted. At the conclusion of the talk, the two exchanged a few words. Fellows then announced that the people in the crowd had been requested to return to their quarters, which he urged them to do. The celebrants dispersed, along with some hisses at the breaking up of the meeting and cheers for Jeff Davis. According to Peel, the prisoners realized that the officer was merely acting under orders. This helped prevent a serious incident, as did the influence of Fellows. Another factor, Peel conceded, was "the recollection of a small 'Six pounder' we had often seen peeping through a loop hole at the upper end of the yard."[31]

If the Washington's birthday celebration was a dramatic diversion, indoor games provided more frequent mental escapes from prison life. Cards, backgammon, checkers, and chess were among the most common. At Rock Island, A. C. Kean passed much of his time playing chess with a set he carved himself. Fort Delaware prisoners formed two chess clubs. This provided not only an activity for the participants but entertainment for those who watched their competitions.[32]

Games of chance inevitably led to gambling among the prisoners. Faro and other card games attracted the most participants—and victims. The stakes included Confederate money, rations, and tobacco. "Some of the prisoners will go without eating at times to gamble off their crackers" Joseph Kern sadly noted at Point Lookout. A. C. Kean recalled that Rock Island prisoners even gambled over rations that sick prisoners were unable to eat. The barracks were generally the scene of this activity, but at some camps prisoners established outdoor gambling booths by driving four poles into the ground and placing blankets around the sides. They attracted several players and even more spectators, although one former prisoner piously noted in his memoirs, "I never was in one, but I looked in." As the remark indicates, not all prisoners approved of the makeshift casinos. "Really the devil seems to be gaining ascendancy over the hearts of a large number confined here," Edmund Patterson wrote from Johnson's Island. "Only a few nights since, while some of the more religiously inclined were holding prayer meeting, another party set up a Faro Bank and carried on the game all through the services in the same room." The division of prisoners to which E. L. Cox belonged at Fort Delaware settled the issue of gambling democratically. "The gambling question was voted on," he wrote on December 15, 1863. "It passed so gambling is in full operation to day."[33]

Prisoners desiring more wholesome diversions were occasionally satisfied by a variety of musicians found among their ranks. "Some nights they will get an old violin & fiddle & dance until lights out," Thomas Beadles wrote of his comrades at Camp Douglas. On one occasion an organization known as the "C. D. string band" favored his barracks with a concert. William Davis wrote that "a couple of violins, an old banjo, and a tambourine, together with a corps of singers," provided an evening's entertainment at Point Lookout. According to Camp Chase prisoner Horace Harmon Lurton, the Columbus depot included "innumerable manufactors of musical instruments, such as violins, banjoes-guitars, flutes &c." Those, combined with a glee club, "enlivened" many evenings.[34]

Sometimes the concerts went beyond the barracks. In addition to providing entertainment, prison concerts were often held to raise funds for sick or destitute prisoners. A single concert at Fort Delaware, Francis Boyle wrote, raised nearly $1,000. At Johnson's Island, the Island Minstrels launched a series of weekly charitable concerts during the summer of 1863. Joseph Kern, who assisted with one of the rehearsals, termed their musical performance "quite creditable." Another group, the Rebelonians, formed the following summer. William Peel described them as "a combination of negro minstrels & Thespian performance." A three-act show that Peel attended opened with the minstrels, who "played & sang a number of sentimental & comic songs, written for the most part in the prison, & got off a number of ludicrous witticisms." The second act consisted of more comic songs, a lecture, and a banjo solo. A play closed the performance. "All seemed well pleased," Peel noted, "except a couple of Yankees who were present, who didn't take a joke so well."[35]

Yankees were apparently not the only residents of Johnson's Island who were less than thrilled with the antics of the minstrel groups. John Dooley was among a group of prisoners who formed the Thespians. "This new association wishes to improve on the Minstrels," he explained, "by abandoning the lees of wine or the glossy black of burnt corks and performing plays worthy of the intelligence and admiration of men of education and enlightenment." The group gave its first performance on September 26, 1863. Dooley commented very little on this debut except to say that it "succeed[ed] very well." Following more successes, including productions of *Pochahontas* and *Box and Cox,* the group began making demands. The members called for their own "dramatic hall," which they offered to erect at their own expense, and refused to perform on extremely cold days. They did not secure a hall, but Block 12 did allow them to erect a stage inside their barracks. Meanwhile actor Dooley was also becoming a critic. " 'Family Jars' is a complete success," he wrote, "but the 'Persecuted Dutchman' hops along on a lame leg. I fear our Dutchman has overdone his acting and in fact played himself out." At least one audience member was well pleased with a production of *The Battle of Gettysburg.* A prisoner penned the play, and Robert Bingham wrote that it "was a really good play & the acting was very creditable to the Thespians."[36]

Warm weather brought the prisoners outdoors, where they enjoyed a variety of childhood games, including seven-up and fox and geese. Even in these pursuits the realities of prison life were never far away. A Confederate captain confined at Camp Chase found this out when he was engaged in a game of fox and geese near the prison wall. He ran across the "dead line," and a sentinel immediately took aim. Fortunately a Union surgeon, who would have had to treat any wound the prisoner received, restrained the guard. According to Curtis Burke, a group of Camp Douglas prisoners raised $3 and persuaded a Yankee sergeant to go into town and purchase a "gum foot ball" for them. "It is now going the rounds in a crowd of some three or four hundred men in the center of this square," Burke observed on March 25, 1864, "and many a skinned and bruised shin will be the result of it."[37]

At Johnson's Island, "base ball" was apparently the sport of choice. It was played at the Lake Erie depot as early as July 5, 1862, when a team of eleven prisoners took on the same number of men "chosen from the whole garrison. They beat us considerably," Edward Drummond of the prisoners' team explained, "which was no more than we expected as they had a greater advantage in the selection." In the spring of 1864, William Peel reported that the game was "raging" at Johnson's Island. That August Edmund Patterson reported that the Southern Base Ball Club defeated the Confederate Base Ball Club 19-11. Although he did not note the length of the game, Patterson did explain that the Confederate team had led until the fifth inning. He also pointed out that betting on the games was popular among prison gamblers. John Thompson, a member of the Confederate team, played his first game on July 14. "I think it an excellent game for exercise," he wrote, "and the very thing I need to preserve good & perfect health." He may have changed his mind two weeks later, when a Confederate captain was seriously injured by a bat striking him in the forehead. The bat had slipped from the hands of a batter who swung and missed a pitch. "He lay quite insensible for several minutes," one spectator reported, before two friends helped him back to his barracks. It was two days before a doctor declared his life to be out of danger.[38]

For prisoners in camps located close to water, swimming and bathing were two other very welcome options in warm weather. This meant excursions to the Delaware River for Fort Delaware prisoners. Those confined at Point Lookout charged into Chesapeake Bay. William Davis wrote that he and a group of his friends went there daily "and passed a delightful hour swimming and romping." Johnson's Island prisoners enjoyed bathing in Lake Erie. According to the diaries of various captives, the officers were allowed to visit the lake two or three times a week. They went in groups of about one hundred and were allowed to remain for about twenty minutes. Although the men looked forward to their time in the lake, Drummond complained of women and children watching the naked men from passing excursion boats.[39]

Winter generally drove the prisoners indoors, but it did not halt outdoor activities altogether. Frozen ponds at Rock Island and Elmira allowed the men who could find skates to go ice-skating. At Johnson's Island, at least three snowball battles, each involving hundreds of prisoners, broke the winter monotony during January 1864. They involved the six upper blocks against the six lower blocks and lasted as long as half a day. According to an onlooker, the participants pinned the numbers of their blocks to their hats so they could tell friend from foe. "Of course several got black eyes, bloody noses &c.," he added. Gen. Thompson, who "commanded one army" in at least one of the contests, later recalled, "I was captured several times, and once nearly pulled in two by my friends trying to rescue me." He added, "Sometimes after our battles the snow would be nearly as bloody as in actual conflict, for bloody noses and teeth knocked loose with snowballs were plentiful." According to Thompson, the Federals were so amused by the proceedings that they requested copies of the "official reports" the combatants prepared after the battles.[40]

As they battled the loneliness of prison life, a number of Confederate captives found comfort in faith. For many, of course, this involved nothing more than a reaffirmation of views long held. For others it involved a new step or a return to values that had lapsed. Anniversaries often prompted reflection and resolutions to lead a more godly life. "One year ago this evening . . . I arrived on Johnson's Island," Patterson wrote on July 20, 1864. "It would be better, it seems to me, to be killed at once on the battlefield," he added. "We can do nothing but pray," Patterson concluded, "but thank God we can always pray for the right, and for the last three months we have had prayer meetings daily, and it does the soul good to hear the warm, earnest petitions that go up day after day and night after night, from the very depths of the hearts of the noble ones who linger here, to God, our Father, that he will have mercy on our bleeding country and save her and our people."[41]

Richard H. Gayle of the Confederate navy spent his thirty-third birthday at Fort Warren. "No better opportunity than I now have, could offer for a man to review his past life," he wrote. Gayle resolved to lessen "sins both of omission and commission and wasted opportunities." John Joyes found himself at Johnson's Island the day he turned thirty. "I have formed new rules for my future guidance," he wrote, "and humbly ask of our Heavenly Father that at the experation of another ten years, if I shall be permitted to live so long, I can then say in every thing I have so lived as to make me worthy of a longer life." Joyes resolved to read at least one chapter of the Bible daily and to continue the habit after his release. William Burgwyn even managed to find comfort as he spent Christmas 1864 at Fort Delaware. "Can not but contrast my situation on this Christmas and that of last," he noted, "and while I am depressed at being in prison and in the complete power of my ruthless and bloody enemies I can not but be thankful and return thanks to Almighty God that he has preserved me to be even here though the numberless dangers I have passed through between this and last Christmas."[42]

Individual expressions of faith took various forms. William M. Jones of the Fiftieth Georgia spent what he otherwise termed a "very foul, lonesome, dreary day" at Point Lookout reading the New Testament. "I have started to peruse it over again and have gone as far as the VI chapter of St. Luke," he wrote. Camp Chase prisoner James Anderson devoted the fall of 1864 to reading the Old Testament. "I sincerely hope to be able to continue the investigation of this Sacred word," he wrote upon finishing the project. While confined at Fort Delaware, George L. P. Wren read *The Bruised Reed,* a book that he hoped would "prove a blessing to me and strengthen me in trying to serve God." Many found strength in prayer. Troubled because "I sometimes think I do not give up enough for God," James Mayo wrote, "God help me to serve him aright for my own eternal salvation." The Johnson's Island prisoner added, "When I get back to my Regiment I will [do so] by example and in religious services and may God help me in this determination."

While confined at Fort Delaware, George Washington Hall wrote, "I have committed every thing into His kind hand & Almighty care." Specifically, he prayed daily for "my dear loved ones at home far away." Thanks to his faith, Hall concluded, "the languishing hours of our imprisonment in this awful and dreary place pass away more pleasant & sweetly than I anticipated."[43]

Inevitably, men of faith sought out each other and formed into groups of believers. Prayer meetings and Bible classes were common. At Johnson's Island, according to William Peel, some prisoners risked all to attend the nightly prayer meetings held in his block. It was not that prison officials objected to the meetings. The problem was that they often occurred after dark, when the men were prohibited from leaving their barracks. Indeed, the bulk of the evidence indicates that Union officers at Johnson's Island and other prisons were prepared to assist—or at least not interfere with—prisoners in their expressions of faith. On one occasion some fifty Johnson's Island prisoners were paroled to the lake so they could participate in a baptism ceremony. Camp officials often allowed religious tracts to be distributed to the prisoners, although James Mayo complained that those received at Johnson's Island were "much tainted with politics."[44]

When there was preaching at the prisons, it was generally done by the prisoners themselves. From time to time outside speakers were brought into the compounds to address the men's spiritual needs. Among them was a local Baptist minister who spoke at Elmira. "He reminded me very much of some of [the] Old Virginia Baptist preachers and the big meetings in Dixie," one prisoner from the Old Dominion wrote. Although an avowed Unionist, the minister generally avoided politics and "prayed that the day was not far distant when north & South would become brothers again." He also spoke of Baptist friends he had made during his travels to Dixie. At Johnson's Island some of the prisoners objected when they learned that a Union chaplain was to preach in one of the blocks. "It is simply out of the question," one prisoner wrote of the proposition. "As for myself, I want no advice on religious matters from any one who at the same time is urging yankees to join in the attempt to subjugate us." William Peel was more understanding, learning that the chaplain had been invited by a group of prisoners with no minister of their denomination. Peel did not attend the service, but he understood that the message was "confined strictly to the gospel." He regretted the fact that some of his comrades verbally abused the pastor as he was leaving the yard. Even Mayo conceded that the chaplain's sermon was "confined to religion and not politics."[45]

Although prison officials were generally supportive of religious activities among the Confederates, there were exceptions to their tolerance. According to the diaries of two prisoners, one guard at Camp Douglas took special delight in breaking up the prisoners' services. After he threatened to attach a ball and chain to anyone he caught, a group of prisoners appealed to the guard's captain. The officer said the guard was not acting under his orders, but he also refused to intercede. At Fort Delaware, Francis Boyle wrote that officers placed unspecified restrictions on a "Christian Association" that had formed at the camp. The group had worked to meet both the spiritual and the physical needs of the prisoners. They had also received from a Philadelphia donor an awning for their well-attended outside services. Boyle did not cite a reason for the restrictions, but they may have had something to do with the group's leader. Rev. Isaac Handy was a political prisoner who had been arrested for remarks he allegedly made about the United States flag. On August 14, 1863, Albin Schoepf reported that Handy had refused to take the oath of allegiance, saying, "I would rather rot in prison than do that." The commandant added, "He has not improved any since his confinement, and preaches to his fellow prisoners regular Rebel sermons every Sunday."[46]

Another group that labored to aid its fellow prisoners was the Masonic Lodge. At Johnson's Island the Masons' efforts were largely devoted to decorating the graves of members of their order and seeing to it that board markers were put in place. A similar association at Camp Chase performed like work. The Masons also attended to brother members in the hospital, bringing them tobacco and other items and visiting them to keep the flies away. At Camp Douglas the Masons not only carried out such charitable activities, they also ended up in their own barracks. According to Curtis Burke, whose father lived in the Masonic barracks, the prison association received contributions from lodges outside the camp. "The guard is a mason," Burke wrote, "and they all appear to be getting along as well as could be expected under the circumstances." A more cynical view came from Camp Douglas prisoner William A. Milton. In a postwar memoir Milton insisted that the Masons received better quarters and rations because of their "influence with the powers that ruled."[47]

As important as faith and associations based upon faith were to the prisoners, they were not the primary weapon in the battle against boredom. Skilled labor was. The purpose was twofold. Not only did pursuing an occupation help pass the time, it was also a way of raising funds to purchase supplemental items from the camp sutler. As Michael P. Gray has pointed out in his excellent study of the Elmira prison, that camp had a regular business district, termed "The Market" by prisoners. There one could find crude placards announcing a wide variety of goods and services, as well as numerous gambling halls. Such businesses were not limited to Elmira. They could be found in every Union prison.[48]

Although there was a great variety of shops and stands, jewelry establishments were easily the most numerous. "The jewelry shops are without number," Joseph Kern wrote from Point Lookout, "and all do a good business." Thomas Taylor observed that nearly every mess at Johnson's Island had several workmen, most of whom turned out rings, buttons, and other items made from gutta-percha. Curtis Burke wrote that there were about thirty ring makers at Camp Douglas. Most, he noted, did not have the necessary tools to manufacture a quality product. One, however, had a variety of tools and a workbench in his barracks. According to Burke, the man turned out numerous styles of rings, breast pins, and other articles. He added ornamentation to them with gold, silver, and pearl, which he was able to acquire, most likely through the assistance of camp guards. At the other end of the spectrum was Lafayette Rogan. In the summer of 1864 the Rock Island prisoner acquired a file for 50¢ and set to work producing shirt studs and breast pins. After two weeks' labor, he had sold $1.50 in stock and had another $1 worth ready for sale. Rogan was pleased with his profit, noting that in prison the time he invested was not a factor.[49]

The raw material to produce jewelry came from a variety of sources. Prisoners scoured the compounds of their camps for discarded bones and buttons. Others purchased what they needed, counting it as one of the costs of doing business. Location gave an advantage to the men at Point Lookout, Fort Delaware, and Johnson's Island, where access to the beach afforded the opportunity to secure shell. Other prisoners had friends on the outside who kept them supplied with the items they needed. Johnson's Island prisoner William Peel began producing rings during the winter of 1864. Within two months he had run out of shell, "getting into a fit of the blues on account of having nothing to do." With bathing weather still a few weeks away, his prospects were grim until friends in Baltimore sent him a supply. Soon he had fashioned a cross that netted him $2.50. Later in the spring his Baltimore suppliers shipped him a large slab of gutta-percha.[50]

Peel was a reluctant jeweler, forced into the business by economic necessity. The need for postage stamps and other items left him with the choice of borrowing from friends or pursuing a trade, and he decided the latter was preferable. One of his biggest sales, made to "a Yankee outside," consisted of a breast pin, nine studs, and a pair of sleeve buttons, all of which earned him $8. A different type of necessity, the need for tobacco, drove many other prisoners into the jewelry business. At Elmira, Henri Mugler wrote, a number of prisoners kept themselves supplied with tobacco thanks to their skill in turning out trinkets. Arriving at Point Lookout in May 1864, Berry Benson discovered that tobacco was the medium of exchange at the camp's marketplace. It came in thumbnail-size sections called "chews," which were equal in value to one hardtack cracker. Although he was confined to Point Lookout's hospital ward, William M. Jones still found the energy to make rings and devoted the money he realized to the purchase of tobacco.[51]

Second perhaps only to jewelry among items manufactured by the prisoners were fans. According to William Haigh, those produced at Point Lookout were made from cedar and white pine and "exceed anything . . . in beauty." The men exposed the wood to steam, Haigh explained, to make it pliant. At Johnson's Island, Peel, who had entered the jewelry trade reluctantly, found his niche in making fans. He began in July 1864 after growing tired of the jewelry trade. Within two weeks he had produced twenty-seven, which he sent through a guard to a friend in Philadelphia to sell. One week later he sent out a shipment of thirty. By late August Peel had made some one hundred. Some he sent as gifts, some he sold at the prison. Most went to either Baltimore or Philadelphia to be sold. Sales were so brisk that he decided to return to ring making, thus expanding his inventory. In November Peel received a letter from his Philadelphia distributor. A shipment of twenty-six fans had sold for $22.50, he learned, and recent jewelry sales totaled $41.50.[52]

The market for items produced by prisoners varied. While some followed Peel's method of shipping their wares to outside friends, most confined their dealings to fellow prisoners or guards who acted as middlemen. Many Union prisons also served as recruiting stations, and young recruits, many with bonus money received for signing up, made inviting targets. In November 1864 several of them arrived at Governor's Island. They paid the prisoners $2 to $3 per ring, H. H. Wiseman observed, while some paid with tobacco. According to C. W. Jones, guards at Point Lookout often purchased jewelry produced by the prisoners. Jones conceded that the men had to be cautious about which guards they approached, but he added that they tended to be polite and were generous in the prices they paid. Prisoners also served as customers. John Thompson sent several pieces of jewelry he purchased from his fellow captives at Johnson's Island to his niece as Christmas presents. Capt. G. Washington Nelson, also a Johnson's Island prisoner, sent his wife a ring. "I had it made expressly for you," he wrote, adding, "I fear it is too large. Wear it for my sake, darling."[53]

At Elmira, as Gray's research revealed, a complex economy emerged involving prisoners, Union officers and guards, and even outside contractors. The men in blue secured the gold, silver, and pearl used to produce the items and sold the finished products to eager customers on the outside. Sales were generally made on a commission basis. This forced the prisoners to trust their enemies, but the bulk of the evidence suggests that the system worked well for those on both sides. Even postwar memoirists conceded that the guards and their officers were generally honest in these transactions. One Federal officer, Capt. John S. Kidder, who was transferred to Elmira after being severely wounded at Spotsylvania, made $500 in about four months by distributing prison-made jewelry before he returned to his regiment. It was such a booming business that Kidder even sent for a friend, who became his partner in the enterprise.[54]

Several prison entrepreneurs offered goods and services that were designed exclusively for their fellow captives. Among them were tailors and shoemakers. Capt. Joseph Julius Wescoat of the Eleventh South Carolina arrived at Fort Delaware in February 1865. Although his stay would prove brief, he was determined to attempt "anything to get a square meal." The captain finally settled on taking in laundry at 5¢ per item. According to Haigh, Point Lookout prisoners could secure the same service for half the price. Haigh also noted that a few vendors sold used clothing, as did Elmira prisoner Wilbur Gramling.[55]

Barbers and dentists also plied their trades at the various camps. Among the latter was a Point Lookout dentist who advertised that he could remove stains caused by the camp's brackish water. He further promised to do so without "injuring the enamel." After suffering "dreadfully" with a toothache, John Thompson engaged the services of "one of our prison dentists." The good doctor "plugged" four of Thompson's teeth. Although Thompson identified his dentist as "Captain Phillips," John Dooley recorded a deal he made with a Lt. Phillips of the Tenth Virginia Cavalry. Dooley loaned the doctor money he needed for instruments to start his prison practice. In return, Dooley received the dentist's promise "to plug and draw all my teeth free gratis, for nothing."[56]

Food and drink were available at many marketplace stands. One opened at Point Lookout when a prisoner received "a nice barrel of eatables" from an acquaintance. Some stands offered baked goods. After coffee was eliminated from the prisoners' rations as a measure of retaliation for the treatment Union soldiers received in Confederate prisons, coffeehouses sprang up. According to Berry Benson, Elmira prisoners purchased coffee, made a large boilerful, and walked around vending it by the cupful. A cracker or a chew of tobacco was the general price. A number of prisoners wrote that stronger beverages were also available. In brief diary references E. L. Cox reported that beer could be purchased at Fort Delaware and Joseph Kern claimed that it was also available at Johnson's Island. Writing after the war, George Nelson recalled that the Fort Delaware prisoners were "great beer drinkers." It was made from molasses and water and sold for 5¢ a glass. Nelson justified the practice by pointing out that the water at Fort Delaware was often very brackish. Luther Rice Mills claimed that Johnson's Island even had a hidden distillery that turned out "an inferior article of corn whiskey." Inferior or not, the whiskey fetched $5 a quart in Union money.[57]

The variety of products and services offered at prison marketplaces was remarkable. On his second day at Elmira, Berry Benson recalled, the sound of fiddle music attracted him—along with several others. The performer was playing an instrument of his own manufacture, likely made from cracker boxes, Benson speculated, and he was offering it for sale. Another Elmira businessman, with a twenty-five-inch homemade grindstone, offered to sharpen knives for a chew of tobacco. Arriving penniless at Camp Chase, R. M. Gray converted a knife into a crude saw and went into the spoon-making business. After he had sold about fifty at 10¢ apiece, others caught on and soon glutted the market. Gray turned his attention to pipes, which sold "tolerably well." Chair making became a popular enterprise at Johnson's Island in late 1864. Some prisoners worked with only pocketknives, while others managed to fashion turning lathes for their work. Their greatest challenge was finding material for the bottoms. "He who can get an old coffee sack is quite fortunate," Peel wrote. The craftsmen pulled the sacks apart, straw by straw, then retied the threads together into cords. Others made leather strings from old shoes and boots. Perhaps the most unusual prison entrepreneur was the Point Lookout inmate who offered to "examine phrenologically the heads of prisoners" and present a lecture to them. The admission for this scientific offering was either 5¢ or a piece of bread or meat.[58]

At Johnson's Island a resourceful Tennessee prisoner, Lt. G. B. Smith, set up his own photography studio and darkroom in the barracks. At least three Johnson's Island diarists visited the establishment. To reach it they had to climb a ladder nailed to the wall, then crawl across rafters to a platform loosely placed over the rafters and joists. Smith had his lens with him when he was captured. Attached to a tobacco box it made a crude camera. Guards purchased the chemicals and plates for him. One prisoner reported that the price of a portrait was $1, while another wrote that it was 50¢. John Dooley was "very well satisfied" with the finished product. Virgil Murphey was disappointed that the plate was too small to capture his entire beard, which reached to his waist. Otherwise he, too, was pleased with his portrait.[59]

As imaginative as many of the prisoners' activities were, they were to a large extent limited to the upper socioeconomic classes of captives. The intellectual pursuits, whether reading, debating, or studying, were largely confined to those with a formal education, a luxury in the antebellum South. This left many men with little to do but walk the narrow limits of the compounds. "Wretched, restless creatures," one prisoner wrote of them, "they wander round the pen from morning to night and are never still." Some engaged in conversation with others, some strolled alone. None enjoyed the mental stimulation that allowed at least a psychological escape from prison life. Even those who did profit from such activities could never totally lose sight of where those activities were occurring. The most imaginative diversions could not entirely eradicate the realization of a boring, lonely life. William Haigh, a generally dispassionate and perceptive observer of prison life, summed up the situation when he recorded a passing remark from a fellow Point Lookout captive. "'I'll never cage a bird again,' said a poor little suffering prisoner the other day. 'I know what it is to be in prison.'"[60]

7
“i had rather bee hear then to bee a marching”
Keepers in Blue

Not only did the collapse of the cartel mean a lengthy stay for Confederate captives in Northern prisons, it also forced Col. Hoffman to face administrative challenges that exchange had temporarily alleviated. Foremost among them was the shortage of qualified officers with whom to staff those prisons. Many of the facilities were training camps that were pressed into service to accommodate the Fort Donelson prisoners. As new Union regiments continued to arrive, their colonels served as camp commanders for a few weeks or months until they departed for the front. The situation had long annoyed Hoffman. As early as February 1862 he had informed Ohio governor Tod, “Much embarrassment results from the frequent changes of the officers in charge of the [Camp Chase] prisoners, and I would respectfully urge that some suitable officer . . . be selected to remain permanently in charge.” Seven months later, Hoffman complained to Adj. Gen. Thomas, “The frequent changes in the commander of [Camp Chase] leads to many irregularities and a proper responsibility can only be arrived at through a permanent commander and permanent guard.” On April 24, 1863, fourteen months after he had first broached the topic, Hoffman pleaded with Gen. Ambrose Burnside, then commanding the Department of the Ohio, to “direct such steps [be] taken as will establish the good order and proper discipline so much needed at the camp. The indispensable requisite in the camp,” Hoffman again emphasized, “is an active and efficient commander with a reliable guard of at least five full companies.”[1]

Camp Chase was not the only facility where a lack of continuity in the command structure plagued the commissary general of prisoners. In May 1863, the U.S. Sanitary Commission issued a damning report about the prisoners’ hospitals at Camp Douglas. In forwarding the report to Stanton, Hoffman used the lack of stability as an excuse for the negative assessment. "When there are such frequent changes of commanders and medical officers as there have been at Camp Douglas," he explained, "it is almost impossible to have instructions properly carried out. There is no responsibility and before neglects can be traced to any one he is relieved from duty." Hoffman was using the confusion of the camp's command structure to excuse a situation that was his responsibility. He was, however, correct about the confusion. From the beginning of 1862 until the end of 1863 Camp Douglas had at least eight commanders. Two of them, Capt. J. S. Putnam and Capt. John Phillips, were paroled Union soldiers sent to the camp from Harpers Ferry.[2]

At Camp Morton, the first change in commanders upset the prisoners more than it did Hoffman. In May 1862, Col. Richard Owen and the Sixtieth Indiana were ordered to the field. Owen had endeared himself to the Confederates with his humane treatment, and word of his imminent departure concerned them. The prisoners went so far as to address a petition to Governor Morton asking that Owen and his regiment be retained. This failed, and the Sixtieth left for Louisville on June 20. Owen's successor, Col. David Garland Rose, was the United States marshal for Indiana. He brought a stricter attitude to the post and remained for a year. After Rose departed in June 1863, Camp Morton had four commanders within the next four months. The first was Col. James Biddle. Most of his regiment, the Seventy-first Indiana, had been captured in Kentucky. While they awaited exchange at the camp, the remainder of the outfit served as guards. In July Governor Morton dispatched them to chase John Hunt Morgan's cavalry raiders out of Indiana, and command of the camp passed first to Capt. Albert J. Guthridge and then to Capt. David W. Hamilton. By then, thanks to the exchange cartel, there were only about twelve hundred prisoners left to be guarded at Camp Morton.[3]

Only at Johnson's Island did Hoffman find stability in the command structure. There Lt. Col. William Pierson, who had been promoted from major, remained in command throughout 1863. Unfortunately, this was one prison where Hoffman desired a change in the top officer. Pierson brought no military experience to the post, and the normally gruff Hoffman was generally patient with the commander of the camp he had personally established. He could not, however, get Pierson to overcome his strong tendency toward nervousness. On June 18, 1862, Pierson reported, "There is among the prisoners here a concerted plan for general revolt with a view of taking the island and take their chances for escape." He blamed the plot on "the restless spirit of a set of very bad rebels," and asked that the leaders be sent to Fort Warren. The next day Pierson wrote that the prisoners had formed into a "military organization," complete with "a general and adjutant and other officers." Hoffman was skeptical about the report, but he did order a dozen prisoners, all colonels and lieutenant colonels, transferred to Fort Warren. One week later Pierson informed Hoffman that a departing Confederate surgeon had warned him of an impending revolt. After launching their attack against the guard, the doctor warned, the desperate prisoners planned to tear down the fences to make rafts to carry them to the mainland. Hoffman considered the story "improbable," but he asked Governor Tod to dispatch another company of guards to Johnson's Island. "I must try and cultivate a little more confidence in the command with less concern about what may be undertaken," he candidly told the governor, "but twenty preventions are better than one cure."[4]

This crisis was past, but the following year, Pierson discovered another alleged plot. On October 1, 1863, he informed the commissary general, "There is a bad spirit among the prisoners. They have the idea that it would be a great thing for the Confederacy for them to escape, and they are talking about it being their duty to make the attempt." Pierson had heard numerous rumors, and he concluded, "I have little doubt it will be only a question of time for them to make a revolt." Five days later Pierson added that the prisoners possessed vast stocks of civilian clothing, which would aid them in any effort to escape. Hoffman denied Pierson's request for additional companies of guards. He explained that prisoners of war "frequently discuss the chances of escape . . . and make plans and threats to accomplish what they so much desire." However, at Johnson's Island, "The difficulties in the way are very great, independent of the guard, and so long as it is vigilant and prepared there is no danger that the prisoners will sacrifice so many lives, as they must do in any such desperate attempt, when, even if they should overcome them, their final escape would be so doubtful."[5]

This did not end the matter. Pierson apparently appealed to Tod, who passed his concerns along to the War Department and joined in the call for more guards at Johnson's Island. Stanton did not send more men, but he did dispatch the ironclad *Michigan* to Sandusky Bay. This did not satisfy the nervous commandant. On October 31 Pierson complained to Hoffman that the vessel would be useless during the winter months, when ice covered the lake. Escaping prisoners, he went on, would face only a two-day march to the Detroit River and the safety of Canada. Pierson complained that his command was overtaxed in its duties and requested the addition of "at least two companies." This appeared to snap Hoffman's patience, and he replied brusquely, "I have no more confidence in the reports of revolt you hear this year than I have of similar reports made to you last year." As to the claim that potential escapees could reach the Detroit River in two days, the commissary general asserted, "I doubt if one-fourth of them could make that journey without assistance if you were to invite them to go." Within two months, Pierson was gone as commander of Johnson's Island, but his concerns would eventually prove prescient. The following year, the *Michigan* would become the target of an actual plot to liberate the prisoners there.[6]

It was the war itself that eventually solved Hoffman's problem of finding capable commandants for Union prisons. War produces wounded soldiers, and the Civil War was anything but an exception. As the conflict went on, dozens of experienced officers suffered wounds that made it impossible for them to retake the field but were not so serious as to preclude them from holding administrative posts. By the middle of 1864 a number of them were staffing Northern prison camps. One of the first was Gen. Albin Schoepf, who assumed command of Fort Delaware in April 1863. In the previous twelve months, the post had four commanders, Capt. Augustus Gibson, Maj. Henry Burton, Col. Delvan Perkins, and Col. Robert Buchanan. Schoepf's arrival ended this revolving-door command structure. The general held the post until the end of the war.[7]

A native of Poland, Schoepf was a graduate of the Military Academy of Vienna. By the time he came to America in 1851, he had seen action in numerous European campaigns, including service with Kossuth in the 1848 revolts in Hungary. Gen. Winfield Scott, the Union general in chief at the outset of the Civil War, was aware of Schoepf's background, and Scott's recommendation was good enough to earn the immigrant soldier a general's star. On October 17, 1861, he was assigned to the Department of the Cumberland brigade of Gen. George H. Thomas. The following spring Thomas brought court-martial charges against Schoepf, charging him with "Fraud, Conduct unbecoming an officer, and Incompetence for military command." Specifically, Thomas accused Schoepf of taking from a Confederate soldier a horse that the soldier had stolen from a citizen and of selling a government horse to "a pedler, name unknown." Thomas further charged that Schoepf, "whilst under the influence of liquor is in the habit of using gross and abusive language to officers." As for the charge of incompetence, Thomas accused Schoepf of allowing bands of Confederate guerrillas to learn of the advance of a Union expedition, thus foiling the mission. The case was never tried. According to Thomas, "Gen. Schoepf, having had an intimation of these charges, resigned and went home." However, a brigade surgeon certified on June 1, 1862, that Schoepf was suffering from "Neuralgia of his leg in consequence of an injury received by being thrown from his horse."[8]

Disabled officers also brought the stability that Hoffman had long desired to Camp Chase. In June 1863 Col. William Wallace of the Fifteenth Ohio arrived in Columbus with an unidentified illness. Gen. John Mason, commanding U.S. forces in Columbus, requested that Wallace be named commander of Camp Chase. He held the post for eight months, which at that point was the longest tenure of any commander of the camp.[9]

On February 10, 1864, Wallace had recovered sufficiently to rejoin his regiment. His successor was Col. William Pitt Richardson. A Pennsylvania native, Richardson had served in the Mexican War before locating to Ohio, where he practiced law. When war broke out again in 1861, Richardson raised two companies that became part of the Twenty-fifth Ohio. In May 1862 he became commander of the regiment. One year later, on May 2, 1863, Richardson received a wound that ended his career as a field officer. At the battle of Chancellorsville, the Twenty-fifth was part of the ill-fated Eleventh Corps, Army of the Potomac, which bore the brunt of Stonewall Jackson's flank attack. Richardson and his outfit held firm, earning the praise of superiors, but in doing so, Richardson suffered a severe wound to his left shoulder. His next assignment came in January 1864, when he was detailed as president of a court-martial that convened at Camp Chase. His appointment to command the following month brought overdue stability to the Ohio camp. He served there until the end of the war.[10]

Richardson was easily the most capable of the Camp Chase commanders. He oversaw a major project to rebuild the prison barracks, and he addressed the long-standing drainage problem, adding markedly to the health of the camp. Richardson was well liked by both the guards and the prisoners. One of the guards, writing to his hometown newspaper, observed that the colonel was "the most capable, efficient, and popular commandant we have ever had." Writing long after the war, Maj. J. Coleman Alderson, a Confederate prisoner, recalled that Richardson would often overrule stricter subordinates. "When we were able to reach Colonel Richardson," Alderson wrote, "our wrongs were righted." Former prisoner John F. Hickey, who worked in the camp hospital, later remembered that Richardson "inaugurated a pacific and humane course of treatment." That humanity, Hickey admitted, extended to sharing a drink from "a bottle of good old Kentucky bourbon" that had been sent to a prisoner "for treatment of his throat trouble."[11]

Camp Morton's final commander was Col. Ambrose A. Stevens. The commander of the Twenty-first Michigan Infantry, Stevens resigned in February 1863 after being wounded at Perryville, Kentucky, four months earlier. He reentered the service the following September and was assigned to Camp Morton. On October 22 he became the commander. Like Richardson, Stevens attempted to make improvements to camp drainage and buildings. He also instituted a program of improved policing and increased hospital capacity. Stevens attempted to accomplish more during the fall of 1864. Unfortunately, he failed to forward cost estimates to the frugal Hoffman, an omission that resulted in fatal delays. Despite the difficulties in dealing with Washington, Stevens did manage to utilize materials he could locate around the camp. As a result, several prisoners moved from tents to more substantial quarters.[12]

On January 14, 1864, Brig. Gen. Henry D. Terry assumed command of Johnson's Island. Lt. Col. Pierson remained in command of the guard force at the prison for a few days before being succeeded by Col. Charles W. Hill. Terry's tenure proved brief. On May 6, Lt. Col. John F. Marsh submitted a generally negative inspection report of the camp to Col. James A. Hardie, inspector general of the Union army. "General Terry is an intelligent, clever gentleman," Marsh wrote, "but quite as fond of a social glass of whisky as of attending to the duties of his command." Marsh went on to report that the grounds and barracks were poorly policed and the sinks were "offensive." He charged Mr. Johnson, owner of the island, with supplying poor-quality wood at inflated prices and accused beef suppliers of similar chicanery.[13]

Five days later Terry was gone and Hill was in command of the camp. In assigning Hill to the post, Hoffman made it clear that he expected the new commander to address a number of problems that Terry had failed to correct. Citing letters that he had previously addressed to Terry, Hoffman wrote, "I request you will at once put all the desired reforms in force." These included cleaning up the sinks, which Hoffman termed a "nuisance," and improving the policing of the camp.[14]

The availability of competent officers unfit for service in the field brought command stability from the outset to the new prisons that were established in 1863 and 1864. Among the wounded veterans to assume command of a Union prison was Brig. Gen. Gilman Marston, who took charge of Point Lookout after that camp was set up in July 1863 to accommodate the huge influx of captives from Gettysburg. A New Hampshire lawyer and politician, Marston had raised the Second New Hampshire Volunteers at the outset of the war. He led the unit at the battle of First Manassas, where he suffered a severe wound to the right arm. Marston eventually rejoined his unit, but in April 1863 he was reassigned to the Department of Washington. On June 16 he was given command of troops in the vicinity of Poolesville, Maryland, with instructions to protect a nearby signal station. Once this danger had passed, Marston was available to establish the new prison. On July 23 he received orders to report to Gen. Meade at Gettysburg, where he was to secure a guard force, including members of his old regiment, and relieve Meade of as many of his captives as possible.[15]

Marston remained in command of Point Lookout until December 1863. Gen. Edward W. Hinks and Col. Alonzo Draper were his successors, each serving for a few months. On July 2, 1864, Brig. Gen. James Barnes assumed command of Point Lookout, remaining until the end of the war. The command, which included Hammond General Hospital, was a large one, and Barnes turned most of the responsibility for the operation of the prison over to Maj. Allen G. Brady. According to surviving reports, Brady was a conscientious officer whose desire for discipline often trumped his humanitarian instincts. Frequently his inspection reports called for more liberal issues of food, clothing, and improved tents for the prisoners. However, he declined to issue a shipment of trousers because he feared their blue color might aid potential escapees. Not surprisingly, the prisoners' views of Brady were mixed. C. W. Jones termed him "an excellent, brave and good soldier," and recalled that it was Brady who allowed the men to gather along the Chesapeake for exercise. Capt. Robert Park had a different view. According to Park, Brady approved when two officers who had attempted to escape were balled and chained and confined to the guardhouse wearing "a peculiar felon's suit." Park continued that this was typical of Brady's habit of treating the prisoners "as if we were criminals of the lowest type."[16]

At Rock Island, Col. Adolphus J. Johnson assumed command on December 5, 1863, just two days after the first shipment of prisoners arrived. He remained in charge of the Illinois prison for the remainder of the war. The former commander of the Eighth New Jersey Infantry, Johnson had resigned his commission in March 1863, when injuries from a wound suffered at the battle of Williamsburg during the Peninsular campaign became unbearable. He reentered the service in July 1863 after recovering sufficiently to perform noncombat duties. After commanding a portion of the Camp Chase guard force, where he apparently learned the basics of prison administration, he was transferred to Rock Island.[17]

Elmira, too, enjoyed a reasonably stable command situation thanks to the availability of officers incapable of serving at the front. The first commander of the New York depot was Lt. Col. Seth Eastman, a graduate of West Point who had spent over three decades in the army. His varied career included command of forts in the Wisconsin, Minnesota, and Utah territories and service against the Seminoles in Florida. For seven years he was an assistant instructor of art at West Point. His often-arduous assignments left him in ill health. As a result, Eastman's Civil War service was limited to duties behind the lines. He assumed command at Elmira in January 1864, when the post was still a draft rendezvous. The added responsibilities that came with the command of a major prison were too much for Eastman, and he resigned in September.[18]

His successor was Col. Benjamin Franklin Tracy of the 109th New York Infantry. An attorney and member of the New York state assembly, Tracy was named to head a recruiting committee in New York's Twenty-fourth Senatorial District when Lincoln put out a call for additional volunteers in the spring of 1862. He soon found himself leading one of the units he helped recruit, the 109th New York. The outfit guarded railroads in the Washington, DC, area for the next two years. Things changed in March 1864. Ulysses S. Grant, now general in chief, was planning what he hoped would be the final campaign for Richmond. He needed all the men he could get, and the 109th found itself part of Ambrose Burnside's Ninth Corps. At the battle of the Wilderness, when a portion of his command faltered under heavy Confederate fire, Tracy personally carried the regimental colors forward. Inspired, his men followed and captured the Confederate trenches. The success was temporary. A fierce Confederate counterattack followed; but Tracy's conspicuous gallantry would thirty years later earn him the Congressional Medal of Honor.[19]

The colonel's heroism also left him suffering from heat prostration. A regimental surgeon pronounced him unfit for field service, and Tracy reluctantly tendered his resignation. He returned home, where a fellow New Yorker considered him well qualified for a vacant position. Henry J. Raymond, editor of the *New York Times* and Tracy's former colleague in the assembly, recommended him to Stanton as commander at Elmira. On September 20, 1864, Tracy assumed the post. By then Eastman was so ill that he could offer no assistance to his young successor. Tracy learned quickly, picking up the administrative skills that would later serve him as secretary of the navy under Benjamin Harrison.[20]

Like other Union prisons, Elmira continued to serve as a recruiting and training camp, leaving the commander with a daunting array of responsibilities. Both Eastman and Tracy were fortunate to have another capable but disabled veteran in the post of prison commander. Maj. Henry V. Colt, whose brother gained fame in the pistol business, was a member of the 104th New York. He arrived at Elmira after injuring himself by falling on his sword during a march. A highly competent officer, Colt eased the burden of the camp commanders. He also endeared himself to the prisoners with his soldierly deportment and his understanding attitude. "My prison comrades considered Major Colt one of the best men they ever knew, even if he was a Union soldier," T. H. Stewart of the Third Georgia later recalled. "He certainly had a Christian heart in him, and showed it by his consideration for the prisoners under him." Stewart's fellow prisoner Anthony Keiley agreed. "Uniformly urbane and courteous in his demeanor," Keiley wrote, "[Colt] discharged the various, and oftentimes annoying, offices of his post with a degree of justice to his position and to the men under his charge, a patience, fidelity, and humanity, that could not be surpassed, and, I fancy, were seldom equaled, either side of the line, in similar positions." Colt departed Elmira in December 1864, sufficiently recovered to return to his regiment. In this one instance, the prisoners at Elmira were fortunate. Colt's successor, Lt. Col. Stephen Moore of the Eleventh New Jersey, also proved popular with the Confederate captives.[21]

This was not the case at every prison. Among the officers in charge of the prison at Camp Chase was Lt. Alexander Sankey. Maj. Alderson remembered him as being "cruel, even brutal, in his treatment of the prisoners." It was not just the prisoners who considered Sankey's methods too extreme. John F. Hickey later wrote that Col. Richardson "at once stopped, in a measure, the inhumanities of Sankey."[22]

Consistency was also an elusive goal in the area of units assigned to guard the prisoners at the various Northern depots. About the only exceptions to this were the two Ohio camps. At Camp Chase the First Battalion of Governor's Guards was mustered into the Federal service on October 27, 1862, and immediately assigned to duty at Camp Chase. The following July the outfit was brought up to regimental strength and rechristened the Eighty-eighth Ohio Volunteer Infantry. Except for a brief assignment to Cincinnati in late 1863, the unit remained as the permanent nucleus of the Camp Chase guard force. According to the Eighty-eighth's postwar history, "The hope was cherished by the officers and men that they would be afforded a chance to display their acquirements at 'the front.' This hope was soon dissipated, orders having been received for the regiment to remain on duty at Camp Chase." Although many members of the guard force may have harbored such thoughts, a recruiting ad placed in the *Delaware (Ohio) Gazette* when the unit was being brought up to regimental strength suggests otherwise. "This regiment is designed exclusively for guard duty at Camp Chase," potential enlistees were promised, "and in no event [is] to be taken out of the state."[23]

On New Year's Day, 1862, a similar ad appeared in the *Sandusky Register,* as officials attempted to staff Johnson's Island. Although the recruits were not guaranteed that they would never leave the state, they were told that they would "receive the same military instruction that enlisted men do in the regular service, and draw the same pay." The potential guards were also promised a $100 bounty for enlisting "in addition to good pay, excellent quarters, and good rations." Ohio governor William Dennison was behind the recruiting effort. Secretary of War Cameron had asked him to raise a unit to serve as guards at the prison. The governor secured four companies, which he christened the Hoffman Battalion, in honor of the officer who was then laboring to complete the facility. In January 1864 six new companies were added, bringing the unit up to regimental strength. The outfit became the 128th Ohio. Col. Hill was placed in command of the regiment, making him available to succeed Terry as post commandant.[24]

This type of consistency was not to be found at other Union prisons. With the most capable outfits serving at the front, prison commanders were often left with untrained, incapable, and sometimes unarmed units assigned to them as guards. On August 5, 1864, Brig. Gen. Joseph Copeland, commanding at Alton, wrote that, when he assumed the post three months earlier, the Tenth Kansas Infantry had been on duty at the Illinois prison. He described it as "a Veteran Regiment that performed all their duties as soldiers in a most creditable and satisfactory manner." Only seventeen days after Copeland took command, the Tenth Kansas was ordered away. Its replacements were two battalions of the Thirteenth Illinois Cavalry. They had only recently been recruited, Copeland noted, and they "were imperfectly armed, were undrilled, and undisciplined." One of these battalions stayed only about three weeks before departing. At about the same time the Seventeenth Illinois Cavalry arrived. Its members, too, lacked discipline, a problem compounded by the fact that Copeland was unable to secure pay for them. The outfit also arrived with only five hundred muskets, making it difficult for the guards to perform their duties even if they desired to do so.[25]

At Elmira, where only two men served as camp commanders during the time that the facility functioned as a prison, guard units came and went as if through a revolving door. New York National Guard units on duty included the Fiftieth, Fifty-fourth, Fifty-sixth, Fifty-eighth, Seventy-seventh, Ninety-eighth, Ninety-ninth, and 102nd. Companies of the Second, Twelfth, and Fourteenth United States Infantry also served at the Chemung Valley camp, as did a battery of the Fourth U.S. Artillery.[26]

The constant shuffling of guard units was caused by a number of factors. Often temporary regiments, raised for only one hundred days of service, filled the ranks of prison guards. Units from Delaware and Maryland often served at Fort Delaware. Officials were concerned that the border-state soldiers might sympathize with the captives they were assigned to guard, a danger that familiarity over time might have enhanced. In June 1864, after inspecting the camp, Hoffman recommended that the Fifth Maryland be replaced by a new guard regiment. "It has too many sympathizers in it to be intrusted with the charge of prisoners of war," he warned Stanton. Two days later a one-hundred-day Ohio regiment was on its way to the camp to replace the Maryland outfit.[27]

At Camp Morton a pair of paroled regiments stationed at the camp helped guard prisoners. The Fifty-first and Seventy-third Indiana Infantry received their exchanges during the summer of 1863. They were immediately assigned to guard duty at the prison. The units were less than sharp. Capture and months of inactivity while on parole had left them demoralized. Their officers were still being held as prisoners of war at Richmond, and this lack of leadership left them undisciplined. On November 9 Col. Stevens complained to Hoffman that the two units, comprising thirteen hundred men, had only seven officers. Although "composed of good material," Stevens concluded that the regiments were "insufficient to perform a duty so important as that required of a guard at this post."[28]

As the war continued, a variety of groups emerged to perform much of the guard duty at the growing number of Union prisons. Among the most unusual was the Thirty-seventh Iowa Infantry. Raised under the authority of Iowa governor Samuel J. Kirkwood, the outfit was mainly composed of men over fifty years old. One was reportedly eighty. The regiment, also known as the "Graybeards" or the "Silver Grays," was mustered into the service in December 1862. After serving as guards at various buildings in the St. Louis area, the Graybeards crossed the river to Alton prison in July 1863. For about four months, beginning in August 1863, the regiment's commander, Col. George Kincaid, also commanded the prison.[29]

The Graybeards' next move came in January 1864, when they relocated to Rock Island. Once there, they made a generally poor impression on officials from both inside and outside the facility. Lt. Col. John F. Marsh, in forwarding an inspection report to Col. James Hardie, inspector general of the army, termed them "a regiment of decrepit old men and the most unpromising subjects for soldiers I ever saw." There were numerous reports of them drinking heavily. The sanitary habits of the outfit were also subject to question. Members of the regiment kept pigs within the limits of the compound, and Surgeon A. M. Clark found their enforcement of sanitary regulations to be lax. Clark complained that the policing of both the grounds and the prisoners' barracks were poor under the Graybeards' watch. He traced the problem to the top. "[I]f it does not exceed my duty," Clark wrote to Hoffman, "allow me most respectfully to suggest that Colonel Kincaid . . . be under no circumstances placed in command of this post. He is altogether too slow and too easy, and his officers and men appear to have no idea of the value of discipline." On May 30, 1864, Johnson informed Hoffman that the Thirty-seventh Iowa was about to depart, to be replaced by a one-hundred-day regiment. He added, "When it takes place, this Depot will be better garrisoned than at present."[30]

From Rock Island the Graybeards headed to Camp Morton and then to Camp Chase. At the latter facility the outfit did not impress Capt. Robert Lamb, the assistant inspector general of the camp. On October 28, 1864, Lamb reported to Richardson that the officer of the guard was "negligent and careless of [his] duty." Lamb explained, "I visited his guard during the afternoon yesterday and discovered them doing very lax duty a number of the guards were allowed to congregate together on the parapet and engage in conversation, some of them with their guns at order arms, while others carried arms in various positions." Many were not even facing the prison, but were gazing at other areas of the camp. As the men headed to their posts for duty, Lamb reported, "Much confusion was observed among the men, such as loud talking and whistling and laughing during the time they were marched from their headquarters until they were assigned to their respective posts."[31]

Much more significant than the Thirty-seventh Iowa were members of the Veteran Reserve Corps, who served as guards at virtually every Northern prison camp. The corps was established on March 20, 1863, as the Invalid Corps. The goal of the outfit was to utilize the services of wounded or otherwise disabled soldiers. They would serve behind the lines, freeing more able-bodied men for the front. The corps was to be divided into three battalions. The first was to consist of those "who were able to bear a musket and do garrison duty." The second would include men who had lost a hand or an arm. Remarkably, the third was to be made up of men in worse condition than those in the second. The latter two were eventually consolidated. Recruits proved hard to come by. By October 31, 1863, 18,255 officers and men had been welcomed into the Invalid Corps.[32]

Of those, over 16,000 had been transferred from other outfits. The lack of volunteers sprang from many reasons. The three-year enlistment came with no bounty, and only men not subject to the draft could enter. Members believed the sky blue uniforms set them apart from their fellow soldiers. They also did not like the name. In addition to eschewing the title "Invalid," they soon realized that the initials "IC" matched the Quartermaster Department's designation for property that had been "Inspected and Condemned." At Camp Chase, one regular guard gleefully noted, the prisoners referred to their Invalid Corps guards as "condemned Yankees." Accordingly, on March 18, 1864, the name was changed to the Veteran Reserve Corps (VRC), removing the offensive title, if not the stigma.[33]

At a few prisons, the commanding officers of VRC units also served as camp commandants. Among them was Camp Douglas, where both Col. James Strong and Col. Benjamin Sweet were members. Perhaps most prominent among them was Col. Johnson, who commanded the Rock Island prison during virtually its entire existence. Johnson was also the commander of the Fourth Regiment, VRC, which served as the primary guard unit. Richard Rush, who briefly commanded the camp when it opened, found the men of the Veteran Reserve Corps to be "very good, steady, obedient, & willing men but entirely without instruction or discipline." Rush considered Johnson to be "a very superior officer [who] will be fully able to carry on this establishment." Col. Stevens, commanding at Camp Morton, also led the VRC's Fifth Regiment. Stevens was satisfied with the performance of his "invalid" soldiers. In fact, in November 1864 he twice requested two additional companies of VRC men to supplement troops from the Forty-third Indiana. The Hoosier outfit needed help, Stevens asserted, because many of its men were absent without leave and because of the "limited knowledge of duty manifested in both officers and men."[34]

Another group that supplied a number of guards to the prisons was the United States Colored Troops (USCT). Like the VRC, the USCT was recruited out of necessity. The need for men led Union officials to put aside their prejudices, and on July 17, 1862, Congress approved an act authorizing the president to enlist black volunteers. None were mustered in for nearly a year, but eventually 186,097 joined. Some 50 percent had once been the property of the Southerners they were enlisted to help defeat. Although a small number ended up at the fighting front, and a few, such as the Fifty-fourth Massachusetts, gained fame for their achievements, most served well behind the lines. Included among that group were guards at Rock Island, Point Lookout, and Elmira.

At Rock Island the 108th USCT arrived on September 24, 1864. The opinions of their superiors were mixed. Col. Johnson was not impressed with his new guard force. "At depots of this character, the enlisted men doing duty in the prison comdg. Rebel Co's must be able to read and write well," the colonel noted. "With our small force of white troops this is a serious difficulty." Following an escape, Johnson lamented, "I feel very insecure and fear they [escapes] are likely to occur as long as we must depend on this class of troops for Prison guard." The white officers of the 108th did not share Johnson's view. "These men are the best guards I ever saw," Capt. Leroy B. House wrote to a friend. "If an order is given to them to guard any thing wo be to the man who attempts to interfere with them." He conceded, however, "I have to look after my Co. more than if it is a Co. of intelligent whites. They cannot figure very much, and if we do not see to it the men that furnish rations cheat them in weight." John Cowgill, the captain of Company A, agreed with the former sentiment. On October 5 he reported, "I join with Officers of the Guard in saying that I have never seen Guard duty better performed."[35]

The prisoners were less charitable. "The Rebel prisoners here swear that they will not submit to be guarded by the d——d nigers," House wrote. Two days after the 108th arrived, Lafayette Rogan wrote in his diary, "8,000 Southern men to day are guarded by their slaves who have been armed by the Tyrant." The prisoners registered their protest with volleys of rocks. This activity had actually begun in July. Both the Forty-eighth Iowa and the 133rd Illinois had been subjected to geological assaults, but the frequency increased once the 108th arrived. The black guards responded by firing upon their attackers, as had the white units before them. The officers generally supported the guards' decision to fire. On September 9 the officer of the day reported, "There was some disturbance going on because of the rebels throwing stones which I found out to my satisfaction to be true as I barely escaped being hit myself." Few of the shots found their mark, but on the night of November 12, 1864, one of them killed a prisoner. The officer of the guard reported that the sentry had fired "in the discharge of his duty," but such was not always the case. On September 28, the conclusion was that the guard fired at a group of prisoners without provocation. On that occasion nobody was hit.[36]

Rocks also came into play during the brief tenure of a black regiment at Elmira. According to T. H. Stewart's postwar memoirs, "We soon got tired of being guarded by negroes, so we began to knock them off the walks with rocks." Maj. Colt ordered two men from each ward to report to his headquarters, and the prisoners expressed their distaste for the black guards. They requested that a Pennsylvania recruiting regiment be sent in their place. According to Stewart, Colt granted the request. Elmira diarist Henri Mugler recorded the events somewhat differently. On July 30, 1864, Mugler wrote that the prisoners had "stoned the negro sentinels near the privy last night. The result of it is that one of the negro sentinels shot one of the prisoners tonight after having halted him several times in vain." Nine days later Mugler wrote that the black regiment had been sent to the front. Its replacement was a white outfit, the Ninety-ninth New York National Guard.[37]

The same attitude generally prevailed among the prisoners at Point Lookout. "Our Regt does not guard the Rebel prisoners as much as they did," John H. Burrill of the Second New Hampshire informed his parents on March 21, 1864. "The niggers do it part of the time. It makes the Rebs pretty mad." Former Point Lookout prisoner B. T. Holliday later recalled of his black guards, "They were the first negro soldiers I had seen. It was a bitter pill for the Southern men to swallow, and we felt the insult very keenly." Holliday termed them "impudent." His fellow Point Lookout captive William H. Haigh labeled them "imperious." Both terms seemed to imply that, in the opinion of the white captives, the black guards placed over them did not know their place, an unusual view for prisoners to hold concerning soldiers placed in authority over them. Joseph Kern offered a different view. "The Negroes as a general thing are better liked than the whites," he wrote on November 11, 1864. Perhaps the most balanced view was offered by Anthony Keiley. On July 7, 1864, Keiley recorded that the soldiers in a new group of black guards were less abusive than their predecessors. He observed, "I attribute this to the circumstance that these are negroes who have been in service; and any soldier will tell you that an active campaign inspires very humane sentiments toward soldiers."[38]

Lt. Edward Bartlett, a white officer of the Fifth Massachusetts Cavalry, one of the black outfits to serve at Point Lookout, was also objective in his assessment. Writing to his wife, Bartlett noted, "I am just learning the names of my men and also their characters and dispositions, who are the good soldiers and who are the shirks, for there are some of the latter, even in the fifth cavalry."[39]

Whether white or black, guards at Union prison camps lived lives that were in many ways little better than those of the prisoners they supervised. "A centinel died on post last night with cold," E. L. Cox wrote in his Fort Delaware diary on January 26, 1864. Arriving at Camp Chase on a frigid night that same month, prisoner George Moffett learned that two sentinels had frozen to death that night. The following month James Mackey observed, "No sentinel stalks on the parapet; the extreme cold has compelled them to crouch behind the wall." At Rock Island and Johnson's Island the bitter winter of 1864 led camp officials to reduce the time on guard duty from two hours to one. At Camp Douglas they brought the guards off the parapets and stationed them in front of the barracks. This followed a bitter night in which, according to Curtis Burke, "Six or seven of the guards froze on their beats last night and this morning, so that they had to be taken to the Yankee hospital." As the following winter dawned, Leroy House wrote that several of the USCT men at Rock Island had frozen their feet while on guard duty. Even at Point Lookout, where the climate was milder, Edward Bartlett complained of being "posted on the top of a high stockade with nothing to break the wind sweeping across from the bay to the river." The cavalryman concluded, "Hurrah for the day that we shall throw aside our muskets for sabres."[40]

The quarters occupied by the guards were often little better than those housing Confederate prisoners. Alexander J. Hamilton was a member of Independent Battery G, Pittsburgh Heavy Artillery, one of the first outfits to stand guard at Fort Delaware. At first the Pennsylvanians occupied decent quarters. However, in November 1862 they were crowded into "a filthy room." There were no bunks, so the men went on an unsuccessful search through deep snow for lumber and tools.

After about a month in their new quarters, the men were provided with bunks. By then some of them had been arrested while building a raft with which to cross the Delaware and desert. Members of the Ninth Delaware Infantry reported that rats were as common in guard quarters as they were in the prisoners' barracks.[41]

At Fort Delaware and other camps, the conditions of the guard quarters contributed to the poor health of the soldiers. On March 8, 1864, George K. Johnson, an army medical inspector, reported that the strength of the Fort Delaware garrison was 1,068. Of that total, the average number of sick men was 44 per day. The yearly death rate was just over 52 per 1,000. During the preceding three months bronchitis, diarrhea, smallpox, and various "malarial fevers" had been the most prevalent diseases. There had also been three cases of scurvy, an entirely preventable malady. In February 1864 Charles F. Johnson, a guard at Camp Morton, informed his wife that his barracks was so cold that "water freezes in every vessil in the quarters to such an extent that it requires a hatchet to cut it in the mornings." He slept well, however, thanks to seven blankets the quartermaster had loaned him. In November 1863 Dr. Ira Brown of the Sixty-fifth Illinois reported that the guard quarters at Camp Douglas were "so constructed that it is impossible to keep them in a healthy condition." He found them dark and poorly ventilated. Worse, they rested directly on the ground instead of being elevated. Brown concluded, "The Quarters indicate a neglect in being properly policed, but to clean them thoroughly should not render them healthy."[42]

The guards themselves were philosophical about their situation. This was particularly true of those who had served at the front. In January 1863 Isaac Marsh reached Camp Douglas after helping escort prisoners from Arkansas Post. He wrote of his new comrades, "They have very good warm quarters here which they shared with us and good beds that is a tick filled with hay." Another Camp Douglas guard, George W. Bisbee of the Ninth Vermont Infantry, found time for an active social life while serving at the Chicago prison. He frequently left camp to attend political meetings or parties in the city, sometimes remaining away overnight. At camp he joined an "Orratory Club" that held frequent debates. Among the topics discussed were "Resolved that the extension of knowledge increases morell evil" and "Resolved that the invention of labor saving machines has been detrimental rather than benefishal to our country." Capt. House informed his friends that he enjoyed duty at Rock Island, particularly during the cold winter months. "We can procure all the fuel [we] can burn by sending a written order to the coal office at Post Head Quarters," he noted. He predicted that with the advent of warmer weather he would yearn for service in the field. Still, House noted, "I am trying to persuade myself that guarding Rebel Prisoners is as healthy business as charging Rebel Breast Works." George Watson of the Twelfth New Hampshire was also pleased with his assignment at Point Lookout. He informed his mother that he got plenty to eat "and that is good a nuf for eney one and a good bed to lay on." Watson concluded, "i had rather bee hear then to bee a marching."[43]

Those views notwithstanding, guarding prisoners was boring duty performed in boring surroundings. To escape the tedium of life in the camps, many men turned to drinking. Indeed, according to Elmira historian Michael P. Gray, "The number of guards arrested for being drunk on and off duty might have left some observers wondering how officials kept escapes to a minimum." Court-martial reports at the camp show that guards were frequently so drunk that they were unable to perform their duties. They were, however, often able to engage in fights and acts of vandalism outside the camp. In one instance, according to the *Elmira Advertiser,* a group of VRC guards, "having imbibed most too freely, concluded to smash some glass and they succeeded to a charm." The men broke every window out of a saloon, broke all of the bottles, and severely injured the owner. They then broke out the windows of several other buildings and assaulted a number of local police before the provost guard arrested seventeen. At Rock Island officials discovered that similar incidents were not limited by age, race, or disability. Members of the Graybeards, the USCT, and the Veteran Reserve Corps were all involved in incidents related to excessive drinking. VRC guard Frances Bishop wrote on July 2, 1864, "Again do we see the fruit of that curse of humanity whiskey." Five or six men from his regiment had gotten into a "drunken row" at a local restaurant. One of them died in the melee. Bishop blamed the establishment. "I just wish some of the boys would tare the thing down for it will be a curse as long as it remains," Bishop concluded.[44]

A. J. Hamilton's Fort Delaware diary is well garnished with accounts of drunken guards, including himself. "Was on duty from 4 to 8," Hamilton wrote on August 21, 1863, "then got dead drunk by stealing whiskey. . . . Went to bed at 10:30, was very sick." On another occasion he got drunk and fell asleep on a table. When his lieutenant awakened him, he was missing $40. Heavy drinking marked Christmas Eve in both 1862 and 1863. The latter year he noted, "Our boys have two or three kegs of lager and are having a good time." At least one who did not was the Pennsylvania sentry who was "badly beaten by six of the 5th Maryland." Holidays were not the only occasions for drinking sprees. On May 26, 1863, Hamilton was a member of a party that presented a sword, belt, sash, and hat to a comrade who had been promoted to lieutenant. After offering his thanks, the newly christened officer "tapped a half barrel of beer over which we had a jollification."[45]

At Point Lookout, Edward Bartlett was part of a squad of men charged not with keeping prisoners in, but with keeping whiskey out. On October 23, 1864, he informed his wife, "Some way the men for the past week got hold of more of the liquor than was good for them, so the Col. posted the guard to keep it out." Everyone approaching the camp was to be inspected. Those found with whiskey were arrested and sent to headquarters. During his twenty-four hours of liquor patrol, Bartlett managed to seize four bottles that were secreted in a wagon. Camp Chase guards captured three beer wagons on May 21, 1863, "but not until a considerable quantity of beer had been sold." According to the camp's guard report, "The drinkers thereof made some trouble during the day; but the Provost Guard was prompt in suppressing disturbances."[46]

On January 31, 1865, Camp Douglas prisoner Curtis Burke wrote that some drunken members of the patrol guard had gone "the grand round" of the camp the previous night, making life miserable for the prisoners. At one barracks they found a few prisoners talking and some others sitting at the stove after lights-out. They marched all two hundred men out of the barracks and made them stand on one foot for an hour. Those sitting by the stove received the additional punishment of being whipped with the guards' belts "just as a negro would be whipped or worse." According to Burke, eight other barracks received similar visits. The inhabitants of one of them were "made to stand out awhile and then bare themselves and sit on the snow and ice till they melted through to the ground." A prisoners' committee complained to camp authorities, "but no satisfactory response was returned, which occasioned considerable excitement among the prisoners."[47]

The opinions the prisoners had of their guards, even when those guards were sober, were seldom high. "The Yankees are very spiteful today," Fort Delaware prisoner E. L. Cox wrote on September 1, 1864. "They broke up preaching this eavening." The guards also dispersed worshipers the next day and prevented the men from cooking their rations. In a letter apparently smuggled from Camp Morton in September 1863, James A. Thomas informed his father, "To be sure we are subjected to all the harsh usage that men for once 'clothed with a little brief authority' see fit to inflict upon us." It was a common attitude. William Peel was disappointed when he learned that the veterans who had been supplementing the guard force at Johnson's Island were returning to the front. He explained, "The news excites a good deal of regret among us since we will then be left again to the Hoffman Battalion, who have never been in the field, & whom we have consequently not had an opportunity of teaching to respect us." Peel's fears were realized several weeks later. A garrison lieutenant pronounced a few names incorrectly during roll call, the prisoners laughed at him, and the lieutenant "flew into a rage & pronounced the party a 'set of damned cowardly puppies.'" He also cut off the entire block's rations, but prisoners from surrounding barracks "sent them rations until they had more than they usually get."[48]

Although specifics varied from camp to camp, and rules at all prisons were subject to change, the prisoners generally were free to move about their compounds during the day. They had to be careful to avoid the "dead line," generally ten to twenty feet from the fence. They were also usually forbidden from gathering in large groups. Otherwise, their freedom of movement was not limited during ordinary circumstances. This was not the case after dark. At every camp, prisoners were expected to remain in their barracks except to visit the sinks. All lights were to be extinguished. Roll call was held twice a day at most camps. At Johnson's Island, however, only a morning roll call was conducted. As Virgil Murphey described it, the men were called from their blocks at 8:00 a.m. and formed into line. Either a commissioned or a noncommissioned officer called the roll. "Long after the role has been called we are compelled to remain in the open air until the drum sounds disperse or retire," Murphey explained. "It generally requires about an hour. When the snow is upon the earth and the thermometer below zero it is a severe and trying ordeal. Indeed it is suffering of the keenest kind."[49]

Officials at the various camps also conducted inspections. They were held every Sunday at Point Lookout and on an irregular basis at other prisons. According to one Point Lookout diarist, prisoners in need of shoes or clothing received them during these inspections "when there are any to be issued." It was much more common, however, for prisoners to forfeit items than to receive them. Blankets were most often sought out by the prison inspectors. Any prisoner found with more than one had to give up the excess. The Yankees also sought out any "extra" clothing that the prisoners might have. Occasionally the inspections were justified by circumstances. They often turned up ladders or even rafts that were being secreted as part of escape plans.[50]

At Camp Douglas a search for weapons revealed instead a number of intoxicated prisoners. Following an incident in which one prisoner stabbed another, Point Lookout officials confiscated all knives. At the other extreme was the incident recorded by Point Lookout prisoner Joseph Kern. The prisoners were marched from their tents, and members of the Fifth New Hampshire proceeded to "sack the camp. . . . Everything was seized. All things of value were carried out, while those of little account were strewn in the street."[51]

The prisoners attempted to hide items they did not wish to lose, with mixed results. "We resorted to every artifice to conceal our blankets, taking up the floor and hiding them, wrapping rocks up in them and sinking them in the tanks from which we drew our drinking water," recalled Fort Delaware prisoner P. H. Aylett. "They were generally found, however, and always confiscated." Charles Warren Hutt recorded one victory at Point Lookout. Following a May 15, 1864, search, Hutt wrote, "Had an inspection but did not loose anything as we secreted our blankets under the floor." At Camp Douglas and Johnson's Island the prisoners decided that their best strategy was to hide their best clothing in plain sight. When rumors spread of an impending inspection at Camp Douglas to seize surplus clothing, Thomas Beadles wrote, "Every man is wearing his best, willing to give them his rags." Noting a similar rumor at Johnson's Island, William Peel wrote, "Our block made, perhaps, the most genteel appearance at roll-call, this morning that they ever have for a long time."[52]

Besides confiscating what they considered surplus clothing and blankets, the Union keepers resorted to a variety of punishments for a wide range of offenses. "The guard is very spiteful," a Fort Delaware prisoner observed on December 5, 1864. "This evening they have had several of the officers double quicking for the most trivial offenses." When a group of prisoners at Camp Douglas shouted "Bread, bread, more bread," at a Union officer passing by their barracks, the officer ordered all the men of the barracks out into line and made them stand there for several hours. The next day he saw to it that they got no bread. He also ordered the prisoners in the other barracks to give them none. A Camp Douglas prisoner on a work detail ended up with six extra days of forced labor after remarking in the presence of a guard that he would "make some Yankee prisoner work with interest some day or other." Camp Douglas prisoners loitering around their compound were occasionally rounded up and required to clean out the guard quarters. This, however, appears to have been less a punishment than an opportunity for lazy guards to secure free labor. Whatever the motivation, there is no record of Camp Douglas officers stopping the practice.[53]

In November 1864 prisoners at Elmira began stealing potatoes from the mess hall. Prison officials cut off all rations until the parties involved confessed. "They soon came to light," one prisoner noted. Soon after a mess hall was built at Johnson's Island, the men of one block stole a table from it and used the lumber to patch their barracks. "You will use every exertion to find out who the men are that committed the depredations refered to," an incredulous Col. Hill ordered the superintendent of prisons. The guilty parties were to be put in close confinement and on half rations for two days. If they were not found, all the men of the barracks were to receive half rations for two days. "The prison regulations must be strictly enforced," Hill concluded.[54]

Close confinement was considered a severe punishment at Johnson's Island. Those sentenced there found themselves in a windowless room about twelve feet square. Often they were in irons with a thirty-two-pound cannon ball attached. According to one prisoner, "The fate of the other prisoners is paradise compared to their situation." While several officers were often crowded into the single room at Johnson's Island, the guardhouse at Elmira was a larger building divided into individual cells. Like the Johnson's Island guardhouse, Elmira's "dungeon" had no windows. After being sent there for an unnamed offense, Wilbur Gramling noted, "Given nothing but bread and water. . . . Pretty lousy hole." The "dungeon" at Camp Douglas was such a horrid place that it drew the wrath of Dr. Clark, Hoffman's medical inspector. "It is a 'dungeon' indeed," Clark wrote after an October 1863 inspection. He described it as "a close room about eighteen feet square, lighted by one closely barred window about eighteen by eight inches. . . . The floor is laid directly on the ground and is constantly damp. A sink occupies one corner, the stench from which is intolerable." Clark found twenty-four prisoners there. He concluded, "The place might do for three or four prisoners, but for the number now confined there it is inhuman. At my visit I remained but a few seconds and was glad to get out, feeling sick and faint."[55]

The ball and chain were common items of punishment at the prisons. One Camp Chase guard wrote, "Sometimes a prisoner refuses to work at cleaning up the Prison, but a little moral suasion in the shape of hand-cuffs and ball and chain with no rations soon brings him to his senses." The prisoners, of course, viewed the situation less blithely. W. C. Dodson later recalled being one of a group of captives thus encumbered. One of his comrades, Dodson wrote, was an older man suffering from a hip wound. "The shackles rendered him practically helpless, and we younger ones had to wait on him like he was a child." Perhaps the only prisoner to turn his ball and chain into a positive situation was A. C. Kean. The Rock Island prisoner had been fitted up with a pair of sixteen-pound cannon balls after striking a guard who was abusing another prisoner. He wore the balls for an entire winter, "but used them to keep warm during the cold nights by throwing them in the fire and heating them up before bed time." Kean recalled, "There were quite a few of us decorated the same way, as they would ball and chain [prisoners] for any little offence."[56]

Curtis Burke made two observations involving the ball and chain at Camp Douglas. On April 12, 1864, he wrote that four men were wearing balls that weighed approximately fifty-six pounds attached to five feet of stout chain. Each came with a leather strap that enabled the victims at least to carry them when they had to move farther than the length of the chain. One man had a "fiddle string" that he used to unlock the clasp fitted around his ankle when the guards were not around. On December 9, Burke observed that a fellow prisoner had returned from the smallpox hospital with his ball and chain still attached. As he had been taken to the hospital, the ball had fallen out of the ambulance, "nearly jerking his leg off before the ambulance could be stopped." In addition to a case of smallpox, the unfortunate man "suffered a great deal with his leg."[57]

At Elmira the "barrel shirt" was a common punishment. The miscreant was marched around the camp with an open-ended barrel resting upon his shoulders. Often there was a sign attached listing the offense. Henri Mugler observed one such prisoner whose sign read "flanker," the term for a man who attempted to secure a second meal from the mess room. On another occasion Mugler, who commanded the prison drum corps, was ordered to supply musicians to play the "Rogue's March" as a prisoner caught stealing was paraded over the compound. J. B. Stamp later recalled seeing a dozen or more men marching in circles over icy ground with the barrels on. "This was often for trifling offenses, and had to be performed so many hours each day of their sentence to the guard house," Stamp added. The latter claim is confirmed by former prisoner T. H. Stewart. Stewart, who admitted in his memoirs to flanking both bread and wood, recalled both time in the guardhouse and wearing the barrel shirt.[58]

Stamp also recalled crueler punishments, such as hanging prisoners by their thumbs and "bucking and gagging" them. Stamp recalled one incident involving the latter punishment. It occurred when a drunken prisoner refused to reveal his supplier. "In this, the instrument used was a block of wood which was forced in his mouth and fastened with a strong cord at the back of the head. The cord was drawn so tight, that incisions, or ruptures, were made in the mouth." Although reports of hanging prisoners by the thumbs are common in postwar memoirs, they are far less common in contemporary diaries. James Marsh Morey noted three such incidents at Hart's Island, a facility north of New York City that was pressed into service as a prison in the waning days of the war. On one occasion the victim was a man caught stealing from the sutler stand. Two men later received the punishment for stealing and fighting. On the third occasion, which occurred more than a month after Appomattox, three prisoners were hung up simply "for some misdemeanors."[59]

One of the most graphic examples of hanging prisoners by the thumbs was recorded by Camp Douglas prisoner Curtis Burke and confirmed by William Milton in his postwar memoirs. Three prisoners had threatened to hang a fellow prisoner who had reported their escape plans to authorities. They were removed from their barracks and hung from the railing of the platform that surrounded the camp's flagpole. There they remained suspended, their toes barely touching the ground, for about an hour. Burke wrote that the men suffered in silence for a half hour, "then commence[d] groaning and hollowing. It made me almost sick to hear them." One man vomited all over himself. Another fainted, and, according to Milton, he was unable to return to the barracks for several hours.[60]

"Riding the mule" was another punishment often employed at Camp Douglas and occasionally at other camps. Prisoners were made to sit upon the sharp edge of a board that was placed on a platform. According to Burke, "Men have set on it till they fainted and fell off." J. S. Rosamond of the Fourth Mississippi wrote after the war that a prisoner on the mule began kicking and asked a guard for a pair of spurs. The guard was not amused. He attached a discarded stove to the man's legs and said, "Now, damn you, kick and spur." The prisoner eventually "began to cry like a child, and begged most piteously for them to be taken off." He was unable to walk for nearly ten days.[61]

As cruel as these punishments may have been, they were not limited to Confederate prisoners. Occasionally the Union used the same methods to punish their own. One Camp Douglas captive wrote, "We Rebels continue to have a little amusement by seeing the Yankees punished by riding a wooden horse about ten feet high, the back of which is a sharp rail." At Camp Chase three Union privates, possibly recruits or parolees, were found guilty of destruction of public property. They were sentenced to two weeks of hard labor with a ball and chain attached. In May 1863 Fort Delaware guard A. J. Hamilton wrote, "Bucking and gagging now has become quite a fashionable amusement with certain officers here." He added, "While such treatment is tolerated who can wonder at the number of deserters from our army?"[62]

Certain guards developed reputations for individual acts of cruelty. At Camp Douglas one of the worst was nicknamed "Old Red." Curtis Burke observed, "He bayoneted several of the men, and we have no particular love for him." In an 1898 article about his time in Camp Morton, J. K. Womack wrote that the sergeant who called the roll for his barracks was "a demon in human flesh. I have seen him walk through our barracks with a heavy stick in his hand, striking right and left on the heads, faces, backs, or stomachs of the poor, starving prisoners, as though they were so many reptiles, crying out: 'This is the way you whip your negroes.'" At Elmira a number of officials failed to follow Maj. Colt's example of kind treatment. Among the most notorious was Capt. J. H. Borden of the Eighty-sixth Pennsylvania. Anthony Keiley recalled the captain's attempt to force a drunken prisoner to tell where he had gotten his liquor. Borden first hung the man by his thumbs, but he refused to talk. He then attempted to gag the prisoner with a tent pin. When the man failed to open his mouth sufficiently, Borden struck him in the mouth with an oak billet, breaking several teeth. In October 1864 one of the few prisoners still confined at Castle Williams on Governor's Island wrote that a guard struck a man with a board. The Yankee sergeant was conducting an inspection, and the captive, who was ill, "did not move fast enough to suit him."[63]

Although tales of excessive punishments are more prominent in postwar memoirs than in contemporary diaries, accounts of the shooting of prisoners are common entries in the diaries of Union captives. Upon arriving at Fort Delaware in July 1864, E. L. Cox was informed that it was "a common occurance" for prisoners to be shot. This may have been an exaggeration, but by the end of the year he had recorded three such instances. One occurred in November. Although Cox did not record what prompted the shooting, he did note that the victim's leg was amputated and that he died the next day. Two more shootings took place in December. After the second, Cox wrote, "It is now that the Yankeys seem to murder prisoners without remors or conscience."[64]

On January 16, 1864, Johnson's Island prisoner Robert Bingham wrote, "The Yankees are getting quite bold. They know they are too strong for us now & these infamous home guards, Hoffman's Battalion, are getting large & shooting at everybody—shot several times last night." In one instance the guard had without any warning fired upon, but missed, a prisoner headed for the sinks. "Some poor rebel being shot nearly every night," Thomas Beadles observed at Camp Douglas in January 1864. "When a man lies down to rest & repose at night there is no surety that he will be alive in the morning as bullets are sailing through the barracks constantly." Prisoners had been shot on two consecutive nights, Beadles added, and he claimed that the average was about three a week. At Rock Island, William Dillon insisted that "one brutal cowardly guard" was responsible for a number of shootings. Among his victims was a man who had stepped outside his barracks after dark. The guard ordered him back inside, according to Dillon's account, then fired as he opened the door.[65]

Between April and August 1864, Bartlett Yancey Malone recorded five shooting incidents in his Point Lookout diary. All involved black sentries. Malone's fellow prisoner Charles Hutt confirmed one of the incidents, saying the man had been killed "for no provocation whatever." Camp records corroborate another account. In that case the sentry, who was transferred before an investigation of the shooting occurred, claimed to have been enforcing the rule that "no nuisance be committed except in the tubs." The situation was serious enough that camp officials addressed the problem on August 29 with a set of orders regulating the conduct of the sentries. "The wanton and unnecessary shooting at prisoners of war for slight offenses will be severely punished," they stated. "The general good order which the prisoners of war at this post have observed entitles them to the protection of the Government, and any trifling or unimportant disobedience of a sentinel's orders on the part of a prisoner can be corrected in some other way than by shooting at him, by which the lives of others entirely innocent of any offense are endangered."[66]

Sometimes carelessness played a role in the shootings. At Camp Morton one prisoner wrote that the guards often fired their weapons to help them remain awake. "One of these balls came uncomfortably close to our heads as we lay in our bunks about midnight," he added. A Johnson's Island prisoner was amused by at least one shooting incident. "[The guard] seems to have converted into a Reb's appearance an old ash barrel, near the Block, upon which he fired into without further ado." The situation was more serious at Rock Island. Guards discharging their weapons when going off duty were so careless that, according to one camp officer, "if life has not been lost it was not for the want of opportunity." Orders were issued requiring the officer of the guard to accompany the sentries to the target ground. Such incidents were not limited to Confederate prisoners. In November 1863 Elmira guard George W. Pearl, who was guarding Union draftees and substitutes, informed his parents, "A sad accident happened at the guard house yesterday." One of the men confined there became drunk and disorderly. The guards attempted to gag him, but he got loose and climbed up onto the beams above the room. An officer ordered a guard to "prick him down with his bayonet." The weapon discharged, killing the man instantly.[67]

Poor marksmanship on the part of Union sentries occasionally resulted in the deaths of innocent prisoners. In one such case a Rock Island guard fired on a prisoner attempting to climb the fence. Instead he hit a man in the barracks. A similar incident occurred at Camp Douglas. In this instance the guard fired at a prisoner who had crossed the dead line. He aimed too high and wounded two men in a nearby barracks. A commission that investigated the incident concluded that the soldier was "strictly performing his duty when he fired." Its only recommendation was that "sentinels be instructed to carefully fire low under such circumstances."[68]

At Camp Chase Lt. Col. August H. Poten of the Invalid Corps dismissed even more blithely an incident that resulted in the death of a prisoner. According to Poten's report, the sentinel fired into a barracks after making repeated calls for the men to extinguish all lights. He wounded Henry Hupman of the Twentieth Virginia Cavalry in the arm. Hupman died a few days later. Poten concluded, "As sad as this case may be, to wound a perhaps innocent man, . . . it has proved to be a most excellent lesson, very much needed in the prison—No. 1—as the rebel officers confined in that prison showed frequently before a disposition to disobey the orders given to them by our men on duty. They have since changed their minds and obey."[69]

This incident was one of four shootings that took place at Camp Chase between September and December 1863. Three resulted in the death of a prisoner, and two occurred after the prisoners allegedly refused to put out lights. This attracted the attention of the commissary general of prisoners. Writing to Col. Wallace, then commanding the camp, he complained, "To justify such an act as this it is necessary to show that all proper means had been tried in vain to put a stop to the burning of lights after hours, and it should be shown that the light was not the accidental blazing up of wood left in the stove." More disturbing was the report Hoffman received from a medical inspector stating that Hupman had received no medical attention until the next morning. This was later confirmed by Camp Chase surgeon G. W. Fitzpatrick, who reported that he did not see the wounded man until late the next morning "while making my usual visit to Prison No. 1." Both reports contradicted Poten's claim that Hupman had received immediate attention, and both left Hoffman appalled. "Such treatment of prisoners, whatever may be the necessity for wounding them, is barbarous and without possible excuse," he informed Wallace.[70]

Following the incidents at Camp Chase, Hoffman ordered commanders at all camps to convene a board of officers to investigate every shooting. The results were to be forwarded to his office. Any guard shooting a prisoner was required to demonstrate that he "was governed strictly by the orders he received, and that the prisoner or prisoners willfully disregarded his cautions of orders." Hoffman concluded, "Rigid discipline must be preserved among the prisoners, but great care must be observed that no wanton excesses or cruelties are committed under the plea of enforcing orders."[71]

The commissions that grew out of Hoffman's orders had a strong tendency to exonerate sentries. One notable exception occurred at Camp Morton in April 1864 following the shooting of James Beatie of the Fourth Florida and Michael Healey of the Thirtieth Mississippi. Stevens concluded that "the shooting in question was a malicious and premeditated act on the part of the guard." Stevens explained that the sentry in question had "repeatedly threatened to 'shoot some rebel,' stating that they had shot two fingers off for him . . . while he was in the field." The camp commander ordered that murder charges be made out against the guard. The outcome of the case is not known.[72]

One order that guards were almost always considered justified in enforcing was firing upon a prisoner who approached too closely to the fence or stepped across the dead line. A row of stakes marked the dead line at Johnson's Island. At Camp Douglas it was a railing about eighteen inches high. Elsewhere a ditch was generally used. However it was designated, the dead line was aptly named. Despite this, many prisoners did not see it as an ending point but as the starting point for a potential journey to freedom. The accounts of those who attempted to challenge it make for some of the Civil War's most exciting and tragic stories.[73]

1. Although its capacity was limited, the Old Capitol Prison in Washington, DC, housed a variety of military and political prisoners during the war. Courtesy National Archives, Washington, DC.

2. The parade ground at Fort Warren in Boston Harbor. A number of prisoners captured during 1861 were incarcerated at Fort Warren. The secure facility later became the destination for high-ranking Confederate officers. Courtesy Massachusetts MOLLUS Collection, United States Army Military History Institute, Carlisle Barracks, PA.

3. Camp Morton, a training camp at the Indiana State Fairgrounds, was one of many western facilities pressed into service as a prison after the Union capture of Fort Donelson in February 1862. Courtesy Massachusetts MOLLUS Collection, United States Army Military History Institute, Carlisle Barracks, PA.

4. Another view of Camp Morton, showing the stream that ran through the middle of the camp. Courtesy Massachusetts MOLLUS Collection, United States Army Military History Institute, Carlisle Barracks, PA.

5. Confederate prisoners at Camp Douglas in Chicago in 1864. Another prison established to handle the Fort Donelson captives, Camp Douglas became one of the Union's largest prisons. Courtesy Massachusetts MOLLUS Collection, United States Army Military History Institute, Carlisle Barracks, PA.

6. Prisoners at Camp Chase Prison No. 3 pose for Columbus photographer Manfred M. Griswold. Despite the steeply sloped streets, drainage was a perennial problem at the prison. Courtesy National Archives, Washington, DC.

7. In addition to serving as a prison camp, Camp Chase was also a Union training facility for the entire war. This view shows the barracks for recruits. Courtesy National Archives, Washington, DC.

8. Established by William Hoffman, the Union commissary general of prisoners, Johnson's Island was the only Union prisoner of war camp designed specifically for that purpose. In 1862 it was set aside for Confederate officers. The prison was on Lake Erie adjacent to Sandusky, Ohio. Courtesy Sandusky County Library, Sandusky, OH.

9. A portion of the Hoffman Battalion, later incorporated into the 128th Ohio Infantry. The unit served as the guard force at Johnson's Island. Courtesy Sandusky Public Library, Sandusky, OH.

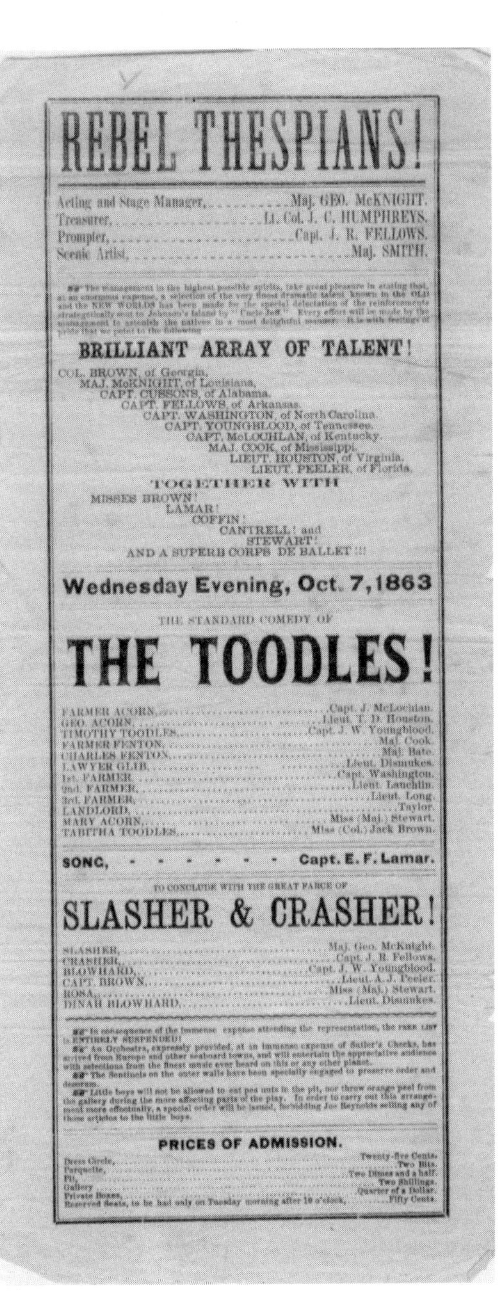

REBEL THESPIANS!

Acting and Stage Manager,............Maj. GEO. McKNIGHT.
Treasurer,..........................Lt. Col. J. C. HUMPHREYS.
Prompter,..........................Capt. J. R. FELLOWS.
Scenic Artist,..........................Maj. SMITH.

The management in the highest possible spirits, take great pleasure in stating that, at an enormous expense, a selection of the very finest dramatic talent known in the OLD and the NEW WORLDS has been made for the special delectation of the reinforcements strategetically sent to Johnson's Island by "Uncle Jeff." Every effort will be made by the management to astonish the natives in a most delightful manner. It is with feelings of pride that we point to the following

BRILLIANT ARRAY OF TALENT!

COL. BROWN, of Georgia,
MAJ. McKNIGHT, of Louisiana,
CAPT. CUSSONS, of Alabama.
CAPT. FELLOWS, of Arkansas.
CAPT. WASHINGTON, of North Carolina.
CAPT. YOUNGBLOOD, of Tennessee.
CAPT. McLOCHLAN, of Kentucky.
MAJ. COOK, of Mississippi.
LIEUT. HOUSTON, of Virginia.
LIEUT. PEELER, of Florida.

TOGETHER WITH

MISSES BROWN!
LAMAR!
COFFIN!
CANTRELL! and
STEWART!
AND A SUPERB CORPS DE BALLET !!!

Wednesday Evening, Oct. 7, 1863

THE STANDARD COMEDY OF

THE TOODLES!

FARMER ACORN,..........................Capt. J. McLochlan.
GEO. ACORN,..........................Lieut. T. D. Houston.
TIMOTHY TOODLES,..........................Capt. J. W. Youngblood.
FARMER FENTON,..........................Maj. Cook.
CHARLES FENTON,..........................Maj. Bate.
LAWYER GLIB,..........................Lieut. Dismukes.
1st. FARMER..........................Capt. Washington.
2nd. FARMER,..........................Lieut. Lauchlin.
3rd. FARMER,..........................Lieut. Long.
LANDLORD,..........................Taylor.
MARY ACORN,..........................Miss (Maj.) Stewart.
TABITHA TOODLES,..........................Miss (Col.) Jack Brown.

SONG, - - - - - - Capt. E. F. Lamar.

TO CONCLUDE WITH THE GREAT FARCE OF

SLASHER & CRASHER!

SLASHER,..........................Maj. Geo. McKnight.
CRASHER,..........................Capt. J. R. Fellows.
BLOWHARD,..........................Capt. J. W. Youngblood.
CAPT. BROWN,..........................Lieut. A. J. Peeler.
ROSA,..........................Miss (Maj.) Stewart.
DINAH BLOWHARD,..........................Lieut. Dismukes.

In consequence of the immense expense attending the representation, the FREE LIST is ENTIRELY SUSPENDED!

An Orchestra, expressly provided, at an immense expense of Sutler's Checks, has arrived from Europe and other seaboard towns, and will entertain the appreciative audience with selections from the finest music ever heard on this or any other planet.

The Sentinels on the outer walls have been specially engaged to preserve order and decorum.

Little boys will not be allowed to eat pea nuts in the pit, nor throw orange peel from the gallery during the more affecting parts of the play. In order to carry out this arrangement more effectually, a special order will be issued, forbidding Joe Reynolds selling any of those articles to the little boys.

PRICES OF ADMISSION.

Dress Circle,..........................Twenty-five Cents.
Parquette,..........................Two Bits.
Pit,..........................Two Dimes and a half.
Gallery..........................Two Shillings.
Private Boxes,..........................Quarter of a Dollar.
Reserved Seats, to be had only on Tuesday morning after 10 o'clock,..........Fifty Cents.

10. Filling the boring hours of captivity was a constant challenge for the prisoners. The performances of the Rebel Thespians provided a diversion for those at Johnson's Island. Courtesy of Sandusky Public Library, Sandusky, OH.

11. Located on Pea Patch Island in the Delaware River, Fort Delaware housed a small number of prisoners within its imposing walls. Courtesy Fort Delaware Society, Delaware City, DE.

12. The majority of Fort Delaware prisoners were housed in barracks adjacent to the fort. The swampy area produced numerous health problems. Courtesy Fort Delaware Society, Delaware City, DE.

13. Located at the confluence of the Potomac River and Chesapeake Bay, Point Lookout prison was established to accommodate the captives taken at Gettysburg. The buildings resembling spokes at the point were the Hammond General Hospital. The prison was on the bay (right) side of the camp. Courtesy Massachusetts MOLLUS Collection, United States Army Military History Institute, Carlisle Barracks, PA.

14. The busy wharf at Point Lookout. A number of prisoners volunteered to help unload the ships, returning to the camp with whatever supplies they could scavenge. Courtesy Massachusetts MOLLUS Collection, United States Army Military History Institute, Carlisle Barracks, PA.

15. Roll call at the Rock Island prison. This prison, established on the island in the Mississippi River, opened in December 1863 just in time to receive a wave of prisoners taken at Chattanooga. Courtesy Rock Island Arsenal Museum, Rock Island, IL.

16. "Riding the mule" was a common punishment at Union prisons. This shot was taken at Rock Island. Courtesy Rock Island Arsenal Museum, Rock Island, IL.

17. Guards from the 108th United States Colored Troops at Rock Island. Black recruits also served as guards at Elmira and Point Lookout. Courtesy Abraham Lincoln Presidential Museum, Springfield, IL.

18. Elmira was another Union prison established in 1864 to handle the dramatic increase in the prison population. At first tents were pressed into service to house the captives at the New York facility. Courtesy Massachusetts MOLLUS Collection, United States Army Military History Institute, Carlisle Barracks, PA.

19. Eventually barracks were built for the Elmira prisoners. Courtesy Massachusetts MOLLUS Collection, United States Army Military History Institute, Carlisle Barracks, PA.

20. Except for a few months in 1864 and 1865, Col. William Hoffman (right) served as the Union's commissary general of prisoners for the entire war. A capable administrator, he combined a penchant for thrift with a genuine concern for the welfare of Confederate prisoners. Courtesy Massachusetts MOLLUS Collection, United States Army Military History Institute, Carlisle Barracks, PA.

21. Gen. Henry W. Wessells served as commissary general of prisoners from November 1864 until February 1865. Although no reason was given for his appointment, he had been an advocate of retaliation against Confederate prisoners. Courtesy Massachusetts MOLLUS Collection, United States Army Military History Institute, Carlisle Barracks, PA.

22. Located near Fredericksburg, Belle Plain, Virginia, served as a holding camp for prisoners taken during Ulysses S. Grant's 1864 campaigns against Robert E. Lee's Army of Northern Virginia. Courtesy Massachusetts MOLLUS Collection, United States Army Military History Institute, Carlisle Barracks, PA.

8
"Don't be so hasty and you may get out"
The Possibility of Escape

As weeks and then months wore on, with nothing more than rumors offering hope for the resumption of exchange, Confederate prisoners realized that escape offered the only hope for a return home. The challenges were daunting. The first came in the form of a wall, patrolled by armed guards, that the men would have to get either under, over, or through. Once beyond the wall, a furtive journey through hundreds of miles of hostile territory lay ahead. For prisoners at Johnson's Island, Fort Delaware, and to a lesser extent, Point Lookout, bodies of water made the beginning of this journey all the more challenging. Even those meeting that challenge would face days of hunger, uncertainty, and often cold.

Although no Union prison commander encouraged escape, at least one recognized the inherent right of the prisoners to make the attempt. In a general order issued in October 1864, Col. Sweet, commanding Camp Douglas, informed the prisoners that he had information of a possible plot to escape. "Captivity is one of the incidents of war," Sweet wrote, "and a prisoner has a right to escape if he can, taking the risks and consequences. The Colonel Commanding blames no man for a desire to go from his custody, and in reversed positions, would beyond all doubt be actuated by the same motives." Having said that, Sweet added, "It is your right to escape, my business and duty to keep you." He would uphold his duty, Sweet wrote, by shooting any individual prisoner making the attempt. He further warned that in the event of an insurrection, he could not guarantee the safety of any prisoner, whether involved in the uprising or not. Although the conclusions were much the same, the language was more bizarre in an order Gen. Schoepf issued at Fort Delaware in August 1863. "Several prisoners have made the attempt to desert from this post," he wrote. "The Genl. Comdg. warns prisoners of war at this post to desist from all such attempts or plans to desert." The consequences, he ominously warned, could include turning the camp's artillery upon the prisoners' barracks.[1]

Whatever the attitude of the commanding officer, and whatever the difficulties and dangers connected with the attempt, prisoners from every Northern camp made efforts to defy the odds and return to Dixie. Their attempts took many forms. Tunneling was a popular although seldom successful method. On a number of occasions prisoners made plans to charge the gates or scale the walls with improvised ladders. Sometimes these attempts involved gathering stones with which to attack the guards. Prisoners also tried to plan these attacks for times when the guard force would be light or otherwise occupied. Clever individuals hid in wagons, barrels, or even coffins. Others fashioned makeshift blue uniforms and tried to pass through the gates as Union soldiers.

Regardless of the method they chose, the prisoners had to be extremely careful in selecting the men to be involved in the effort. Camp commanders often brought in detectives to infiltrate the ranks of the prisoners. Would-be escapees were often betrayed by their fellow captives, men who planned to take the oath of allegiance or simply hoped to secure extra rations or privileges. Dubbed "razorbacks" by their fellow prisoners, these men often rendered worthless the work of several weeks. On the night of June 2, 1864, Johnson's Island guards prevented the escape of a group of tunnelers. The work was completed, and the prisoners were only waiting for the evening to grow dark before departing. "They came straight to the spot without waiting to look around at all," prisoner Edmund Patterson wrote of the guards. "Some spy had told them all about it." One month earlier, the same scene had played out at Rock Island. The project was almost finished when the guards arrived on the scene. "I think some traitors reported them," surmised prisoner William Dillon. The next day four prisoners were placed in balls and chains for the attempt. Wilbur Gramling reached a similar conclusion when a nearly completed tunnel at Elmira was discovered that October. So did Camp Chase prisoner Henry Mettam, who was part of a group that spent three weeks digging with case knives. The men had removed the bricks in front of the stove in their barracks, dug down four feet, then headed for the fence. They believed they were close when the officer of the guard suddenly appeared at about midnight. He informed the men that their rations would be suspended until the tunnel was filled back in. "Even in prison there were traitors," Mettam concluded.[2]

Other Camp Chase prisoners found out that dumb luck could be just as effective as "traitors" in betraying tunnels. Heavy rains caused one tunnel at the Columbus depot to cave in. Writing after the war, R. M. Gray recalled a similar bit of bad fortune. "But for an accident," Gray wrote, a tunnel he helped dig "would have doubtless opened the outside world to our longing eyes." In this case, too, wet weather played a role in the prisoners' misfortune. So did the fact that their tunnel passed under a road used for daily wood deliveries. One of the wagon wheels broke through, betraying their plans.[3]

Burrowing out of camp did not always involve digging lengthy tunnels. Peter Williams of the Fifty-first Alabama made his escape from Camp Morton on September 1, 1864, by crawling up the stream running through the camp and digging under the floodgate. A heavy rain covered his effort, although a second prisoner who attempted to follow was captured. A North Carolina prisoner escaped from Camp Douglas in August 1864 by crawling to the fence and digging a hole under it. Ten prisoners used the same method to liberate themselves from Rock Island in October 1864. In reporting the incident to Hoffman, Johnson took pains to blame the "glaring negligence" of the black guards for the escape. Nevertheless, seven of the prisoners were quickly recaptured. Two months later six Rock Island prisoners crawled through a sewer that was being constructed at the camp. This time Johnson blamed the superintendent in the Quartermaster Department, who, the commander claimed, had improperly installed an iron gate where the trench intersected the prison fence.[4]

Ten Rock Island prisoners made their escape from an unoccupied hospital barracks on June 14, 1864. This time Johnson could find no one else to blame, which may explain why he failed to notify Hoffman of the incident until the 25th. The camp commander conceded that he had ordered trenches dug on the north, east, and west sides of the compound to prevent tunneling. On the south side, where the rock came close to the surface of the ground, he had considered a trench to be unnecessary. The escapees proved him wrong. Johnson was eventually able to report that all ten had been recaptured. Guards tracked down seven within a few hours of the escape. The other three were recaptured on June 29. Johnson also informed Hoffman that one of the ten, who was originally reported to have drowned in the slough, was among the first seven brought back. Prisoners had reportedly seen him struggle in the water then disappear. As it turned out, the man had collapsed from exhaustion, falling to his knees but not drowning.[5]

On the night of February 11, 1864, prisoners at Camp Morton put a carefully planned escape plot into effect. According to Col. Stevens, "several" prisoners had escaped the previous night. That occurrence, as well as information from unnamed sources that a second escape had been planned for the 11th, led him to strengthen the guard. Despite his effort, eighteen prisoners got away. The tunnel commenced at a barracks that was located eleven feet from the fence. The prisoners kept it concealed by nailing down the flooring over the opening each day. They got rid of the dirt by placing it in buckets mixed with ashes from the stove and the sweepings from the barracks floor. The night of the escape was especially dark, but the guards managed to shoot and kill one of the escapees. At the same time, a second group attempted to scale the fence at another point. The guards there opened fire. Although they did not hit anybody, their quick action prevented anyone in the second group from getting away. Only two of the eighteen men who made their escape through the tunnel were recaptured. To discourage future attempts, Stevens had a trench dug near the barracks closest to the fence and removed twenty feet from the end of those barracks. He also apparently instructed the guards to increase their vigilance. On March 13 Stevens informed Hoffman that four tunnels had been discovered since the escape.[6]

At Camp Douglas, too, successful tunnel escapes were occasionally followed by the discovery of other subterranean projects. One of them came closely on the heels of one of the largest mass escapes of the war. On December 3, 1863, Camp Douglas commandant Charles De Land reported to Hoffman that a large number of prisoners belonging to John Hunt Morgan's cavalry command had exited through a tunnel the previous night. They had begun crawling through at about 8:00, continuing at various intervals for an hour and a half, before they were discovered. "As near as I can ascertain now not far from 100 prisoners passed out. If there had been less hurry among them many more could have escaped," he added, a detail that he might have wisely omitted. An incredulous Stanton ordered Gen. William W. Orme to investigate. He discovered that the tunnel commenced under a barracks and continued for ninety feet. The men had deposited the dirt under the floor between the beams on which it rested. Orme exonerated De Land and the guards. "From my own experience and knowledge of the camp, I do not feel that I can censure any one for this escape. The camp is badly arranged for the custody of prisoners of war." He further reported that the night had been "very dark and in every way favorable to the escaping prisoners." Several had subsequently been recaptured, Orme informed Stanton, but he did not say how many.[7]

De Land decided to do all he could to prevent future escapes, regardless of the consequences. He informed Hoffman that he had ordered the flooring removed in all the barracks and cookhouses and the spaces between the support beams filled with dirt. "This will undoubtedly increase sickness and mortality," he blithely conceded, "but it will save much trouble and add security." If Hoffman objected, there is no record of it. According to Curtis Burke, the colonel also threatened to "turn us all out in the weather if we did not quit digging out." He added that the prisoners enjoyed "jumping around" on the exposed beams. De Land's increased security measures did pay some dividends. On December 18 guards discovered another tunnel. Morgan's men were also responsible for this one. Two of them admitted to being the instigators. Their confession kept the other men in the barracks out of the dungeon.[8]

Barracks were not the only starting points for Camp Douglas tunnels. Two months earlier, twenty-six prisoners had made their escape from the dungeon. De Land did not report the incident until prompted by a telegram from Hoffman, who had apparently learned of the escape from other sources. In his reply, De Land informed the commissary general that the prisoners had cut through the plank flooring and tunneled into an old sink that had been used for slops from a kitchen. From there they continued their tunnel, about ten feet below the ground, to a point outside the fence. De Land devoted the rest of his report to excuses. "We have lost quite a number of men this month besides these," he conceded, but asked Hoffman to "be patient a moment or two over it." He had arrived at the camp on August 18, the colonel wrote. "The whole thing, barracks, fences &c., were out of repair and very unsafe," he continued. Prisoners began arriving the next day, soon reaching five thousand in number. Since then numerous building, fencing, and sewer projects had taken place. The result was gaps in sections of fence and holes in the ground that provided tempting targets for escapees. De Land asserted, "I tell you frankly this camp has heretofore been a mere rookery; its barracks, fences, guard houses, all a mere shell of refuse pine boards; a nest of hiding places instead of a safe and compact prison, and my guard has never yet numbered over 900 effective men." The repair projects were nearly completed, the colonel concluded, and this he promised would bring an end to the escapes.[9]

This promise proved to be untrue, as the December escape demonstrated; and the tunneling continued into 1864. On March 21 a group of twelve prisoners was sent to the dungeon for tunneling under a barracks they were helping to build. The following night twelve men escaped from the dungeon. It is not known if any of the new arrivals were included. According to Curtis Burke, three did not get away until after dawn, and daylight prevented the escape of many others. Four days after these men made their getaway, an officer discovered a tunnel under a cooking stove in a barracks. Burke wrote that the tunnel was one night away from completion. Adding to the frustration of the men was the fact that seeping water from recent rains had delayed the work for two days.[10]

One of the most successful tunnel escapes took place at Elmira during the night of October 6–7, 1864. Ten prisoners made their exit, none of whom was recaptured. Although no detailed report of the escape survives among camp records, two of the participants, Washington Brown Traweek and Berry Benson, wrote thorough accounts following the war.

Traweek was a member of the Jeff Davis Artillery, an Alabama outfit. He had been captured on May 12, 1864, at the battle of Spotsylvania Court House. After spending a few weeks at Point Lookout, Traweek was among a group of prisoners transferred to Elmira in early July. A few days after their arrival, Traweek formed an alliance with John Fox Maull and John P. Putegnat, both members of his outfit, to start a tunnel. They began the operation on August 24. Digging in a vacant tent close to theirs, the men carefully removed the thick sod so it could be used to conceal their work.[11]

Traweek and his comrades dug down six feet before starting their horizontal shaft toward the wall. They worked at night, digging with pocketknives. To determine the distance they would have to tunnel, the men wrapped a thread around a stone, threw it to the wall, and reeled it back when the guards were not watching. It proved to be sixty-eight feet. They disposed of the dirt by placing it in sacks fashioned from one of Putegnat's shirts. These they hid under their clothing and carefully emptied into Foster's Pond. As stains from the clay in which they were working began to appear on the diggers' clothing, they turned their clothes inside out after completing a shift in the tunnel.[12]

It soon became obvious that more men would be needed to complete the project. The trio carefully recruited additional members. All were required to swear a solemn oath upon a Bible not to reveal the project and to "aid in putting to death any one of the party who became guilty of revealing the existence of the tunnel." The group soon grew to include Frank E. Saurine, S. C. Malone, Gilmer G. Jackson, William H. Templin, J. P. Scruggs, and Glenn Shelton. All proved to be safe choices, and two proved to be critical to the effort. One of the group was the "sick sergeant" of the ward. This position gave him access to the cook room, allowing him to sneak extra food to the hungry workers. Another was the ward sergeant. He kept the men abreast of impending inspections.[13]

Benson recruited himself. Like Traweek, Benson, a member of McGowan's South Carolina Brigade, was a former Point Lookout prisoner. He had escaped from the Maryland facility but was recaptured. As soon as he arrived at Elmira, Benson began to seek ways of liberating himself from his new prison. He discovered Traweek at Foster's Pond, disposing of dirt and stones from the tunnel. Approaching him, Benson said, "You'd better be careful; some fellow may see you and tell on you." Traweek tried to deny what he was doing, but when Benson offered to shield him from the sight of other prisoners, he quickly emptied his sacks. A few minutes later, Benson became the tenth member of the party.[14]

As work continued on the original tunnel, Traweek and Putegnat commenced a second shaft beneath a new hospital that camp officials were erecting. This nearly resulted in the end of the entire operation. The second tunnel was discovered, as was another one being worked under another hospital building by a separate party. Traweek soon found himself under arrest. Questioned by Maj. Colt, he remained true to his oath, revealing nothing. He was relieved to learn, through Colt's questioning, that officials knew nothing of the original tunnel. Placed in the dungeon, Traweek befriended James W. Crawford, who had been arrested for his participation in the other hospital tunnel. He swore Crawford in as the eleventh and final member of the group. Traweek's friends soon smuggled in a file, but he did not need it. After three weeks of confinement, he was able to persuade Colt to release him and Crawford. As he did so, Colt offered a piece of advice. "My lad," he said, "you were too hasty. If you had been more cautious and taken more time, you would have made your escape. Next time don't be so hasty and you may get out."[15]

During his confinement, Traweek had gotten word to the other tunnelers that prison officials knew nothing of their shaft. With this knowledge they resumed their effort. The men worked in pairs. The digger went in first, removing dirt and rock with a butcher knife the group had secured. Air was at a premium, and according to Benson, "A minute [at the end of the shaft] was enough to give one the most violent, racking headache." When the digger had scraped away so much dirt that it was in his way, he set down the knife and crawled backward, scooping dirt as he went. After dragging it the length of his body, he returned to his digging. Meanwhile, his partner removed the dirt. Although they still deposited much of the dirt in the pond, Benson devised several methods of getting rid of larger rocks. Some he tossed under buildings. Others he dropped down rat holes. Occasionally Benson and his comrades joined other Elmira prisoners in their frequent rat hunts, tossing the surplus rocks at real or imaginary rodents.[16]

As the work neared completion, the tramp of the guards overhead appeared to be some distance away. A few members of the party took a piece of tin to a spot in the yard that should have been directly above the end of the tunnel. They pounded on it as if they were fashioning a spoon, a common prison occupation, while a colleague listened below. The tin workers appeared to be far to the left of the proper location. A second experiment confirmed this. Benson located a prisoner with a ramrod, which he asked to borrow. One of the party drove it upward from the tunnel, while the others gathered at the presumed spot. As the ramrod emerged from the ground, one of the men stepped on it. The test confirmed that the men, all of whom were right-handed, had deviated ten feet from a straight line. A side benefit of the experiment was a hole that supplied fresh air to the diggers. The men covered it with a stone when it was not needed. The tunnelers soon worked well beyond this "ventilator," but they still managed to take advantage of it. The man working behind the digger remained beneath the air hole. He raked the dirt back to that spot then placed it in a wooden box attached to two cords. A man at the entrance of the shaft then pulled the box back to be emptied.[17]

On October 5 a measurement indicated that the men were near their objective. This time the sound of guards overhead confirmed their location. Ten men set the next night at 10:00 p.m. as the time of departure. The eleventh, the ward sergeant, who suffered from a shoulder wound, elected to remain behind. Camp rumors suggested that the sick and wounded were soon to be exchanged, and he chose to await this safer means of departure. Meanwhile, Benson and Traweek, battling headaches and nausea, worked feverishly to complete the tunnel. By the time they finished, it was well past midnight. They notified the other men, and as a sentinel shouted, "Half past three o'clock and all is well," Traweek emerged outside the wall. Crawford accompanied him. The others followed, exiting at intervals to diminish the chance of being spotted. For all, the journeys that lay ahead would be lengthy, circuitous, and dangerous. None were recaptured, although one member of the group was never heard from again. Benson reached Virginia on October 20. Traweek also headed for the Old Dominion, swimming the Potomac to reenter the Confederacy.[18]

For claustrophobic Confederates, scaling the fence provided another opportunity for escape. As did those who attempted to tunnel under the fence, prisoners trying to get over it had to conduct their activities surreptitiously or risk betrayal. As 1864 came to a close, a group of Camp Chase prisoners planned to make a break by clambering over the fence. "Such projicks look foolish to me," prisoner James Anderson wrote. Their plan was ruined on January 3, 1865, when a group of guards arrived and uncovered a variety of ladders, ropes, and hooks, which they required the conspirators to carry out of the barracks. "It was rather amusing to see the long faces of the Hook & Ladder Co as they went forward with their implements," Anderson wrote. He added, "I should hate to be the man that reported their project."[19]

On May 15, 1864, Camp Douglas guards confiscated what one prisoner termed "a ladder made of a splendid pattern." The man who made it ended up in the dungeon. At Johnson's Island a similar search conducted that same month yielded no ladders, although the guards did confiscate a pair of Confederate flags. Watching the thorough search through a window, Edmund Patterson reflected, "I could not help thinking that a carpet sack or a letter box was a rather strange place to look for a ladder."[20]

Getting over the fence, of course, was only the first step toward freedom, and for many prisoners it was as far as they got. Prisoners who made it over the north gate of Point Lookout shortly before midnight on July 28, 1864, soon found themselves in the hands of outside pickets and on their way to the guardhouse. On the night of December 12–13, 1864, a group of about twenty-five Johnson's Island prisoners made the attempt. The first shots chased all but about ten back to the barracks. One of those who continued, Lt. John Bowles of Louisville, Kentucky, was shot and killed, leaving his father, a prisoner at the same camp, to mourn his loss. According to Henry Parsons, a guard with the 128th Ohio, two others were wounded. Six made it over the fence, Parsons wrote, and four crossed the frozen lake to the mainland. All were recaptured by citizens and members of the 128th. According to William Peel, who was not a member of the escape party, the lack of cover hindered the escapees. The guards pursued them across open fields, and the alerted citizens had all roads covered. One prisoner, Peel wrote, numbed by the cold, lay down after reaching the mainland. This actually worked in his favor, as the guards passed by. Regaining his strength, the fugitive walked seven or eight miles during the night. When the cold again overcame him, he decided to risk all and stop at a farmhouse to seek aid. He asked the farmer for permission to come inside and get warm. "You cannot," the farmer told him, "I don't wish to arrest you, but I can't give you shelter." The desperate prisoner, knowing he could press on no farther, surrendered to the farmer, trading his freedom for shelter and warmth. That afternoon the farmer returned him to the camp.[21]

On three occasions, diarists at Camp Douglas recorded at least partially successful efforts to escape over the fence, although it cannot be said for certain that none were ever recaptured. On February 27, 1864, Curtis Burke wrote that four men using two ladders had made the attempt the previous night. Two succeeded, one was mortally wounded, and the fourth scampered back to his quarters undetected. The following June a pair of captives made their way into the camp's Union garrison and escaped over an unguarded section of fence. Thomas Beadles offered no details when he noted on December 27, 1864, that three prisoners had escaped the previous night "by running over the fence."[22]

On September 28, 1864, Col. Johnson reported to Hoffman that two prisoners confined to the hospital at Rock Island had escaped by placing a board against the fence. Only seven days earlier another patient had somehow secured a ladder and made good his escape. "The arrival of more troops has enabled us to double the guard around the hospital and increased security is anticipated," Johnson assured his boss. This apparently did not apply to the rest of the camp. On Christmas Day, 1864, Johnson reported that three prisoners had escaped with the aid of "a hastily constructed ladder." The men timed the guards on their beats to get over the fence before they were spotted. Despite what Johnson termed a "gauntlet of fire" from the guards, all three got to the frozen river and made it safely across.[23]

On a few occasions the desperation of the prisoners to escape reached the point that they attempted direct charges of the guards and the prison fence. One such incident, carried out by a dozen members of the Tenth Kentucky Cavalry, occurred at Camp Douglas on June 1, 1864. They assaulted the guards with a volley of bricks and used the same weapons to knock out one of the lamps in the prison yard. Col. Sweet placed much of the blame for the attempt on the guards' faulty weapons and the inability to secure replacements. He wrote Hoffman, "This attempt was encouraged by a knowledge gained on the part of the prisoners of war that the guns with which the [guards] on duty at the camp are armed are worthless." Four sentinels had attempted to fire, he informed the commissary general, but only one weapon had discharged. Fortunately a patrol guard armed with revolvers quickly arrived and quelled the disturbance. Sweet went on to insist that he had made the proper reports and requisitions to the ordinance office several months earlier and had received no response. The colonel asked for Hoffman's assistance in securing replacements. In the meantime, Sweet concluded, he would order every guard to be armed with a revolver.[24]

Securing proper weapons did not guarantee that the guards would use them properly. This fact was demonstrated on the evening of September 6, 1864, when another group of Confederate prisoners charged the fence at Camp Douglas. Six made their escape. A commission that investigated the incident concluded that the officer of the guard was derelict in his duty for not making sure that the guards' guns were loaded and in good condition before each relief was posted. The guards had fallen into the habit of exchanging their unused firing caps when relieving each other rather than discharging their weapons as required by regulations. The men did so to avoid cleaning their pieces. This practice rendered the caps useless. As a result, several weapons failed to discharge when the prisoners rushed the fence.[25]

The next assault against the fence at Camp Douglas occurred on the evening of September 27. Twelve prisoners, representing five different states, were involved in the attack. An unknown member of the party spearheaded the assault, throwing a blanket over either the fence or a lamp, depending upon which account one chooses to believe. Pvt. Lewis H. Moore of the Seventh Florida followed with a plank of wood, intended either to breach the fence or to allow the escapees a means of getting over it. Moore's designs can never be known because a guard shot him in the face and mortally wounded him before he could carry out the plan. Although one prisoner claimed to have heard some twenty-five shots, nobody else was injured. Moore's shooting thwarted the charge, and none of the prisoners escaped.[26]

Camp Morton was also prone to uprisings among the prisoners. In August 1864 Col. Stevens received reports of a "conspiracy among the prisoners in camp, the object of which was to rise on the guard and break out." The colonel ascribed the activity to a group of "influential" prisoners. Receiving orders to transfer five hundred Confederates to Fort Delaware, Stevens made it a point to include those he considered the leaders of the movement. He also doubled patrols inside and outside the camp and obtained four mountain howitzers with a supply of canister and other ammunition.[27]

These precautions were not enough. On the night of September 27, a night chosen for its extreme darkness, a group of approximately twenty prisoners assaulted the sentries on the platforms with a volley of stones. After drawing the guards' fire, they charged the fence with ladders. Some were fashioned from tent poles. Others consisted of the prisoners' short bunk ladders, which they had connected together. Two prisoners were shot and killed. Three escaped, although blood trails suggested that at least two had been hit. After the escape, camp officials found four ladders against the fence and five more lying nearby.[28]

The bloodshed did not serve long as a deterrent. On the night of November 14, another cloudy and dark night, forty-eight prisoners made their escape. The method was similar. While one group of prisoners attacked the sentinels with "stones and other missiles," another party rushed the fence between Posts 21 and 24 on the north side of the camp. They got over with ladders made from boards taken from the bottoms of their bunks. By November 23, when Stevens made his report to Hoffman, seventeen had been recaptured. The camp commander blamed the incident on the withdrawal of Veteran Reserve Corps troops, men "who had been long accustomed to this kind of duty." They had been replaced with men from the Sixtieth Massachusetts, a one-hundred-day regiment, whose term of service had actually expired at the time of the escape. This, Stevens asserted, had "emboldening effects on the prisoners."[29]

Camp Chase was the scene of a failed plot to charge the gate. Had bad luck not intervened, the July 4, 1864, effort could have been the camp's most successful escape, and one of the biggest from any Northern prison. The prisoners began to hatch their plot when they learned that many of their guards planned to attend an Independence Day picnic that morning. They knew the regularly scheduled arrival of the bread wagon was 10:00 a.m., at which time the gate would be thrown open. The conspiracy was a large one. One hundred men were selected to follow the wagon closely as it departed. When the vehicle reached the gate, the leader of this first wave would shout, "Fresh fish!" That was the signal for successive waves of prisoners, armed with rocks, to follow. Prison rules prevented large numbers of men from gathering, so they clustered in smaller groups, standing as near to the gate as they safely could. Remarkably, neither camp spies nor "razorbacks" betrayed the plot. It was the driver of the bread wagon who unintentionally foiled the plan. He, too, planned to attend the picnic, and he arrived one hour early that day. The first wave made the charge as planned, but the second group was caught unprepared. About twenty-one prisoners bolted through the open gate, where several guards, mounted and ready to depart for the picnic, met them. They quickly rounded up the escapees, shooting one in the arm, a wound that required amputation.[30]

For prisoners detailed on work parties, often beyond the walls, the temptation to attempt an escape was especially strong. Some of the resulting efforts appear to have been impromptu. For example, Col. Johnson reported on July 30, 1864, that Pvt. Henry Withen of the Forty-second Alabama managed to become separated from his fellow Rock Island workers. He hid in a nearby woods until it was safe for him to bolt for freedom. A Johnson's Island prisoner escaped from a watering party on December 24, 1864, and apparently made his way safely across the frozen lake and beyond to freedom. A group of prisoners working in the Garrison Square at Camp Douglas on June 20, 1864, made a sudden dash for the fence. Two got over, but both were soon recaptured. Elmira prisoner H. H. Wiseman did not elaborate when he recorded in his diary on December 30, 1864, "One of the Rebs who was on detail doing some work for the Yanks made his escape today."[31]

On at least three occasions members of prison work parties overpowered guards in their attempts to escape. One occurred at Camp Morton on September 2, 1864. Pvts. W. T. Davidson and T. J. Norman, both of the Ninth Tennessee Cavalry, were detailed to help haul garbage from the camp. One guard accompanied them. When the wagon was about two hundred yards from the camp, concealed by a ravine, the pair overpowered the guard, took away his weapon, and made their escape through a wooded area. An incident involving several more prisoners took place at Alton on September 9, 1864. Forty-six prisoners attacked their nine-man guard detail and managed to wrest away some of their weapons. The remainder of the detail responded promptly, killing seven and wounding five. All but two of the prisoners were recaptured. On May 30, 1864, seven prisoners received permission to go to a pump for a drink while doing landscaping work just outside the walls of Camp Chase. A lone guard accompanied them. The prisoners jumped him, relieved him of his weapon, and headed for a nearby woods. Guards quickly recaptured four of the men, but the other three, including two civilian prisoners, got away. In reporting the incident to Hoffman, Col. Richardson placed the blame on the officer in charge of the work party, who had permitted the men to separate from the group without adequate supervision.[32]

Rather than attacking guards, the prisoners occasionally resorted to attempts to bribe their keepers. On October 13, 1863, Col. De Land reported a "streak of bad luck" at Camp Douglas in the form of the escape of twelve prisoners over the course of two nights. De Land strongly suspected "collusion and bribery." He went so far as to arrest the guards he believed to be involved, placing them in irons. If he ever uncovered any proof of their culpability, De Land did not report it. Later that month a Camp Chase guard admitted in a letter home that one of his fellow sentinels was under arrest, charged with accepting a bribe from a prisoner and aiding him in escaping. The writer was quick to add that such attempts seldom succeeded.[33]

Prisoner diaries suggest that the guard was correct in his assessment. While such efforts at bribery usually helped line the pockets of the guards, they also generally resulted in the recapture of the prisoners. On September 8, 1864, Thomas Sharpe, a citizen prisoner at Camp Chase, wrote that the morning dawned with the shout of "Fresh fish!" It did not signal the arrival of new prisoners. Instead it marked "the return of some of our boys that thought they had the sentinels bribed to let them over the wall." They did make it over the wall, but that was as far as they got. The guards had armed men waiting beneath the parapet, and they quickly marched the five escapees back into the camp.[34]

In December 1863 a Johnson's Island guard pulled what one prisoner termed a "real yankee trick" when he accepted a gold watch and $100 from a group of prisoners. That guard, too, had men stationed outside the wall to recapture the entire party. At least one guard did not even bother to enlist the aid of his comrades. On January 13, 1864, six prisoners bribed a Camp Douglas sentinel. As they were about to depart the camp, the guard ordered them to halt, and for good measure shot one of the escapees, breaking his thigh.[35]

Throughout the war there were reports and rumors of outside parties aiding prisoners in escaping or assisting them once they had gotten beyond the prison walls. Hoffman addressed this issue in early 1862 when he ordered Col. Mulligan at Camp Douglas to admit no visitors. Mulligan ignored the order. In the fall of 1863, Hoffman backed De Land when he refused to honor passes issued by department headquarters to visit friends and family members of prisoners. In November 1863, Brig. Gen. Speed S. Fry, writing from Camp Nelson, Kentucky, informed his superiors that several prisoners who had recently escaped from Camp

Chase had been recaptured. According to Fry, the escapees boasted that Confederate sympathizers in Kentucky and other states had raised a fund "for the purpose of bribing the guard at Camp Chase and Camp Douglas to allow prisoners to escape." In May 1864, a recaptured Camp Douglas escapee informed Louisville's provost marshal that a woman living near the depot was "the principal instrument in assisting prisoners to escape. This she manages," the Kentucky official reported, "through her little daughter, who plays around in the vicinity unsuspected and manages to slip into the prisoners letters containing money & other articles."[36]

A much more serious plot was uncovered in late 1864. The elaborate affair involved the potential release of the prisoners at Johnson's Island as well as possible attacks upon various Lake Erie cities. This scheme had its genesis in April 1864, when President Jefferson Davis dispatched Jacob Thompson and two other agents to Canada. Once there, Thompson, who had served as secretary of the interior under James Buchanan, received word from Davis to "carry out the instructions you have received from me verbally." What those previous instructions were cannot be positively determined. What Thompson did was hatch a plot for the capture of the USS *Michigan.* The United States Navy's first ironclad ship, built in 1844, the *Michigan* was the only U.S. vessel patrolling Lake Erie during the Civil War. Its main duty was providing security for Johnson's Island.[37]

In July Thompson sent Capt. Charles H. Cole, formerly of Gen. Nathan Bedford Forrest's Cavalry Corps, to Sandusky. Posing as the secretary of a Pennsylvania oil company, Cole became a fixture in Sandusky society. He befriended officers from the *Michigan,* gaining such information as he could. Cole apparently enlisted Sandusky residents sympathetic to the South. He also made arrangements for several more conspirators to arrive at Sandusky by train the night of the operation to provide assistance once the vessel was captured. Finally, Cole met with John Yates Beall, whom Thompson had selected to assist Cole with the project. They set the date for September 19. On that evening Beall was to capture a vessel on the lake and direct it to the *Michigan.* Cole would already be aboard the Union ironclad, having scheduled a "wine drinking" with the officers. According to Thompson's subsequent report to Judah Benjamin, the Confederate secretary of state, once the *Michigan* was captured, a cannon shot through the officers' quarters at Johnson's Island "was to signify to the prisoners that the hour for their release had come." The prisoners would then somehow be mounted, making their way to Virginia via Cleveland and Wheeling.[38]

Although none of the conspirators were aware of it, the plot began to fall apart on September 17, when one of their members betrayed the plan. He was a former Confederate soldier who had become a refugee in Canada. He sought out Lt. Col.

Bennett Hill, commander of the District of Michigan, at Hill's Detroit hotel. "The plots are constantly being made here," Hill later reported, but the earnestness of the informant impressed him. He decided to alert Capt. John C. Carter of the *Michigan.* The informer also apparently revealed Cole's role in the plot because, after conferring with Col. Charles Hill at Johnson's Island, Carter had Cole arrested. Cole cooperated, revealing the identities of his Sandusky coconspirators and telling officials about the pending arrival by rail of some fifty others.[39]

Unaware of these developments, Beall and a group of men he had enlisted seized two Lake Erie passenger ferries, the *Philo Parsons* and the *Island Queen.* The unusual activity on the lake aroused the suspicion of John Brown Jr., son of the fanatic abolitionist, who owned a vineyard on South Bass Island. With three other men, Brown rowed across a dangerously choppy lake from Put-in-Bay to warn Col. Hill at Johnson's Island that something was afoot. Beall's first inkling that things had gone wrong came when he failed to receive an expected signal from Cole. Although he wanted to see the plan through, his crew members did not, and it was their view that prevailed. They attempted to scuttle both vessels before returning safely to Canada. The cooperative Cole was confined at Fort Lafayette, where he remained until 1866. Beall was captured, convicted as a spy, and hanged on February 24, 1865.[40]

Although Thompson had reported that a cannon shot from the *Michigan* was intended to alert the prisoners to their liberation, there is no evidence that they were directly involved in the plot. Indeed, Johnson's Island diarists recorded the events as if they had no prior knowledge. "Yankees terribly frightened at the discovery of a plot to capture the Michigan (Gun Boat) and release the prisoners confined here," Edmund Patterson wrote on September 21. After noting that the plot had been exposed, Patterson added, "I hope they will try it again." John Joyes wrote, "Great excitement prevails in regard to a supposed conspiracy to relieve all of the prisoners on this island by sympathizers. It is believed within the 'Bull Pen' to be a hoax." According to William Peel, the prisoners first believed that the men brought over to the island from Sandusky on September 20 had been arrested for opposition to the draft. Only later did they learn that "they were implicated, or supposed to be, in a scheme to take the island and release the prisoners. There seems to have been such a project on foot," he added. Peel discovered more details the next day in a Sandusky newspaper.[41]

The Johnson's Island plot had ripple effects in Chicago. On September 22 Col. Sweet informed Hoffman that "simultaneous with" the Lake Erie incident, "a plot was discovered on the part of the prisoners of war here to make a concerted and combined attempt to overcome the guard and escape." The alleged attack, Sweet continued, was to be made in conjunction with a draft call scheduled to take place in the city. According to Sweet, he had determined to allow the prisoners to make the attempt "and make dispositions accordingly." The instigators became suspicious, however, and failed to carry through with the plot. Sweet concluded, "It is observable that the prisoners are restive and inventive to an uncommon degree of late."[42]

Sweet's report was lacking in details, most likely because the commander had few to offer. Despite that fact, Sweet eventually oversaw a series of arrests. Included in the November roundup were several Chicago residents, many allegedly members of the "Sons of Liberty," a pro-Southern organization operating in the North. Others were listed as "bushwhackers, guerrillas, and rebel soldiers." A military trial, held in Cincinnati, followed. The prosecution case hinged largely on the testimony of John T. Shanks of the Fourteenth Kentucky Cavalry. A Texan, Shanks had spent time in the penitentiary for fraud. Later, after enlisting to get out of prison, he had deserted from the Fifteenth Texas Cavalry. He ended up with Morgan's Raiders, service that landed him in Camp Douglas. Research conducted by Camp Douglas historian George Levy demonstrates that Sweet employed Shanks as a detective. The trial resulted in three convictions, including George St. Leger Grenfell, a native of England, who received the death sentence. This was later commuted to life in prison. The show trial, Levy concludes, played into the desires of individuals on both sides eager to believe that a dangerous conspiracy had existed. "Confederate agents wished themselves into believing they had created one," he concluded, "and General Sweet made their dreams come true."[43]

With conspiracies generally failing, whether they originated within or without their prison fences, many Confederate captives resorted to individual ingenuity. Johnson's Island prisoner Theodore P. Hamlin of the Eighteenth Tennessee tried a unique but woefully naive tactic in November 1864. "My term of service was out the first of May last," he informed his father in a letter, "and as I did not reinlist, and am now captured, I would like to quit the service, if you can arange it in any way so I can be releised." Two months later a disappointed Hamlin asked his father to try to secure a parole for him. A more dangerous naiveté was demonstrated by the brother of an escaped Rock Island prisoner. In January 1865 he sent a letter to camp officials asking that a box of provisions he had sent to his brother be returned. He explained that his brother was no longer at the camp. Johnson concluded that the man could not have known that fact unless he had seen—and was possibly harboring—the escapee. The colonel believed this information might lead to the recapture of the prisoner. If it did, no record of it remains.[44]

One of the most common methods employed by individual prisoners was to sneak out of camp in disguise. These efforts took a variety of forms. In 1862 a number of Gratiot Street prisoners escaped from the St. Louis pen "in disguise as negroes." Officials offered no details, but one suggested that black prisoners no longer be housed at the facility. Soon after his arrival at Camp Douglas, Curtis Burke noted that escapes were "a common nightly occurrence." Two had gotten away on the night of September 6, 1863, in civilian clothing. Burke added his suspicion that bribery was also a factor in the escape. The following May Burke wrote of a similar attempt foiled by the stupidity of a fellow prisoner. A group of thirty visitors was enjoying a tour of the camp. One of the prisoners donned civilian clothing and joined the party as it departed. He was nearly out when his fellow prisoner greeted him, thus alerting the otherwise unsuspecting guards. A similar disappointment befell a Johnson's Island prisoner who passed out in dress similar to the camp sutler's. He got aboard the ferry to Sandusky and was bound for freedom when a guard recognized him.[45]

During the fall of 1864 a pair of Rock Island prisoners combined disguise and forgery to effect their escape. Contract surgeons at the camp were given passes, which they were required to present when entering and leaving the facility. The two prisoners made fake passes, dressed as the civilian surgeons, and were allowed to pass beyond the gates. Johnson reported to Hoffman that the passes were "correct imitations of those issued by proper authority." He suspected that a disloyal surgeon had provided the escapees with a pass to copy, but he had no proof.[46]

Despite frequent searches, prisoners occasionally managed to conceal homemade blue uniforms that they used to escape. This method was especially favored by the officers confined at Johnson's Island. James Mayo wrote that "some" had used that method to depart the island on February 21, 1864. The men were part of the water detail and apparently wore the uniforms beneath their clothing. The lake was frozen, and they walked to freedom. Another tried the same tactic a month later, but the ice was too thin, and he had to return.[47]

On August 8, 1864, Col. Hill received a "confidential note from a prisoner vaguely cautioning me that a plot was on hand requiring my immediate attention." Hill ordered the guard force increased and had a patrol of eighty men ready to conduct a search if necessary. The commander then questioned the sentinels at the gates and discovered that one had allowed several men to pass out. Hill's patrol scoured the island, discovering eighteen Confederates. All wore regulation blue trousers and shirts that were similar to Federal uniforms. A search of the barracks uncovered several more articles of blue clothing. A roll call further revealed that two prisoners were missing. The pair, Hill later learned, had escaped on the 6th. Other prisoners had answered for them at roll calls as they made their way to Canada.[48]

According to Edmund Patterson, the first escapee had secured a shovel and passed out with a work party. This proved to be an inspiration, and the next day groups of about half a dozen accompanied every wagon exiting the camp. William Peel confirmed Patterson's account, noting, "Every body that could raise a suit was trying the trick." The scheme came to an abrupt end when a prisoner in a red shirt made the attempt. A sentinel challenged him. The prisoner insisted that he was a Union soldier, but when the guard asked him to identify his company, the man hesitated. Contradicting Hill's story of the anonymous note, Peel insisted that it was this incident that led to the search of the island.[49]

No Johnson's Island prisoner was more persistent in his efforts to get away than Charles Pierce. On December 12, 1864, he was part of a group that attempted to scale the wall of the camp. Pierce made it over but was recaptured a few miles away. Undeterred, he joined a tunneling party. The group was caught, and a guard informed Pierce that he had known of the effort within a half hour after it began. He proved this by telling Pierce what time the digging had started. At this point Pierce decided to resort to deviousness. He not only secured a genuine Federal uniform but also fashioned a prop rifle with a wooden stock and a tin barrel. On the night of January 15, 1865, Pierce told a sentinel that a mass breakout was being planned for 8:00. Guards quickly descended upon the barracks in question, searching for ladders and other tools. Finding none, they decided the report was false. As they departed, Pierce fell in with the squad. He had nearly made it to the gate when an officer asked him where his cartridge box was. Pierce replied that he had forgotten it in the rush to get to the barracks. At that point another member of the squad said, "That's a hell of a gun you've got anyhow." The game was up, and Pierce soon found himself in Col. Hill's office. According to one prisoner, the commander "laughed very heartily when the case was laid before him," complimenting Pierce on his ingenuity.[50]

At Rock Island a prisoner in a Northern uniform secured Federal transportation to get beyond the gates. In September 1864 Sgt. David H. Ross of the Eighth Georgia Infantry disguised himself as a Union soldier and wrapped himself in a blanket. He then climbed into an ambulance that was transporting sick members of the garrison to a hospital outside the camp. A second prisoner, taking advantage of the dark night, concealed himself beneath the carriage of one of the doctors and also gained a ride for the first leg of his journey home.[51]

Other means of escape were even more ingenious. On September 30, 1864, Curtis Burke wrote that a Morgan cavalryman had himself lightly nailed inside a vinegar barrel. A burly fellow prisoner carried the barrel to a junk pile inside the garrison square. After dark the man kicked out the weakly secured barrelhead. The patrol was light, and the prisoner, clad in blue, quickly made his way out of camp. In November 1864 an Elmira prisoner rode out in the "dead wagon," the vehicle used to transport bodies from the camp to the nearby cemetery. Prisoners recorded two versions of the incident. According to diarist Henri Mugler, the man paid the driver a bribe of $8. Writing after the war, J. B. Stamp offered a more entertaining version of the story. Stamp wrote that the prisoner concealed himself inside a coffin. After the wagon had passed a safe distance outside the camp, the lid sprang open, and the escapee bolted away—as did the frightened driver.[52]

At Point Lookout, the waters of Chesapeake Bay discouraged most prisoners from attempting to escape. Others, however, saw the bay as a means toward an end, and some of those prisoners fashioned homemade boats to attempt a voyage to Virginia. On February 14, 1864, Charles Hutt wrote that a routine search of the prison resulted in the discovery of two such vessels. Prison records leave no report of such an attempt succeeding. However, in a postwar account, former Point Lookout prisoner C. W. Jones wrote that on one occasion a group of prisoners got away aboard a sailboat they had made from cracker boxes.[53]

The Delaware River held out similar opportunities for daring Fort Delaware prisoners. Depending on the tides, the Delaware shore was between twelve hundred and two thousand yards away. Swimming was a possibility, but the risks were great. Sharks frequented the river, and there were floating chunks of ice during the winter months. Strong tidal currents that could carry a swimmer out into Chesapeake Bay posed an additional hazard. Despite the risks, men occasionally made the attempt. On July 15, 1862, A. F. Williams recorded that some thirty had made it to the beach and "speedily constructed a small raft out of some rubbish." A heavy wind swamped the impromptu vessel. Two drowned, and at least eighteen more were recaptured. Guard A. J. Hamilton noted two unsuccessful attempts in 1863. On August 13 he wrote that a schooner used to patrol the river returned four prisoners found attempting to swim to freedom. At least two, Hamilton added, were "in a drowning condition." On November 14 five Confederate captives attempted to get away on a raft. Although Hamilton did not record the details, he wrote that three drowned in the effort and the other two were recaptured. Diarist George Washington Hall wrote that many of his fellow prisoners made the attempt during the summer of 1864. Guards confiscated all canteens, he noted, after learning that some of the swimmers had used them as flotation devices.[54]

If such methods were unusual, the results were far from being atypical. Despite the resourcefulness of the prisoners in plotting and executing their escape attempts, the odds against them generally proved to be too great. From July 1862, when prison records were first recorded, until the end of the war, 1,210 Confederate captives escaped from Union prisons. Of this number, 310 escaped from Camp Douglas and 231 from the small prison facility at New Orleans, representing nearly 45 percent of the total. This suggests that prisoners not fortunate enough to be held in either the Windy City or the Crescent City faced especially daunting challenges in getting away. Although the successful attempts make for exciting narratives, they represent the efforts of a fortunate few whose dreams of freedom became a reality.[55]

9
"Almost starving in a land of plenty"
Rations and Retaliation

In general, there were two methods of preparing and eating rations at Union prison camps. At about half of the camps prisoners cooked and ate in their own barracks. At other facilities there were mess rooms into which the prisoners paraded for their meals. Prisons in the former group included Camp Chase, Camp Douglas, Camp Morton, and for most of the war, Johnson's Island. A similar system was used at Rock Island, where the prisoners ate in separate rooms connected to their barracks. At those camps rations were issued anywhere from daily to every ten days. Prisoners in each barracks divided the mess chores. At Curtis Burke's Camp Douglas barracks this included drawing the rations, cooking, washing the dishes, fetching water, and sawing and splitting wood. Johnson's Island prisoner Edmund Patterson dreaded his turn for mess duty. "Each day we have three men detailed whose duty it is to set the table[s], clear them off, sweep the rooms, scour the knives and forks, receive and divide the rations, and etc., and all this to do three times during the day, and this is what I have been doing today, and those who have had experience in the matter will agree that it is no small job, where there are between eighty and one hundred men to feed."[1]

The supplies for cooking and eating were skimpy. Former Camp Chase prisoner Joseph Kern recalled being in a barracks where each of the thirty-six prisoners received a plate, cup, knife, and fork. There was also an ample supply of pots, frying pans, and coffeepots, Kern insisted. His, however, was a minority view. Another Camp Chase prisoner, James Mackey, wrote upon his arrival that his mess of twenty men had to share just six knives and forks. Rock Island prisoner William H. Davis noted that his barracks, containing 120 men, was furnished with nothing more than twenty tin cups. At Camp Douglas Burke supplemented his insufficient store of cooking supplies on two occasions, once through purchase and once by stealing them from a hospital building that was not being used.[2]

Cooking at virtually every camp was done with "farmer's boilers." Hoffman described them as "the most economical and convenient [means] for cooking for prisoners," and he urged all camp commandants to use them. "Those in which the boiler sits inside an outer case are much better than the kind where the boiler is placed on top of the furnace," he further instructed one camp commander. By "better" the frugal commissary general was speaking solely in terms of expense. To Stanton he explained, "I found at all the camps camp-kettles, skillets, and frying pans in general use, which wasted the rations, and in consequence of the numerous fires used required an extravagant quantity of fuel." The boilers, he promised would "remedy this great evil." Hoffman remained almost obsessed with the devices, even in the face of commanders who disagreed with their utility. When Col. De Land pronounced them "a failure," Hoffman shot back, "The Farmer boilers are in use in several camps under my charge and are found to be the most convenient mode of cooking, and if they have failed at Camp Douglas it is because those who used them did not want [them] to succeed." At Camp Chase Richardson described the boilers as "worthless," prompting Hoffman again to extol their virtues and insist that they "have been very successfully introduced into all [other] prison camps." At one camp, at least, the prisoners disagreed. When the boilers replaced cooking stoves at Camp Douglas, forty-one members of one barracks signed a petition to retain the stoves. The hospitals were crowded, the prisoners noted, meaning that many men had to be cared for in the barracks. "By means of the cooking stoves, delicacies suitable to their condition can be prepared," they explained. "But the boiler would be totally inadequate to this purpose!"[3]

However the rations were prepared, the system of cooking in the barracks was universally criticized by inspectors who visited the various prisons. "There is no good system for cooking, each man being left to arrange for himself," an inspector sent by Stanton wrote of the situation at Camp Douglas. A medical inspector dispatched to the Chicago prison agreed, writing, "the arrangements for cooking are deficient or entirely wanting, and the food is improperly prepared, and much waste prevails." At the small Gratiot Street and Myrtle Street prisons in St. Louis the surgeon in charge of the hospital wrote, "The practice of cooking and eating in the rooms should be discontinued. It produces filth and confusion. In one room at Myrtle street I found two men roasting pork over the stove, the fumes filling the room and the fat soaking the floor."[4]

These reports were generally ignored by Union officials, and the prisoners continued to eat in their quarters. An exception was Point Lookout, where Hoffman granted permission to Marston to erect mess houses in October 1863. That, however, was only because Stanton refused to allow barracks to be constructed to replace the tents in which prisoners were housed. Elmira had mess halls from its inception as a prison. They went up at Fort Delaware in late 1863, when barracks were also erected to accommodate a dramatic increase in the prison population.[5]

Only at the officers' prison at Johnson's Island did a medical inspector's warnings produce a change in eating arrangements. On July 23, 1864, Surgeon Charles T. Alexander wrote that the erection of two large mess halls would improve both the policing and the health of the camp. Five days later Hoffman ordered Hill to have the structures built. The work was to be done quickly and cheaply, with either gravel or "rough board" floors. They were to be equipped, of course, with farmer's boilers. The mess halls were occupied in early September. According to Lt. Col. Edward Scovill, the superintendent of prisons, they led to "a decided improvement in the police of the quarters."[6]

Although prison inspectors preferred mess halls to cooking in barracks, not all prisoners shared this view. "The eating arrangements I do not like," wrote Point Lookout prisoner Robert Bingham, who had been transferred from Johnson's Island. "We have a large dining room & are marched out, dinner on plates, regular convict style." E. L. Cox, confined at Fort Delaware, complained, "The dining room is a large hall about sixty by eighty feet with tables running length wise placed so near together that two men cannot go abreast between them." Guards were posted at each door, Cox added, to prevent the prisoners from "flanking" extra rations. For the same reason, Fort Delaware prisoners had to wait until everyone had eaten before they could leave the mess hall. When they entered mess sergeants chosen from their barracks made sure that prisoners from other squads did not sneak in.[7]

For most of the war rations at Union prisons were sufficient but little more. After visiting all the western prisons in the fall of 1863, Brig. Gen. William W. Orme used such terms as "abundant" and "good quality" in describing the rations. At Camp Douglas he listed the rations as "three quarters of a pound of bacon (1 pound of fresh beef three times a week), good well-baked wheat bread, hominy, coffee, tea, sugar, vinegar, candles, soap, salt, pepper, potatoes, and molasses." He reported that the same rations were issued at Camp Morton. Medical inspector G. K. Johnson visited Fort Delaware in February 1864. He found that during the previous month the 2,747 prisoners had received 48,675 pounds of fresh beef, 20,113 pounds of potatoes, and 74,734 pounds of flour. Also included were salt pork, bacon, cornmeal, beans, rice, coffee, sugar, vinegar, salt, pepper, and molasses. This diet, he concluded, could be "considered fair, both as to quantity and quality," but he recommended that more vegetables be issued to arrest a recent outbreak of scurvy. In forwarding the report to Schoepf, Hoffman wrote, "Such vegetables may be purchased as you may deem necessary."[8]

The prisoners' views of their rations were more mixed. Recalling his imprisonment at Camp Chase, Joseph Kern wrote that his fare included "flour, or hard tack, or corn meal—beef, or bacon, or mess pork, rice, hominy, & potatoes, coffee, sugar, salt and occasionally molasses. They were generally of good quality and enough to supply our wants," Kern added. Former Elmira prisoner J. B. Stamp recalled, "Our breakfast consisted of about five ounces of bread, or five or six small crackers; three or four ounces of boiled beef, or salt pork, and a cup of weak coffee. Dinner was the same amount of bread, and a pint of rice or bean soup." As at other camps, Elmira prisoners received only two meals a day. However, Stamp noted, "The prisoner who was so fortunate as to get a small piece of meat in his soup was regarded with envy by his comrades, and he considered that he was in a good condition to do without supper." Camp Chase prisoner James Anderson considered his rations, which were similar to Stamp's, to be sufficient. Because of the prisoners' idle lives, he noted, more food could "breed diseases."[9]

Johnson's Island prisoner Virgil Murphey was philosophical about the rations he and his fellow officers received. The bread, prepared in a prison bakery, he termed "heavy and of a liquid mushy character. The authorities doubtless think it much better and more preferable than any we can make," he wrote. "In this way they are sadly in error." As to the quantity, "To assert that the ration is sufficient and that we are never annoyed with the pangs of hunger would be to contradict the experience of every denizen in the 'pen.' That it will support and maintain life is equally true and unquestionably." He further asserted that a man's stomach "demands more in prison than at home or in the army. It is true that we undergo no labor, no hardships, no exposure, no violent exertions to weary our strength," he conceded, "and yet we crave more food than when we were subjected to the above occurrences. It's because we think more of it."[10]

The quality of rations was often more a source of complaint than the quantity. "We draw fresh beef every other day," a Camp Douglas prisoner wrote, "but it is not the number one article being mostly neck, flank, bones and shanks." Johnson's Island prisoner John M. Porter was indignant when he received rations that were spoiled to the point that they could not be eaten. "The generous Yankees always feed us well, they say, yet here is truth to be pushed in their teeth," he wrote. "Do our men at Richmond give yankees spoiled provisions?" Thomas Sharpe had better luck. When his Camp Chase mess drew spoiled beef, they were able to exchange it for some that was better.[11]

Problems with inferior rations—and the men who provided them—often proved difficult for prison officials to deal with. Early in the war Lazelle reported to Hoffman that Capt. Benjamin Walker, the commissary officer at Camp Chase, was lax in performing his duties. As a result contractors were getting away with supplying inferior provisions to the prisoners. The charges were so serious and so well substantiated that Walker was dismissed from the service. The disgraced officer, however, numbered among his friends Schuyler Colfax, a powerful Republican representative from Indiana. Colfax pulled strings, and Lincoln ordered Walker restored. Numerous scandals concerning the quality and quantity of rations swirled about Camp Douglas. All centered on Capt. Ninian W. Edwards, who allowed contractors to supply rations directly to the prisons without regard to the camp commissary. The evidence against Edwards was serious, but his wife was the sister of Mary Todd Lincoln. Eventually five subcontractors were required to refund $1,416.89 for "deficiencies in Beef Soap and Molasses." Edwards avoided any penalties.[12]

Officials at Johnson's Island battled with both their own officers and Sandusky contractors to see to it that the government and the prisoners were not cheated. On August 22, 1864, Hill informed the camp's commissary of subsistence, "I have it upon reliable authority that your subordinates issue necks, shanks, hearts and livers quite generally to prisoners, and shanks, hearts, and livers occasionally to [Federal] troops, weighed up in each instance with 'beef', and accounted for as beef in provision return." Hill demanded that the problem be corrected. "It is your duty and my duty and the duty of all of us to see that the prisoners are faithfully, and honestly dealt with," the commander added. Three months later Hill directed that the beef contractors in Sandusky be warned to quit sending an inferior product to the island. Writing on Hill's behalf, a junior officer informed the supplier, "The quality of the lot of fresh beef yesterday inspected and ordered to be thrown back on your hands was disgraceful to you, and it will not be condusive to your interest to repeat the experiment."[13]

If they found either the quality or the quantity of their rations to be insufficient, prisoners could occasionally find ways to supplement what was issued. One option was to secure a place on a prison work detail. In the summer of 1864 Rock Island officials needed help to construct a sewer. Johnson sought guidance from Hoffman, who responded with a circular establishing policies for prison labor. It set wages for mechanics at 10¢ a day and for laborers at 5¢ a day. The prisoners had the option of receiving the wage in tobacco. They would also receive extra rations. There were risks, however. Adam D. Thompson of the Forty-fifth Tennessee died while working on the Rock Island sewer project. He failed to get to safety while blasting and was struck in the back of the head with a sharp piece of wood that killed him instantly.[14]

At Point Lookout, which was remotely located, prisoners made up for a shortage of labor. One of their chief duties was unloading supply ships at the wharf. "The prisoners very cheerfully volunteer to be so employed, as it relieves them from the ennui of confinement," Hoffman reported to Stanton. Prisoner William Haigh suggested that extra coffee, sugar, and tobacco, which the prison laborers received weekly, were stronger incentives. George Peyton found an even better reason to volunteer. Filling in for a friend on October 3, 1864, Peyton found himself carrying empty barrels from the bakery to the dock. He returned with three loaves of bread, which a friend had sneaked to him, and two empty bags that he planned to make into a bed tick. Several weeks later Peyton got "an armful of hay." He sold it in camp for 10¢ and used the money to purchase stamps. He later spent a cold December morning shoveling coal onto a boat, returning with a few chunks for fuel. Peyton's biggest windfall came on New Year's Day, 1865. A shipload of beef arrived late in the day, and the Yankees offered a drink of whiskey to anyone who would help unload it. "To this we agreed and we made the beef fly." In addition, Peyton recorded, "We brought in a lot of plunder. Wood, apples, beef, crackers, and flour."[15]

Short of exchange, there was perhaps no happier news in the life of a prisoner than word that a box of provisions had arrived. With it came the likelihood of clean clothes, reading material, and most important, delicacies not otherwise available. "I had the pleasure of receiving by express a couple of boxes which upon being opened proved to be filled with the greatest variety of niceties," William Peel noted on March 31, 1864. "An elegant ham, several pounds of sausage, quite a number of oranges & lemons, & several pounds of sugar presented themselves in one, while the other contained quite a supply of chewing & smoking tobacco, a lot of candy, & several dozen new biscuits." The next day Peel's Johnson Island block enjoyed "a splendid dinner . . . in which several friends & myself indulged to such an excess as to render our conditions rather uncomfortable during the ballance of the day."[16]

"I am Lucky about boxes now," Robert Bingham wrote from Johnson's Island in September 1863. One contributor had sent clothing and handkerchiefs. From a group of friends and relatives he received peaches, tomatoes, a ham, and ketchup. Another Johnson's Island prisoner, James Archer, informed a friend that he had "dined out (not outside the prison) with the mess of Col. Jones who had received a present from some friends near Chicago of Catawba wine." He added that he planned to eat with another mess that had also been sent "a box of good things."

Charles Hutt wrote that his cousin had been "very kind to me since my imprisonment." Reading material, oranges, and lemons composed one of the boxes she sent to the Point Lookout prisoner. James Anderson later wrote that a colonel in his Camp Chase mess often received "a box of choice provisions" from family members. The supplies were so bountiful that "all together we lived too well for prisoners."[17]

Not every prisoner enjoyed such windfalls. Many came from families who simply could not afford to purchase and ship such luxuries. According to one Camp Douglas prisoner, geography also played an important role. William Milton recalled, "The poor fellows from Florida, Georgia, and the other [deep] southern states had no friends to send them clothing or good things to eat, and consequently they fared much worse than the men from Missouri, Maryland, Tennessee and Kentucky." At least one Elmira prisoner confirmed this claim. Wilbur Gramling, a Florida native, wrote in his diary, "Boxes of clothing, etc. and money are being sent in daily to the men from their relatives and friends but I am somewhat among the unfortunate."[18]

The sutler stand offered another option for hungry soldiers. Rock Island prisoner Lafayette Rogan enjoyed a New Year's dinner in 1864 that included meats, oysters, cheese, cakes, pies, fruits, and milk. All had been purchased from the sutler by Rogan's three hosts, who had enough left over to invite him back the following night. Other prisoners used the sutler stand to supplement their rations on a day-to-day basis. Inmates of Robert Bingham's Johnson's Island block combined their resources, at a cost of 8¢ to 10¢ a man per day, to purchase butter and milk for breakfast and potatoes and onions for supper. William J. Davis was the cook for his mess at Fort Delaware in July 1864. After securing the rations of bread and meat he purchased an onion or some other item from the sutler to create "a hash or 'cush,' which, with coffee or tea likewise obtained, forms our principal diet."[19]

All of this, of course, came at a price. Sutlers enjoyed a monopoly and a captive market. As a result, their prices were often considerably inflated. At Johnson's Island L. B. Johnson, who owned the island, also served as sutler for much of the war. In addition to charging exorbitant prices, Johnson developed a knack for creativity in cheating the Confederate captives. On one occasion he required prisoners to purchase pictures of the island at $3 apiece before he would sell them anything else. Camp officials soon stopped the practice. Another time he offered oil lamps for sale. They proved to be a popular item. However, when the prisoners returned to replenish their supply of lamp oil, they were informed that the oil was contraband and could no longer be purchased. This may not have been Johnson's fault, but his refusal to take the lamps back on exchange angered his customers. One was so upset that he struck the sutler in the head with the useless item, smashing the lamp and dropping Johnson to the ground. According to one prison diarist the attacker got away before the sutler could recover to identify him.[20]

Prisoners without money were very limited in their options if they desired to supplement the rations issued to them. The same laissez-faire system that gave the captives almost unlimited freedom to pursue various vocations worked against prisoners lacking in those abilities. This resulted in a cultural Darwinism that produced a stratified society of haves and have-nots. Randolph Shotwell, whose postwar memoirs were anything but kind to the Yankees, indicted his fellow prisoners for this situation. "It must be confessed," Shotwell wrote, "that a portion of the officers [at Fort Delaware] were reprehensible in their thoughtlessness, or want of consideration, for the sufferings of their less fortunate circumstanced fellow prisoners." Shotwell claimed that many who received all they wanted to eat from boxes sent from home and purchases made at the sutler stand declined to share even their prison rations with those in need.[21]

Two Fort Delaware diarists confirmed much of what Shotwell claimed. "Those who have meens of geting money here almost board themselves from the sutler," E. L. Cox wrote. George Washington Hall, who was on the wrong side of the equation, wrote poignantly of his plight. "Those of the prisoners who were fortunate enough to have green backs in their possession when captured & also those who have friends or relatives inside the Federal lines, have every thing they want in abundance but us who have no friends nor money are in a deplorable & lamentable condition." He added, "It is a most miserable life to live & always be hungry & also to see a plenty of good things to eat all around you every day & for it to be impossible for you to get any of them."[22]

Thomas Taylor wrote of the same situation at Johnson's Island. He noted, "Even in prison, where are a common cause and suffering in common, can be seen that difference in society that is seen other places, those who have ample means clinging together, with the usual number of toadies and dependents eagerly picking up the crumbs that their bounty lets fall to them." Taylor placed himself in the former group, writing of his fellow prisoners, "They are upon the whole a motley crew." Robert Bingham also considered himself and his friends to be among the higher class at Johnson's Island. Writing about their trips to the sutler, he noted, "We go down after the crowd is done & thus avoid being pushed & crammed by the rabble—and really many of the officers are the veriest rabble I ever saw." Although just a private himself, James Anderson was unimpressed with his original messmates at Camp Chase. "I don't think a much ruffer set of fellows could be found than this was," he later wrote. Anderson cheered when the Yankees punished one of them who refused to keep himself clean. "It was not my misfortune to have to stay long in this miserable dirty squad," he wrote. A friend invited him to join his more upscale mess.[23]

Perhaps no Confederate captive described his less fortunate fellow prisoners more vividly—and less charitably—than did Henri Mugler. Selected to recruit a drum corps among Elmira prisoners, Mugler lamented, "Found any number of 'musicians' but none to answer the purpose. There is evidentally very little musical talent amongst the poorer classes of the Southern States." He added, "There are some hard & dirty & ignorant cases amongst them. A great many do not hesitate to put themselves on perfect equality with the negro soldiers begging chews of tobacco from them and trading and conversing with them."[24]

Soon Mugler was referring to these prisoners as "Goopers" and "Snuffies" and making frequent references to them in his diary. Passing one, he observed, "The general expression of his countenance showed any thing but human intelect." On another occasion he referred to them as "the most indolent, dirty, filthy & ignorant people in the world, the Digger indians of California scarcily excepted." When an August 1864 cold snap compelled many of the poorer prisoners to crowd around fires, Mugler was unsympathetic. "They are very much like cornfield negroes in this respect," he wrote. "Give them a little fire to set by and some corn beef and they are fixed. I have often doubted whether these people are civilized." After going outside the camp on a wood detail, he observed, "It is a pleasure to be any where away from amidst these uncivilized heathens and 'dirt eaters.'" Only when the extreme weather began to result in death did Mugler find room for compassion. In November he wrote, "Some of them are mere boys, not more than 16 & 17 years of age. There are also some very old men amongst the prisoners. Some of these boys & old men look very pitiful. A man in here can see some of the horrors of war."[25]

The horrors of war became even greater for Confederate prisoners during the summer of 1864 when the Union government adopted a policy of retaliation, reducing rations and limiting the ability of prisoners with the means to subsist themselves. The first significant discussion of such a policy came late in 1863. On October 30 Col. Adrian R. Root, commanding Camp Parole, reported to Hoffman on the condition of Union prisoners arriving from Richmond. The cartel was dead, but both sides had agreed to informal limited exchanges of sick and invalid prisoners. "These invalids arrived here in a pitiable condition of mind and body, having experienced extreme suffering from a want (apparently) of proper food," he wrote. Five had died en route from City Point. After mulling this over for five days, Hoffman forwarded Root's message to Stanton. The war secretary responded with a brief message to Gen. Hitchcock, the commissioner of exchange: "You will please report what measures you have taken to ascertain the treatment of United States prisoners by the rebels at Richmond, and you are directed to take measures for precisely similar treatment toward all prisoners held by the United States, in respect to food, clothing, medical treatment, and other necessities."[26]

Hitchcock replied that he had already threatened Confederate officials that the Union might resort to retaliation. He advised against the policy, however, citing not humanitarian concerns but worries over security. Hitchcock feared uprisings at Camp Chase, Camp Morton, and perhaps other depots "where the means of security are very slender."[27]

Stanton considered Hitchcock's counsel and treaded carefully. On November 23 Hoffman issued orders that prisoners could receive clothing only from members of their immediate family, not from "disloyal friends or sympathizers." The following week he ordered the sutler stands at all prison camps closed to Confederate captives. On Christmas Eve Hoffman ordered the molasses ration reduced from four quarts per hundred rations to one quart, although this appears to have reflected a similar reduction in the issue for Union soldiers.[28]

After taking these steps toward retaliation, Stanton suddenly shifted his views. Believing that the treatment of Union captives in Richmond had "been materially improved," he granted Hoffman authority to reopen the sutler stands on December 29. For reasons that are not clear, Hoffman waited until March 3, 1864, to pass the word on to camp commanders. It came with a list of items that could be sold to the prisoners. Shoes and underclothing were included, but no outerwear was permitted. Several food items were on the list, including vegetables and canned meats and fish. Eight days later Hoffman granted permission for prisoners to receive boxes "containing nothing hurtful or contraband." Specifically excluded were uniform clothing, weapons, and liquor.[29]

The respite proved temporary. Soon after the prison sutlers opened up again, more reports of Southern abuse of Union prisoners reached Stanton's office. This time the war secretary determined to get to the truth of the situation. Learning on May 1 that four hundred sick prisoners were on their way to Annapolis, he dispatched Hoffman to Camp Parole. The commissary general found the officers to be in generally good condition. The plight of the enlisted men, however, was such that it moved the normally staid officer. He reported, "Some of these poor fellows were wasted to mere skeletons and had scarcely life enough remaining to appreciate that they were now in the hands of their friends. . . . Many faces showed that there was scarcely a ray of intelligence left." Hoffman added, "That our soldiers when in the hands of the rebels are starved to death cannot be denied." His advice was stark. "I would very respectfully urge that retaliatory measures be at once instituted by subjecting the officers we now hold as prisoners of war to a similar treatment."[30]

This was all the urging Stanton needed. He quickly forwarded Hoffman's report to Benjamin F. Wade, a powerful Republican senator and chairman of the Joint Committee on the Conduct of the War. At the war secretary's suggestion, the committee was soon on its way to Camp Parole to meet with the returned captives in person. Its conclusions were similar to Hoffman's but much more widely distributed in Northern newspapers and pamphlets that Wade ordered printed. Utilizing new technology, the Republicans also distributed photographs of many of the emaciated parolees. At least one Union soldier was not totally impressed with this process. Frank Wilkeson of the Eleventh New York Artillery Battery later wrote, "It is true that many of [the paroled prisoners] were diseased and almost dead when they were delivered to us, and these soldiers were grouped and photographed, very unfairly I think, and the illustrated papers which reproduced these photographs were widely circulated throughout the United States."[31]

Having secured his political flank with the legislative branch and presumably gained public support, Stanton went to work on Lincoln. He pleaded his case against the background of the Fort Pillow Massacre. On April 12, 1864, Confederate forces under Gen. Nathan Bedford Forrest captured the Tennessee fortification and allegedly murdered a number of its defenders, including black troops and Tennesseans belonging to Union outfits. Details of the affair remain hazy, and therefore contentious, but in 1864 the Northern response was one of outrage. On May 5, at the president's request, Stanton submitted a report containing a number of opinions concerning the proper response to the massacre. He then turned to prison policy in general. Stanton asserted that no Confederates taken in battle should be released "while our prisoners are undergoing ferocious barbarity or the more horrible death of starvation." He further suggested that Confederate officers should receive "precisely the same rations and treatment" to which the Confederates subjected Union captives. The next day Hoffman hinted at things to come. In a message sent to all commandants the commissary general of prisoners wrote, "It is possible that from circumstances which may soon occur more than ordinary vigilance will be required from the troops in charge of prisoners of war."[32]

Those circumstances began to materialize on May 19, when Hoffman submitted a proposal to Stanton that would reduce the rations received by Confederate prisoners by approximately 20 percent. Although Stanton had proposed retaliation only against Confederate officers, Hoffman's plan applied to all captives held by the Union. It quickly made the rounds of the military hierarchy. Halleck approved the reduced rations and further suggested that tea, coffee, and sugar be eliminated. At the suggestion of Surgeon General J. K. Barnes, those items were restored for sick prisoners. Otherwise, Barnes saw no problem with the plan, and on May 27 Stanton approved the proposal. Retaliation was now the policy of the Union.[33]

On June 1 Hoffman issued a circular making everything official. The savings from the reduced rations were to be added to the prison fund. On August 10 another circular severely limited sutler sales and the contents of boxes sent to prisoners. All food and clothing items were prohibited at the sutler stand. Friends and relatives could send food to prisoners only in cases of illness. Such shipments had to be approved by the prison surgeon. "Near relatives" could send limited items of clothing to "destitute prisoners" with the approval of the camp commandant.[34]

The prisoners' reactions to these new policies were—at least at first—rather understated. Among the first prisoners to notice were the officers at Johnson's Island. On June 5 William Peel wrote, "I understand our rations, already quite limited enough for those who have not the means of purchasing from the Sutler, are to be very materially shortened." Three days later he reported that this prison rumor was true. In early August, when he was apparently short on funds, Peel lamented, "I have been, for a week past, confined strictly to Govt rations, & my experience is that a man thus dependent, must be a very small eater not to suffer from hunger." The meat ration that had been issued the previous Saturday and intended to last three days only got the men through Sunday's breakfast. After that they were limited to a small amount of dry bread. Edmund Patterson attempted to put the change in a positive light. Noting the absence of coffee and sugar, he observed, "I know we will be healthier without them, especially the villainous compound called coffee." By the time the limits on sutler sales and boxes came, Patterson had changed his mind. "I am afraid that there will be much suffering this winter if the order is enforced, for the rations we receive from the Yankees are not sufficient to keep body and soul together."[35]

At Rock Island William Dillon first remarked briefly on the shorter rations on June 25. By July 5 he observed that they were producing "a great deal of murmuring and complaining" among the prisoners, adding, "of course this does no good." His November 25 entry read, "My rations make me some small meal per day. I stay hungry all the time. . . . This is our actual condition at the present time, almost starving in a land of plenty with no hope whatever of an exchange." Fort Delaware prisoner E. L. Cox first remarked on the limited fare on July 27, writing, "Rations is short." Specifically, he wrote that the morning meal consisted of a small amount of bread and "a piece of bacon or pork frequently no larger than my two fingers." In the afternoon the prisoners received a piece of beef slightly larger than the pork ration and a cup of rice or bean soup. A month later he noted, "Rations is growing frightfully less every day." George Washington Hall, also confined at Fort Delaware, wrote on November 2, "Our meat rations now will average a piece of lean boiled beef the size of a man thumb twice a day, our bread rations is from 4 to 6 ounces a day & some days we get half [a] pint of soup to day we got none & some days we get no meat."[36]

It was not until August that Camp Chase diarists first mentioned the reduced rations. "For several days our rations have been short in meat," Thomas Sharpe wrote on August 25. Sharpe was not one to complain, but on October 13 he noted, "Bread rations are short, and we are all the time hungry." He added, "Some healthy men are actually suffering for lack of food." James Anderson, who also generally eschewed emotionalism, complained, "What's left on my plate would starve a snow bird. A cat tried it in here but passed away of starvation." More ominously, Anderson continued, "If any body should ever read these notes they will worry over my complaints of hunger, and, for all I speak, often yet I do not tell half the suffering I see."[37]

Not only was the quantity of the prisoners' rations reduced at Camp Chase, so too, in their opinion, was the quality. "For two days we have had a new sort of ration, salt fish, said to be the white fish of the lakes," Sharpe recorded on September 3. Over the next two months the fish rations frequently reappeared. Maj. J. Coleman Alderson later recalled, "Sometimes when the head[s] of the barrels were knocked out we smelled them in any part of the prison." Marylander Henry Mettam improved somewhat upon the fish by boiling it with cornmeal and potatoes when available and then baking the entire concoction. This, he claimed, resulted in a dish that was "beautiful and brown." Fish were also included in the rations at Johnson's Island, but the prisoners there were apparently less creative. On September 8 Edmund Patterson wrote, "No rations today but bread and rotten fish, which we would none of us eat only as a matter of necessity to keep body and soul together." The fish was so salty, he added, that it had to be boiled three times, leaving "as much nutriment in them as there would be in the same quantity of boiled shavings."[38]

For prisoners with either means or friends, the limits on sutler purchases and items that could be received proved a more severe blow than the reduction of rations. Those most affected were the officers confined at Johnson's Island. The policy on boxes went into effect at the Lake Erie facility on August 22. "And great was the indignation & Many the curses heaped upon the Yankees," John

Thompson noted. According to William Peel a large express shipment arrived that day, but all the clothing and food it contained was confiscated. Peel was expecting two hams and twenty-five pounds of flour that he had ordered several weeks before, and he considered the sudden implementation of the order to be "a piece of great injustice." On this one occasion the story had a happy ending. A Union lieutenant looked the other way, giving many prisoners opportunities "for carrying off unobserved a good many such things." As a result, Peel gratefully wrote, "My prospect for biscuit and ham for breakfast is highly flattering."[39]

Confederate prisoners were resourceful, and many found ways of supplementing their suddenly limited rations. Their methods ranged from the clever to the desperate. At Point Lookout Chesapeake Bay provided the prisoners with crabs. There and at Fort Delaware they sometimes had luck in catching fish. Although far from the coast, Camp Morton had small streams that supplied crawfish. According to one prisoner they were made into "most excellent soup." A cluster of small oak trees provided Rock Island prisoners with acorns. A. C. Kean recalled, "We would get up early and go out at the crack of day to gather these acorns to eat. Not daring to do so in the day time as the guards would shoot at any one climbing a tree." Elmira, at least in the early days, had lush green spaces that provided knowledgeable gleaners with lamb's quarter and other edible plants.[40]

A group of Johnson's Island prisoners tapped one of the numerous sugar maple trees in the yard during the early spring of 1864. After two days they had collected about seven gallons of sap, which they proceeded to boil. Although their intention was to make maple syrup, the prisoners were admittedly "inexperienced" in the process. Instead, they ended up with "about two pounds of a very tolerable quality of maple sugar." As summer approached several of the blocks planted gardens. Even after the War Department instituted its policy of retaliation, camp officials did not interfere with this means of supplementing rations. There was, however, another concern. On September 17 Peel observed "some of the finest tomato bushes here I ever saw." They were not yet ripe, and he feared "the frost will catch them." If prisoners at other camps planted gardens, they were not noted by diarists, which seems unlikely. In an article written in 1900, former Camp Douglas prisoner T. M. Page claimed that a group of Chicago women had provided seeds to the prisoners. When the crops ripened they were confiscated by the guards.[41]

By the autumn of 1864 prisoners at virtually every camp were resorting to less palatable options. On October 10 Sharpe wrote in his Camp Chase diary, "Our mess were so near out of anything to eat that 3 of them made their breakfast on a big grey rat caught in a dead fall." Other members of the mess had a second rodent salted down for an upcoming meal. As a former Camp Chase prisoner later explained, "Fresh meat, regardless of species, was too much of a rarity among these hungry men to be discarded on account of an old prejudice." William Dillon wrote that rats were so popular an item of fare at Rock Island that they eventually became scarce. When the barracks at Camp Douglas were raised, prisoners captured and ate thousands, according to a former prisoner—who insisted that he was not among those partaking. Even the officers confined on Johnson's Island made this desperate resort. After eating his first, on November 25, Peel conceded, "They proved palatable in my half starved condition."[42]

No animal was safe inside the prison compounds. William Milton wrote after the war that a dog belonging to a Union officer at Camp Douglas "wandered into our midst and disappeared." The next evening Milton was invited by some friends to dine with them on roast pig. He soon learned the true identity of the dinner, and "my stomach refused the inviting morsal." Thomas Beadles may have been referring to the same incident when he recorded in his diary that a puppy, "three months old & very fat," met the same fate. According to his account, Capt. Wells Sponable learned about the incident and confined the offenders to the dungeon for about an hour. The prisoners had the last word, posting on the bulletin board such anonymous messages as "For want of meat, The dog was eat." One Rock Island diarist wrote that four dogs had been consumed there by the end of November. One of them, according to a postwar account, was the camp sutler's pet bulldog. According to Rock Island historian Benton McAdams, the sutler found the hide nailed to a tree accompanied by a note asking prison officials to "send in another dog."[43]

Visiting Block 12 at Johnson's Island, E. John Ellis discovered a freshly cooked cat. "I placed it close enough to my olfactories to get the scent and was tempted to taste it, but my prejudices were too strong." At Camp Chase Henry Mettam overcame his prejudices, helping his messmates consume a cat. They soaked the animal in salt water overnight and added onions and potatoes before cooking. According to Mettam the dish was much like rabbit stew. He added, "I have never been able to eat a rabbit since."[44]

"I have seen men eat anything that they could lay their hands on," C. W. Jones recalled of his time at Point Lookout. This included Jones himself, who wrote that he once traded his pocketknife for a pie "seasoned with skimmings from the slop tubs at the cook house." The meal "gave me a spell of sickness which came very near sending me to the 'peach orchard.'" On another occasion, Jones watched a comrade retrieve a dead gull that had washed up on the beach. The bird had been dead over a month, but the prisoner devoured it "with a gusto." At all camps men made daily searches of the grounds seeking out bones or any scrap of refuse. Beef bones were especially prized. The men broke them, boiled them, and skimmed away the grease. The result, which they termed "bone butter," was eagerly spread on bread. Fort Delaware guard A. J. Hamilton observed, "Was amused at the Johnnies snatching and grabbing at the slops from the cook house." At Camp Chase the men gathered around the open sewer that ran through the camp for the daily flushing. Included in the flow were scraps of food from the hospital. According to former prisoner M. A. Ryan, "Our boys would be strung along the sides of the ditch, and as it came floating by they would grab it and eat it like hungry dogs."[45]

The most graphic accounts of desperate prisoners came from Henri Mugler's Elmira diary. "Saw several 'bone pickers' going their rounds this morning," he recorded. "These fellows go arround camp and pick up every old bone provided it has a little meat on it. They also pick old jews [chews] of tobacco." Worse was his entry for September 26, 1864. "Morrison threw up his Supper on his blankets during the night. He cleaned off his blanket to day. He found several pieces of meat which he threw up on the night in question among his blanket; These he threw out to day. He had no Sooner thrown them out than a 'Gooper' came along, picked them up, and eat them."[46]

A different type of retaliation occurred in June and August 1864. The first case took place when Gen. Sam Jones, in command of Confederate forces at Charleston, South Carolina, received permission from the Southern War Department to place fifty Union prisoners in the city. The Union was shelling the city from nearby Morris Island, and Jones believed the presence of the prisoners might put a stop to it. Gen. John G. Foster, commanding Union troops on the island, urged retaliatory action. The Union responded by sending five Confederate generals and forty-five field officers to Morris Island. The incident had a happy ending for the men placed under fire. When the fifty Confederates arrived Foster realized that he did not have secure facilities for housing them. Eventually Jones and Foster agreed to exchange their hostages.[47]

In late July the Confederates shipped six hundred more captives to Charleston. Their motives appear to have been different on this occasion. The Union prisoners were transferred from a Macon facility that Confederate officials considered unhealthy and lacking in security. Nothing in surviving Confederate records suggests that the prisoners were regarded as hostages. Foster, of course, did not have access to Confederate records, and to him the motives of the enemy forces appeared obvious. He requested that six hundred Confederate hostages be sent. Stanton ordered Halleck, Halleck ordered Hoffman, and Hoffman ordered Schoepf to ship six hundred officers from Fort Delaware.[48]

At Fort Delaware the prisoners selected to be placed under enemy fire were considered lucky. Thanks to the prison "grape" news of the fate of the fifty sent in June had already reached the prison. "Reports are current in Camp to day that six hundred Officers are to leave here soon," E. L. Cox wrote on August 12. "Every one hopes he will be lucky enough to get off. If they are for retaliatory measures it is believed that they will be the first exchanged." Cox was disappointed, writing two days later, "I am one of the unfortunate ones as we are considered by those who are going to leave." Francis Boyle noted that the prisoners were unsure whether those departing were destined for retaliation or exchange. "Most of us however, seemed to think it a sure road to Dixie." Some were so certain, George Nelson later recalled, that they traded gold watches to be able to go in the places of those selected.[49]

"Great rejoicing and speculating as to who will be the fortunate ones," Lt. James R. McMichael of the Twelfth Georgia wrote in his diary when Fort Delaware officials made the announcement. Once aboard the ship he quickly changed his mind. The prisoners were crowded into the hold of the U.S. steamer *Crescent*. Only a few were allowed up on the deck at a time, and the conditions in the hold were awful. "I am sure I have never seen men suffer for air, space, and food as we have," McMichael wrote. "I have lost in one week fifteen pounds and feel as I have before when recovering from a severe spell of fever." The August heat, Nelson wrote, was intense. "Perspiration rolled from us in streams all the time, clothes and blankets were saturated with it and it dripped constantly from the upper to the lower bunks." A. J. Hamilton, who served as a guard on the ship, wrote, "The sun is very hot and the shade is scarce so that I am almost roasted." Hamilton admitted that the condition of the prisoners was "absolutely horrible."[50]

The Confederate hostages arrived at Charleston on August 26. Foster reported to Halleck that they were transferred to the island four days later. Despite having reached their destination, they had to remain aboard the *Crescent* for another week. Foster was again proving to be an inefficient jail keeper, failing to complete facilities for his prisoners. As his men worked on the stockade, the captives continued to swelter aboard the crowded ship. When they finally disembarked, McMichael noted that the Confederate batteries could not open fire "without playing great havoc with us. This is retaliation in the extreme, yet I am proud to be off the Steamer Crescent, for we can stand here in the day time and wash our faces." Added Samuel H. Hawes, "Any change is pleasant compared with our horrible condition on board the boat."[51]

Foster informed Halleck that the hostages were quartered in tents. "Many of the officers express themselves well satisfied with the novelty of the change," he added, "and have little fear of their own shells, which they watch with interest." Nelson confirmed the latter point. "One of our greatest pleasures was to watch the shells at night, darting through the air like shooting stars. And in predicting how near to us they would explode." On the night of September 8, McMichael wrote, "For the first time Gen. Sam Jones appeared determined to kill us. It was a beautiful sight to see the red balls of iron flying (apparently) among the stars and bursting immediately over the Batteries around us but fortunately none of us were hurt, although two of our shells (prematurely) exploded immediately over our heads and scattered their fragments down among us. We had no chance to dodge, nothing to protect us but the merciful God who made us." Despite this and other close calls, none of the prisoners were killed or wounded. According to Nelson, the only casualty was a black sentry who "had his leg knocked off by a shell." Before long, McMichael was observing, "The gnats are more annoying this morning than shell."[52]

The shelling bothered the men much less than did the rations supplied them. Hawes wrote, "The rations given us are abominable, rancid meat, with hard crackers, in which we can see the worms and bugs crawling through; we are weak and suffering on account of this detestable manner of living." Nelson claimed that the mush that the men occasionally received was full of worms also. Insisting that he was "too hungry to be dainty," Nelson consumed both mush and worms. "But I knew several fastidious men, who attempted to pick out the worms, and after throwing out from fifty to eighty, stopped, not because the worms had come to an end, but because all the little bit of mush was going with them." The rations grew skimpier with the passage of time. On September 24, McMichael reported, "Rations reduced to three little crackers a day. All are becoming very weak and it really seems that many will die for want of food."[53]

On October 13 Gen. William J. Hardee, who had succeeded Jones, informed Foster that all Union prisoners had been removed from Charleston. Foster responded that his hostages would be taken from Morris Island. They departed for Fort Pulaski, along the Georgia coast, on October 21. The prisoners' quarters in the casemates of the fort were cold and damp, but otherwise comfortable. After a few days the captives received bunks and stoves. Richard Henry Adams wrote that they got "almost a soldiers rations," a definite improvement. Boxes from friends also began to arrive. One contained two hams, potatoes, coffee, clothing, and "a ten gallon keg of nice Dixie syrup."[54]

On November 19 two hundred of the prisoners were shipped away to Hilton Head. They arrived during a heavy rain and were quartered in tents. After two days the storm abated, only to be followed by a strong northwest wind. Then came conditions so cold that the water in the tents froze. "I have undergone severe exposure in the field, but no hardship there ever tried me as severely as this," Hawes wrote. After a week in the tents, the men were moved to prison quarters that Hawes described as "more like a jail than any prison that I have yet been in." Rations were much as they had been on Morris Island, generally consisting of bread and a small quantity of pickles. Adams wrote that he and his messmates had supplemented their rations with three cats and that felines were "in demand—everybody after them." Hawes noted that the rations improved somewhat in late January. On February 20 he wrote that the officers had received "the full prison ration." Adams termed them "big rations," including "10 oz. meat, 16 oz. of bread stuff (meal & flour), beans, peas & soap."[55]

Meanwhile, conditions at Fort Pulaski deteriorated after the first of the year. A small quantity of meal and pickles composed the ration. McMichael wrote that it was "not sufficient to keep us from that degree of suffering never before endured." Soon shipments from home were cut off. Nelson recalled, "Our guard were not allowed to relieve our sufferings, though they frequently expressed their sympathy. The Colonel himself told us it was a painful duty to inflict such suffering—but that we knew he was a soldier and must obey orders." As did the prisoners at Hilton Head, the Fort Pulaski captives found cats the only means of supplementing their rations. Nelson wrote that he helped consume several, one of which was sneaked to him by a sympathetic guard. By mid-February, according to a tabulation made by McMichael, 156 of the 311 prisoners confined in the fort were sick. Of that number, 42 were suffering from scurvy.[56]

By then Union officials in South Carolina wanted rid of the Confederate captives. On January 8 Foster sought permission from Halleck to return them north. His successor, Gen. Quincy Gillmore, repeated the request on February 13. Finally, on March 4, the prisoners left Fort Pulaski. Those at Hilton Head rejoined them the next day and all set out for Fortress Monroe. The men at first believed they were going to be exchanged but later learned to their disappointment that, after all they had endured, they were returning instead to Fort Delaware. They arrived on the 12th. "I had no idea what a miserable looking set of men we were until contrasted with the Fort Delaware prisoners, our old companions," Nelson recalled. "I thought they were the fattest, best dressed set of men, I had ever seen."

Both Boyle and Cox were shocked by the condition of the men that they had watched depart with envy a few months before. "Their sufferings have been awful," Boyle wrote. Cox noted that about sixty were immediately taken to the hospital. By the 17th he reported that "several" had died.[57]

As time went on more and more Confederate prisoners opted to take the oath of allegiance to the Union. Many enlisted in the Federal service. The hopelessness of exchange and the retaliatory policies of the Union government combined to make the decision more attractive. Another factor, according to some prisoners, was Yankee exploitation of the gullibility of many prisoners. In July 1863 Robert Bingham asserted that Fort Delaware officials were taking advantage of bad war news "by operating on the C.S. privates." Many, he added, were taking the oath of allegiance and marching off in Union uniforms. "No wonder, poor fellows—they hear nothing but Yankee news, and no one of us [officers] is allowed to speak to them." William Dillon observed one recruiting call at Rock Island for three hundred men to join the Union navy. "I regret to be compelled to add that they got nearly or quite nearly the required number by using the most dishonorable means that ever was used," he added. "Their officers all went amongst our men and coaxed, argued and bribed and commanded all who they could influence to desert the cause of their country and enlist themselves in the ranks of their brutal enemies."[58]

On October 27, 1863, Hoffman wrote to the Union prison camp commandants, "You will please inform all prisoners of war under your charge that for the present no more discharges will be granted." Although there were some exceptions, this remained the Union policy for the remainder of the war. There were, however, other incentives for prisoners to accept the oath. One was the opportunity to work for camp officials, which meant extra rations.[59]

Another motivation was assignment to better quarters. Oath takers who ended up in the Union military were referred to as "Galvanized Yankees." As a result, the section they occupied at Fort Delaware was called the "galvanized pen" by the prisoners. "They are treated about the same as the other prisoners except they eat three times a day," observed a prisoner who did not join them. A guard at Rock Island informed a friend that the camp was divided into two sections. One, the "bull pen," contained Confederates who refused to take the oath. The other, termed the "calf pen," housed those who had taken the oath and enlisted for the frontier service. At Johnson's Island Block 1 was considered prime real estate. The barracks was divided into small rooms, each with its own stove. Because of this there was a great deal of resentment when its occupants were turned out to make room for a group of oath takers. Word that they were to receive extra rations only increased the indignation. Watching them head to their new quarters, Virgil Murphey wrote, "They marched amid horid groans and biting sarcasm with penitent heads abjectly bowed, eyes fastened intently upon the earth as if it would open its ponderous jaws and swallow them for apostasy, with pallid looks indicating their fear of vengeance." He added, "Even the Yankees are undisguised in their aversions to these neophytes, for they hate the traitor when benefitted by their treason."[60]

Abuse of oath takers was not limited to verbal taunts. On January 8, 1864, several Johnson's Island prisoners learned the identity of the latest "traitor" and pursued him across the compound. The man was kicked, cuffed, hit with snowballs, and "used roughly" before being rescued by a Union officer with a squad of reinforcements. At Camp Douglas a group of prisoners ganged up on a member of the Twenty-eighth Alabama who had not only agreed to enlist in the Union navy but was also recruiting among the men captured with him. The mob "pounced on him & beat him considerably" before Union guards put a stop to the proceedings. Sometimes the guards did more than simply stop the men engaged in abusing oath takers. At Fort Delaware a group of officers threatened to hang one of their disloyal comrades. Finally they tossed him around with a blanket and threw him out of the barracks. Those involved were taken to the galvanized pen "and tossed by [guards] in a blanket by way of retaliation for half an hour."[61]

Most disturbing, although unsubstantiated, was the prison rumor that Henri Mugler recorded in his Elmira diary. "It is the opinion of a good many of the prisoners that Union men have been poisoned in here." They believed this was occurring in the hospital, where Confederate stewards worked. According to Mugler, one of the workers, whom he described as "a strong rebel," told him that many oath takers had died in his ward but none of the loyal Confederates had.[62]

Despite the hazards the opportunity to get out of their prison camps was too tempting for a number of men. In June 1863 Hamilton observed that recruiting was going on "briskly" at Fort Delaware. In March 1864, some two hundred naval recruits departed from Point Lookout. Four months later officials at Camp Chase informed Hoffman that 111 prisoners had signed up for the Union navy, a fact confirmed by a guard in a letter home. A naval officer was soon headed to Columbus to get them.[63]

Nowhere did recruiting go on with more zeal than at Rock Island. On January 9, 1864, William Davis wrote that Tennesseans had been offered the opportunity to return to their native state as home guards. Two weeks later a major recruiting drive for the Union navy took place at the Illinois camp. On the 18th

Johnson informed Hoffman that six hundred had volunteered. Eight days later a guard writing to his brother claimed that the number had reached twelve hundred. "They are still enlisting & I think as many more will yet enlist," he added. Even the disapproving prisoners admitted that the Yankee recruiters were making inroads upon their ranks. Lafayette Rogan, who was working as a clerk, wrote in his diary on February 9, "Navy Roll of 664 traitors to our country completed to day." William Dillon was disappointed that three members of his company had enlisted, "but this is the place to try men—base metal will show itself when tried by fire."[64]

Late that summer the army got its turn to recruit at Rock Island. Recruiters offered inducements of a $100 bounty for one year, $200 for two years, and $300 for three years of service against frontier Indians. Rogan predicted that between fifteen hundred and two thousand would enlist. Dillon wrote, "I firmly believe that 19 out of every 20 will go for to desert at the first opportunity and thus get out of prison." One detachment left the bull pen on September 30, prompting Rogan to observe, "Oh how depraved the men of the present generation are become." When another contingent departed on October 15, Dillon noted, "The number gone out up to this time will probably reach 1,000, a very large number of traitors for the number of prisoners here, and still the Yankee officers say that they will have another 800 or reduce our rations yet more."[65]

The men in the calf pen soon found themselves in a bureaucratic no-man's-land, which added to their suffering. On November 18, 1864, Johnson explained the situation to James B. Fry, the Union provost marshal general. The pen was "full to repletion" with galvanized Yankees. As a result, "This pen is close and tiresome and the men are becoming disspirited." Worse, their clothing was of "the poorest description." Since they were no longer prisoners, Johnson could not issue better clothing to them. Since they had not yet been organized into Union army units, neither could the quartermaster. "Consequently these cold nights find them shivering around the Barrack stoves." The following month Johnson made two similar appeals to Hoffman. "Their condition is deplorable," Johnson wrote of the new Union recruits. These pleas, too, apparently fell upon deaf ears. These galvanized Yankees had gained little and lost much. Except for a few more rations, their abandonment of the Southern cause brought them virtually no benefits. They had engendered the enmity of their former comrades; and their quest for freedom had carried them only a few feet to the calf pen. Figuratively and literally, this had proven to be cold comfort.[66]

10

"Inevitable death awaited its victims"

The Health of the Prisoners

Of the 214,865 Confederates who found themselves confined in Union prisons, 25,976 died. This was just over 12 percent. Many factors combined to produce this result. Poor sanitary conditions in all military camps, not just prisons, plagued Civil War soldiers. Still, the numbers did not have to be this high; and the lethargy with which Union officials addressed health concerns in their prisons was inexcusable.[1]

Among the problems facing Confederate captives who arrived in Northern prisons was climate. Many men, particularly those from the Deep South, had never experienced the type of bitter cold weather they now encountered. The evidence suggests that Union prison officials did not do nearly enough to protect them from the elements. In 1900 Pvt. T. M. Page, who had been a captive at Camp Douglas, wrote that Col. De Land had established a medical corps of ten Confederate surgeons. One of them, Dr. C. S. Brunson, named Page his secretary. "It thus became my daily duty to fill out reports of sick, tickets of admission to the 'dead house,' . . . and superintend all writing in the office of the prison hospital." According to Page, the doctors saw frequent cases of prisoners freezing to death in their bunks. They tended to list "debilitas" as the cause of death in their reports. However, when a boyhood friend of Dr. Brunson succumbed, the angry surgeon ordered his secretary to write "Frozen to death" on the report. "It fell like dynamite in the headquarters office," Page recalled. Brunson stood his ground, demanding an inquest "of reputable Chicago surgeons," and the prison officials backed down.[2]

Neither prison diaries nor camp records at Camp Douglas substantiate Page's claim that men were freezing to death "every cold night." Thomas Beadles, however, did offer some corroboration. "Last night was severe—so much so that one Confederate soldier froze to death," he wrote in his diary on November 23, 1864. On December 8 he recorded, "Last night was the coldest of the season. Many suffered & some froze to death."[3]

At other camps prisoners' diary references to men freezing to death were rare but not unheard of. On December 16, 1863, William Davis wrote that six prisoners at Rock Island had recently succumbed to the cold. Three days later William Dillon wrote that the temperature had reached eight degrees below zero and that a man in his barracks had died. He did not directly link the two but he noted, "We are suffering terribly from the cold being all very poorly clad. A great many have their feet and ears frozen." On January 29, 1865, Joseph Kern wrote briefly and starkly in his Point Lookout diary, "During last night several prisoners froze to death." In November and December 1864 E. L. Cox wrote that men remained up all night at Fort Delaware to keep from freezing to death and that they had resorted to dancing as a way of staying warm.[4]

Even if the cold killed but few, it left many of the prisoners suffering. Observing contingents arriving at Rock Island, one guard wrote, "I do realy pity the poor fellows as they stand shivering in the cold wintery blast their feet almost naked to the biting frost." At Elmira Wilbur Gramling complained on January 22, 1865, that his feet were "frostbitten again." Camp Chase prisoner James Anderson observed on December 11, 1864, a particularly cold day, "It's a hard time on Prisoners born and raised in Southern lands." In a letter that may have been smuggled out of camp, Johnson's Island prisoner Daniel S. Printup wrote in January 1864, "I myself have experienced colder weather but at least half of the prisoners never before knew what it was to be exposed to cold more than a few degrees below the freezing point. These suffered & could hardly realize the fact that cold could be so intense." According to Virgil Murphey the cold froze the Johnson's Island prisoners "almost into a lethargic state." On another occasion the weather conditions simply made one of them angry. In the spring of 1864 John Porter wrote in his diary, "Snowing all yesterday—2nd of May—What a country. Yanks."[5]

At no time during the war did the cold compare with that experienced on New Year's Day in 1864. According to weather historians Thomas and Jeanne Schmidlin, it was a cold snap that survived in people's memories well into the twentieth century. It was on this evening that Curtis Burke recorded that six or seven guards "froze on their beats" and had to be hospitalized. According to Thomas Beadles, several prisoners were also "frozen badly." Burke wrote that the wind blew the snow that accompanied the cold in the upper Midwest into five-foot drifts. Although wood and coal had always been delivered to the barracks before, on this occasion the prisoners had to go some four hundred yards to fetch it, "and some came near freezing at it." Camp officials pulled the sentinels from the fences and stationed them at the barracks doors. Prisoners were required to remain in the barracks after dusk. Burke concluded, "The night was very cold, but the guards kept the coal stoves red hot all night, which kept the barracks warm, and we slept well."[6]

At Rock Island twenty-seven prison barracks ran out of coal during the blizzard. When local teams could not be hired to replenish the supply, camp officials sent a detachment to impress them. "Soon the Island was alive with vehicles," one guard wrote. "Military power put in force." This decisive action likely saved several lives, although William Davis wrote, "Men are actually freezing to death." Davis placed the temperature on New Year's Day at twenty-eight below zero, William Dillon at minus thirty-one. According to Dillon, water froze within five feet of the stove in his barracks. He added, "It is utterly impossible for me to describe the suffering of the prisoners the last five or six days but when I say that not half of the men have any coats and only ragged jackets and thin cotton shirts, a man may imagine the sufferings of the men."[7]

On Lake Erie there was no snow, but the cold and wind were intense. At least three Johnson's Island diarists wrote that it was the most bitter weather they had ever experienced. One of them wrote, "All of nature's powers seem to be taken up in order to bring to our minds by this temperature that man's works are finite." Robert Bingham wrote that the ice was half an inch thick on the windows of his block. Two of the prisoners got their hands badly frostbitten going out for wood. According to James Mayo, a man strayed from a wood detail and attempted to escape. He did not get very far across the frozen lake before the cold forced him to turn back to the prison.[8]

Returning to Johnson's Island saved the man's life, but it did not guarantee that he would be warm and comfortable. At no camp did the hastily erected barracks afford complete protection from the elements, but some were worse than others. A medical inspector dispatched to Camp Douglas in October 1863 found them greatly in need of repair. All doors and most windows were missing. Returning four months later, he still found them to be "much dilapidated." At least one prisoner agreed with the assessment. On October 4, 1863, George Weston wrote, "Exceedingly cold. The wind blowing lustily from the NE & every one of us nearly frozen to death. In a wooden shanty like we are in, the glass out of the windows, the cracks of the building open . . . it's enough to freeze a mule, much less a man." The situation was the same at Camp Morton. According to one inspector, the only ventilation in the prisoners' quarters there was provided "by dilapidation and by insufficient doors and windows."[9]

One problem the prisoners generally did not have was a lack of fuel in their barracks. Wood and coal rations were never restricted under Union retaliation orders, and camp officials were usually not inclined to carry retaliation beyond orders received from Washington. Johnson's decisive action during the New Year's blizzard of 1864 was one example. In the fall of 1864 wood became scarce at Fort Delaware. The prisoners endured a cold October, although those with money were able to purchase old barrels for 25¢. Finally, on November 1, camp officials secured coal for the prisoners. Point Lookout captives were not so fortunate. "The ground is covered with snow and we have not the first stick of wood for it is our day to miss," Charles Hutt wrote on February 3, 1864. Even when Point Lookout prisoners could get wood, it was of poor quality, coming from a stand of pines located near the camp.[10]

At other prisons it was water that posed a problem. For a time only three hydrants served the needs of Camp Douglas inhabitants, and one was set aside for Union soldiers. The situation was alleviated somewhat in 1863, when Meigs relented and allowed construction of the sewer he had denied the previous year. At Alton a six-mule team and a single wagon hauled water from the Mississippi to the prison. It was February 1864 before a medical inspector pronounced the arrangement "entirely insufficient" and ordered a second wagon employed. Although they were surrounded by water, Johnson's Island prisoners often found it difficult to obtain. Wells on the island frequently went dry, and the pumps that brought water from the lake tended to freeze in cold weather or break down at any time. When this happened camp officials allowed the prisoners to go down to the lake under a heavy guard to fetch water in buckets.[11]

On Pea Patch Island, Fort Delaware prisoners got their water from large iron tanks that collected runoff from prison buildings. When this was not enough boats were dispatched to haul water from nearby Brandywine Creek. Prisoners pronounced it "brackish." George Hall wrote, "The water we have to use is verry bad worse than any I ever saw used before & the use of it bring on various diseases." Hall's complaints did not matter, but on July 4, 1863, Surgeon General William Hammond received a similar report from Senator Reverdy Johnson of Maryland. Johnson had heard that poor water was responsible for ten to fifteen deaths a day. "Can this be so?" he asked. A prominent "War Democrat," Johnson's concerns did matter. The surgeon general quickly sent John M. Cuyler, a medical inspector in his office, to the prison. His report has not survived, but two inspectors who visited the camp that autumn pronounced the water good, one claiming it was "as sweet as Potomac Creek or James River water."[12]

Water was not the only health problem facing the prisoners at Fort Delaware. The island was flat and marshy, and the drainage ditches that traversed it were inadequate to their task. Following nearly a week of autumn rains in 1864 one prisoner wrote, "The black mud on this island has become stirred up so deep we can hardly walk out of the barracks without miring up." Perhaps the strongest indictment of the conditions on the island came from a panic-stricken Schoepf. On July 7, 1863, the commandant informed Meigs that the newly erected prison barracks had begun to sink as soon as the prisoners occupied them. Some had sunk as much as a foot, and Schoepf feared that they might collapse. Meigs dispatched a man to correct the construction flaw, but nobody seemed concerned over the effects the location might have on the prisoners' health. Medical inspectors who later visited the camp complained of "zymotic influences" and land that was "low, damp, and to some extent miasmatic." A third even wrote, "the last monthly report shows miasmatic disease largely predominating and most fatal." By then the collapse of the cartel had placed at a premium space in which to house prisoners. Questions of health were secondary.[13]

The same was true at Camp Chase. Drainage at the hastily erected training camp was poor from the outset. One Fort Donelson prisoner termed the camp "the filthiest, muddiest place I ever saw human beings in." Another described the facility as "a wooden wall enclosing about 1/2 acre of the wettest mudiest ground." In July 1862 Governor Tod urged Hoffman to build a new prison between Camp Chase and Columbus, although he was mainly concerned about having recruits and prisoners at the same post. Stanton rejected the plan. The exchange cartel had just been signed, and the war secretary believed Camp Chase's days as a prison were numbered. The matter resurfaced in August 1863, when Dr. D. Stanton, military superintendent of hospitals in Columbus, reported that the selection of the site "was a most unfortunate one. It is low, flat, and not susceptible of drainage." He concluded, "The occupation of a camp so situated for so long a time . . . has made Camp Chase a very unhealthy place." Tod repeated his appeal to relocate the camp, and Stanton forwarded it to Meigs. The quartermaster general replied that the project would be too expensive. Instead he suggested that Hoffman travel to Columbus to confer with Tod. No more was heard of the proposal.[14]

Instead it fell to Col. Richardson to address the problems. In April 1864 he proposed to move Prison 3 away from the eastern area of the camp, a section he said was "rendered almost uninhabitable by the stench from the ditch that carries off the filth of this prison." Stanton had denied a similar project the previous year.

This time Richardson forwarded a report from the post surgeon, who reported that the sinks in the prison were overflowing, their contents running through the camp. Hoffman's endorsement was likely more important in influencing Stanton's decision. Putting aside his pecuniary concerns, the commissary general reminded the war secretary that Governor Tod, among others, had "several times" complained of the situation. Outflanked, Stanton approved the plan. By utilizing prison labor, Richardson kept the cost down. By initiating the project and seeing it through he improved the health of the camp markedly. In addition to relocating Prison 3 and rebuilding the barracks, Richardson oversaw construction of a large reservoir that was emptied each day to wash away accumulated filth. The prison was also graded and the drainage improved. It had taken over three years, but Richardson was likely not exaggerating when he asserted that his efforts had made Camp Chase "as good a camp as any other in the West."[15]

Although Hoffman supported Richardson's improvements, he again counted nickels and dimes when an even more serious health threat was brought to his attention. Almost from the moment the prison at Elmira opened, the commissary general received warnings of the potentially deadly effects of Foster's Pond. Dr. Charles T. Alexander, a Union medical inspector, first raised the issue in a July 14 report. One month later the commander, Lt. Col. Seth Eastman, warned that the pool had become "very offensive, and may occasion sickness unless the evil is remedied very shortly." He sought permission to dig a drainage ditch to alleviate the problem. The warning was repeated one week later in a report of the camp inspector, which was forwarded to Hoffman. Col. Benjamin Franklin Tracy took up the issue when he assumed command in September. That month the death toll at Elmira reached 385, more than Camp Chase, Camp Douglas, Fort Delaware, and Rock Island combined.[16]

It was October before Hoffman finally approved the project, and then only after downsizing the scope of the work to hold down expenses. Prisoners were to perform all the labor, and the cost, which Hoffman felt should not exceed $120, was to be paid out of the prison fund. Soon a crew of 125 prisoners, working eight-hour days, was digging the ditch and laying pipe. Hoffman's foot-dragging, however, had exacted a high human price. Heavy rains delayed the project, as did "waste and quicksand in the bottom of the cutting" and "coarse gravel of what seems once to have been the river's bottom." As a result, the work was not completed until late December. By then over twelve hundred Elmira prisoners had died.[17]

Frequently Union officials placed some of the blame on the prisoners themselves for their lack of good health. As early as November 1862 Capt. Freedley claimed the captives at Alton were so "excessively indolent" that they had to be forced to clean themselves. The following August a Camp Chase guard wrote, "Much sickness is prevailing among the rebs, which is not to be wondered at when we take into consideration the filth amid which they live." Many, he added, died from "the greybacks and other vermin with which they are covered."[18]

After visiting Fort Delaware in November 1863, medical inspector A. M. Clark termed the prisoners "indolent" and wrote that they "can hardly be roused to take necessary exercise." He concluded, "At present I am convinced that idleness and ennui are more pregnant sources of disease than any other to be found in our various prisons." As incredible as that statement was, Dr. Alexander, who inspected the prison the following June, agreed with his colleague's assessment of the Fort Delaware captives. "The quarters of the prisoners are fairly policed and could be kept in good condition if the inmates were not too lazy to consult even self-interest and comfort," he wrote. The two inspectors also agreed that the same situation existed among the Confederate officers confined at Johnson's Island. Alexander expressed surprise that "men calling themselves gentlemen should be willing to live in such filth." Clark noted that camp officials shared the blame, reporting that the prisoners policed their quarters "as they see fit, no organized system being in force."[19]

Although some prisoners did express disgust with their less sanitary fellow captives, it is difficult to discern the percentages of the apathetic and the concerned. Surviving diaries indicate that the literate prisoners were largely in the latter category. This was especially true when the subject was lice. "Devoted the entire morning to examining my underclothing for vermin an abominable nuisance in prison that it seems almost impossible to get rid of," John Thompson wrote from Johnson's Island on January 17, 1864. Robert Bingham noted that he had boiled his clothing three days out of four. Two days later his garments were again infested. Camp Douglas diarist George Weston approached the topic with wry humor. "Feeling something nibbling at me last night I concluded I would search my self to see if I could not find any boogers," he wrote on October 14, 1863. "I did not think such was the case as I dressed very clean yesterday but Lo when I looked 16 large Greybacks were found in the seemes of the shirt I put on. I succeeded in dispatching them, but it is no use to kill a louse, a dozen will come to his funeral." William Haigh found absolutely no humor in the situation. Recalling his first encounter with the vermin at Point Lookout, he wrote, "I don't belive that I ever premeditated suicide before—but if such a thought be ever pardonable, it would be under such circumstances as I then found myself."[20]

Even if the prisoners deserved a portion of the blame for the poor sanitary conditions in their camps, culpability for one health problem rested squarely on the shoulders of Union officials. At the majority of large Northern prisons medical inspectors reported scurvy among the captives. Although Hoffman would frequently criticize camp commanders for making minor mistakes in forwarding reports, there is almost no record of the commissary general of prisoners issuing orders to arrest this highly preventable condition. The results of this neglect were pathetic. One prisoner who remembered observing the disease's effects later wrote, "Lips were eaten away, jaws became diseased, and teeth fell out." Another, who fell victim to the disease, recalled, "My gums sloghed away from my teeth. With my fingers I could have removed any tooth from my mouth without pain, for they were ready to drop out."[21]

In January 1864 Clark reported from Johnson's Island that "although there are no declared cases of this disease at present in camp, . . . many, perhaps a majority of the prisoners, are more or less strongly tainted with it." Hoffman ignored the warning. Writing to Terry a week later, he made no mention of scurvy. His only reference to Clark's inspection was an insistence that the prisoners be required to police the camp. Seven months later Alexander reported that the disease had actually broken out at the camp. This time, in a message to Hill, Hoffman spoke again of the need for better policing. He also complained about the sutler system, ordered that the sinks be improved, and called for the erection of a washhouse. According to one prisoner, Alexander took the matter into his own hands. Isaiah Steedman, who worked in the prison hospital, later recalled, "Whenever [Dr. Alexander] visited our prison, and the wholesale prevalence of scurvy . . . was exhibited to him, he promptly and cheerfully ordered additional rations of fresh meat and vegetables, especially onions and cabbages."[22]

Clark reported "several cases of scurvy" at Camp Morton in October 1863. Three months later he said the disease was "prevalent" at the Indiana prison, a claim he repeated in April. Charles J. Kipp inspected the camp in July 1864. Reporting on the twenty-four deaths that had occurred in just one week, he concluded, "The cases which terminated in death were complicated with decided symptoms of scurvy and of malarial poisoning." Similar reports came from Fort Delaware in March and June 1864. As with the Johnson's Island cases, there is no record of Hoffman ordering any direct action to combat the outbreaks. He did, however, send a message to all commandants on August 1, 1864, informing them that antiscorbutics could be purchased "whenever in the judgment of the surgeon they are necessary." They were to be paid for from the hospital fund.[23]

This order led to complications at Elmira. On August 26, 1864, Dr. Eugene Sanger, the chief prison surgeon at the camp, reported that there were 793 cases of scurvy. Unfortunately the hospital fund at the recently opened prison was limited, and Eastman sought permission to use money from the prison fund instead. Maj. George Blagden, who worked in Hoffman's office, replied that this would be acceptable under the circular. This apparently proved insufficient. On September 30 Tracy, who had succeeded Eastman, bluntly informed Hoffman, "Scurvy prevails to a great extent. Few if any vegetables have been recently issued. Greater efforts should be made to prevent scurvy." In November Dr. William Sloan inspected the camp and forwarded his findings to the surgeon general. The report, which was highly critical, was then forwarded to Gen. Henry Wessells, who had temporarily succeeded Hoffman. Perhaps unaware of Eastman and Tracy's appeals to Hoffman, Wessells demanded to know "what is about being commenced to remedy the evils mentioned in [the] report." As the bureaucrats engaged in verbal fencing, the prisoners paid the price. On September 29 Henri Mugler wrote, "There are a great many cases of Scurvy among the prisoners." T. H. Stewart later recalled that, despite the prevalence of smallpox, "We lost more men from scurvy than anything else."[24]

Hoffman was pursuing a harder line, which appears to have been a result of the Union's retaliation policy. One year earlier, when commander Brig. Gen. Gilman Marston informed him that many of the prisoners at Point Lookout were afflicted with scurvy, the commissary general had approved a plan to purchase vegetables. Cost, he wrote, was "not a material consideration." Soon a schooner load of vegetables reached the camp. A second shipment was delayed when the revenue collector in Massachusetts discovered "two or three cases of bitters," which the Point Lookout commissary had ordered. By the following July they had apparently stopped altogether because Alexander found that the disease had again broken out at the prison. One month later Point Lookout surgeon James H. Thompson reported a "rapid increase in Scurvy in the Prisoners." He urged Brig. Gen. James Barnes, then in command, to increase the amount of vegetables issued. Barnes forwarded the recommendation to Hoffman, who had become much less understanding. "No change can be made except so far as to make it conform to the recent law fixing the ration," he wrote.[25]

Besides scurvy, medical reports from Union prisons indicate frequent cases of pneumonia, measles, and various fevers. There were also rare cases of cholera. Most common were the camp diseases that plagued virtually all Civil War encampments, particularly diarrhea and dysentery. One or both diseases are mentioned in the overwhelming majority of inspections conducted by Drs. Clark and Alexander. They also appear in the prisoners' letters and diaries. "There were two candles burning all night, and several men sat up with the sick flux patients,"

Curtis Burke observed from Camp Douglas on August 6, 1864. Flux is a form of dysentery. The next day Burke reported two deaths from the disease. Fellow prisoner R. W. Davis confirmed the flux was "very bad in camp" in a letter home. The following month Henri Mugler wrote, "A great many of the prisoners are dying from the effects of chronic diarhia." Recalling his work in the Johnson's Island hospital, Steedman wrote, "Chronic bowel diseases, the greatest enemy of armies, and especially prisons, prevailed to an alarming extent among us. Prison diet and treatment could do nothing for it; inevitable death awaited its victims."[26]

No disease was dreaded more by the prisoners than smallpox. Although Edward Jenner had developed the vaccine in 1796, and despite the nearly universal endorsement of physicians, many Americans remained dubious. Army regulations called for vaccination in training camps. This was overlooked in many states, at which level most Civil War regiments were raised. As a result Union prisons were packed with both captives and guards who were susceptible to the deadly disease.[27]

Outbreaks occurred at every major prison camp, but some were worse than others. The disease struck Camp Chase in January 1864. Fortunately the energetic Dr. Clark was there at the time on one of his frequent inspection trips. He immediately ordered that enough vaccine be secured for "every person in or connected with, or who may hereafter become connected with the prison camps." The surgeon of one of the regiments training at the camp insisted that the floors and bunks in his men's barracks be removed and the ground sprinkled with lime. Col. Wallace, then commanding the camp, shook his usual lethargy to see to it that the work was carried out. The disease continued into February, peaking at about ninety cases. There were few deaths. One of them was a member of the camp's guard force.[28]

The next outbreak, which began about eight months later, proved more difficult to stem. On September 6, Thomas Sharpe wrote in his diary that there was "some uneasiness" among the prisoners because of smallpox. Camp rumors placed the number of cases at about twenty. On October 17 a guard at the camp wrote, "The prisoners have the small-pox quite bad, and many of them are dying." Three days earlier Richardson had gotten around to informing Hoffman of the outbreak. He reported that there was an average of ten new cases each day. The total had reached 168. The commissary general replied, "You will appreciate the necessity of doing all in your power to abate and remove smallpox from the camp." Beyond stating the obvious, Hoffman offered no assistance. On November 26, after the disease had claimed 105 prisoners in a two-week period, Richardson reported that it was abating. Ten days later he predicted that it would soon be eradicated. The prisoners were less positive. As late as December 21, Pvt. Anderson recorded in his diary, "The air here is perfectly impregnated with smallpox, and no man knows at what hour he is to be struck with this loathsome disease." His views proved to be correct. On January 21, Richardson was forced to admit that smallpox was still plaguing the camp.[29]

The disease also struck the Alton prison. It first appeared in December 1862, and by the following July one camp official was reporting that it had "become an almost established disease in the prison." The guard force had also become infected, as had the city of Alton. Smallpox was so prevalent that Maj. Thomas Hendrickson, the commanding officer, virtually begged that no more prisoners be sent "so that we may have an opportunity to rid the prison of this most loathsome disease." He reported that the vaccine had been ineffective. Apparently camp officials redoubled their efforts, because in October Dr. Clark reported that only five cases remained. He credited this to the "energetic and well-directed efforts of the present surgeon in charge." Despite this, smallpox soon reemerged at Alton. In February 1864 Clark reported again that the disease was "rapidly disappearing." Fifty cases remained, and "every precaution is taken to prevent the spread of smallpox."[30]

On Christmas Day 1864 Tracy reported that smallpox was "on the increase" at Elmira. Two weeks later the camp's inspecting officer offered the ironically positive report that the disease was "not on the increase so much as last week." Still, the week had produced 126 cases and ten deaths. As at Camp Chase, the prisoners did not view things so optimistically. Wilbur Gramling first mentioned the outbreak on December 19, adding, "Prisoners are very sickly as a general thing." Four days later he wrote that the disease was "raging." By the 24th there had been forty cases and four deaths, and Gramling observed, "Prospects are bad for Christmas." Camp surgeons apparently agreed. On Christmas Day Henri Mugler observed, "Small pox is rapidly on the increase here. . . . One or two of the Fed surgeons have become afraid of catching it & have asked to be relieved from duty here." By mid-January Gramling reported that new cases were arriving at the hospital daily. Mugler placed the total number at 180 on January 12 and 250 on March 16. On February 28 Gramling reported that more cases were proving fatal. By then there were between twenty and thirty deaths a day from a variety of diseases. It was April 22 before Gramling wrote, "Health of camp a great deal better and smallpox departing." By May 2 the number of cases was down to thirty-six.[31]

At Rock Island camp officials had to deal with a smallpox outbreak within three days of the opening of the prison. The fault lay with officials at Louisville, where Confederate captives were temporarily held before being sent on to western prison camps. The large body of prisoners that arrived in the wake of the Union victory at Chattanooga taxed the facility in the extreme. One of the corners the Louisville officers cut was to send trainloads of prisoners, including Confederates with smallpox, quickly on to Rock Island. On at least one occasion an officer at Louisville informed Col. Johnson that a shipment of 550 prisoners on their way included some smallpox cases. He blithely added the suggestion that they be quarantined. The first case was reported at Rock Island on December 6, 1863. Six days later Johnson informed Hoffman that there were 136 sick prisoners in the makeshift hospital that had been established and a "large number" in the barracks. Two medical officers were present for duty. Johnson did what he could, scrambling to locate vaccine and converting barracks into temporary hospitals. By January he had ten such hospitals with forty-two bunks each. All were filled, he informed Hoffman, "and a sufficient number [are] sick in quarters to fill five more." According to William Davis, the prisoners were ordered to burn the straw they used for bedding and to sun their blankets daily. Smallpox killed forty-six in January. By February 17 there were 381 cases among the prisoners.[32]

The busy Dr. Clark arrived at Rock Island on February 3. One week later he reported to Hoffman, "I find that there has been much remissness on the part of medical officers of the prison in not taking proper measures to prevent the spread of the smallpox." Specifically, Clark charged that upon his arrival he had found thirty-eight prisoners afflicted with the disease still in the barracks. "This is inexcusable," he asserted. Clark reported that the three surgeons at the camp were competent professionally but unaware of their duties as military officers. "A medical officer of experience and executive ability should be at once assigned to duty here," he advised. Clark also called for construction of a hospital, a proposal that would prove to be controversial.[33]

As bad as smallpox was, many prisoners feared the results of vaccination almost as much as they did the disease itself. A number of captives complained of "impure matter" being administered, resulting in frightful consequences. On July 12, 1864, Thomas Beadles wrote from Camp Douglas that his arm was "just well from effects of impure vaccine matter which was [given] the first of March." J. B. Stamp, who termed the hospital at Elmira "worthy of commendation," nevertheless recalled that the vaccine administered there produced "loathsome sores completely covering the arm." He heard that in some cases amputation had been necessary. J. Coleman Alderson later noted that similar incidents had occurred at Camp Chase. During a smallpox outbreak in the summer of 1864, Fort Delaware diarist E. L. Cox wrote, "Several men have bad arms from vaxination. I have heard of several who have lost their arms by it. Others have died of it." Although such reports were numerous, the cause of these symptoms is less clear. Eczema and other skin conditions can result in severe complications, including death, when smallpox vaccine is administered.[34]

Other than vaccination, isolation was the main weapon in the battle against smallpox. For camps located close to populous communities this often posed problems. In early 1863 a group of Chicago residents complained to the city's board of health about the Camp Douglas smallpox hospital. The board dispatched three local physicians to study the situation and make a report. The trio suggested moving the facility a short distance and stationing a guard force there to ensure absolute quarantine. They also called for vaccinations. "With these precautions [we] feel that our citizens may yield all alarm," the trio concluded. The hospital was relocated, but the issue came up again in the fall of 1864. The site was near the home of Adele Douglas, widow of the senator, and the University of Chicago. Sweet informed Hoffman that the hospital "has broken up two terms of school at the University and materially injures the [Douglas] estate." Hoffman granted permission to relocate the smallpox hospital again.[35]

At Alton, not only was Hendrickson overwhelmed by the number of smallpox cases, he was unable to locate a place to send the afflicted men. "The people who own property in the vicinity of the city are averse to having a smallpox hospital placed on or near their grounds," he explained. As he searched for a site, the smallpox patients remained in the regular prison hospital. One former prisoner recalled that this facility was some twenty feet from his quarters, "so that we could easily see through the open windows and even converse with the sick." Hendrickson finally had to settle for an island in the Mississippi, where he ordered hospital tents to be pitched. Dr. Clark pronounced the location adequate, although he noted that ice on the river had rendered it unreachable for up to two days. As a result, patients often had to wait to be transferred to the hospital.[36]

At least one Alton prisoner was less impressed than Dr. Clark with the smallpox hospital. During the winter of 1864, D. C. Thomas found himself "prostrated with a severe fever" that turned out to be smallpox. The river was frozen, and he was taken to the hospital in a sled. There was no bed waiting for him, but he learned that one would soon be available as a man had just died. He was limited to two blankets and found the rations to be uneatable. The scene, as he recalled it in 1898, was ghastly. "All day and all night, day after day and night after night, the groans and prayers of the poor, suffering prisoners could be heard piteously begging for water or for some trivial attention from the cold-hearted nurses." Thomas was lucky. He recovered in two weeks and returned to the prison.[37]

Curtis Burke was another survivor. On October 5, 1864, the Camp Douglas captive was loaded on an ambulance and taken to the smallpox hospital near the university. The facility did not impress him. The ward in which he was placed had two stoves, but only one was working, and the roof had "two holes that I could crawl out." Worse, the blankets on his cot were covered with scabs. "I turned the cover back and the smell nearly staggered me," he wrote. The rations were skimpy, but the nurses were kind. They assured Burke that his case was mild. Somebody distributed a "religious paper with the Stars and Stripes in color at its head." Few were read, being used instead "mostly to cover our faces to keep the flies off." On the 19th Burke was well enough to return to the prison, where he was "kept busy for awhile receiving the congratulations of my friends on my recovery and in answering questions concerning the remaining boys of the regiment." Their congratulations were prescient. A month later returning patients informed Burke that the smallpox hospital had become crowded to the point that many were forced to lie on the floor. The stoves were short of coal, and the men were in "a deplorable condition." There was an average of eight deaths a day.[38]

Surviving accounts of prisoners indicate that their opinions of Union medical care, though more often negative, were mixed. Stamp recalled that Elmira surgeons were both accessible and competent. In addition, "The office of chief surgeon was inside the walls, and also a full line of medical stores, which were in charge of competent druggists, and accessible at all hours of the day and night. The strictest rules of cleanliness were enforced in the management of the hospitals." Following a stay in the Elmira prison hospital, H. H. Wiseman wrote, "The Federals deserve credit for the treatment of our sick." He insisted that the hospital was warm and comfortable, the diet was good, and the facility had "a good clock." These views were far from universal. One former Elmira prisoner remembered an incident in which a junior physician asked the chief surgeon how to treat three sick prisoners. He was told to administer four or five drops of an arsenic solution. The doctor wrote it down as "45 drops," and an orderly gave that dosage. The result was three dead prisoners. Anthony Keiley, whose work in the prison office often took him to the hospital, also disagreed with Stamp's view. He charged the doctors with stealing quinine and whiskey and labeled chief surgeon Sanger "simply a brute." According to Keiley, Confederates who served as ward doctors eventually refused to send patients to the hospital. Keiley himself cited one of his own diary entries in which he recorded twenty-nine deaths in one day. He concluded, "The men are being deliberately murdered by the surgeon, especially by either the ignorance or the malice of the chief."[39]

Sanger's list of critics was not limited to prisoners. Rumors that he was addicted to either medicines or alcohol spread both inside and outside the camp. His relations with Tracy were also cool. In October 1864 the camp commander wrote to Hoffman, "The mortality in this camp is so great as to justify, it seems to me, the most rigid investigation to its cause." In addition to diet, clothing, and the effects of Foster's Pond, Tracy also wanted the investigation to include "the competency and efficiency of the medical officers on duty here." The result was Dr. Sloan's visit, which, although critical of conditions at the camp, generally exonerated Sanger. In December, likely to everyone's relief, Surgeon General Joseph K. Barnes granted Sanger's repeated requests for a transfer.[40]

At Johnson's Island Virgil Murphey wrote, "The Hospital for the accomodation of our sick . . . is one of the best regulated institutions I ever saw." Robert Bingham held a decidedly different view. On December 22, 1863, he termed it "a disgrace to the Yankee nation & an outrage to humanity." Bingham continued, "This hospital is a death house, worse provided [for] all the surgeons say than any hospital in the south." He charged that the hospital rations were actually worse than those received in the barracks. Bingham soon moderated his views somewhat. "The hospital is improving," he wrote on January 11, 1864. The beds now had sheets and pillows, and the medical staff was "worth all the surgeons in the army." Isaiah Steedman, the Confederate surgeon confined at Johnson's Island, recalled that the Union surgeons "did their duty as humane men; while they could not change or disobey orders from higher authority, they did their best to ameliorate our condition."[41]

Elsewhere, prisoners did not always feel that the doctors were working their hardest to ameliorate the captives' condition. William Dillon wrote on December 28, 1863, that the orderly sergeant in his barracks had received orders to move all the sick men into middle bunks. The reason was that the doctor did not feel like climbing up or stooping down to attend to a patient. "The medical department is carried on very extensive," George Weston wrote from Camp Douglas. "The [sick] men are all assembled together, the Doctor comes around, feels the pulses looks at their tongues, & goes through a lot of medical preliminaries re. the 1st batch of men gets salt or pills, the 2nd batch gets opium & the 3rd batch gets quinine . . . no matter what kind of disease a man has." The prisoners did not limit this opinion to Union physicians. According to a Point Lookout captive, "Any little reb quack, who has poked his nasal organ inside of an apothecary shop, or whose privilege it was to drive an ambulance in the war, is at once made an M. D." He added, "It is a miracle how many escape [death]." Views concerning poor medical care were not restricted to prisoners. In 1862 a Fort Delaware guard wrote, "We have again

2000 prisoners here, about 300 wounded and one doctor who does not know anything."[42]

Among the worst hospital facilities were those at Camp Morton. Following an October 22, 1863, inspection, Dr. Clark reported that there were two hospitals at the camp. One was in good condition, although overcrowded. The other was "dilapidated and utterly unfit for use." There were six hospital tents in use, all lacking stoves, and 125 sick men in the barracks. The medical officer was Dr. David Funkhouser of Indianapolis, who was employed as a contract surgeon. "This officer is utterly unfit for the post he holds," Clark charged. He accused Funkhouser of maintaining his local private practice, which was extensive, and visiting Camp Morton a half hour or less a day. As a result, most medical matters at the camp were left in the hands of an enlisted man who had "paid some attention to the study of medicine." Clark requested that Funkhouser be replaced, and Hoffman ordered it done.[43]

Funkhouser did not go down without a fight. He insisted that any medical problems at Camp Morton could be traced to poor facilities, a situation beyond his control. It did him no good, but to an extent he was right. A prisoner who arrived at Camp Morton in late 1863 recalled that the tents were always full. "A sick or wounded man would have to wait until a vacancy occurred, by recovery or death (most generally the latter), before he could get a cot." Although two new hospitals went up by the end of 1863, illness increased at a more rapid rate than did medical facilities. Despite the new construction, when Clark returned in January 1864 he found 706 sick prisoners in quarters. Sixteen unfloored tents were still being used, and six more were about to go up. As late as August 1864, Dr. Alexander found the "hospital accomodations much too small." There were still 256 sick prisoners in the barracks and 228 in thirty-eight hospital tents.[44]

One of the most bizarre chapters in hospital construction occurred at Rock Island. It may have begun with a misunderstanding. On February 11, 1864, Col. Johnson sent Hoffman a plan for a prison hospital. He added, "The creation of these buildings has been contracted for at $18,000.00 with the understanding that the expenses are to be repayed by the Prison Saving Fund in case the Q. M. Deptnt declines to erect them." Hoffman apparently misread the figure as $1,800. When he realized the error the commissary general balked. "I find them much more extensive than I thought them to be," he wrote of the plans. He explained, "The pressing necesity for hospital accomodations at the time Surg. Clark was at Rock Island made it unavoidable that all that was possible should be done to provide for the sick, but as such a state of things could not long continue, it was only necessary in permanent arrangements to provide for what might be required under ordinary circumstances." Hoffman insisted that the work be stopped when the project reached "a sufficiency of room for the average number of sick."[45]

Johnson defended the project. He pointed out that there had been 1,490 cases of sickness in February, resulting in 330 deaths. Johnson further asserted, "The fact that many patients remained in Barracks too long, or were never removed for want of accomodations, does in a great degree account for the startling number of deaths." The commissary general of prisoners also received a lecture from Surgeon General Barnes. After reading an inspection report from Rock Island, Barnes wrote to Hoffman, "The necessity for ample hospital accomodations is greater with prisoners than with an equal number of persons under other circumstances, and the immediate completion of the proposed buildings is recommended." Hoffman relented, although he urged that Johnson observe "the closest economy in all things."[46]

This did not happen. Within a few weeks Johnson's estimates rose to $24,000 and then $30,000. The prison fund would not cover the cost, so Johnson proposed to have his quartermaster pay the construction costs and to reimburse him with monthly installments drawn from the prison fund. Hoffman found this arrangement irregular and refused to approve it. The commissary general reminded the commandant of the original $18,000 estimate. He demanded immediately "a detailed statement of the amount of the prison fund thus far expended on the buildings erected and in progress, showing the quantity and cost of the different articles purchased and the amount paid for labor." He also desired to be informed of how much work lay ahead. Johnson responded by first lying about the original estimate, claiming to know nothing of it. He then went on to review the general history of the project, although it was far from the detailed report of expenditures Hoffman had demanded. A follow-up report, supplied by Capt. Charles Reynolds, the Rock Island quartermaster, also did not appease Hoffman. Hoffman complained about specific expenses, but it was one of his generalities that was most troubling. "Of the other items I cannot well judge, but they seem to be on a too liberal scale," he wrote, "much more so than is proper in providing for rebel prisoners."[47]

It was a rare statement for the commissary general of prisoners. Although he never endorsed extravagance—and his standard of what was extravagant was set very low—Hoffman tended to support all that was necessary to prevent suffering. Strangely, in the area of the prisoners' health he often made exceptions. Whether it was the Rock Island hospital, his reluctance to address the nuisance of Foster's Pond at Elmira, or penny-pinching policies that allowed scurvy to emerge and prevail at numerous camps, Hoffman failed the captives most in need of compassion. Medicine was far from a perfect science during the 1860s; and sanitary practices now taken for granted were just beginning to gain acceptance. Where groups of men gathered for long periods of time, disease and death were very likely to follow. Still, the commissary general of prisoners could have acted more decisively to keep those numbers as low as possible in the prisons that were his responsibility.

11
"Our honor could in no way be compromised"
The Road to Release

On October 7, 1864, William Hoffman received a brevet promotion to brigadier general. On November 11 the commissary general of prisoners received what could only be considered a demotion. Brig. Gen. Henry W. Wessells was named commissary general of prisoners for the entire country east of the Mississippi River. Hoffman was relegated to the same position west of the Mississippi. No official reason for the change, which was ordered by Stanton, was given. One piece of evidence suggests that the war secretary may have felt that Wessells would be more amenable than Hoffman to a policy of harsh retaliation. Wessells had been held by the Confederates as a prisoner of war. For a time he was among the Union captives placed under fire at Charleston Harbor. When the Union retaliated by sending the "Immortal 600" from Fort Delaware, Wessells and four other generals had sent a message through the lines, asking that the Confederate hostages be treated kindly. "We think it is just to ask for these officers every kindness and courtesy that you can extend to them, in acknowledgment of the fact that we, at this time, are as pleasantly and comfortably situated as is possible for prisoners of war."[1]

Wessells returned north one month later, part of a special exchange. Upon reaching New York his views abruptly changed. In a letter to Adj. Gen. Lorenzo Thomas, Wessells wrote, "While prisoners in our hands are well fed, clothed, and sheltered, and are treated humanely, our own officers and soldiers are habitually robbed and starved until rendered unfit for further service." He strongly endorsed a policy of retaliation, writing, "As a measure of economy, if not even justice, this is respectfully urged." Wessells proposed the appointment of a commission, composed of Union officers who had been held by the Confederacy. They would visit

Northern prisons "to compare carefully the treatment adopted, and to draw up a code of instructions for the government of our commanders of prisons and others interested, particularly with respect to transportation, shelter, clothing, and subsistence." The commission was never appointed, but the restrictions on sutler sales and boxes that prisoners could receive quickly followed the general's proposals. Two months later Wessells succeeded Hoffman. The reassignment proved temporary, and Hoffman was back at his original post in February.[2]

The commissary general of prisoners departed with a decidedly ambivalent record in the area of retaliation. A good career soldier, he had carried out Stanton's policies to the letter. To an extent these policies had reflected Hoffman's own views. That he was obsessed with frugality is beyond doubt. Still, he approached his position with a sense of humanity, often overlooked by scholars, that made it difficult for him to impose harsh treatment even on enemy soldiers. For example, historians eager to indict Hoffman like to cite a message he sent to Col. Stevens at Camp Morton on November 12, 1863. "So long as a prisoner has clothing upon him, however much torn, you must issue nothing to him," Hoffman wrote, "nor must you allow him to receive clothing from any but members of his immediate family, and only when they are in absolute want." These same historians ignore the fact that just one week earlier Hoffman had asked Meigs to set aside, "out of humane considerations," fifteen thousand suits of inferior clothing, fifteen hundred blankets, and extra shirts for prisoners expected to arrive soon at western depots. Later that same month Hoffman informed Gen. Marston that he had received a negative report about conditions at Point Lookout. "From the report it appears that there is a great want of clothing among the prisoners," he wrote. "Though it is the desire of the War Department to provide as little clothing for them as possible, it does not wish them to be left in the very destitute condition which this report represents." Hoffman instructed Marston to send in requests for whatever clothing was needed.[3]

Still, Hoffman's passion for economy and Stanton's passion for revenge proved a problematic combination for Confederate prisoners. The former was most strongly demonstrated by the establishment and management of the prison fund. Formally announced in a July 7, 1862, circular from Hoffman's office, the fund became almost an obsession with the commissary general of prisoners. It was formed from "surplus" rations that were withheld and resold to the commissary. A tax on sutlers was also intended to go into the fund. The savings were to be used to purchase such things as tables, cooking utensils, items for policing, bed ticks and straw, enlargements of barracks, and to pay prisoners employed as clerks. Although ostensibly established solely for "the health and comfort of the prisoners," the fund was often used for other purposes. Hoffman allowed Johnson to use it to purchase furniture, stationery, and lamps for his Rock Island office. He informed Orme at Camp Douglas that money from the fund could be used to purchase lamps for the prison grounds and the guardhouses. At Johnson's Island the fund was used routinely to purchase such office supplies as lamps, chairs, and ink, as well as tables, stoves, and bunks for the guard quarters. While commanding Camp Chase, Col. William Wallace went too far, buying carpeting and curtains for his office with the fund. When Hoffman found out he recommended a court-martial, but by then Wallace had returned to field duty and it is doubtful that he was tried.[4]

After the war ended Hoffman returned to the government $1,845,125.99 in savings from prison and hospital funds. The fund at Point Lookout, where prisoners lived in tents, was over $500,000. Fort Delaware reported a savings of over $300,000. At Rock Island, where Hoffman had quibbled over the cost of building a hospital, the fund had a surplus of $174,000. Although Hoffman had informed one commander, "It is not desirable to accumulate any large fund on hand," it appears that Union commandants had taken their cues from Hoffman's frugality.[5]

Although officially responsible for prisons west of the Mississippi, Hoffman's new position instead took him to Louisville. There he supervised the transportation of the last great wave of prisoners taken in the West. Confederate general John Bell Hood had led the Army of Tennessee on an ill-fated campaign that included severe defeats at Franklin on November 30 and Nashville on December 16. A civilian described the retreating Confederates as "the most broken down set I ever saw." A participant wrote of "the bare & bleeding feet of the men." The plight of the prisoners appealed to Hoffman's sense of compassion. On December 22 he asked the War Department if, under the terms of a recent agreement, shoes could be provided for them out of funds raised by the Confederates. As usual, Stanton was in no mood to be compassionate. Inspector General James Hardie replied, "The Secretary of War desires to know whether the prisoners whom you suggest should be supplied with shoes . . . are any part of that rebel army recently engaged in killing Union troops at Nashville, and whether they are more destitute or worse provided for now in food, shelter, and raiment than when engaged in that work." Hoffman stood his ground. He reminded Hardie that Union policy had been to provide all necessary clothing. "My impression is that the order for the issue of clothing has not yet been countermanded. If it has, I have not received the order." Hoffman made his point, but the Confederates remained shoeless.[6]

The prisoners from Hood's army ended up at Camp Chase, Camp Douglas, and Johnson's Island. Many died from the effects of the trying campaign, complicated by Stanton's obstinacy. Officials at Louisville reported on at least two occasions that the captives they were forwarding were "in a very destitute condition." Both prisoners and Union officials at the camps to which the prisoners were forwarded agreed. The inspecting officer at Camp Douglas reported that they were "poorly clad, many of them are nearly barefoot, and destitute of blankets." One resident prisoner noted that the newly arriving captives were "suffering severely from frost bitten feet." Another noted, "Seven hundred prisoners arrived today, frost-bitten, naked, & hungry. Awful picture." A veteran Camp Chase guard wrote, "They are the most destitute and spiritless of any perhaps that have ever arrived here, many of them being entirely barefooted and others suffering from scarcity of clothing." Richardson reported that the captives had been "very much exposed, and great mortality prevails." The bluntest assessment was offered by Capt. Edward Allen, Camp Chase's inspecting officer. On March 11, 1865, he reported, "A very large decrease in numbers of sick and deaths since my last [report] is attributable to the fact that those brought here in an almost dying condition have died."[7]

On October 30, 1864, Confederate officials sent an unusual proposal through Union lines. Robert Ould, the Confederate agent of exchange, sought permission from Gen. Grant to ship a load of cotton to the North. The cotton would be sold and the proceeds used to purchase items for Confederate prisoners. Grant immediately gave tentative approval. Administration officials added their consent, and on November 11, the general in chief informed Ould that a shipment of one thousand bales of cotton from Mobile would be received in New York. As part of the arrangement the Union would be permitted to send supplies to its prisoners held in the South.[8]

Had matters then proceeded in a timely way, the arrangement would have prevented a great deal of suffering as another Northern winter approached. Unfortunately, problems quickly arose that delayed the operation. Under the original agreement a paroled Confederate prisoner was to make arrangements for the sale of the cotton and the purchase of the supplies. Maj. Gen. Isaac Trimble, a prisoner at Fort Warren, was originally selected. Stanton objected to Trimble, however, and Brig. Gen. William N. R. Beall, whom Stanton termed "unexceptionable," was chosen in his place. Beall set up headquarters in New York at 75 Murray Street and put up a small sign reading, "Brig. Gen. W. N. R. Beall, C.S. Army, Agent to Supply Prisoners of War." This attracted some attention in the press, enough that Beall offered to remove "C.S. Army" from the sign. Instead Stanton ordered Beall's parole revoked until the cotton arrived. Halleck ordered Brig. Gen. Halbert E. Paine, the Union official chosen to accompany Beall in the work, to place Beall in Fort Lafayette.[9]

Meanwhile, there were delays at Mobile. First Union officials refused to accept the shipment because they had not received the necessary declaration of readiness. Then bad weather caused the Confederate vessel bearing the cotton to run aground. The cargo was transferred to flatboats, enabling the main vessel to pass. However, one of the flats broke adrift, causing two more days of delay. The next problem to plague the operation was a shortage of men to load the cotton onto the Union ship. Some of the cotton was damaged amid all this confusion. Finally, on January 16, 1865, 830 bales of cotton were on their way to New York. The shipment arrived eight days later.[10]

By then winter was one month old and the prisoners were desperate for clothing. As he awaited the shipment Beall sought permission, with Paine's support, to purchase supplies on credit. Stanton denied the request, viewing it as "an application to purchase goods on the credit of the so-called Confederate Government." At the same time Union officials were citing the impending shipment as a reason for not supplying the needs of prisoners. Officers had been selected at each prison to ascertain the needs of the captives and forward a report to Beall. On December 27 Col. William Hawkins, a prisoner at Camp Chase, informed Beall that twenty-five hundred prisoners greatly in need of clothing and blankets were on their way from Tennessee. Camp officials had been instructed to issue no clothing to them because "the Confederacy will supply them." Beall could do nothing more than urge Hawkins to have other prisoners share supplies with them until the shipment arrived. The same week Fort Delaware's inspecting officer reported that the prisoners had submitted a requisition to Beall. It had not arrived, "hence the increase in sickness and deaths."[11]

At Elmira a series of miscommunications left a large number of prisoners to suffer for two months. On December 1 Tracy submitted a requisition for clothing. A few days later he received a portion of what he asked for but was still short by one thousand jackets, twenty-five hundred shirts, three thousand pairs of trousers, seven thousand socks, and eight thousand drawers. Soon after that Tracy received word of the impending cotton deal. On January 5 Tracy informed Wessells that thousands of prisoners at Elmira were growing desperate for clothing while awaiting the arrival of the cotton. Fourteen days later Wessells replied that the original requisition had been held at his office because Tracy had failed to report his views "on the necessity of such issue," as requested. The clothing Tracy had received had been sent by mistake. More time was consumed as Tracy replied that he had not made the report because he had believed at the time that supplies from the cotton sale would soon arrive. On January 27, after Tracy had forwarded the report in question, he was informed that the requisition was denied. Maj. George Blagden, an assistant to Wessells, explained, "As the cotton for the purchase of supplies for rebel prisoners has arrived at New York, it is supposed that clothing will be forwarded by General Beall nearly or quite as soon as it could be furnished by the Quartermaster's Department."[12]

Another result of the delays was that less money was realized from the sales. As 1865 dawned the plight of the Confederacy appeared desperate, and the anticipation of peace drove cotton prices down. After taxes and other expenses, Beall had $331,789.66 with which to purchase supplies. He dispatched items to fourteen Union camps. The prisoners received 13,248 blankets, 12,218 coats and jackets, 13,636 pairs of pants, 15,140 shirts, 9,608 drawers, 13,625 pairs of socks, and 11,175 pairs of shoes. Prison diarists made little mention of the arrival of the items, which reached most of the camps in March. Thomas Beadles, who helped distribute the clothing at Camp Douglas, noted only that, thanks to the position, he got to stay up late and "write as much & when I please." At Elmira Henri Mugler complained that the "long looked for and much talked of Confederate clothing" did not begin to meet the needs of the prisoners. Indeed, about the only prisoner to remark positively about the shipments was Washington Pickens Nance, who was confined at Camp Chase. Writing on March 12, Nance observed, "The prisoners look considerably improved dressed up in the new clothing Col. Hawkins distributed."[13]

The operation impressed Stanton even less than it did the prisoners. He particularly objected to the fact that Beall had purchased only blankets and clothing with the proceeds. "The result," Halleck wrote to Grant, "is that we feed their prisoners and permit the rebel Government to send cotton within our lines . . . to purchase and carry back the means of fitting out their own men for the field." Because of this, Stanton decided against allowing any future shipments.[14]

Stanton's concern about goods being carried back to the South was justified because prisoner exchange had finally been resumed. It started with a proposal from Gen. Benjamin Butler. The officer that Jefferson Davis had proclaimed "a felon deserving of capital punishment" had been named "special agent of exchange" in late 1863. Despite the South's enmity toward him, the publicity-hungry general worked hard to arrange a resumption of exchanges. In doing so he went against the expressed wishes of his general in chief. In 1862, when he had to deal with the deluge of prisoners from Fort Donelson, Grant had favored a policy of immediate parole. For equally practical reasons, Grant had paroled the Vicksburg garrison in 1863. Now, with Lee's army under siege before Petersburg, pragmatism did not favor exchange. As Grant explained the situation to Butler, "It is hard on our men held in Southern prisons not to exchange them, but it is humanity to those left in the ranks to fight our battles. Every man we hold, when released on parole or otherwise, becomes an active soldier against us at once either directly or indirectly. If we commence a system of exchange which liberates all prisoners taken, we will have to fight on until the whole South is exterminated. If we hold those caught they amount to no more than dead men."[15]

There were, however, other factors to consider. One was the fact that 1864 was a presidential election year and the public clamor for a resumption of exchange was growing. On September 9 Butler made a proposal to Robert Ould that took into account both political considerations and Grant's military concerns. He suggested an exchange "from time to time" of sick and wounded prisoners who would likely remain unfit for duty for sixty days. Ould agreed, and Hoffman soon sent word to the Northern commandants to prepare to ship invalid enlisted prisoners who were well enough to travel.[16]

On September 15 a Johnson's Island prisoner wrote, "There was considerable of pleasure & excitement caused this morning by the appearance at the Hospital of the Yankee Doctors who announced that their mission was to examine the patients for the purpose of selecting twenty of the worst cases, who were to be sent on exchange to Dixie." The physicians approved twenty-two more the next day, and that afternoon all forty-two "passed out of the detestable prison yard, & went on their way rejoicing." At Elmira the examinations began two weeks later. On October 11 a group of fourteen hundred departed the New York pen, thus missing a bitter winter of captivity. Although they were supposed to include only those unable to fight in the ranks, Henri Mugler observed, "There were many hearty looking rebs among them."[17]

Anthony Keiley had a ready explanation for the healthy appearance of the allegedly invalid prisoners. According to Keiley, his fellow captives resorted to a number of schemes to "corrupt the integrity" of the examiners. One of them informed the doctor that an arm wound would preclude him from service for the required sixty days. He took the physician aside and rolled up his sleeve, exposing a $5 greenback. As he removed the note, the doctor instructed his clerk to "enter Mr. B, gunshot wound in left arm."[18]

Such shenanigans were not limited to Elmira. At Fort Delaware three diarists wrote that bribery was practiced extensively. The rate generally ranged from $50 to $100, "the highest price having the best chance" for a quick release. The system was not without its flaws. William Burgwyn gave a fellow prisoner $40 to pass along to one of the examiners. The next day the Federal surgeon said the prisoner, who had already departed for exchange, had never given him any money. Burgwyn believed him, concluding that the prisoner had absconded with his money. This view seemed confirmed when he later discovered that the man had also stolen a handkerchief and a pair of woolen drawers from him.[19]

Those undeserving of a medical exchange proved to be less of a problem than those unable to stand the trip. On September 25 Butler sent a message to Hoffman, chiding the commissary general because nearly thirty out of five hundred had died in an early group. "The occurrence does not speak well either for the Government or its officials," Butler complained. Four days later Hoffman sent instructions to Elmira. He called for a careful examination by medical examiners and specifically instructed Tracy to send none who were "too feeble to endure the journey." Despite this clear order, at least five prisoners died before the trains reached Baltimore en route to City Point. Many others had to be transferred to hospitals in the city.[20]

Anthony Keiley, who accompanied the contingent as a nurse, placed some of the blame on the Northern Central Railroad. The line took forty hours to deliver the men, crammed into boxcars, the 260 miles to Baltimore. Josiah Simpson, an army surgeon and Baltimore's medical director, knew where to place the bulk of the responsibility. "The condition of these men was pitiable in the extreme and evinces criminal neglect and inhumanity on the part of the medical officers making the selection of men to be transferred," he wrote in a message to Hoffman. Simpson backed up his contention with reports from two medical inspectors he had dispatched to investigate the situation. One reported from the railroad depot, "These men were debilitated from long sickness to such a degree that it was necessary to carry them in the arms of attendants from the cars to the ambulances, and one man died in the act of being thus transferred." Another visited the steamer that was about to depart with the men not sent to local hospitals. He found forty who were so feeble that he did not believe they should continue. However, he heeded their pleas to be allowed to continue on toward freedom and home. Still, he concluded, "Someone, in my opinion, is greatly censurable for sending such cases away from camp even for exchange." Their reports moved Hoffman, who forwarded them to Stanton. Tracy and Sanger, he wrote, had "neglected the ordinary prompting of humanity," and he suggested that they "be immediately ordered to some other service."[21]

The issue of exchange suddenly reemerged in the winter of 1865. By then Grant had dispatched the troublesome Butler and was largely handling exchange negotiations himself. The last days of the Confederacy were clearly on the horizon, allowing the general in chief to moderate his strident position. On January 13 he approved a proposal made by the Confederates four months earlier that all prisoners in close confinement be released. On February 2 he informed Stanton, "I am endeavoring to make arrangements to exchange about 3,000 prisoners per week." Grant had not totally abandoned his practical concerns. He asked that Confederates from Missouri, Kentucky, Arkansas, Tennessee, and Louisiana, states firmly under Union control, be released first. After observing that the Rebels were sending their returned prisoners directly to Lee's army, he instructed Hoffman to make certain that men unfit for duty were returned first.[22]

In one area Grant's practicality went too far even for Stanton. At most camps large numbers of prisoners did not want to return to the Confederate army. Thomas Beadles placed the number at Camp Douglas somewhere between twenty-five hundred and three thousand. Rock Island prisoner William Dillon predicted that fewer than one-half of his comrades would return South, although he included in his predictions those who had died. At Camp Chase Col. Richardson addressed a detachment of prisoners and asked those not wishing to leave to step forward. Some 260, mostly members of Hood's army, did. Word of this incident reached Grant, who disapproved of the procedure. "Those who do not wish to go back are the ones whom it is most desirable to exchange," he wrote to Gen. Hitchcock. "If they do not wish to serve in the rebel army they can return to us after exchange and avoid it." Stanton referred the matter to Halleck, who concluded that it was "contrary to the usages of war to force a prisoner of war to return to the enemy's ranks." This view became Union policy, and orders went out to all commandants against sending away prisoners who preferred not to be exchanged.[23]

Despite all this there were still many Southerners eager for exchange. As rumors began to swirl, Camp Chase prisoner Samuel Beckett Boyd wrote that the "prospect of exchange creates quite an excitement." He added, "Willing to be exchanged for Negroes." When the official word came it broke up preaching services in one of the barracks. To this news Boyd added, "Great joy." Over the next three weeks Boyd's fellow prisoner Washington Pickens Nance recorded five departures of five hundred prisoners each. Beadles observed the same pattern at Camp Douglas, writing after one departure, "Excitement grand." Although Dillon had predicted that most Rock Island prisoners would refuse exchange, he wrote of the announcement, "This news has elevated the spirits of the men very much."[24]

As in September, release brought hazards to prisoners in poor health. Once again Elmira provided the most dramatic case. On February 5, one day after Tracy received orders from Hoffman to prepare three thousand prisoners for exchange, the commandant offered a suggestion. Recalling the events of four months earlier, Tracy proposed shipping the men to New York City aboard the Erie Railroad. The line had an abundance of passenger cars on which to transport the prisoners, and the journey would be much quicker. Despite Tracy's assurances that there would be no extra cost, Hoffman failed to act upon the recommendation. The prisoners were again shipped aboard the Northern Central, and the journey was again a slow one. This time three died on their way to Baltimore. Tracy blamed the railroad, but this did not explain the fact that one Elmira prisoner arrived in Baltimore suffering from smallpox.[25]

Suffering was not limited to Elmira prisoners. Henry Hays Forwood, who left Camp Morton on February 26, informed his brother that the men were "crowded up 40 and 50 in one of those old filthy [boxcars] like a lot of hogs." Rations were so skimpy, he wrote, that three or four died of starvation. Forwood avoided that fate by trading his pocketknife during the layover in Baltimore for two loaves of bread. Troubles on the railroads plagued Curtis Burke and a group of fellow Camp Douglas captives. Leaving on March 2, their train got just seventy-two miles from Chicago when it collided with another train. Injuries were minimal. Reaching the Baltimore & Ohio at Wheeling the men were transferred from passenger to boxcars. At Fairmont they had to walk a short distance because Confederate forces had burned a bridge across the Monongahela River. Although Burke did not write of anyone starving, he did observe that the prisoners' rations were gone by the time they reached Cumberland, Maryland. They were apparently not supplemented until the train reached Baltimore, and then by civilians. For John Dooley and some two hundred comrades, the worst part of the exchange trip from Johnson's Island was the first. The lake was frozen solidly, "and the poor bewildered fellows [were] almost tempted to return to prison" rather than venture out onto the ice. It was a new experience for a large number of the Southerners. Many slipped and fell during the march, but none were seriously injured.[26]

On February 27, nearly three months after his attempt to get out by bribery had failed, William Burgwyn "left and I hope forever all the privations of Fort Delaware." His privations were not quite over. Six hundred Confederates were crowded aboard the steamer *Cressandra* "in bunks so close together you could not sit up." Guards were posted to ensure that the prisoners did not leave their cramped quarters. They reached the exchange point near City Point on March 1 but had to remain aboard for another day. Once off the ship he left behind what was to him the last annoying symbol of Northern rule, noting, "my feelings as we passed the last Negro picket were undescribable." The next day he received a furlough home until formally exchanged.[27]

For thousands of Confederate captives exchange did not come soon enough. One of the saddest ironies of the Union prison camp system was the fact that the number of deaths peaked in February 1865, only two months before Lee's surrender at Appomattox. During that month 1,646 prisoners died at the Union's eight largest camps. Camp Chase had the most deaths with 499. Elmira was a close second at 426. The totals were 243 at Camp Douglas, 223 at Point Lookout, 133 at Camp Morton, and 60 at Fort Delaware. All of these figures were greater than during the previous February. Indeed, only 18 prisoners had died at Camp Chase and 54 at Camp Douglas during February 1864. Only at Johnson's Island and Rock Island were the numbers lower than the year before. Rock Island went from 346 deaths in February 1864 to 56 in February 1865. At Johnson's Island the number dropped from 17 to 6.[28]

By this time most prison diarists did not even bother to record the deaths of their comrades. Those who did noted it in a very matter-of-fact manner. "There were twenty dead men hauled out in the dead waggon today," Mugler wrote from Elmira on March 8. Seven days later, Camp Chase prisoner Samuel Boyd wrote, "Another carried out this morning." Boyd, who did not arrive at Camp Chase until January 1865, explained, "The prisoners pay no more, if as much, attention to a dead body as they would to a dead dog."[29]

On April 2, 1865, following a siege of ten months, Robert E. Lee's lines at Petersburg collapsed. The next day Union forces entered Richmond. Six days later Lee surrendered his Army of Northern Virginia to Grant at Appomattox Court House. These events presaged the end of the war and the emptying of the prisons, but among the Confederate captives they produced a mixed reaction. "This day news has arrived of the fall of Richmond and spread a general gloom over the prisoners," Boyd wrote from Camp Chase. Although noting, "It was nothing more than I have for some time expected," Camp Douglas prisoner Thomas Beadles still termed the news "appalling." When word of Lee's surrender arrived one week later, Beadles added, "The more sanguine say now that the war is over & we lost the cause that we battled for, for the last four years." As artillerists fired salutes at Fort Delaware celebrating Lee's surrender, Pvt. Henry Robinson Berkeley, himself a Confederate gunner, wrote, "The firing of these guns makes my heart sink within me. To think that all the blood and treasure, which the South has so unsparingly poured on the altar of our country, should have been shed in vain."[30]

At Elmira news of the surrender was posted on the bulletin board. "Some seem to rejoice—while others lament the capture of so noble an army," Gramling wrote of his fellow prisoners. A premature report of Lee's surrender reached Fort Delaware on April 7, according to prisoner James Bennington Irvine. He added that the guards offered ten-to-one odds, betting that it was true, and found several takers. When the official report arrived, punctuated by the firing of salutes, Irvine wrote, "It would be a hard task to analyse or define my feelings today. The prisoners seem to have made up their minds to bear with philosophy what they cannot help. Some bluster & talk but most are quiet awaiting further developments." A Point Lookout guard wrote that the prisoners there were not at all ambivalent. "They cheered loud and long when they heard that Lee had surrendered," he informed his wife. "They are tired of the war." Prisoner James T. Meade partially confirmed the guard's observations, writing, "I am sorry to say that some of our men appeared as much rejoiced as the Yanks."[31]

Few captives were "rejoiced" on April 17, when word of the assassination of President Lincoln reached the Union prisons. "A few of the prisoners shouted," Rufus Barringer wrote from Fort Delaware, "but nearly all look sad, solemn, & many with fear and alarm." E. L. Cox observed, "Instead of a general rejoicing amongst the prisoners there seems to be a settled sadness upon the countenances of almost every man." From Elmira Henri Mugler wrote, "I have not heard a single prisoner express gratification that the President has met with his death. Very many express deep regret that it has happened and hope that the perpetrator of the worse than fiendish act will meet with deserving punishment."[32]

The sadness was as much practical as it was emotional. "I am afraid that we poor devils will have to suffer for his death," Capt. Joseph Wescoat wrote from Fort Delaware. "It is pretty generally believed that the assassination of President Lincoln has deprived the South of a friend," Mugler observed. "President Lincoln is known to have expressed a great desire and a determination to treat the South with moderation." According to John Joyes, the prisoners at Johnson's Island felt the same way. "Our officers all regard the death of Mr. L. as a sad blow to our future—for we were fully impressed with the belief that his policy would be lenient." Another Johnson's Island prisoner, E. John Ellis, wrote, "If the South is too weak to prolong and carry to a successful terminus her struggle, Mr. Lincoln's death was a misfortune to her people, for he was disposed to be conciliatory and magnanimous. If the struggle is prolonged, she has lost a dangerous enemy."[33]

In isolated cases the consequences of the assassination were more immediate. Pvt. Berkeley wrote that a Yankee guard came into his barracks at Fort Delaware "beastly drunk," brandishing a club. Two or three prisoners were badly beaten, but most were able to evade him. According to Irvine, the guns of the fort were turned toward the prisoners. He also wrote that a Union corporal had been overheard instructing a sentinel "to shoot any of us if they had half a chance." In a letter to his mother, Point Lookout guard George Pearl reported that a Confederate major had been "severely pounded and kicked" for endorsing the deed. He added that there had been other similar incidents. Isaiah Steedman's exchange trip took him to Point Lookout. He later wrote that the black guards there "were wild with rage and thirsting for revenge." Steedman claimed that the guards' white officers warned the prisoners to remain in the barracks and do nothing provocative. A prisoner at Old Capitol who was awaiting transfer to Johnson's Island later claimed that "a vast mob of negroes and the lower grades of whites" thronged to the prison seeking revenge. Infantry, cavalry, and six pieces of artillery were called out to maintain order. Still, the man recalled, "How we did wish for muskets!"[34]

The collapse of Petersburg and Grant's pursuit of Lee resulted in the final surge of Confederate prisoners. More arrived from the Carolinas as Gen. Sherman sparred with Gen. Joseph Johnston's Confederate forces. Even with exchanges again taking place, the deluge taxed Union prison facilities. Hoffman addressed the challenge by opening two new prisons. The first was at Hart's Island. Located in Long Island Sound, the facility had served as a draft rendezvous. Gen. Wessells, the former commissary general of prisoners, commanded the camp. On April 7 he received the first contingent, of 2,027 prisoners. Four days later the prison population swelled to 3,413. Within a few weeks 1,847 were sick, and 217 had died. A Union medical inspector dismissed these figures, asserting that one detachment of prisoners had been "nearly all broken on arrival." He did concede that hospital facilities were inadequate. They consisted of six hospital tents, each with 48 beds, and the post hospital, which had 111 beds.[35]

James Marsh Morey of the Thirty-second Tennessee reached Hart's Island on April 10. He had been captured by Sherman's forces in South Carolina on February 12. For the next six weeks he and his fellow prisoners endured almost daily marches of twelve to twenty-two miles, often through rain and mud. On March 27 they reached Kinston, North Carolina, where they boarded a train for New Berne. From there the prisoners took steamers first to Fort Monroe, then to New York. "We are very much crowded not having room to sit down," he noted. The men also suffered from a lack of water and fresh air. Morey did not mention the poor health of the Hart's Island prisoners, although he did write that one death resulted from one of the numerous fights between the captives. "The rations are enough to sustain life, but they lack a great deal of satisfying our appetites," he noted on April 15. Within a month he was writing, "This life has come to be very disagreeable to me, for I am hungry most of the time."[36]

The last Union prison to open was at Newport News, Virginia. Hoffman sought permission from Grant to establish the depot on April 8 and received Grant's approval the next day. Col. J. H. Davidson of the 122nd United States Colored Troops was placed in command of the camp, and his outfit served as the guard force. On April 11 Davidson and an engineer officer surveyed the ground and selected a site for the prison. The colonel offered the quaint assurance that "no pains will be spared to make it a healthy and safe retreat for Southern gentlemen of rebellious proclivities." He had little time to do so. Three days later the first 2,000 prisoners arrived. By April 25 the number would reach 3,290. Hoffman informed Davidson that the prisoners would have to construct their own barracks. In the meantime, camp officials gave the captives the freedom of the enclosure and instructed them to "use the beach for sinks."[37]

Davidson worked hard to honor his promise to make the prison healthy and safe. He called for the establishment of a hospital and virtually begged Hoffman to send a competent medical officer. When the officer of the day included the words "Prison Filthy" in his report of April 27, the colonel conducted his own inspection and found the prison to be in "a shameful condition." He informed the superintendent of the prison that he had found everything from old rags to human excrement in the spaces between the encampments. "You will be held accountable for the condition of everything inside the enclosure and will at once take steps to secure a thorough cleansing of every foot of ground within the enclosure," he ordered. Despite his efforts, seventy-eight prisoners died at Newport News during April and May. One prison diarist wrote on April 20, "I do not believe there are a hundred well men in the camp."[38]

One of the greatest threats to the well-being of the prisoners turned out to be Davidson's own outfit. "They abuse the prisoners in a most infamous manner," Creed Thomas Davis wrote of the 122nd USCT. He recorded three incidents in his diary in which the guards shot and killed prisoners. On another occasion he wrote that one of the sentinels bayoneted a prisoner, killing him instantly. Davis's observations were perhaps tainted by his personal views. When the Fifth Maryland, a white outfit, replaced the 122nd, Davis wrote, "I know they will not be so wanton in their cruelty. Besides they are white. The angels in Heaven are white." Davis's prejudices aside, his fellow prisoner Smith Kitchin agreed that the Maryland troops were more liberal in their treatment of the prisoners.[39]

Camp records confirm two of the shooting incidents recorded by Davis, although neither was fatal. In both cases the evidence presented tended to exonerate the sentinels. Authorities ruled that one of the shootings was accidental. A guard had been examining his weapon following a brief rain shower when it discharged. The ball struck a prisoner, badly shattering his arm above the wrist. According to the officer of the day, several prisoners confirmed that the shooting was accidental. During the night of April 20, shots were fired at two guard posts. Both times officers reported that they had heard the guards order prisoners to halt at least twice, as required by their orders, before shooting. A single guard fired the first time but did not hit anybody. The second time Thomas M. Tyree was fired upon and hit by three sentinels, although he was not seriously hurt. Tyree claimed that he had diarrhea and was going to the sinks. He also insisted that he had halted as ordered before he was shot. All three guards testified that other prisoners were following Tyree and that they believed all of them were trying to escape.[40]

On March 27 Hoffman reported to Grant that the Union had delivered 24,200 paroled prisoners to the Confederates. The North had received only 16,700 in return. In response the general in chief issued instructions to slow deliveries but not to halt them altogether. This, combined with the surrender of Lee and the fall of Richmond, made the oath of allegiance a more palatable option. Subsequent bad news from the fighting front only increased the trend. On April 26 Johnston surrendered his forces to Sherman. When this news reached Fort Delaware, one diarist wrote, "This settles the matter many applications have been made by those who answered no to change it to yes." Another added that the oath was "growing more popular" among the enlisted prisoners. As for the officers, "Few were in the humor to take it" at that point.[41]

Such ambivalence is easy to understand. For many prisoners the decision to accept the oath was an agonizing one. According to Thomas Beadles, the question was put to the prisoners at an April 27 roll call. Only eighty refused. "I waited to the last hour without final decision, but answered in the affirmative," he wrote. The previous day Gramling had accepted the oath at Elmira. "Most all have applied to take the oath and I was weak enough to do so also." One day later Gramling added, "Am feeling troubled today, afraid I have done wrong." At Fort Delaware "several little fights" broke out over the issue, but the vast majority of prisoners accepted. Diarist James Irvine wrote on May 1 that 2,000 officers and nearly 6,000 enlisted men had taken the oath. Only 146 were still refusing. Outside pressure was also a factor. According to E. L. Cox, many of the prisoners received letters from friends urging them to acquiesce.[42]

At Point Lookout delegations from the various Confederate states met to determine what course of action they should pursue. According to prisoner George Washington Nelson, the meetings grew out of a difficult conclusion reached by most of the prisoners. "The surrender of Johnston's army, together with the voluntary surrender of one or two members of President Davis' Cabinet have combined to force upon us the conclusion that the Southern Confederacy is now a thing of the past." Nelson attended the meeting of the Virginia prisoners, which he termed the "most affecting meeting at which I was ever present." All questions were thoroughly discussed, all opinions freely expressed. In the end the men concluded that "our government no longer existed in fact, that therefore our obligations to it were at an end, and our honor could in no way be compromised by any course we might pursue." The following day camp officials called the roll of officers to determine whether they were willing to take the oath. Nelson wrote that out of 2,300 only 161 refused. He was with the majority.[43]

Regardless of the decisions made by the Confederate prisoners, their fate remained in the hands of Union authorities. On May 8 the War Department announced its policy. All prisoners below the rank of general who had agreed to take the oath of allegiance before the fall of Richmond could be released upon taking the oath. Grant appeared to prefer an even more sweeping policy. "I hope early means may be devised for clearing our prisons as far as possible," he wrote Stanton on the 18th. "By going now they may still raise something for their subsistence for the coming year and prevent suffering next winter." Hoffman proposed going more slowly, calling for the release of about fifty men per day from each of the Union's seventeen prison camps. As he explained it to Grant, this would take about two months. His reason for allowing large numbers of prisoners to languish in the camps much of the summer was that the process would not be "too much hurried, and [would] save much labor in your office, and this one also." Andrew Johnson favored Grant's approach, and as president he had the power to speed up the process. On June 6 Johnson ordered that the prisoners be discharged as quickly as the rolls could be prepared. On July 20 he called for the immediate release of all remaining Confederate prisoners. The only exceptions were those captured with Jefferson Davis and "any others where special reasons are known to exist for holding them."[44]

Surviving evidence suggests that the Federal commandants did all they could to release their prisoners quickly and start them for home. As early as May 13, Beadles wrote that 200 were leaving Camp Douglas each day. Still, it was a slow process. Beadles was part of a contingent that departed exactly one month later. In the meantime, he wrote, "Monotony still rules the camp. The anxiety to get home exceeds everything else." On May 17 Richardson announced that he had released 1,470 Confederates from Camp Chase in nine days. On June 12 Col. Hill addressed the anxiety of the Johnson's Island prisoners. In a notice to the Confederates Hill explained that he had just devoted twenty-six consecutive hours to working on releases. During this time he had completed 219 cases. It had been his hope, Hill asserted, to dispose of 200 cases each day, but the paperwork required by regulations made this impossible. One problem, he explained, was the large number of prisoners insisting that they had agreed to take the oath before the fall of Richmond. They were informed that substantial proof would be required. Despite such problems Hill gave his assurance that "there shall be no want of effort to dispatch cases." At Rock Island Col. Johnson took advantage of an opportunity to dispatch 400 cases. On June 18 an empty steamer reached the island, returning to St. Louis after delivering a group of soldiers to St. Paul. The captain offered to take away the prisoners at a savings of $2.68 per man. Johnson reasoned that Hoffman would appreciate the bargain and sent away the last of his captives.[45]

On May 16 Gen. Barnes informed Hoffman that 1,859 Confederates remained in the large Hammond Hospital adjacent to Point Lookout. Some 1,600, he estimated, could be discharged if the government would provide them with transportation to their homes. Barnes, too, had learned how to appeal to Hoffman, noting, "Many are disabled by loss of limbs and otherwise by wounds and the expense of taking care of them here is considerable." Hoffman forwarded the message to Stanton, agreeing that the cost of sending them home would soon be offset by the savings. The war secretary gave his approval. On June 2 this policy became general as the War Department issued orders that released prisoners were to be provided with transportation. Nine days later all of the hospitalized prisoners at Fort Delaware were released. As they prepared to depart E. L. Cox observed, "Some of them is scarcely able to travel and would not attempt [to] under different circumstances."[46]

Transportation cleared the biggest hurdle for the thousands of Southerners desperate to return home; but even this did not guarantee that the trip would be easy. Many prisoners ended their diaries with their release from prison, but a few continued to record their thoughts and experiences until they reached home. One was Luther Rice Mills. After being released from Johnson's Island on June 19, Mills gradually made his way to Baltimore by train. Having only $1.50, he ate little and slept on platforms while waiting for connections. The inconvenience was worth it. When he reached home six days later, "the old 'rooster' in the morello-cherry tree crowed me a cordial welcome." Sustenance was the biggest problem for Francis Asbury Burrows, who was released from Point Lookout on May 12. When his rations ran out two days later, he tried unsuccessfully for the next two days to secure rations from a provost marshal. He finally succeeded on the 16th. His diary ended the next day as he awaited transportation to Charleston. The trip back to a war-ravaged South was also a journey into the unknown. Although he did not elaborate, Paul McMichael of Orangeburg, South Carolina, alluded to this when he wrote on August 9, "About 2 P. M. reached what is left of Orangeburg." Still, "Much rejoiced to get home again and find all well."[47]

These feelings were echoed by William G. B. Morris of the Sixty-fourth North Carolina. When he was released from Johnson's Island on June 12, Morris wrote, "Oh what a happy day to be at Liberty once more." Two days later he crossed the Ohio River at Bellaire. The Baltimore & Ohio Railroad delivered him to Baltimore the next day. From there he boarded a crowded steamer for Fortress Monroe. Successive railroad connections then took him to Burkeville, Danville, Salisbury, Charlotte, and Greenville. He reached his home in Henderson County on June 25. He undoubtedly spoke for thousands of fellow captives when he wrote, "How happy I am to be at home sweet home with my kind friends once more. Bless the Lord he has brought me safe home again."[48]

On July 5 Hoffman reported to Grant that, except for 150 officers at Johnson's Island, the Union prisons were virtually empty. The few sick prisoners remaining had been transferred to post hospitals, where they were no longer under guard. By October 31 only four prisoners remained in Union hands. All were political prisoners, and all were incarcerated at Fort Lafayette. The last of them was released the following March. Meanwhile, on November 3, 1865, Hoffman was relieved from his duties as commissary general of prisoners and ordered to rejoin his regiment. He remained in the army until 1870, retiring with the rank of major general. Hoffman then relocated to Rock Island, Illinois, got married, and lived for twelve years within sight of one of the prisons he had supervised.[49]

As for the prisons themselves, most quickly vanished. A few, such as Elmira, Camp Douglas, Camp Chase, and Camp Morton, were used to muster out volunteers before being abandoned. Those along the East Coast, including Forts Delaware and Warren, reverted to their prewar function of protecting their section of the coast. Both continued to serve through World War II. Today both are parts of state park systems. Point Lookout became the site of a Coast Guard station that lasted into the 1930s, and later a state park. Erosion has claimed much of the original prison land. Rock Island's prison was incorporated into the federal arsenal that remains in operation. There, as at most prison locations, some historic markers and a Confederate cemetery are the only tangible signs of the site's Civil War heritage. Whatever words appear on the former, the presence of the latter says more.[50]

Notes

Abbreviations

ADAH—Alabama Department of Archives and History, Montgomery
CGPLTS—Office of the Commissary General of Prisoners, Letters and Telegrams Sent, Record Group 249, National Archives
CWMC—Civil War Miscellaneous Collection
CWTI—Civil War Times Illustrated
Duke—Rare Book, Manuscript, and Special Collections Library, Duke University, Durham, NC
Filson—Filson Historical Society, Louisville, KY
GDAH—Georgia Department of Archives and History, Morrow
LC—Library of Congress, Washington, DC
MARBL, Emory—Manuscript, Archives, and Rare Book Library, Emory University, Atlanta
MDAH—Mississippi Department of Archives and History, Jackson
NA—National Archives and Records Administration, Washington, DC
OHS—Ohio Historical Society, Columbus
OR—U.S. War Department, *The War of the Rebellion: A Compilation of the Official Records of the Union and Confederate Armies,* 128 vols. (Washington, DC, 1880–1901). Unless otherwise noted, all references will be to series 2.
RG—Record Group
SHC, UNC—Southern Historical Collection, University of North Carolina Library, Chapel Hill
TSLA—Tennessee State Library and Archives, Nashville
USAMHI—United States Army Military History Institute, Carlisle Barracks, PA
UVA—Special Collections, University of Virginia Library, Charlottesville
VHS—Virginia Historical Society, Richmond
VT—Digital Library and Archives, University Libraries, Virginia Polytechnic Institute and State University, Blacksburg

WHMC—Western Historical Manuscript Collection, University of Missouri, Columbia
WVU—West Virginia Regional Collection, West Virginia University, Morgantown

Chapter 1

1. Paludan, *"A People's Contest,"* 51–55.

2. Weigley, *Quartermaster General of the Union Army,* 164–68.

3. *OR,* 3:8.

4. Ibid., 3:48–49.

5. Hunter, "Warden for the Union," 2–3, 23–24.

6. Ibid., 25–26, 30–32.

7. Sanders, *While in the Hands of the Enemy,* 68; Hunter, "Warden for the Union," 4–15.

8. *OR,* 3:54–55.

9. Ibid., 3:55–58.

10. Ibid., 3:122–23; historians stressing Hoffman's frugality include Benton McAdams, "Unnecessary Expense," *Civil War Magazine* 59 (December 1996), 58–65 and Speer, *Portals to Hell,* 11–12.

11. *OR,* 3:135–36.

12. Ibid., 3:123–24; Frohman, *Rebels on Lake Erie,* 6.

13. *OR,* 3:163, 171, 479–80; Hunter, "Warden for the Union," 34.

14. Hunter, "Warden for the Union," 34–35.

15. Neely, *The Fate of Liberty,* 14–31; Hyman, *A More Perfect Union,* 65–70.

16. Robertson, "Old Capitol," 394–97, 400–2.

17. Ibid., 395–96.

18. Griffith, "Fredericksburg's Hostages," 395–96, 404–8.

19. Ibid., 413, 420, 424.

20. Ibid., 412, 416–17, 425; entries for June 20, 21, 1862, George L. P. Wren Diary, MARBL, Emory.

21. *OR,* 3:9–10; Sanders, *While in the Hands of the Enemy,* 58.

22. Sanders, *While in the Hands of the Enemy,* 56; Speer, *Portals to Hell,* 37.

23. *OR,* 3:32–34.

24. Ibid., 3:33; entries for August 30–September 2, 1861, Thomas Sparrow Diary, SHC, UNC.

25. *OR,* 3:39.

26. Entries for September 20, 30, October 7, 8, 1861, Sparrow Diary, SHC, UNC.

27. *OR,* 3:45–46, 50.

28. Entries for September 25, October 10, 19, 26, 1861, Sparrow Diary, SHC, UNC.

29. Entries for October 9, 10, 12, 1861, Sparrow Diary, SHC, UNC.

30. Entry for September 24, 1861, Sparrow Diary, SHC, UNC.

31. Ibid.

32. Entry for October 28, 1861, Sparrow Diary, SHC, UNC; Speer, *Portals to Hell,* 41–42.

33. McLain, "The Military Prison at Fort Warren," 34–35; entry for November 1, 1861, Sparrow Diary, SHC, UNC.

34. *OR,* 2:110–11.

35. Entries for November 1, 3, 10, 19, 27, 1861, Sparrow Diary, SHC, UNC; Thomas W.

Hall to mother, November 3, 1861, Thomas W. Hall Papers, Maryland Historical Society, Baltimore.

36. Entries for November 1, 3, 1861, Sparrow Diary, SHC, UNC.

37. Entries for November 7, 14, 16, December 25, 1861, Sparrow Diary, SHC, UNC.

38. Entry for November 8, 1861, Sparrow Diary, SHC, UNC.

39. Memorandum on Arrest of George William Brown, Fort Warren Records, Maryland Historical Society, Baltimore; George William Brown to Dr. George Shuttuck, January 31, February 9, 1861, George William Brown Collection, Maryland Historical Society, Baltimore.

40. *OR,* 1:667–75.

41. Entries for November 20, 24, December 3, 9, 29, 1861, Sparrow Diary, SHC, UNC.

42. Pickenpaugh, *Camp Chase,* 13–14.

43. *London National Democrat* (Ohio), December 19, 1861; John A. Smith to family, December 25, 1861, John A. Smith Papers, Bentley Historical Library, University of Michigan, Ann Arbor; Mungo P. Murray to family, September 24, 1861, Mungo P. Murray Letters, *CWTI* Collection, USAMHI.

44. *OR,* 2:39, 42, 3:219.

45. Ibid., 4:348, 690; Galloway's cases can be found in Correspondence between the Special Commissioner and Judge Advocate General relating to the Release of Confederate Political Prisoners, RG 249, NA.

46. Hesseltine, "Military Prisons of St. Louis," 380–83.

47. *OR,* 3:185–86.

48. Lt. Col. William Hoffman to Gen. Montgomery Meigs, January 27, 1862, CGPLTS, RG 249, NA.

49. *OR,* 3:317, 326–27.

Chapter 2

1. *OR,* series 1, 7:161, series 2, 3:271–72.

2. Ibid., 3:267, 269–70, 274, 277, 280.

3. Whitely, "Civil War Journal of James E. Paton," 227–28.

4. Entry for February 19, 1862, Randal W. McGavock Diary, in Allen, *Pen and Sword,* 596; entries for February 19, 20, 1862, Andrew Jackson Campbell Diary, in Garrett, *Diary of Campbell,* 21–22; entry for February 18, 1862, James Calvin Cook Diary, vol. 593, OHS.

5. *OR,* 3:281, 291–92; entry for February 22, 1862, McGavock Diary, in Allen, *Pen and Sword,* 597.

6. Entry for February 21, 1862, Cook Diary, OHS; entries for February 20–23, 1862, Campbell Diary, in Garrett, *Diary of Campbell,* 21–23.

7. *OR,* series 1, 7:120, series 2, 3:355, 365; George William Brown to George Shattuck, July 29, 1862, George William Brown Collection, Maryland Historical Society, Baltimore.

8. Thomas W. Hall to mother, February 10, 1862, Thomas W. Hall Papers, Maryland Historical Society, Baltimore; Brown to Eleanor Shattuck, June 18, 1862, Brown Collection, Maryland Historical Society, Baltimore.

9. Entries for March 6, 7, 17, 28, April 17, July 4, 19, 1862, McGavock Diary, in Allen, *Pen and Sword,* 601–2, 604, 609, 614, 647, 653.

10. *OR,* 3:169, 216, 236–38.

11. Ibid., 3:421–23.

12. Ibid., 3:277, 288.

13. Peterson, "A History of Camp Butler," 75–76.

14. *Illinois State Register,* February 24, 1862, and *Illinois State Journal,* February 24, 1862, quoted in Quinn, "Forgotten Soldiers," 36.

15. Quinn, "Forgotten Soldiers," 37–38; *OR,* 3:363, 364–65, 367–68.

16. Ibid., 3:367–68; Peterson, "A History of Camp Butler," 80.

17. Quinn, "Forgotten Soldiers," 41; entry for May 13, 1862, Josephus C. Moore Diary, in Bowman and Scroggs, "Diary of a Confederate Soldier," 30; *OR,* 3:647–48, 8:986–87.

18. Levy, *To Die in Chicago,* 28–34, 53–55.

19. *OR,* 3:277–78, 297, 315; Levy, *To Die in Chicago,* 31.

20. *OR,* 3:316.

21. Ibid., 3:360–61.

22. Entries for April 23, 27, 28, May 1, 14, 1862, Willie Micajah Barrow Diary, in Stephenson and Davis, "Civil War Diary," 722–25.

23. Entries for June 4, 5, 1862, Barrow Diary, in Stephenson and Davis, "Civil War Diary," 726–27.

24. *OR,* 4:111.

25. Ibid., 4:106–8, 110–11, 129.

26. Hall, "Camp Morton," 6.

27. *OR,* 3:270; entry ca. May 10, 1862, J. K. Farris Diary, MARBL, Emory.

28. Entries for May 12–17, 1862, Farris Diary, MARBL, Emory.

29. *OR,* 3:518–19.

30. Ibid., 3:348–49, 375.

31. Ibid., 3:355, 366–67, 423–24.

32. Ibid., 3:280, 288; *Delaware Gazette* (Ohio), March 7, 1862.

33. *OR,* 3:344.

34. Col. Granville Moody, General Orders for the Government of Prisoners at Camp Chase, n.d., RG 393, NA.

35. *OR,* 3:337, 346.

36. Entries for March 1–3, 1862, Cook Diary, OHS.

37. Entries for March 1–3, 8, 1862, Campbell Diary, in Garrett, *Diary of Campbell,* 25–27; entry for May 1, 1862, John Henry Guy Diary, in Curle, "Diary of John Henry Guy," 29; Pickenpaugh, *Camp Chase,* 33.

38. *OR,* 3:384–85, 405, 448; Hoffman to Commanding Officer, Camp Douglas, June 21, 1862, CGPLTS, RG 249, NA.

39. Entry for April 29, 1862, Guy Diary, in Curle, "Diary of John Henry Guy," 22–23.

40. Entries for June 21, 24, July 5, 1862, Edward William Drummond Diary, in Durham, *Confederate Yankee,* 73–74, 81.

41. Entry for July 13, 1862, Richard L. Gray Diary, MSS 4882, UVA; entry for June 22, 1862, William Henry Asbury Speer Diary, in Murphy, "A Confederate Soldier's View," 107.

42. *OR,* 3:445–46, 462–63.

43. Entries for April 24, May 9, 10, 1862, Drummond Diary, in Durham, *Confederate Yankee,* 46, 51.

44. Entries for May 15, 31, June 1, 11, 24, 1862, George Bell Diary, in Bell, "Diary of George Bell," 174–79; entry for May 12, 1862, J. C. Bruyn Diary, MARBL, Emory.

45. *OR,* 3:471, 4:23, 28, 143, 160, 165; Keen, "Confederate Prisoners," 1.

46. Entries for July 12, 27, 1862, Bell Diary, in Bell, "Diary of George Bell," 183; entries for July 16, 27, 1862, Bruyn Diary, MARBL, Emory; entry for July 12, 1862, A. F. Williams Diary, Collection no. 246, East Carolina Manuscript Collection, J. Y. Joyner Library, East Carolina University, Greenville, NC.

47. *OR,* 3:297, 365–66, 379–80, 517–18.

48. Pickenpaugh, *Camp Chase,* 25–26; Charles Barrington Simrall to wife, September 10, 1862, Charles Barrington Simrall Papers, SHC, UNC.

49. Pickenpaugh, *Camp Chase,* 26–27.

50. *OR,* 3:410–11.

51. Ibid., 3:280, 412, 420, 427–28.

52. Ibid., 3:428; Pickenpaugh, *Camp Chase,* 27–28; Gov. David Tod to Col. Granville Moody, April 22, 1862, Camp Chase, Ohio, Special Orders, RG 393, NA.

53. Entry for April 1, 1862, Campbell Diary, in Garrett, *Diary of Campbell,* 32; entry for March 4, 1862, McGavock Diary, in Allen, *Pen and Sword,* 599–600; entry for May 4, 1862, Drummond Diary, in Durham, *Confederate Yankee,* 48; entry for May 15, 1862, Guy Diary, in Curle, "Diary of John Henry Guy," 36.

54. Hunter, "Warden for the Union," 51, 57–58.

55. Thomas and Hyman, *Stanton,* 155–58.

56. *OR,* 3:156, 327, 389–90.

57. Ibid., 3:417–18, 462, 4:1, 15, 20, 30.

58. Ibid., 4:130–31, 155–58, 216–17, 262–63.

59. Ibid., 4:734–35, 740, 763–65.

60. Ibid., 4:195–208.

61. Ibid., 4:198–208, 304–6.

62. Ibid., 3:509.

63. Ibid., 3:526, 540–41, 586, 4:422–23.

Chapter 3

1. Klein, *Days of Defiance,* 416–20.

2. Thomas, "Prisoner of War Exchange," 24–26.

3. Ibid., 27–32.

4. *OR,* 3:51–52, 155, 158, 165, 167.

5. Ibid., 3:175–77, 181, 183–84; Sanders, *While in the Hands of the Enemy,* 82–83.

6. *OR,* 3:128, 171, 753; Thomas, "Prisoner of War Exchange," 50–51.

7. Paludan, *Presidency of Abraham Lincoln,* 53.

8. Sanders, *While in the Hands of the Enemy,* 33–37.

9. *OR,* 3:157, 183, 211.

10. Thomas, "Prisoner of War Exchange," 64–71; *OR,* 3:253, 789.

11. Ibid., 3:254, 301–2, 322.

12. Ibid., 4:53, 169, 210; Thomas, "Prisoner of War Exchange," 87–90.

13. *OR,* 4:174, 265–68, 815–16; Bridges, *Lee's Maverick General,* 87.

14. Entry for June 11, 1862, Josephus C. Moore Diary, in Bowman and Scroggs, "Diary of a Confederate Soldier," 31; entries for June 24, 27, 28, July 14, 17, September 5, 1862, Edward William Drummond Diary, in Durham, *Confederate Yankee,* 74–77, 86–87, 100–1.

15. Entry for July 29, 1862, J. C. Bruyn Diary, MARBL, Emory; entry for July 29, 1862, George L. P. Wren Diary, MARBL, Emory.

16. *OR,* 4:308, 312–13, 321, 331.

17. Meier, "Confederate Private," 482; Joseph W. Westbrook Memoirs, CWMC, USAMHI; entry for May 24, 1862, Randal W. McGavock Diary, in Allen, *Pen and Sword,* 629.

18. Entry for August 15, 1862, J. K. Farris Diary, MARBL, Emory; entry for March 31, 1862, Timothy McNamara Diary, MDAH; entry for March 4, 1863, J. K. Ferguson Diary, Special Collections Department, University of Memphis Libraries.

19. Meier, "Confederate Private," 482; entry for August 20, 1862, Farris Diary, MARBL, Emory; entries for August 28, September 1, 2, 1862, Moore Diary, in Bowman and Scroggs, "Diary of a Confederate Soldier," 32–33.

20. Entries for July 9, 13, August 10, 11, 1862, Drummond Diary, in Durham, *Confederate Yankee,* 83, 85, 94–95; entry for August 10, 1862, Andrew Jackson Campbell Diary, in Garrett, *Diary of Campbell,* 51; entry for August 27, 1862, John Henry Guy Diary, in Curle, "Diary of John Henry Guy," 65.

21. Entry for July 30, 1863, A. F. Williams Diary, Collection no. 246, East Carolina Manuscript Collection, J. Y. Joyner Library, East Carolina University, Greenville, NC.

22. *OR,* 4:289, 291–92, 414, 645; Hesseltine, *Civil War Prisons,* 69–71, 84.

23. *OR,* 4:419–22, 428–30, 435–37, 454, 458–59, 470–71, 484–85.

24. Ibid., 4:436–37, 512.

25. Entries for September 6, 7, 8, 1862, Farris Diary, MARBL, Emory.

26. Entry for September 5, 1862, Drummond Diary, in Durham, *Confederate Yankee,* 100–1; entry for September 5, 1862, Richard L. Gray Diary, MSS 4882, UVA.

27. Entry for September 5, 1862, Drummond Diary, in Durham, *Confederate Yankee,* 100–1; entry for September 5, 1862, Gray Diary, UVA.

28. Entries for September 8, 9, 1862, Gray Diary, UVA; entry for September 9, 1862, Farris Diary, MARBL, Emory.

29. Entry for September 12, 1862, Gray Diary, UVA; Meier, "Confederate Private," 483; entry for September 10, 1862, Farris Diary, MARBL, Emory.

30. Entry for September 15, 1862, Farris Diary, MARBL, Emory; Roland K. Chatam to sister, December 2, 1862, Roland K. Chatam Letters, Filson; Hoffman to Gen. Charles W. Hill, March 19, 1863, CGPLTS, RG 249, NA.

31. Entries for September 12–16, 1862, Guy Diary, in Curle, "Diary of John Henry Guy," 66–67; entries for September 17, 18, 20, 1862, Farris Diary, MARBL, Emory; entry for September 19, 1862, Gray Diary, UVA.

32. Entries for July 31, August 1–5, 1862, McGavock Diary, in Allen, *Pen and Sword,* 657–60.

33. Entries for August 2–7, 1862, Wren Diary, MARBL, Emory; entry for August 6, 1862, Bruyn Diary, MARBL, Emory.

34. *OR,* 5:179–80; entries for April 11, 12, 13, 29, May 2, 1863, Ferguson Diary, Special Collections Department, University of Memphis Libraries.

35. Entries for May 4, 9, 1863, Ferguson Diary, Special Collections Department, University of Memphis Libraries.

36. Entries for May 12, 14, 17, 19, 1863, Ferguson Diary, Special Collections Department, University of Memphis Libraries.

37. Moss, "A Missouri Confederate in the Civil War: The Journal of Henry Martyn Cheavens," 17–18, 33–34. Despite the title of the article, Cheavens's work reads more like a memoir than a journal.

38. Ibid., 34–37.

39. Ibid., 45; *OR,* 6:92–93, 97.

40. Moss, "A Missouri Confederate," 45–46.

41. Ibid., 19, 47–48.

42. *OR,* 5:967, 6:198, 206, 224, 273–74.

43. Ibid., 6:232–33, 299.

44. Ibid., 6:542–43, 558–59.

Chapter 4

1. *OR,* series 1, 12: pt. 3, 435, 473–74, series 2, 4:271, 329–30, 836–37, 938–39.

2. Ibid., 4:600–3.

3. Ibid., 4:328–29, 770–71; Sanders, *While in the Hands of the Enemy,* 130.

4. Sanders, *While in the Hands of the Enemy,* 145–46.

5. *OR,* 5:128, 795–97.

6. Ibid., 5:178, 186–87, 286.

7. Sanders, *While in the Hands of the Enemy,* 149–50; *OR,* 5:394, 397.

8. *OR,* 5:456, 469, 541–42, 691.

9. Ibid., 5:940–41.

10. Ibid., 6:17–18.

11. Ibid., 5:696, 701, 6:112, 126; Sanders, *While in the Hands of the Enemy,* 155.

12. *OR,* 6:226, 523, 647–49.

13. Hesseltine, *Civil War Prisons,* 76–77; *OR,* 4:360, 499.

14. *OR,* 4:94.

15. Ibid., 4:499.

16. Ibid., 4:522; Wallace, *Autobiography,* 2:632–34; Gen. Lew Wallace to Gen. Lorenzo Thomas, September 21, 1862, Letters Sent from Headquarters, U.S. Paroled Forces, Columbus, RG 393, NA.

17. Pickenpaugh, *Camp Chase,* 48–50; *OR,* 4:569–71.

18. Entries for October 30, November 4, 1862, William L. Curry Diary, James S. Schoff Collection, William L. Clements Library, University of Michigan, Ann Arbor; Abner Royce to parents, October 3, 1862, Royce Family Papers, MSS 1675, Western Reserve Historical Society Library, Cleveland; Benjamin Franklin Heuston to wife, March 15, 1863, Benjamin Franklin Heuston Letters, Wisconsin Historical Society, La Crosse MSSJ.

19. *OR,* 4:295–300, 727, 749, 771.

20. Circular, January 21, 1863, Headquarters, U.S. Paroled Forces, Columbus, General and Special Orders, RG 393, NA.

21. Levy, *To Die in Chicago,* 109–13; entry for September 28, 1862, Charles E. Smith Diary, in Cryder and Miller, *A View from the Ranks,* 79.

22. Entries for October 1, 2, 3, 16, 1862, Smith Diary, in Cryder and Miller, *A View from the Ranks,* 81–83, 87.

23. *OR,* 8:991–94.

24. Ibid., series 1, 27: pt. 1, 27, 118; pt. 3, 514.

25. Ibid., series 2, 6:98–99, 132–33, 141–42; Gilman Marston to Adjutant General, United States Army, August 3, 1863, District of St. Mary's, Letters Sent, RG 393, NA.

26. *OR,* 6:243; Marston to Hoffman, October 8, 1863, District of St. Mary's, Letters Sent, RG 393, NA.

27. Hoffman to Brig. Gen. John H. Martindale, August 18, 1863, CGPLTS, RG 249, NA; Stamp, "Ten Months Experience," 491; B. T. Holliday, "Account of My Capture," UVA.

28. William H. Haigh to Kate, May 24, 1865, diary entry for May 27, 1865, William H. Haigh Papers, SHC, UNC; James A. Low to Charles F. Low, August 3, 1864, Charles F. Low Papers, Duke.

29. Entry for April 5, 1864, Bartlett Yancey Malone Diary, in Pierson, *Whipt 'em Everytime,* 100; entry for February 10, 1864, Charles Warren Hutt Diary, in Beitzell, "Diary of Charles Warren Hutt," 418; entries for November 17, 18, December 19, 1864, George Quintas Peyton Diary, MSS 5031, UVA; entry for April 10, 1864, Joseph Mason Kern Diary, Joseph Mason Kern Papers, SHC, UNC.

30. Entries for January 1, May 2, 5, 1864, Hutt Diary, in Beitzell, "Diary of Charles Warren Hutt," 415, 425; entry for June 10, 1864, Kern Diary, SHC, UNC; entry for January 6, 1865, Malone Diary, in Pierson, *Whipt 'em Everytime,* 117.

31. *OR,* 6:115, 196, 281; McAdams, *Rebels at Rock Island,* 12, 23.

32. *OR,* series 1, 31: pt. 2, 36, series 2, 6:626.

33. McAdams, *Rebels at Rock Island,* 30; Col. Richard H. Rush to Hoffman, November 24, 1863, Rush to Jacob Ammen, November 25, 1863, Rush to Meigs, November 26, 1863, Rush to Col. James Fry, November 26, 1863, Rock Island Barracks, Illinois, Letters Sent, RG 393, NA; Rush to Hoffman, November 30, 1863, November 30, 1863, Rock Island Barracks, Illinois, Telegrams Sent, RG 393, NA.

34. Rush to Hoffman, December 4, 1863, Rock Island Barracks, Illinois, Telegrams Sent, RG 393, NA; Capt. Arnott D. Collins to Hoffman, January 9, 1864, Rock Island Barracks, Illinois, Letters Sent, RG 393, NA.

35. A. C. Kean Reminiscences, Cabarrus and Slade Family Papers, SHC, UNC.

36. Entries for November 27, December 14, 15, 16, 19, 29, 1863, William H. Davis Diary, MARBL, Emory; entries for January 3, 11, 12, 13, 1864, Lafayette Rogan Diary, in Hauberg, "Confederate Prisoner," 31–32.

37. Hoffman to Lazelle, June 12, 1862, CGPLTS, RG 249, NA; *OR,* 4:64–84, 7:146.

38. *OR,* 7:152.

39. Ibid., 7:157.

40. Ibid., 7:394, 424–25; *Elmira Daily Advertiser,* July 7, 11, 13, 29, August 1, 1864.

41. Entries for July 24, 29, 1864, Henri Jean Mugler Diary, A&M 1335, WVU; entries for July 26, 31, 1864, Wilbur Wightman Gramling Diary, Florida State Archives, Tallahassee.

42. *OR,* 7:465.

43. Ibid., 7:603–5, 676–77, 878, 1003–5; Gray, *The Business of Captivity,* 57–58.

44. *OR,* 4:344, 370; Hoffman to David Tod and Richard Yates, September 11, 1862, CGPLTS, RG 249, NA.

Chapter 5

1. D. C. Thomas, "Dark Chapter in Prison Life," *Confederate Veteran* 6 (1898): 71–72.

2. George H. Moffett, "War Prison Experience," *Confederate Veteran* 13 (1905): 105.

3. Isaac Marsh to wife, ca. January 20, 25, 1863, Isaac Marsh Papers, Duke.

4. Entries ca. July 1863, Thomas Jones Taylor Journal, in Wall and McBride, "'An Extraordinary Perseverance,'" 339–41.

5. W. C. Dodson, "Stories of Prison Life," *Confederate Veteran* 8 (1900): 121.

6. William H. Young to family, March 18, 1865, William H. Young Letters, Special Collections Department, Mitchell Memorial Library, Mississippi State University; undated entry, Richard Henry Adams Diary, MS 94-013, VT; James W. Anderson to son, December 1, December ? 1864, in Osborn, "Writings of a Confederate Prisoner of War," 77–78.

7. Anderson to son, December 1864 (three letters), January 1865 (three letters), in Osborn, "Writings of a Confederate Prisoner of War," 78–83.

8. *OR,* 6:1044–46, 8:994–1001.

9. Anderson to son, January 1865, in Osborn, "Writings of a Confederate Prisoner of War," 83–84.

10. Young to family, March 18, 1865, Young Letters, Special Collections Department, Mitchell Memorial Library, Mississippi State University; entries for December 5–9, 1863, William H. Davis Diary, MARBL, Emory.

11. Entries for January 1–8, 1865, Samuel Beckett Boyd Diary, TSLA.

12. Entry ca. January 1865, Virgil S. Murphey Diary, SHC, UNC.

13. A. C. Kean Reminiscences, Cabarrus and Slade Family Papers, SHC, UNC.

14. Ibid.; entry for January 9, 1865, Boyd Diary, TSLA; Anderson to son, January 1865 (two letters), in Osborn, "Writings of a Confederate Prisoner of War," 84–85.

15. Entry ca. January 1865, Murphey Diary, SHC, UNC.

16. *OR,* 5:34–35, 6:436–38, 865–66.

17. Ibid., series 1, 27: pt. 1, 24–28.

18. Entry for July 3, 1863, William Peel Diary, MDAH.

19. Entries for July 3–5, 1863, John Dooley Journal, in Durkin, *John Dooley,* 107–12.

20. Entries for July 5–August 22, 1863, Dooley Journal, in Durkin, *John Dooley,* 117–32.

21. Entries for July 2–3, 1863, Edmund DeWitt Patterson Journal, in Barrett, *Yankee Rebel,* 117–18.

22. Entries for July 4–16, 1863, Patterson Journal, in Barrett, *Yankee Rebel,* 119–22.

23. Hoffman to Grant, May 13, 14, 1864, CGPLTS, RG 249, NA; *OR,* 7:145.

24. Stamp, "Ten Months Experience," 486–89.

25. Ibid., 490–91.

26. Entry for May 12, 1864, George Washington Hall Diary, LC.

27. Entries for May 13–16, 1864, Hall Diary, LC.

28. Wilbur Fisk Davis Memoir, Papers of Wilbur Fisk Davis, MSS 7396, UVA.

29. Entries for May 18, 21, 1864, Hall Diary, LC.

30. Entries for June 6–11, 20–27, July 12, 23, 1864, Wilbur Wightman Gramling Diary, Florida State Archives, Tallahassee.

31. W. Gart Johnson, "Prison Life at Harper's Ferry and on Johnson's Island," *Confederate Veteran* 2 (1894): 242.

32. Entries for July 10, 19, 23, 1863, Henri Jean Mugler Diary, A&M 1335, WVU.

33. Entries for July 1, 2, 4, 6, 8, 12, 16, 23, 1864, E. L. Cox Diary, VHS.

34. Entries for July 23, 24, 1864, Cox Diary, VHS.

Chapter 6

1. Entry ca. April 1864, Thomas A. Sharpe Diary, MARBL, Emory; James W. Anderson to W. Thomas Anderson, January 1865, in Osborn, "A Confederate Prisoner at Camp Chase," 45; entry for January 18, 1864, James T. Mackey Diary, TSLA.

2. Entry for January 18, 1864, Mackey Diary, TSLA; Anderson to W. Thomas Anderson, January 1865, in Osborn, "A Confederate Prisoner at Camp Chase," 45.

3. Entry for July 24, 1863, Curtis R. Burke Journal, in Bennett, "Curtis R. Burke's Civil War Journal," 66:113–14.

4. Entry ca. January 1865, Virgil S. Murphey Diary, SHC, UNC; entry for August 23, 1863, Dooley Journal, in Dunkin, *John Dooley,* 137.

5. Beitzell, "In Prison at Point Lookout," 5; entry for August 18, 1863, Burke Journal, in Bennett, "Curtis R. Burke's Civil War Journal," 66:120–21.

6. Entry for July 10, 1863, Joseph E. Purvis Diary, MSS 3867, UVA; entry for November 29, 1864, John Alexander Gibson Diary, VHS; entry for April 29, 1864, Lafayette Rogan Diary, in Hauberg, "Confederate Prisoner," 39.

7. Entry for June 12, 1864, Edmund DeWitt Patterson Journal, in Barrett, *Yankee Rebel,* 171–72; entries for September 12, 1863, January 10, 1864, James Mayo Diary, LC; entry ca. January 1865, Murphey Diary, SHC, UNC.

8. Entry for June 4, 1864, George Washington Hall Diary, LC; Thomas Gibbes Morgan to brother, December 16, 1863, Thomas Gibbes Morgan Letters, Duke; entry for October 23, 1864, John Joyes Jr. Diary, Filson; Daniel S. Printup to wife, October 3, 1863, Daniel S. Printup Papers, Duke; entry for August 8, 1864, Sharpe Diary, MARBL, Emory; entry for October 31, 1864, Wilbur Wightman Gramling Diary, Florida State Archives, Tallahassee.

9. Entry for June 9, 1864, Burke Journal, in Bennett, "Curtis R. Burke's Civil War Journal," 66:160; entry for May 9, 1862, Edward William Drummond Journal, in Durham, *Confederate Yankee,* 51; entry for July 25, 1863, Purvis Diary, UVA; entry for September 11, 1864, Gramling Diary, Florida State Archives, Tallahassee.

10. William G. Woods to "Cousin Eliza," October 26, 1864, William G. Woods Papers, Duke; entry for July 15, 1864, Francis Atherton Boyle Diary, in Thornton, "Prison Diary," 65.

11. Entry for November 24, 1863, Patterson Journal, in Barrett, *Yankee Rebel,* 145–46; A. M. Bedford to wife, October 31, 1863, Bedford Family Papers, 1849–70, 1940s, WHMC;

Meriwether Jeff Thompson Memoirs, Meriwether Jeff Thompson Papers, 1854–1935, WHMC; T. J. Pitchford to Addie Burr, March 25, 1865, Thomas Jefferson Green Papers, SHC, UNC.

12. Entries for September 19, 20, 1863, Robert Bingham Diary, SHC, UNC.

13. James R. Ervin Sr. to father, September 21, 1864, James R. Ervin Sr. Papers, Duke; Otis Johnson to brother, September 20, 1864, Richardson-Davis Papers, Duke; B. E. Priest to sister, July 8, 1864, Priest Family Letters, 1863–64, WHMC; Daniel S. Printup to wife, December 3, 1863, Printup Papers, Duke; William Lambert Campbell to Zoe Jane Campbell, January 16, 1865, Zoe Jane Campbell Papers, Duke; James A. Riddick to cousin, February 5, 1864, James A. Riddick Papers, Duke.

14. James A. Thomas to sister, December 16, 1863, James A. Thomas Letters, Filson; Henry E. Parberry to sister, May 18, 1864, Henry E. Parberry Papers, 1829–65, WHMC; entry ca. March, 1865, E. John Ellis Diary, in Buck, "A Louisiana Prisoner-of-War," 236.

15. Henry Massie Bullitt Reminiscences, Bullitt-Chenoweth Family Papers, Filson; entry for August 8, 1863, Mayo Diary, LC; entry for August 21, 1864, Henri Jean Mugler Diary, A&M 1335, WVU.

16. Entry for July 11, 1863, Purvis Diary, UVA; entries for June 6, 28, 1862, Drummond Diary, in Durham, *Confederate Yankee,* 64, 77; entry for July 6, 1862, William Henry Asbury Speer Diary, in Murphy, "A Confederate Soldier's View," 109; entry for May 5, 1864, William Peel Diary, MDAH; entry ca. January 1865, Murphey Diary, SHC, UNC.

17. Entry for May 26, 1864, Hall Diary, LC; entries for September 11, 18, 1864, Sharpe Diary, MARBL, Emory; William Jonathan Davis to "Cousin Frank," July 8, 1864, William Jonathan Davis Papers, Filson.

18. Entry for May 3, 1864, Dooley Journal, in Durkin, *John Dooley,* 160.

19. Entry for February 27, 1865, Boyle Diary, in Thornton, "Prison Diary," 79; entry for July 7, 1863, Joseph Mason Kern Diary, Joseph Mason Kern Papers, SHC, UNC; entry for December 28, 1864, Thomas R. Beadles Diary, MDAH; entry for December 26, 1864, E. L. Cox Diary, VHS.

20. Entry for December 16, 1864, H. H. Wiseman Diary, William F. Howard Collection, USAMHI; entry ca. August 1864, Sharpe Diary, MARBL, Emory; entry for September 5, 1864, Mugler Diary, WVU; entry for May 22, 1864, Rogan Diary, in Hauberg, "Confederate Prisoner," 40; entries for November 21–22, 1862, Charles Warren Hutt Diary, in Beitzell, "Diary of Charles Warren Hutt," 441; entry for January 22, 1865, Dooley Diary, in Durkin, *John Dooley,* 165.

21. Entries for September 2, November 7, 1864, Mugler Diary, WVU; entry for August 26, 1864, Rogan Diary, in Hauberg, "Confederate Prisoner," 45; entry for August 31, 1864, Sharpe Diary, MARBL, Emory; entry for November 8, 1864, Peel Diary, MDAH.

22. Entry for November 19, 1864, Gramling Diary, Florida State Archives, Tallahassee; entry for November 10, 1864, John Philip Thompson Diary, MSS 3527, UVA; entry for November 8, 1864, Thomas Jones Taylor Diary, in Wall and McBride, "'An Extraordinary Perseverance,'" 356; entry for November 11, 1864, William H. S. Burgwyn Diary, in Schiller, *A Captain's War,* 162.

23. Entry for October 23, 1864, Cox Diary, VHS; entries for April 13, 26, May 31, June 7, 1864, Peel Diary, MDAH; entry ca. January 1865, Murphey Diary, SHC, UNC.

24. Entry for March 19, 1864, Beadles Diary, MDAH; entry for June 11, 1864, Hutt Diary,

in Beitzell, "Diary of Charles Warren Hutt," 428; entry for May 21, 1864, Peel Diary, MDAH; entry for May 28, 1864, Patterson Journal, in Barrett, *Yankee Rebel,* 168; entry for April 4, 1864, Burke Journal, in Bennett, "Curtis Burke's Civil War Journal," 66:147; entry for May 13, 1864, Kern Diary, SHC, UNC.

25. Entry ca. January 1865, Murphey Diary, SHC, UNC; entry for August 12, 1864, Burke Journal, in Bennett, "Curtis R. Burke's Civil War Journal," 66:324; Beitzell, "In Prison at Point Lookout," 104.

26. Joseph Mason Kern, Unpublished Memoirs, Kern Papers, SHC, UNC; entry for July 30, 1864, Cox Diary, VHS; Edward D. Dixon Reminiscences, SHC, UNC; entry for January 8, 1864, John M. Porter Diary, John M. Porter Papers, Filson.

27. Arthur H. Edey to E. D. Battelle, August 27, 1864, Finney Family Papers, VHS; entry for December 17, 1864, Gramling Diary, Florida State Archives, Tallahassee; entry for July 14, 1864, Kern Diary, SHC, UNC; John Malachi Bowden Reminiscences, Duke.

28. Entries for July 29, September 28, October 8, 1864, Cox Diary, VHS; entry for March 30, 1864, Peel Diary, MDAH; entries for October 21, 1864, January 18, 1865, Boyle Diary, in Thornton, "Prison Diary," 70, 74; entry for April 6, 1865, James Bennington Irvine Diary, ADAH.

29. Entry for January 18, 1865, Boyle Diary, in Thornton, "Prison Diary," 74; entries for August 31, September 2, 7, 9, 11, 1863, Mayo Diary, LC.

30. Entry ca. November 1863, Taylor Journal, in Wall and McBride, "'An Extraordinary Perseverance,'" 346; entry for September 9, 1863, Bingham Diary, SHC, UNC; entry for September 25, 1863, Patterson Journal, in Barrett, *Yankee Rebel,* 138.

31. Entry for February 22, 1864, Mayo Diary, LC; entry for February 22, 1864, Dooley Journal, in Durkin, *John Dooley,* 159; entry for February 22, 1864, Peel Diary, MDAH.

32. A. C. Kean Reminiscences, Cabarrus and Slade Family Papers, SHC, UNC; entry for March 18, 1865, Cox Diary, VHS.

33. Entry for June 10, 1864, Kern Diary, SHC, UNC; Kean Reminiscences, SHC, UNC; Wilbur Fisk Davis Memoir, Papers of Wilbur Fisk Davis, MSS 7396, UVA; entry for July 24, 1863, Bingham Diary, SHC, UNC; entry for August 25, 1863, Patterson Journal, in Barrett, *Yankee Rebel,* 131; entry for December 15, 1863, Cox Diary, VHS.

34. Entries for January 24, 1864, March 21, 1865, Beadles Diary, MDAH; Davis to "Dear Frank," May 29, 1864, Davis Papers, Filson; Horace Harmon Lurton to "My Dear Allen," July 18, 1863, Horace Harmon Lurton Letters, LC.

35. Entry for April 1, 1865, Boyle Diary, in Thornton, "Prison Diary," 82; entry for September 4, 1863, Kern Diary, SHC, UNC; entry for September 11, 1863, Dooley Journal, in Durkin, *John Dooley,* 142; entry for June 23, 1864, Peel Diary, MDAH.

36. Entries for September 22, 26, November 30, December 12, 1863, Dooley Journal, in Durkin, *John Dooley,* 144–45, 146, 152, 153; entry for November 13, 1863, Bingham Diary, SHC, UNC.

37. Entry for February 1, 1864, Thompson Diary, UVA; entry for February 9, 1864, Mackey Diary, TSLA; entry for March 25, 1864, Burke Journal, in Bennett, "Curtis Burke's Civil War Journal," 66:143.

38. Entry for July 5, 1862, Drummond Journal, in Durham, *Confederate Yankee,* 81; entries

for April 19, July 29, 31, 1864, Peel Diary, MDAH; entry for August 27, 1864, Patterson Journal, in Barrett, *Yankee Rebel,* 190; entries for July 14, 16, 30, 1864, Thompson Diary, UVA.

39. Entry for July 7, 1862, George L. P. Wren Diary, MARBL, Emory; Davis to "Dear Frank," May 25, 1864, Davis Papers, Filson; entry for May 13, 1864, Kern Diary, SHC, UNC; entry for June 17, 1864, Patterson Journal, in Barrett, *Yankee Rebel,* 172; entry ca. November 1863, Taylor Journal, in Wall and McBride, "'An Extraordinary Perseverance,'" 344; entry for June 18, 1864, Peel Diary, MDAH; entries for July 24, 26, 1862, Drummond Journal, in Durham, *Confederate Yankee,* 90–91.

40. Entries for December 29, 30, 1864, Rogan Diary, in Hauberg, "Confederate Prisoner," 48; entry for December 20, 1864, Gramling Diary, Florida State Archives, Tallahassee; entry for January 20, 1864, Bingham Diary, SHC, UNC; entries for January 20, 21, 1864, Thompson Diary, UVA; Thompson Memoirs, WHMC.

41. Entry for July 20, 1864, Patterson Journal, in Barrett, *Yankee Rebel,* 181.

42. Entry for February 26, 1865, Richard H. Gayle Diary, in Vandiver, "Extracts from the Diary of Richard H. Gayle," 88; entry for November 14, 1864, Joyes Diary, Filson; entry for December 25, 1864, Burgwyn Diary, in Schiller, *A Captain's War,* 167.

43. Entry for January 31, 1864, William M. Jones Diary, GDAH; entry for December 15, 1864, James W. Anderson Diary, in Osborn, "Writings of a Confederate Prisoner of War," 164; entry for July 12, 1864, Wren Diary, MARBL, Emory; entry for March 7, 1864, Mayo Diary, LC; entries for May 23, 25, 1864, Hall Diary, LC.

44. Entry for December 1, 1864, Anderson Diary, in Osborn, "Writings of a Confederate Prisoner of War," 168; entries for September 11, 18, 1864, Sharpe Diary, MARBL, Emory; entries for February 25, 28, March 5, 6, June 26, 1864, Peel Diary, MDAH; entry for March 4, 1864, Mayo Diary, LC.

45. Entry for August 14, 1864, Mugler Diary, WVU; entry for March 2, 1864, Patterson Journal, in Barrett, *Yankee Rebel,* 158–59; entries for March 5, 6, 1864, Peel Diary, MDAH; entry for March 6, 1864, Mayo Diary, LC.

46. Entries for September 16, 18, 1864, Beadles Diary, MDAH; entry for September 16, 1864, Burke Journal, in Bennett, "Curtis Burke's Civil War Journal," 66:332; entry for September 14, 1864, Boyle Diary, in Thornton, "Prison Diary," 68–69; entry for August 30, 1864, Wren Diary, MARBL, Emory; entry for September 8, 1864, Cox Diary, VHS; Schoepf to Lt. Col. William H. Chesebrough, August 13, 1863, Fort Delaware, Letters Sent, RG 393, NA.

47. Entry for June 6, 1864, Peel Diary, MDAH; entry ca. July 1864, Sharpe Diary, MARBL, Emory; entry for July 14, 1864, Beadles Diary, MDAH; entry for November 30, 1864, Burke Journal, in Bennett, "Curtis Burke's Civil War Journal," 66:351; William Agun Milton Memoirs, Filson.

48. Gray, *The Business of Captivity,* 75–76.

49. Entry for June 10, 1864, Kern Diary, SHC, UNC; entry ca. July 1863, Taylor Journal, in Wall and McBride, "'An Extraordinary Perseverance,'" 344; entry for March 28, 1864, Burke Journal, in Bennett, "Curtis Burke's Civil War Journal," 66:144; entry for August 13, 1864, Rogan Diary, in Hauberg, "Confederate Prisoner" 43.

50. Gray, *The Business of Captivity,* 79; entries for February 4, 5, April 12, 15, June 8, 1864, Peel Diary, MDAH.

51. Entries for February 4, May 8, 1864, Peel Diary, MDAH; entry for July 27, 1864, Mugler Diary, WVU; Benson, *Berry Benson's Civil War Book,* 94; entry for February 19, 1864, Jones Diary, GDAH.

52. William H. Haigh to Kate, May 24, 1865, William H. Haigh Papers, SHC, UNC; entry for May 26, 1864, Hall Diary, LC; entry for July 27, 1864, Mugler Diary, WVU; entries for July 7, 20, 27, August 25, November 23, 1864, Peel Diary, MDAH.

53. S. H. Davis to Ella Smith, January 11, 1865, George W. Smith Papers, A&M 427, WVU; entry for November 21, 1864, Wiseman Diary, William F. Howard Collection, USAMHI; Beitzell, "In Prison at Point Lookout," 104; entry for December 18, 1864, Thompson Diary, UVA; G. Washington Nelson to wife, March 8, 1864, Nelson Family Papers, MS 89-021, VT.

54. Gray, *The Business of Captivity,* 78–82.

55. George W. Nelson Memoirs, VHS; entry for June 10, 1864, Kern Diary, SHC, UNC; entry for March 28, 1865, Joseph Julius Wescoat Diary, in Gregorie, "Diary of Captain Joseph Julius Wescoat," 93; Haigh to Kate, May 24, 1865, Haigh Papers, SHC, UNC; entry for October 31, 1864, Gramling Diary, Florida State Archives, Tallahassee.

56. Haigh to Kate, May 24, 1865, Haigh Papers, SHC, UNC; entries for May 17, 18, 1864, Thompson Diary, UVA; entry for October 27, 1863, Dooley Journal, in Durkin, *John Dooley,* 146–47.

57. Entry for December 2, 1864, Hutt Diary, in Beitzell, "Diary of Charles Warren Hutt," 442; Haigh to Kate, May 24, 1865, Haigh Papers, SHC, UNC; Benson, *Berry Benson's Civil War Book,* 133; entry for August 4, 1864, Cox Diary, VHS; entry ca. July 1863, Kern Diary, SHC, UNC; Nelson Memoirs, VHS; Luther Rice Mills Reminiscences, SHC, UNC.

58. Benson, *Berry Benson's Civil War Book,* 133; entry for September 27, 1864, Mugler Diary, WVU; R. M. Gray Reminiscences, SHC, UNC; entry for September 7, 1864, Peel Diary, MDAH; Mills Reminiscences, SHC, UNC; Haigh to Kate, May 24, 1865, Haigh Papers, SHC, UNC.

59. Entry for February 21, 1865, Dooley Journal, in Durkin, *John Dooley,* 166–67; entry for February 2, 1865, Murphey Diary, SHC, UNC; entry for February 4, 1864, Thompson Diary, UVA; Robert C. Crouch, "Picture Made on Johnson's Island," *Confederate Veteran* 17 (1909): 28–29.

60. Hamilton, *The Papers of Randolph Shotwell,* 2:144–45; entry for June 8, 1865, Haigh Diary, Haigh Papers, SHC, UNC.

Chapter 7

1. *OR,* 3:337, 4:504, 5:517.

2. Ibid., 5:686–87; Levy, *To Die in Chicago,* 133–35, 141, 207.

3. Winslow and Moore, *Camp Morton,* 47–48, 50–52, 80, 86–91; Hall, "Camp Morton," 9–12.

4. *OR,* 4:37–38, 51, 87–88.

5. Ibid., 6:333, 353, 368.

6. Ibid., 6:402, 415, 448–49, 490–91.

7. Keen, "Confederate Prisoners," 15.

8. Temple, *Union Prison,* 32; the court-martial charges against Schoepf can be found in Generals' Papers, RG 94, NA.

9. Gen. John S. Mason to Gen. William S. Rosecrans, June 3, 1863, Mason to Hoffman, November 23, 1863, Camp Chase, Ohio, Telegrams Sent, RG 249, NA.

10. Headquarters, Northern Department, Columbus, Ohio, Special Orders, February 10, 1864, RG 249, NA; *OR,* series 1, 25: pt. 1, 638.

11. Miller, "War within Walls," 50–51; *Delaware Gazette* (Ohio), June 17, 1864; J. Coleman Alderson, "Prison Life in Camp Chase, Ohio," *Confederate Veteran* 20 (1912): 295; John F. Hickey, "With Col. William S. Hawkins in Camp Chase," *Confederate Veteran* 11 (1903): 23–24.

12. Winslow and Moore, *Camp Morton,* 97, 106, 120–22; Hall, "Camp Morton," 12.

13. *OR,* 6:853, 922–23, 7:122.

14. Ibid., 7:140–41, 178.

15. Gilman Marston, Pension and Service Records, RG 94, NA; *OR,* series 1, 25: pt. 2, 242, 27: pt. 3, 152, series 2, 6:141.

16. *OR,* 7:435; Beitzell, *Point Lookout,* 23, 101, 181; Beitzell, "In Prison at Point Lookout," 101.

17. McAdams, *Rebels at Rock Island,* 29.

18. Horigan, *Elmira,* 22–26, 77.

19. Ibid., 77–82; Cooling, *Benjamin Franklin Tracy,* 13–21.

20. Ibid., 22–23.

21. Gray, *The Business of Captivity,* 11–13, 65; T. H. Stewart Memoirs, MARBL, Emory; Keiley, *In Vinculis,* 131–32.

22. Alderson, "Prison Life in Camp Chase," 295; Hickey, "With Col. Hawkins," 23–24.

23. Reid, *Ohio in the War,* 2:492–93; *Delaware Gazette* (Ohio), July 3, 1863.

24. *Sandusky Register,* January 1, 1862, quoted in Frohman, *Rebels on Lake Erie,* 6; Downer, "Johnson's Island," 105–6.

25. Brig. Gen. Joseph T. Copeland to Capt. J. F. Bennett, August 5, 1864, Alton, Illinois, Letters Sent, RG 393, NA.

26. Gray, *The Business of Captivity,* 130.

27. Keen, "Confederate Prisoners," 15; *OR,* 7:187, 193.

28. Winslow and Moore, *Camp Morton,* 91; *OR,* 6:143–44, 492–93.

29. McAdams, *Rebels at Rock Island,* 65–66; Orders No. 3, July 30, 1863, Alton, Illinois, Special Orders and Orders, RG 393, NA; *OR,* 6:160, 195.

30. McAdams, *Rebels at Rock Island,* 67–69; *OR,* 6:1002, 7:23, 65; Johnson to Hoffman, May 30, 1864, Rock Island Barracks, Illinois, Letters Sent, RG 393, NA.

31. Winslow and Moore, *Camp Morton,* 127; Capt. Robert Lamb to Richardson, October 28, 1864, Camp Chase, Ohio, Letters Received, RG 249, NA.

32. *OR,* series 3, 5:543–50, 560–66.

33. Ibid., 549–52; *Delaware Gazette* (Ohio), June 17, 1864.

34. McAdams, *Rebels at Rock Island,* 29; Rush to Col. James Fry, November 26, 1863, Rock Island Barracks, Illinois, Letters Sent, RG 393, NA; Stevens to Capt. A. C. Kemper, November 21, 27, 1864, Camp Morton, Indiana, Letters Sent, RG 393, microcopy 598, NA.

35. Johnson to Hoffman, October 5, 1864, Johnson to Col. W. P. Chapman, November 12, 1864, Rock Island Barracks, Illinois, Letters Sent, RG 393, NA; Leroy B. House to "Friend B.," September 26, 1864, Leroy B. House Collection, Ives Family Papers, Connecticut Historical Society Museum, Hartford; Rock Island Barracks, Illinois, Guard Reports, RG 393, NA.

36. House to "Friend B.," September 26, 1864, House Collection, Ives Family Papers, Connecticut Historical Society Museum, Hartford; entry for September 26, 1864, Lafayette Rogan Diary, in Hauberg, "Confederate Prisoner," 46; Rock Island Barracks, Illinois, Guard Reports, RG 393, NA.

37. Stewart Memoirs, MARBL, Emory; entries for July 30, August 8, 1864, Henri Jean Mugler Diary, A&M 1335, WVU.

38. John H. Burrill to parents, March 21, 1864, John H. Burrill Letters, *CWTI* Collection, USAMHI; B. T. Holliday, "Account of My Capture," UVA; entry for May 29, 1865, William H. Haigh Diary, William H. Haigh Papers, SHC, UNC; entry for November 11, 1864, Joseph Mason Kern Diary, Joseph Mason Kern Papers, SHC, UNC; Keiley, *In Vinculis,* 113;

39. Edward J. Bartlett to wife, October 23, 1864, Edward J. Bartlett Correspondence, Massachusetts Historical Society, Boston.

40. Entry for January 26, 1864, E. L. Cox Diary, VHS; George H. Moffett, "War Prison Experience," *Confederate Veteran* 13 (1905): 105; entry for February 18, 1864, James T. Mackey Diary, TSLA; report for January 1, 1864, Rock Island Barracks, Illinois, Guard Reports, RG 393, NA; entry for January 1, 1864, James Mayo Diary, LC; entry for January 1, 1864, Curtis R. Burke Journal, in Bennett, "Curtis R. Burke's Civil War Journal," 66:135; House to "Dear Friends," December 28, 1864, House Letters, Ives Family Papers, Connecticut Historical Society Museum, Hartford; Bartlett to family, November 26, 1864, Bartlett Correspondence, Massachusetts Historical Society, Boston.

41. Entries for November 21, December 6, 12, 29, 1862, Alexander J. Hamilton Diary, in Wilson, *A Fort Delaware Journal,* 15–17; Layton, "Delaware's Forgotten Regiment," 34.

42. *OR,* 6:1040; Charles F. Johnson to wife, February 20, 1864, Charles F. Johnson Papers, USAMHI; Report of Dr. [Ira] Brown, November 1, 1863, Camp Douglas, Illinois, Register of Letters relating to Prisoners of War, RG 393, NA.

43. Isaac Marsh to wife, January 30, 1863, Isaac Marsh Papers, Duke; entries for January 4, 12, 22, 24, 26, February 16, 1863, George W. Bisbee Diary, Special Collections and Archives, Ralph Brown Draughan Library, Auburn University, AL; House to "Dear Friends," December 28, 1864, House Letters, Ives Family Papers, Connecticut Historical Society Museum, Hartford; George Watson to mother, October 2, 1863, April 16, 1864, George Watson Letters, MS 89-024, VT.

44. Gray, *The Business of Captivity,* 132–38; *Elmira Daily Advertiser,* January 3, 1865; McAdams, *Rebels at Rock Island,* 53–54, 68, 79–80, 174; entry for July 2, 1864, Frances Bishop Diary, Denver Public Library.

45. Entries for December 24, 1862, May 26, August 21, December 21, 24–25, 1863, Hamilton Diary, in Wilson, *A Fort Delaware Journal,* 17, 29, 36, 43.

46. Bartlett to wife, October 23, 1864, Bartlett Correspondence, Massachusetts Historical Society, Boston; report for May 21, 1863, Camp Chase, Ohio, Guard Reports, RG 249, NA.

47. Entry for January 31, 1865, Burke Journal, in Bennett, "Curtis R. Burke's Civil War Journal," 67:134–36.

48. Entries for September 1–2, 1864, Cox Diary, VHS; James A. Thomas to father, September 26, 1863, James A. Thomas Letters, Filson; entries for April 5, August 14, 18, 1864, William Peel Diary, MDAH.

49. General Orders No. 9, January 1, 1864, Camp Douglas, Illinois, General Orders, RG 393, NA; entry for December 10, 1863, William Sylvester Dillon Diary, J. D. Williams Library, University of Mississippi, Oxford; entry for April 3, 1865, James T. Meade Diary, in Minnigrode and Minnigrode, *Journal of Prison Life,* 4; entry ca. January 1865, Virgil S. Murphey Diary, SHC, UNC.

50. Entries for August 24, November 2, 1864, Cox Diary, VHS; entry for November 27, 1864, Francis Asbury Burrows Journal, South Caroliniana Library, University of South Carolina, Columbia; entry for November 6, 1864, Francis Atherton Boyle Diary, in Thornton, "Prison Diary," 71.

51. Entry for February 25, 1864, Thomas R. Beadles Diary, MDAH; entry for March 11, 1864, William M. Jones Diary, GDAH; entry for February 14, 1864, Kern Diary, SHC, UNC.

52. P. H. Aylett Memoirs, P. H. Aylett Papers, Duke; entry for May 15, 1864, Charles Warren Hutt Diary, in Beitzell, "Diary of Charles Warren Hutt," 426; entry for April 15, 1864, Beadles Diary, MDAH; entry for June 14, 1864, Peel Diary, MDAH.

53. Entry for December 5, 1864, Cox Diary, VHS; entries for June 16, October 2, 12, 1864, Beadles Diary, MDAH; entry for May 6, 1864, Burke Journal, in Bennett, "Curtis R. Burke's Civil War Journal," 65:154.

54. Entry for November 10, 1864, Wilbur Wightman Gramling Diary, Florida State Archives, Tallahassee; Hill to Lt. Col. E. A. Scovill, December 17, 1864, Johnson's Island, Ohio, Letters Sent, RG 393, NA.

55. Entries for February 14, September 18, 1864, Peel Diary, MDAH; entry ca. July 1863, Thomas Jones Taylor Journal, in Wall and McBride, "'An Extraordinary Perseverance,'" 346; Gray, *The Business of Captivity,* 124; entry for December 13, 1864, Gramling Diary, Florida State Archives, Tallahassee; *OR,* 6:374.

56. *Delaware News* (Ohio), October 23, 1863; W. C. Dodson, "Stories of Prison Life," *Confederate Veteran* 3 (1900): 121; Kean Reminiscences, SHC, UNC.

57. Entries for April 12, December 9, 1864, Burke Journal, in Bennett, "Curtis R. Burke's Civil War Journal," 66:148, 353.

58. Entries for October 9, December 19, 1864, Mugler Diary, WVU; Stamp, "Ten Months Experience," 495; Stewart Memoirs, MARBL, Emory.

59. Stamp, "Ten Months Experience," 495; entries for April 29, May 13, 23, 1865, James Morey Diary, TSLA.

60. Entry for November 22, 1863, Burke Journal, in Bennett, "Curtis R. Burke's Civil War Journal," 66:131; William Agun Milton Memoirs, Filson.

61. Entry for June 28, 1864, Burke Journal, in Bennett, "Curtis R. Burke's Civil War Journal," 66:164; J. S. Rosamond, "In Camp Douglas Prison in 1865," *Confederate Veteran* 16 (1908): 421.

62. Entry for December 15, 1863, Beadles Diary, MDAH; General Orders No. 5, Camp Chase, Ohio, General Orders, RG 393, NA; entry for May 24, 1863, Hamilton Diary, in Wilson, *A Fort Delaware Journal,* 28–29.

63. Entry for April 3, 1864, Burke Journal, in Bennett, "Curtis R. Burke's Civil War Journal," 66:146; J. K. Womack, "Treatment of Prisoners at Camp Morton," *Confederate Veteran* 6 (1898): 571; Gray, *The Business of Captivity,* 125–26; Keiley, *In Vinculis,* 134–35; entry for October 16, 1864, J. L. J. Lear Diary, MARBL, Emory.

64. Entries for July 24, November 12–13, December 20, 1864, Cox Diary, VHS.

65. Entry for January 16, 1864, Robert Bingham Diary, SHC, UNC; entries for January 16–17, 1864, Beadles Diary, MDAH; entry for June 9, 1864, Dillon Diary, J. D. Williams Library, University of Mississippi, Oxford.

66. Undated entries for April, May, August 1864, Bartlett Yancey Malone Diary, in Pierson, *Whipt 'em Everytime,* 101–2, 108; entry for August 7, 1864, Hutt Diary, in Beitzell, "Diary of Charles Warren Hutt," 433; *OR,* 7:163–65, 698.

67. Entry for August 6, 1863, Burke Journal, in Bennett, "Curtis R. Burke's Civil War Journal," 66:116; entry for June 12, 1864, Peel Diary, MDAH; General Order No. 1, January 13, 1865, Rock Island Barracks, Illinois, General Orders, RG 393, NA; George W. Pearl to parents, November 17, 1863, George W. Pearl Letters, Hamilton College Library, Clinton, NY.

68. Report for October 4, 1864, Rock Island Barracks, Illinois, Guard Reports, RG 393, NA; *OR,* 8:66–67.

69. *OR,* 6:854.

70. Ibid., 6:868, 892, 1061.

71. Ibid., 6:1073.

72. Stevens to Hoffman, April 21, 1864, Camp Morton, Indiana, Letters Sent, microcopy 598, RG 393, NA.

73. Entry ca. July 1863, Taylor Journal, in Wall and McBride, "'An Extraordinary Perseverance,'" 345; entry for April 10, 1864, Burke Journal, in Bennett, "Curtis R. Burke's Civil War Journal," 66:147.

Chapter 8

1. General Orders No. 95, October 1, 1864, Camp Douglas, Illinois, General Orders, RG 393, NA; Special Orders No. 148, August 14, 1864, Fort Delaware, General, Special, and Post Orders, RG 393, NA.

2. Entry for June 3, 1864, Edmund DeWitt Patterson Journal, in Barrett, *Yankee Rebel,* 170; entries for May 15–16, 1864, William Sylvester Dillon Diary, J. D. Williams Library, University of Mississippi, Oxford; entry for October 24, 1864, Wilbur Wightman Gramling Diary, Florida State Archives, Tallahassee; Miller, "Civil War Memoirs," 165.

3. J. Coleman Alderson, "Prison Life in Camp Chase, Ohio," *Confederate Veteran* 20 (1912): 294; R. M. Gray Reminiscences, SHC, UNC.

4. Stevens to Hoffman, October 13, 1864, Camp Morton, Indiana, Letters Sent, RG 393, microcopy 598, NA; entry for August 22, 1864, Thomas R. Beadles Diary, MDAH; Johnson to Hoffman, October 5, 1864, Johnson to Henry W. Wessells, December 6, 1864, Rock Island Barracks, Illinois, Letters Sent, RG 393, NA.

5. *OR,* 7:415; Johnson to Hoffman, June 29, 1864, Rock Island Barracks, Illinois, Letters Sent, RG 393, NA.

6. *OR,* 6:946–47, 1043–44; Stevens to Hoffman, February 29, 1864, Camp Morton, Indiana, Letters Sent, RG 393, microcopy 598, NA.

7. *OR,* 6:637–38, 860–61.

8. Ibid., 6:638; entry for December 3, 1863, Curtis R. Burke Journal, in Bennett, "Curtis R. Burke's Civil War Journal," 66:132–33; entry for December 18, 1863, Beadles Diary, MDAH.

9. *OR,* 6:434–35.

10. Entries for March 23, 27, 1864, Burke Journal, in Bennett, "Curtis R. Burke's Civil War Journal," 66:142–44; entries for March 22, 23, 1864, Beadles Diary, MDAH.

11. Moore, "Break Out!" 26, 52. This article is Traweek's first-person account of the escape.

12. Ibid., 52–53.

13. Ibid., 53; Benson, *Berry Benson's Civil War Book,* 138.

14. Ibid., 136–37.

15. Moore, "Break Out!" 53–59.

16. Benson, *Berry Benson's Civil War Book,* 139–40.

17. Ibid., 141–43, 145.

18. Ibid., 146–49, 167; Moore, "Break Out!" 59, 61.

19. Entries for December 28, 1864, January 3, 1865, James W. Anderson Diary, in Osborn, "Writings of a Confederate Prisoner of War," 173, 178.

20. Entry for May 15, 1864, Beadles Diary, MDAH; entry for May 29, 1864, Patterson Journal, in Barrett, *Yankee Rebel,* 168–69.

21. Capt. John Barnes to Gen. J. Barnes, July 30, 1864, District of St. Mary's, Letters Received, RG 393, NA; entry for December 13, 1864, John Joyes Jr. Diary, Filson; entries for December 12, 13, 1864, Henry Parsons Journal, vol. 641, OHS; entry for December 13, 1864, William Peel Diary, MDAH.

22. Entries for February 27, June 17, 1864, Burke Journal, in Bennett, "Curtis R. Burke's Civil War Journal," 66:138–39, 161; entry for December 27, 1864, Beadles Diary, MDAH.

23. Johnson to Hoffman, September 21, 28, 1864, Johnson to Wessells, December 25, 1864, Rock Island Barracks, Illinois, Letters Sent, RG 393, NA.

24. *OR,* 7:187; entry for June 1, 1864, Beadles Diary, MDAH.

25. Entry for September 7, 1864, Beadles Diary, MDAH; General Orders No. 85, September 15, 1864, Camp Douglas, Illinois, General Orders, RG 393, NA.

26. *OR,* 7:897; General Orders No. 94, September 28, 1864, Camp Douglas, Illinois, General Orders, RG 393, NA; entry for September 28, 1864, Beadles Diary, MDAH.

27. Stevens to Hoffman, September 5, 1864, Camp Morton, Indiana, Letters Sent, RG 393, microcopy 598, NA.

28. *OR,* 7:915–17.

29. Stevens to Hartz, November 23, 1864, Camp Morton, Indiana, Letters Sent, RG 393, microcopy 598, NA.

30. R. H. Strother, "Attempt to Escape from Camp Chase," *Confederate Veteran* 4 (1901): 553–54; *OR,* 7:474.

31. Johnson to Hoffman, July 30, 1864, Rock Island Barracks, Illinois, Letters Sent, RG 393, NA; *OR,* 7:1275; entry for June 21, 1864, Beadles Diary, MDAH; entry for December 30, 1864, H. H. Wiseman Diary, William F. Howard Collection, USAMHI.

32. Stevens to Hoffman, October 13, 1864, Camp Morton, Indiana, Letters Sent, RG 393,

microcopy 598, NA; *OR,* 7:813–14; Richardson to Hoffman, June 3, 1864, Camp Chase, Ohio, Telegrams Sent, RG 249, NA.

33. De Land to Ammen, October 13, 1863, Camp Douglas, Illinois, Letters Sent, RG 393, NA; *Delaware Gazette* (Ohio), October 23, 1863.

34. Entry for September 8, 1864, Thomas A. Sharpe Diary, MARBL, Emory.

35. Entry for December 23, 1863, Patterson Journal, in Barrett, *Yankee Rebel,* 151; entry for January 14, 1864, Beadles Diary, MDAH.

36. Levy, *To Die in Chicago,* 151, 158; Brig. Gen. Speed S. Fry to Brig. Gen. J. L. Boyle, November 3, 1863, Camp Chase, Ohio, Letters Received, RG 249, NA; Capt. Stephen E. Jones to Commanding Officer, Camp Douglas, May 6, 1864, Camp Douglas, Illinois, Register of Letters relating to Prisoners of War, RG 393, NA.

37. Frohman, *Rebels on Lake Erie,* 72–74.

38. Ibid., 73; *OR,* series 1, 43: pt. 2, 922.

39. *OR,* series 1, 43: pt. 2, 233–34, series 2, 7:901–2.

40. Ibid., series 2, 7:903; Frohman, *Rebels on Lake Erie,* 74–80.

41. Entry for September 21, 1864, Patterson Journal, in Barrett, *Yankee Rebel,* 195; entry for September 20, 1864, Joyes Diary, Filson; entries for September 20, 21, 1864, Peel Diary, MDAH.

42. Sweet to Hoffman, September 22, 1864, Camp Douglas, Illinois, Letters Sent, RG 393, NA.

43. Levy, *To Die in Chicago,* 264–77.

44. Theodore P. Hamlin to father, November 6, 1864, January 18, 1865, Theodore P. Hamlin Letters, SHC, UNC; Johnson to Hoffman, 27 January, 1865, Rock Island Barracks, Illinois, Letters Sent, RG 393, NA.

45. *OR,* 4:145; entries for September 7, 1863, May 5, 1864, Burke Journal, in Bennett, "Curtis R. Burke's Civil War Journal," 66:123, 154; entry for August 10, 1864, Peel Diary, MDAH.

46. Johnson to Hoffman, November 5, 1864, Rock Island Barracks, Illinois, Letters Sent, RG 393, NA.

47. Entry for February 21, 1864, James Mayo Diary, LC; entry for March 24, 1864, Peel Diary, MDAH.

48. Hill to Hoffman, August 26, 1864, Johnson's Island, Ohio, Letters Sent, RG 393, NA.

49. Entries for August 6–7, 1864, Patterson Journal, in Barrett, *Yankee Rebel,* 186–87; entries for August 7–8, 1864, Peel Diary, MDAH.

50. Entries for December 13, 1864, January 16, 1865, Joyes Diary, Filson; entry for January 16, 1865, Peel Diary, MDAH.

51. Johnson to Hoffman, September 5, 1864, Rock Island Barracks, Illinois, Letters Sent, RG 393, NA.

52. Entry for September 30, 1864, Burke Journal, in Bennett, "Curtis R. Burke's Civil War Journal," 66:334; entry for November 20, 1864, Henri Jean Mugler Diary, A&M 1335, WVU; Stamp, "Ten Months Experience," 498.

53. Entry for February 14, 1864, Charles Warren Hutt Diary, in Beitzell, "Diary of Charles Warren Hutt," 419; Beitzell, "In Prison at Point Lookout," 103.

54. Keen, "Confederate Prisoners," 16; entry for July 15, 1862, A. F. Williams Diary, Col-

lection no. 246, East Carolina Manuscript Collection, J. Y. Joyner Library, East Carolina University, Greenville, NC; entries for August 13, November 14, 1863, Alexander J. Hamilton Diary, in Wilson, *A Fort Delaware Journal,* 36, 42; entries for July 3, 25, 1864, George Washington Hall Diary, LC.

55. *OR,* 8:986–1001.

Chapter 9

1. Entry for March 22, 1864, Curtis R. Burke Journal, in Bennett, "Curtis R. Burke's Civil War Journal," 66:142; entry for August 26, 1863, Edmund DeWitt Patterson Journal, in Barrett, *Yankee Rebel,* 131–32.

2. Joseph Mason Kern Memoirs, SHC, UNC; entry for January 19, 1864, James T. Mackey Diary, TSLA; entry for December 29, 1863, William H. Davis Diary, MARBL, Emory; entries for August 24, November 14–15, 1863, Burke Journal, in Bennett, "Curtis R. Burke's Civil War Journal," 66:122, 130–31.

3. *OR,* 6:158, 462–63, 490, 702, 7: 823; entry for August 18, 1864, Burke Journal, in Bennett, "Curtis R. Burke's Civil War Journal," 66:325–26.

4. *OR,* 6:660, 848–49, 992–93.

5. Ibid., 6:390, 516, 918–19.

6. Ibid., 6:484, 504, 803, 840.

7. Entry for February 14, 1864, Robert Bingham Diary, SHC, UNC; entry for July 27, 1864, E. L. Cox Diary, VHS; entry for October 29, 1864, William H. S. Burgwyn Diary, in Schiller, *A Captain's War,* 160; Wilbur Fisk Davis Memoirs, UVA.

8. *OR,* 6:660–63, 7:1039–41.

9. Kern Memoirs, SHC, UNC; Stamp, "Ten Months Experience," 491; entry for December 12, 1864, James W. Anderson Diary, in Osborn, "A Confederate Prisoner at Camp Chase," 49.

10. Entry ca. December 1864, Virgil S. Murphey Diary, SHC, UNC.

11. Entry for October 21, 1863, Burke Journal, in Bennett, "Curtis R. Burke's Civil War Journal," 66:128; entry for February 1, 1864, John M. Porter Diary, John M. Porter Papers, Filson; entry for August 29, 1864, Thomas A. Sharpe Diary, MARBL, Emory.

12. Pickenpaugh, *Camp Chase,* 43–44; Levy, *To Die in Chicago,* 153–55, 188–90; Special Order No. 175, Camp Douglas, Illinois, Special Orders, RG 393, NA.

13. Hill to Capt. Ellmaker, August 22, 1864, Capt. & a.a.a.g. to A. P. & D. Kelley, December 3, 1864, Johnson's Island, Ohio, Letters Sent, RG 393, NA.

14. McAdams, *Rebels at Rock Island,* 116–18; *OR,* 7:366–67; Johnson to Hoffman, July 14, 1864, Rock Island Barracks, Illinois, Letters Sent, RG 393, NA.

15. *OR,* 7:154; William H. Haigh to Kate, May 24, 1865, William H. Haigh Papers, SHC, UNC; entries for October 3, November 25, December 13, 1864, January 1, 1865, George Quintas Peyton Diary, MSS 5031, UVA.

16. Entries for March 31, April 1, 1864, William Peel Diary, MDAH.

17. Entry for September 26, 1863, Bingham Diary, SHC, UNC; James Jay Archer to "My Dear Nannie," September 15, 1863, James Jay Archer Collection, Maryland Historical Society, Baltimore; entry for April 30, 1864, Charles Warren Hutt Diary, in Beitzell, "Diary of Charles

Warren Hutt," 425; Anderson to W. Thomas Anderson, January 1865, in Osborn, "A Confederate Prisoner at Camp Chase," 47.

18. William Agun Milton Memoirs, Filson; entry for October 31, 1864, Wilbur Wightman Gramling Diary, Florida State Archives, Tallahassee.

19. Entries for January 4–5, 1864, Lafayette Rogan Diary, in Hauberg, "Confederate Prisoner," 31; entry for July 30, 1863, Bingham Diary, SHC, UNC; entry for July 15, 1864, William Jonathan Davis Diary, William Jonathan Davis Papers, Filson.

20. Entry for February 1, 1864, Patterson Journal, in Barrett, *Yankee Rebel,* 157; entry for March 8, 1864, Peel Diary, MDAH; entry for March 9, 1864, James Mayo Diary, LC.

21. Hamilton, *The Papers of Randolph Shotwell,* 2:140–41.

22. Entry for October 19, 1864, Cox Diary, VHS; entry for August 21, 1864, George Washington Hall Diary, LC.

23. Entry ca. July 1863, Thomas Jones Taylor Journal, in Wall and McBride, "'An Extraordinary Perseverance,'" 339; entry for July 30, 1863, Bingham Diary, SHC, UNC; Anderson to W. Thomas Anderson, January, 1865, in Osborn, "A Confederate Prisoner at Camp Chase," 46–47.

24. Entries for August 4–5, 1864, Henri Jean Mugler Diary, A&M 1335, WVU.

25. Entries for August 27, September 19, 23, November 23, December 2, 1864, Mugler Diary, WVU.

26. *OR,* 6:446, 485.

27. Ibid., 6:486.

28. Ibid., 6:554–55, 602, 625, 628, 640–41, 754.

29. Ibid., 6:774, 1014–15, 1036.

30. Ibid., 7:101, 110–11.

31. Ibid., 7:110, 115; Sanders, *While in the Hands of the Enemy,* 242–44; Wilkeson, *Turned Inside Out,* 224.

32. *OR,* 7:113–14, 123–24.

33. Ibid., 7:150–51.

34. Ibid., 7:183–84, 573–74.

35. Entries for June 5, 8, August 12, 1864, Peel Diary, MDAH; entries for June 10, August 20, 1864, Patterson Journal, in Barrett, *Yankee Rebel,* 171, 188.

36. Entries for June 25, July 5, November 25, 1864, William Sylvester Dillon Diary, J. D. Williams Library, University of Mississippi, Oxford; entries for July 27, August 29, 1864, Cox Diary, VHS; entry for November 2, 1864, Hall Diary, LC.

37. Entries for August 25, October 13, 1864, Sharpe Diary, MARBL, Emory; entries for December 22, 27, 1864, Anderson Diary, in Osborn, "A Confederate Prisoner at Camp Chase," 50.

38. Entries for September 3, 9, 16, 22, 27, October 13, 14, 20, 22, 23, 1864, Sharpe Diary, MARBL, Emory; J. Coleman Alderson, "Prison Life in Camp Chase, Ohio," *Confederate Veteran* 20 (1912): 296; Miller, "Civil War Memoirs," 164; entry for September 8, 1864, Patterson Journal, in Barrett, *Yankee Rebel,* 192.

39. Entry for August 22, 1864, John Philip Thompson Diary, MSS 3527, UVA; entry for August 22, 1864, Peel Diary, MDAH.

40. Entry for September 17, 1864, Hutt Diary, in Beitzell, "Diary of Charles Warren Hutt,"

436; entry for November 18, 1864, Peyton Diary, UVA; entry for July 11, 1863, Joseph E. Purvis Diary, MSS 3867, UVA; Elder J. K. Womack, "Treatment of Prisoners at Camp Morton," *Confederate Veteran* 6 (1898): 571; A. C. Kean, Reminiscences, Cabarrus and Slade Family Papers, SHC, UNC; Benson, *Berry Benson's Civil War Book,* 134.

41. Entries for March 25, 27, June 10, July 26, September 17, 1864, Peel Diary, MDAH; T. M. Page, "The Prisoner of War," *Confederate Veteran* 8 (1900): 63.

42. Entry for October 10, 1864, Sharpe Diary, MARBL, Emory; George H. Moffett, "War Prison Experience," *Confederate Veteran* 13 (1905): 106; entry for November 25, 1864, Dillon Diary, J. D. Williams Library, University of Mississippi, Oxford; Milton Memoirs, Filson; entries for September 12, November 25, 1864, Peel Diary, MDAH.

43. Milton Memoirs, Filson; entry for October 25, 1864, Thomas R. Beadles Diary, MDAH; entry for November 25, 1864, Dillon Diary, J. D. Williams Library, University of Mississippi, Oxford; McAdams, *Rebels at Rock Island,* 149.

44. Undated entry, E. John Ellis Diary, in Buck, "A Louisiana Prisoner-of-War," 237–38; Miller, "Civil War Memoirs," 164.

45. Beitzell, "In Prison at Point Lookout," 102; entry for March 9, 1865, Alexander J. Hamilton Diary, in Wilson, *A Fort Delaware Journal,* 75; M. A. Ryan Memoirs, MDAH.

46. Entries for September 26, December 5, 1864, Mugler Diary, WVU.

47. Hesseltine, *Civil War Prisons,* 163–64; *OR,* 7:371, 381, 388, 447.

48. Hesseltine, *Civil War Prisons,* 163–64; *OR,* 7:418, 463, 472, 567–68, 597–98.

49. Entries for August 12, 14, 1864, Cox Diary, VHS; entry for August 21, 1864, Francis Atherton Boyle Diary, in Thornton, "Prison Diary," 66; George W. Nelson Memoirs, VHS.

50. Entries for August 12, 20, 1864, James Robert McMichael Diary, GDAH; Nelson Memoirs, VHS; entries for August 21, 23, 1864, Hamilton Diary, in Wilson, *A Fort Delaware Journal,* 58.

51. *OR,* 7:683, 712, 819; entry for September 7, 1864, McMichael Diary, GDAH; entry for September 7, 1864, Samuel Horace Hawes Diary, VHS.

52. *OR,* 7:819; Nelson Memoirs, VHS; entries for September 8, 30, 1864, McMichael Diary, GDAH.

53. Entry for September 20, 1864, Hawes Diary, VHS; Nelson Memoirs, VHS; entry for September 24, 1864, McMichael Diary, GDAH.

54. *OR,* 7:981–82, 1006–7; Nelson Memoirs, VHS; entry for October 25, 1864, Hawes Diary, VHS; entry for November 7, 1864, Richard Henry Adams Diary, MS 94-013, VT; entries for October 23, November 4, 1864, McMichael Diary, GDAH.

55. Entries for November 19–26, 1864, January 27, February 20, 1865, Hawes Diary, VHS; entries ca. January 1865, February 20, 1865, Adams Diary, VT.

56. Entries for January 8, 20, February 12, 1865, McMichael Diary, GDAH; Nelson Memoirs, VHS.

57. *OR,* series 1, 47: pt. 2, 27–28, 412–13; entries for March 4, 13, 1865, McMichael Diary, GDAH; entries for March 5, 11, 1865, Hawes Diary, VHS; Nelson Memoirs, VHS; entry for March 15, 1865, Boyle Diary, in Thornton, "Prison Diary," 80; entries for March 12, 17, 1865, Cox Diary, VHS.

58. Entry for July 30, 1863, Bingham Diary, SHC, UNC; entry for May 20, 1864, Dillon Diary, J. D. Williams Library, University of Mississippi, Oxford.

59. *OR,* 6:427; entry for September 13, 1864, Beadles Diary, MDAH; Stamp, "Ten Months Experience," 496.

60. Entry for November 29, 1864, John Alexander Gibson Diary, VHS; Daniel T. Ellis to "Friend Thomas," February 24, 1865, Daniel T. Ellis Letters, LC; entries for January 21, 30, 31, February 2, 1865, Peel Diary, MDAH; entries for January 30, February 1, 1865, Murphey Diary, SHC, UNC.

61. Entry for January 8, 1864, Mayo Diary, LC; entry for January 8, 1864, Thompson Diary, UVA; entry for January 8, 1864, Bingham Diary, SHC, UNC; entry for August 16, 1864, Beadles Diary, MDAH; entry for March 8, 1865, Boyle Diary, in Thornton, "Prison Diary," 79; entry for March 8, 1865, Hamilton Diary, in Wilson, *A Fort Delaware Journal,* 75.

62. Entry for January 2, 1865, Mugler Diary, WVU.

63. Entries for June 24–25, 1863, Hamilton Diary, in Wilson, *A Fort Delaware Journal,* 33; Marston to Gideon Welles, January 27, 1864, District of St. Mary's, Letters Sent, Benjamin Butler to Marston, March 22, 1864, District of St. Mary's, Letters Received, RG 393, NA; Richardson to Hoffman, August 6, 1864, Camp Chase, Ohio, Telegrams Sent, John D. Hartz to Richardson, July 15, 16, 1864, Camp Chase, Ohio, Letters Received, RG 249, NA; *Delaware Gazette* (Ohio), July 15, 1864.

64. Entries for January 9, 26, 1864, Davis Diary, MARBL, Emory; Johnson to Hoffman, January 18, May 16, 1864, Rock Island Barracks, Illinois, Letters Sent, RG 393, NA; Addison W. McPheeters to brother, January 26, 1864, McPheeters Family Papers, USAMHI; entry for February 9, 1864, Rogan Diary, in Hauberg, "A Confederate Prisoner," 34; entry for January 24, 1864, Dillon Diary, J. D. Williams Library, University of Mississippi, Oxford.

65. Entries for September 12, 30, 1864, Rogan Diary, in Hauberg, "A Confederate Prisoner," 46–47; entries for September 12, October 15, 1864, Dillon Diary, J. D. Williams Library, University of Mississippi, Oxford.

66. Johnson to Brig. Gen. James B. Fry, November 18, 1864, Rock Island Barracks, Illinois, Letters Sent, RG 393, NA; *OR,* 7:1245, 1280–81.

Chapter 10

1. Sanders, *While in the Hands of the Enemy,* 1.

2. T. M. Page, "The Prisoner of War," *Confederate Veteran* 8 (1900): 63.

3. Ibid.; entries for November 23, December 8, 1864, Thomas R. Beadles Diary, MDAH.

4. Entry for December 16, 1863, William H. Davis Diary, MARBL, Emory; entry for December 19, 1863, William Sylvester Dillon Diary, J. D. Williams Library, University of Mississippi, Oxford; entry for January 29, 1865, Joseph Mason Kern Diary, Joseph Mason Kern Papers SHC, UNC; entries for November 23, December 13, 1864, E. L. Cox Diary, VHS.

5. Entry for January 2, 1864, Frances Bishop Diary, Denver Public Library; entry for January 22, 1865, Wilbur Wightman Gramling Diary, Florida State Archives, Tallahassee; entry for December 11, 1864, James W. Anderson Diary, in Osborn, "Writings of a Confederate Prisoner," 88; Daniel S. Printup to wife, January 6, 1864, Daniel S. Printup Papers, Duke; entry for January 25, 1865, Virgil S. Murphey Diary, SHC, UNC; entry for May 3, 1864, John M. Porter Diary, John M. Porter Papers, Filson.

6. Thomas W. Schmidlin and Jeanne Appelhans Schmidlin, *Thunder in the Heartland: A*

Chronicle of Outstanding Weather Events in Ohio (Kent, OH, Kent State University Press, 1996), 86; entry for January 1, 1864, Curtis R. Burke Journal, in Bennett, "Curtis R. Burkc's Civil War Journal," 66:135; entry for January 1, 1864, Beadles Diary, MDAH.

7. Entry for January 1, 1864, Bishop Diary, Denver Public Library; entries for January 1–2, 1864, Davis Diary, MARBL, Emory; entries for December 31, 1863–January 2, 1864, Dillon Diary, J. D. Williams Library, University of Mississippi, Oxford.

8. Entry for January 1, 1864, Porter Diary, Filson; entries for January 1–2, 1864, Robert Bingham Diary, SHC, UNC; entries for January 1–2, 1864, James Mayo Diary, LC.

9. *OR,* 6:373, 878, 908; entry for October 4, 1863, George Harry Weston Diary, Duke.

10. Entries for September 25, October 9, 17, 28, November 1, 1864, Cox Diary, VHS; entry for November 2, 1864, George Washington Hall Diary, LC; entry for February 3, 1864, Charles Warren Hutt Diary, in Beitzell, "Diary of Charles Warren Hutt," 418; Beitzell, "In Prison at Point Lookout," 103; entry for March 6, 1864, William M. Jones Diary, GDAH; B. T. Holliday, "Account of My Capture," UVA.

11. Levy, *To Die in Chicago,* 146–47; *OR,* 6:4, 372, 968; entry ca. January 1865, Murphey Diary, SHC, UNC; entry for July 24, 1864, William Peel Diary, MDAH; entry for December 4, 1863, Bingham Diary, SHC, UNC.

12. Keen, "Confederate Prisoners," 4; entry for July 18, 1864, Hall Diary, LC; entry for November 29, 1864, John Alexander Gibson Diary, VHS; *OR,* 6:80–81, 516, 653.

13. *OR,* 6:88, 105–6, 516, 1041, 7:421; entry for October 4, 1864, Hall Diary, LC.

14. Entry for March 1, 1862, Andrew Jackson Campbell Diary, in Garrett, *Diary of Campbell,* 27; entry for February 26, 1862, Timothy McNamara Diary, MDAH; *OR,* 4:164, 250, 6:227; D. Stanton to Mason August 3, 1863, Camp Chase, Ohio, Letters Received, RG 249, NA.

15. *OR,* 6:389–90, 7:51–52, 382, 698–99, 764–65; Miller, "War within Walls," 50–51.

16. *OR,* 7:465, 603–4, 677, 878, 8:998.

17. Ibid., 7:1003–4, 1025, 1146, 8:4; Horigan, *Elmira,* 134–35.

18. *OR,* 4:764; *Delaware Gazette* (Ohio), September 4, 1863.

19. *OR,* 6:517–18, 826–27, 7:421, 484.

20. Entry for January 17, 1864, John Philip Thompson Diary, UVA; entry for August 14, 1863, Bingham Diary, SHC, UNC; entry for October 14, 1863, Weston Diary, Duke; William H. Haigh to Kate, May 24, 1865, William H. Haigh Papers, SHC, UNC.

21. R. T. Bean, "Seventeen Months at Camp Douglas," *Confederate Veteran* 22 (1914): 270; Holliday, "Account of My Capture," UVA.

22. *OR,* 6:827, 852–54, 7:485, 504–5; Isaiah G. W. Steedman to son, June 1, 1891, Isaiah G. W. Steedman Papers, *CWTI* Collection, USAMHI.

23. *OR,* 6:425, 879, 1041, 7:96, 421, 512–13, 521.

24. Ibid., 7:682–83, 785, 878, 1133–36; entry for September 29, 1864, Henri Jean Mugler Diary, WVU; T. H. Stewart Memoirs, MARBL, Emory.

25. *OR,* 6:473, 489, 7:450, 835; Marston to Benjamin F. Butler, January 22, 1864, District of St. Mary's, Letters Sent, James H. Thompson to Barnes, August 20, 1864, District of St. Mary's, Letters Received, RG 393, NA.

26. Entries for August 6–7, 1864, Burke Journal, in Bennett, "Curtis R. Burke's Civil War Journal," 66:323; R. W. Davis to brother, August 9, 1864, Davis Family Papers, Filson; entry

for September 21, 1864, Mugler Diary, WVU; Steedman to son, June 1, 1891, Steedman Papers, *CWTI* Collection, USAMHI.

27. Adams, *Doctors in Blue,* 219.

28. A. W. Clark to Commandant, Camp Chase, January 7, 1864, G. W. Brooke to Lt. Col. Bentley, January 8, 1864, Camp Chase, Ohio, Letters Received, RG 249, NA; *Delaware Gazette* (Ohio), February 12, 1864.

29. Entry for September 6, 1864, Thomas A. Sharpe Diary, MARBL, Emory; *Delaware Gazette* (Ohio), October 21, 1864; *OR,* 7:972, 1069, 1161, 1182, 1236, 8:106; entry for December 21, 1864, Anderson Diary, in Osborn, "Writings of a Confederate Prisoner," 169.

30. *OR,* 6:61, 70, 96, 393, 968.

31. Ibid., 7:1272–73, 8:39; entries for December 19, 23, 24, 1864, January 12, 15, 19, February 28, April 22, May 2, 1865, Gramling Diary, Florida State Archives; entries for December 25, 1864, January 12, March 16, 1865, Mugler Diary, WVU.

32. McAdams, *Rebels at Rock Island,* 49–50, 52–53; Stephen E. Jones to Johnson, December 31, 1863, Rock Island Barracks, Illinois, Letters Received, Johnson to Hoffman, December 12, 1863, January 18, February 17, 1864, Rock Island Barracks, Illinois, Letters Sent, RG 393, NA; entry for January 25, 1864, Davis Diary, MARBL, Emory.

33. *OR,* 6:938–39.

34. Entry for July 12, 1864, Beadles Diary, MDAH; Stamp, "Ten Months Experience," 494, 498; J. Coleman Alderson, "Prison Life in Camp Chase, Ohio," *Confederate Veteran* 20 (1912): 296; entry for July 26, 1864, Cox Diary, VHS. I am grateful to Dr. Rick Nelson of the Ohio State University Hospitals for information concerning smallpox vaccination.

35. Levy, *To Die in Chicago,* 129; *OR,* 5:346, 7:795; Sweet to Hoffman, September 4, 1864, Camp Douglas, Illinois, Letters Sent, RG 393, NA.

36. *OR,* 6:160, 179, 191, 393, 969; Lewis F. Levy, "Two Years in Northern Prisons," *Confederate Veteran* 14 (1906): 122.

37. D. C. Thomas, "Dark Chapter in Prison Life," *Confederate Veteran* 6, (1898): 72–73.

38. Entries for October 5, 7, 9, 19, November 21, 1864, Burke Journal, in Bennett, "Curtis R. Burke's Civil War Journal," 66:335–44, 349.

39. Stamp, "Ten Months Experience," 494–95; entry for February 10, 1865, H. H. Wiseman Diary, William F. Howard Collection, USAMHI; Robertson, "The Scourge of Elmira," 91; Keiley, *In Vinculis,* 138, 144–45, 174–75.

40. Gray, *The Business of Captivity,* 51–52; *OR,* 7:996–97, 1134–35.

41. Entry ca. January 1865, Murphey Diary, SHC, UNC; entries for December 22–23, 1863, January 11, 1864, Bingham Diary, SHC, UNC; Steedman to son, June 1, 1891, Steedman Papers, *CWTI* Collection, USAMHI.

42. Entry for December 28, 1863, Dillon Diary, J. D. Williams Library, University of Mississippi, Oxford; entry for September 25, 1863, Weston Diary, Duke; Haigh to Kate, May 24, 1865, Haigh Papers, SHC, UNC; Franz Wilhelm von Schilling to William, September 22, 1862, Franz Wilhelm von Schilling Letters, VHS.

43. *OR,* 6:425, 442.

44. Winslow and Moore, *Camp Morton,* 95; W. S. Dundas, "Life in Camp Morton," *Confederate Veteran* 13 (1905): 265; *OR,* 6:879, 7:555–56.

45. Johnson to Hoffman, February 11, 1864, Rock Island Barracks, Illinois, Letters Sent,

RG 393, NA; Hoffman to Johnson, March 10, 1864, CGPLTS, RG 249, NA. See also McAdams, *Rebels at Rock Island,* 60.

46. Johnson to Hoffman, March 22, 1864, Rock Island Barracks, Illinois, Letters Sent, RG 393, NA; *OR,* 7:11–16.

47. *OR,* 7:59–60, 77–78, 132–33, 196–97; McAdams, *Rebels at Rock Island,* 101–2, 123.

Chapter 11

1. Hunter, "Warden for the Union," 177; *OR,* series 1, 35: pt. 2, 163, series 2, 7:1117.

2. Ibid., series 2, 7:570–74.

3. Ibid., 6:503–4, 585; among those citing Hoffman's November 12, 1863, message are Speer, *Portals to Hell,* 11; and Sanders, *While in the Hands of the Enemy,* 180–81.

4. *OR,* 4:152–53, 5:367; Hoffman to Johnson, December 11, 1863, Hoffman to Orme, January 5, 1864, Hoffman to Stanton, March 9, 1864, CGPLTS, RG 249, NA; Capt. John Lewis to Capt. L. M. Brooks, June 3, 15, August 27, September 19, 22, 1864, Lewis to Capt. J. J. McClellan, November 11, 1864, Johnson's Island, Ohio, Letters Sent, RG 393, NA.

5. *OR,* 5:367, 8:767–68.

6. McMurry, *John Bell Hood,* 180–82; *OR,* 7:1260–61.

7. *OR,* 7:1275, 8:36, 106, 107, 381; entry for December 23, 1864, Curtis R. Burke Journal, in Bennett, "Curtis R. Burke's Civil War Journal," 66:358; entry for December 22, 1864, Thomas R. Beadles Diary, MDAH; *Delaware Gazette* (Ohio), January 13, 1865.

8. *OR,* 7:1063, 1101, 1122.

9. Ibid., 7:1117, 1131, 1295, 8:13–15; Powell, "Cotton for the Relief of Confederate Prisoners," 29.

10. *OR,* 7:1281, 1286, 8:27, 67–68, 77, 123; Powell, "Cotton for the Relief of Confederate Prisoners," 32–33.

11. *OR,* 7:1246–47, 1249, 1285, 1288–89.

12. Ibid., 8:23–24, 90, 105–6, 137.

13. Ibid., 8:227, 241–42, 257, 313–15, 318; Powell, "Cotton for the Relief of Confederate Prisoners," 33; entry for March 9, 1865, Beadles Diary, MDAH; entry for February 15, 1865, Henri Jean Mugler Diary, WVU; entry for March 12, 1865, Washington Pickens Nance Diary, ADAH.

14. *OR,* 8:227, 241–42.

15. Ibid., 7:607.

16. Sanders, *While in the Hands of the Enemy,* 259–60; *OR,* 7:793, 818, 907.

17. Entries for September 15–16, 1864, William Peel Diary, MDAH; entries for September 30, October 11, 1864, Wilbur Wightman Gramling Diary, Florida State Archives, Tallahassee; entries for September 29–30, October 11, 1864, Mugler Diary, WVU.

18. Keiley, *In Vinculis,* 185.

19. Entry for October 21, 1864, Francis Atherton Boyle Diary, in Thornton, "Prison Diary," 71; entries for October 24, December, 5, 6, 11, 1864, William H. S. Burgwyn Diary, in Schiller, *A Captain's War,* 158, 164–65; entries for October 5, 6, 30, 1864, E. L. Cox Diary, VHS.

20. *OR,* 7:872, 891–94.

21. Keiley, *In Vinculis,* 191; *OR,* 7:891–94.

22. *OR,* 8:63, 170, 363.

23. Entry for February 17, 1865, Beadles Diary, MDAH; entry for February 5, 1865, William Sylvester Dillon Diary, J. D. Williams Library, University of Mississippi, Oxford; *Delaware Gazette* (Ohio), February 10, 1865; *OR,* 8:234, 239–40, 301.

24. Entries for January 24, 31, February 5, 1865, Samuel Beckett Boyd Diary, TSLA; entries for February 12, 17, 24, March 2, 4, 1865, Nance Diary, ADAH; entries for February 21, 24, 27, March 2, 14, 1865, Beadles Diary, MDAH; entry for February 6, 1865, Dillon Diary, J. D. Williams Library, University of Mississippi, Oxford.

25. *OR,* 8:182, 231–32.

26. Henry Hays Forwood to brother, August 25, 1865, William Stump Forwood Papers, SHC, UNC; entries for March 2, 5, 6, 1865, Burke Journal, in Bennett, "Curtis R. Burke's Civil War Journal," 67:140–43; entry for February 27, 1865, John Dooley Journal, in Durkin, *John Dooley,* 168–69.

27. Entries for February 27, March 1, 2, 3, 1865, Burgwyn Diary, in Schiller, *A Captain's War,* 175–76.

28. *OR,* 8:994–1001.

29. Entry for March 8, 1865, Mugler Diary, WVU; entry for March 15, 1865, Boyd Diary, TSLA.

30. Entry for April 3, 1865, Boyd Diary, TSLA; entries for April 3, 10, 1865, Beadles Diary, MDAH; entry for April 11, 1865, Henry Robinson Berkeley Diary, in Runge, *Four Years in the Confederate Artillery,* 133.

31. Entry for April 13, 1865, Gramling Diary, Florida State Archives, Tallahassee; entries for April 7, 10, 1865, James Bennington Irvine Diary, ADAH; J. E. Crowder to Kate, April 11, 1865, J. E. Crowder Letters, Thomas R. Stone Collection, USAMHI; entry for April 10, 1865, James T. Meade Diary, in Minnigrode and Minnigrode, *Journal of Prison Life,* 7.

32. Entry for April 15, 1865, Rufus Barringer Diary, SHC, UNC; entry for April 16, 1865, Cox Diary, VHS; entry for April 15, 1865, Mugler Diary, WVU.

33. Entry for April 16, 1865, Joseph Julius Wescoat Diary, in Gregorie, "Diary of Captain Joseph Julius Wescoat," 94; entry for April 15, 1865, Mugler Diary, WVU; entry for April 15, 1865, John Joyes Jr. Diary, Filson; entry ca. April 15, 1865, E. John Ellis Diary, in Buck, "A Louisiana Prisoner-of-War," 241.

34. Entry for April 15, 1865, Berkeley Diary, in Runge, *Four Years in the Confederate Artillery,* 133–34; entry for April 15, 1865, Irvine Diary, ADAH; George W. Pearl to mother, April 17, 1865, George W. Pearl Letters, Hamilton College Library, Clinton, NY; Isaiah G. W. Steedman to son, June 1, 1891, Isaiah G. W. Steedman Papers, *CWTI* Collection, USAMHI; Luther Rice Mills Reminiscences, SHC, UNC.

35. *OR,* 8:480, 664–66.

36. Entries for February 12–May 10, 1865, James Morey Diary, TSLA.

37. *OR,* 8:477, 488; Col. J. H. Davidson to Lt. R. Dale Benson, April 11, 1865, Davidson to Brig. Gen. B. L. Ludlow, April 25, 1865, Newport News, Virginia, Letters Sent, RG 393, NA; Report of Capt. Daniel H. Herr, April 14, 1865, Newport News, Virginia, Reports of the Officer of the Day, RG 393, NA.

38. *OR,* 8:493–94, 1001–2; Davidson to Hoffman, April 26, 1865, Davidson to Maj. A. A.

Monroe, April 27, 1865, Newport News, Virginia, Letters Sent, RG 393, NA; entry for April 20, 1865, Creed Thomas Davis Diary, VHS.

39. Entries for April 21, 23, May 8, 1865, Davis Diary, VHS; entry for May 13, 1865, Smith Kitchin Journal, South Caroliniana Library, University of South Carolina, Columbia.

40. Report of Capt. Alpheus D. Clark, April 20, 1865, Report of Capt. Daniel H. Herr, April 22, 1865, Newport News, Virginia, Reports of the Officer of the Day, RG 393, NA; *OR,* 8:508–10.

41. *OR,* 8:435–36; entry for April 29, 1865, Irvine Diary, ADAH; entry for April 27, 1865, Paul A. McMichael Diary, SHC, UNC.

42. Entry for April 27, 1865, Beadles Diary, MDAH; entries for April 26–27, 1865, Gramling Diary, Florida State Archives, Tallahassee; entries for April 27, May 1, 1865, Irvine Diary, ADAH; entry for May 4, 1865, Cox Diary, VHS.

43. Nelson to wife, May 3, 1865, Nelson Family Papers, VT.

44. *OR,* 8:538, 556, 585, 641, 709–10.

45. Entries for May 13, 24, June 13, 1865, Beadles Diary, MDAH; Richardson to Hoffman, May 17, 1865, Camp Chase, Ohio, Letters Sent, RG 249, NA; Col. Charles Hill, Notice to Prisoners of War, May 13, June 12, 1865, Johnson's Island, Ohio, Letters Sent, RG 393, NA; Johnson to Hoffman, June 24, 1865, Rock Island Barracks, Illinois, Letters Sent, RG 393, NA.

46. *OR,* 8:557–58, 633; entry for June 11, 1865, Cox Diary, VHS.

47. Mills Reminiscences, SHC, UNC; entries for May 12–17, 1865, Francis Asbury Burrows Diary, South Caroliniana Library, University of South Carolina, Columbia; entry for August 9, 1865, McMichael Diary, SHC, UNC.

48. Entries for June 12–29, 1865, William G. B. Morris Diary, USAMHI.

49. *OR,* 8:693–94, 700–1, 784, 1004; McAdams, *Rebels at Rock Island,* 205.

50. Sanders, *While in the Hands of the Enemy,* 292; Speer, *Portals to Hell,* 303–10.

Bibliography

Note on Sources

Even before the end of the Civil War, the war of words concerning prisoners and their treatment was well under way. Over the next five decades numerous accounts of captivity were churned out by veterans from both sides of the Mason-Dixon Line. Some purported to be written directly from prison diaries, others from memory. The best of them tended to be exaggerated. The worst were outright fabrications. With few exceptions, these works have been avoided as sources for this book.

Among those few exceptions to this rule are a few works produced soon after the war ended. Perhaps the two most reliable among them are Anthony Keiley, *In Vinculis; or, The Prisoner of War* (Petersburg, VA: Daily Index Office, 1866) and Griffin Frost, *Camp and Prison Journal* (Qunicy, IL: Quincy Herald Book and Job Office, 1867). Both have been reprinted in recent years.

In 1893 *Confederate Veteran* began publication. This journal was composed largely of reminiscences by former Confederate soldiers, including a number of ex-prisoners of war. Some of their articles were used in this work, particularly when their claims were corroborated, at least in part, by manuscript sources. *Confederate Veteran* articles remain useful for the first two decades of publication. In the years that follow they go from questionable to outrageous.

Besides first-person accounts, the only significant work on a Union prison during the first sixty years after the war was Clay W. Holmes, *The Elmira Prison Camp: A History of the Military Prison at Elmira, N.Y., July 6, 1864, to July 10, 1865* (New York: Knickerbocker, 1912). An unabashed apologia for the Union prison keepers at Elmira, Holmes's work is little more reliable than the memoirs of former prisoners.

It was not until 1930 that Civil War prisons received their first serious scholarly treatment with the publication of William Best Hesseltine, *Civil War Prisons: A Study in War Psychology* (Columbus: Ohio State University Press, 1930). Growing out of Hesseltine's doctoral dissertation, the work was largely based upon *The War of the Rebellion: A Compilation of the Official*

Records of the Union and Confederate Armies, 128 vols. (Washington, DC: Government Printing Office, 1880–1901). Eight volumes of this valuable primary source work deal with prisons and prisoners. Hesseltine made extensive use of the *Official Records.* Despite a strong Southern orientation and a lack of manuscript sources, Hesseltine's work remains the standard starting point for the study of Civil War prisons.

For the next sixty years the topic of Civil War prisons was largely ignored by historians. Edited diaries and memoirs showed up from time to time in scholarly journals. So, too, did occasional journal articles on particular camps, but book-length studies were rare. In 1940 Hattie Lou Winslow and Joseph R. H. Moore published *Camp Morton, 1861–1865* (repr., Indianapolis: Indiana Historical Society, 1995). Twenty-five years later Charles E. Frohman published a study of Johnson's Island, *Rebels on Lake Erie* (Columbus, Ohio: Historical Society, 1965). Both were solid, scholarly works, but they, too, were largely lacking in manuscript sources.

Hesseltine returned to the topic in 1962 when he edited an issue of the journal *Civil War History* devoted to prison camps. It was reprinted as *Civil War Prisons* (Kent, OH: Kent State University Press, 1962). Included were valuable scholarly articles on Fort Warren, Rock Island, Elmira, and Johnson's Island, as well as various Southern camps.

The last ten years have witnessed the publication of a number of books on individual prisons. Among the best are Benton McAdams, *Rebels at Rock Island: The Story of a Civil War Prison* (DeKalb: Northern Illinois University Press, 2000) and Michael P. Gray, *The Business of Captivity: Elmira and Its Civil War Prison* (Kent, OH: Kent State University Press, 2001). Both deal not only with the camps themselves but also with their impacts on the communities in which they were located. Other recent works include George Levy, *To Die in Chicago: Confederate Prisoners at Camp Douglas, 1862–65* (Gretna, LA: Pelican, 1999); Michael Horigan, *Elmira: Death Camp of the North* (Mechanicsburg, PA: Stackpole, 2002); and Roger Pickenpaugh, *Camp Chase and the Evolution of Northern Prison Policy* (Tuscaloosa: University of Alabama Press, 2007).

Two recent works have tackled the daunting subject of Civil War prisons on both sides of the Mason-Dixon Line. Lonnie R. Speer, *Portals to Hell: Military Prisons of the Civil War* (Mechanicsburg, PA: Stackpole, 1997), provides a useful introduction to the topic. The work is especially strong in detailing the histories of all major and many minor camps. In assessing what went on in those camps, it largely eschews manuscript sources and relies instead on agenda-driven postwar published accounts of prisoners.

Charles W. Sanders, Jr., *While in the Hands of the Enemy: Military Prisons of the Civil War* (Baton Rouge: Louisiana State University Press, 2005) examines the topic from the top. Based on the papers of high-ranking military and government officials, Sanders asserts that leaders North and South abused prisoners as a matter of policy. Sanders's work is solid and provocative. If he falls a bit short of conclusive proof for his contention, he makes a strong case for negligence that at least borders on the criminal.

Manuscript Sources

Alabama Department of Archives and History, Montgomery
James Bennington Irvine Diary
Washington Pickens Nance Diary

Auburn University, Auburn, AL, Special Collections and Archives, Ralph Brown Draughan Library
George W. Bisbee Diary
Connecticut Historical Society Museum, Hartford
Leroy B. House Collection, Ives Family Papers
Denver Public Library
Frances Bishop Diary
Duke University, Durham, NC, Rare Book, Manuscript, and Special Collections Library
P. H. Aylett Papers
John Malachi Bowden Reminiscences
Zoe Jane Campbell Papers
James R. Ervin Sr. Papers
Charles F. Low Papers
Isaac Marsh Papers
Thomas Gibbes Morgan Letters
Daniel S. Printup Papers
Richardson-Davis Papers
James A. Riddick Papers
George Harry Weston Diary
William G. Woods Papers
East Carolina University, Greenville, NC, East Carolina Manuscript Collection, J. Y. Joyner Library
A. F. Williams Diary
Emory University, Atlanta, Manuscript, Archives, and Rare Book Library
J. C. Bruyn Diary
William H. Davis Diary
J. K. Farris Diary
J. L. J. Lear Diary
Thomas A. Sharpe Diary
T. H. Stewart Memoirs
George L.P. Wren Diary
Filson Historical Society, Louisville, KY
Henry Massie Bullitt Reminiscences, Bullitt-Chenoweth Family Papers
Roland K. Chatam Letters
William Jonathan Davis Papers
Davis Family Papers
John Joyes Jr. Diary
William Agun Milton Memoirs
John M. Porter Papers
James A. Thomas Letters
Florida State Archives, Tallahassee
Wilbur Wightman Gramling Diary
Georgia Department of Archives and History, Morrow
William M. Jones Diary

James Robert McMichael Diary
Hamilton College Library, Clinton, NY
George W. Pearl Letters
Library of Congress, Washington, DC
Daniel T. Ellis Letters
George Washington Hall Diary
Horace Harmon Lurton Letters
James Mayo Diary
Maryland Historical Society, Baltimore
James Jay Archer Collection
George William Brown Collection
Fort Warren, Massachusetts, Records
Thomas W. Hall Papers
Massachusetts Historical Society, Boston
Edward J. Bartlett Correspondence
Mississippi Department of Archives and History, Jackson
Thomas R. Beadles Diary
Timothy McNamara Diary
William Peel Diary
M. A. Ryan Memoirs
Mississippi State University, Starkville, Special Collections Department, Mitchell Memorial Library
William H. Young Letters
National Archives and Records Administration, Washington, DC
Record Group 94, Records of the Adjutant General's Office, 1780–1917
Civil War, Generals' Papers and Books
Record Group 249, Records of the Office of the Commissary General of Prisoners
Camp Chase, Ohio, Guard Reports
Camp Chase, Ohio, Letters Received
Camp Chase, Ohio, Telegrams Sent
Columbus, Ohio, Special Orders
Correspondence between the Special Commissioner and Judge Advocate General relating to the Release of Confederate Political Prisoners
Office of the Commissary General of Prisoners, Letters and Telegrams Sent
Record Group 393, Part IV, Records of the United States Army, Continental Commands
Alton, Illinois, Letters Sent
Alton, Illinois, Special Orders and Orders
Camp Chase, Ohio, General Orders
Camp Chase, Ohio, Special Orders
Camp Douglas, Illinois, General Orders
Camp Douglas, Illinois, Letters Sent
Camp Douglas, Illinois, Register of letters relating to Prisoners of War
Camp Douglas, Illinois, Special Orders
Camp Morton, Indiana, Letters Sent
District of St. Mary's, Letters Received
District of St. Mary's, Letters Sent

Fort Delaware, General, Special, and Post Orders
Fort Delaware, Letters Sent
Johnson's Island, Ohio, Letters Sent
Newport News, Virginia, Letters Sent
Newport News, Virginia, Reports of the Officer of the Day
Rock Island Barracks, Illinois, General Orders
Rock Island Barracks, Illinois, Guard Reports
Rock Island Barracks, Illinois, Letters Received
Rock Island Barracks, Illinois, Letters Sent
Rock Island Barracks, Illinois, Telegrams Sent

Ohio Historical Society, Columbus
James Calvin Cook Diary
Henry Parsons Journal

Tennessee State Library and Archives, Nashville
Samuel Beckett Boyd Diary
James T. Mackey Diary
James Morey Diary

United States Army Military History Institute, Carlisle Barracks, PA
John H. Burrill Letters, *Civil War Times Illustrated* Collection
J. E. Crowder Letters, Thomas R. Stone Collection
Charles F. Johnson Papers
McPheeters Family Papers
William G. B. Morris Diary
Mungo P. Murray Letters, *Civil War Times Illustrated* Collection
Isaiah G. W. Steedman Papers, *Civil War Times Illustrated* Collection
Joseph W. Westbrook Memoirs, Civil War Miscellaneous Collection
H. H. Wiseman Diary, William F. Howard Collection

University of Memphis Libraries, Special Collections Department
J. K. Ferguson Diary

University of Michigan, Ann Arbor
William L. Curry Diary, James S. Schoff Collection, William L. Clements Library
John A. Smith Papers, Bentley Historical Library

University of Mississippi, Oxford, J. D. Williams Library
William Sylvester Dillon Diary

University of Missouri, Columbia, Western Historical Manuscript Collection
Bedford Family Papers
Henry E. Parberry Letters
Priest Family Letters
Meriwether Jeff Thompson Memoirs

University of North Carolina Library, Chapel Hill, Southern Historical Collection
Rufus Barringer Diary
Robert Bingham Diary
Edward D. Dixon Reminiscences
William Stump Forwood Papers
R. M. Gray Reminiscences

Thomas Jefferson Green Papers
William H. Haigh Papers
Theodore P. Hamlin Letters
A. C. Kean Reminiscences, Cabarrus and Slade Family Papers
Joseph Mason Kern Papers
Paul A. McMichael Diary
Luther Rice Mills Reminiscences
Virgil S. Murphey Diary
Charles Barrington Simrall Papers
Thomas Sparrow Diary
University of South Carolina, Columbia, South Caroliniana Library
Francis Asbury Burrows Journal
Smith Kitchin Journal
University of Virginia Library, Charlottesville, Special Collections
Wilbur Fisk Davis Memoir
Richard L. Gray Diary
B. T. Holliday, "Account of My Capture"
George Quintas Peyton Diary
Joseph E. Purvis Diary
John Philip Thompson Diary
Virginia Historical Society, Richmond
E. L. Cox Diary
Creed Thomas Davis Diary
Finney Family Papers
John Alexander Gibson Diary
Samuel Horace Hawes Diary
George W. Nelson Memoirs
Franz Wilhelm von Schilling Letters
Virginia Polytechnic Institute and State University, Blacksburg, Digital Library and Archives, University Libraries
Richard Henry Adams Diary
Nelson Family Papers
George Watson Letters
Western Reserve Historical Society, Cleveland
Royce Family Papers
West Virginia University, Morgantown, West Virginia Regional Collection
Henri Jean Mugler Diary
George W. Smith Papers
Wisconsin Historical Society, La Crosse
Benjamin Franklin Heuston Letters

Newspapers and Journals

Confederate Veteran
Delaware Gazette (Ohio)
Elmira Daily Advertiser

Published Primary Sources

Allen, Jack, ed. *Pen and Sword: The Life and Journals of Randal W. McGavock.* Nashville: Tennessee Historical Commission, 1959.

Barrett, John G., ed. *Yankee Rebel: The Civil War Journal of Edmund DeWitt Patterson.* Chapel Hill: University of North Carolina Press, 1966.

Beitzell, Edwin W., ed. "The Diary of Charles Warren Hutt." *Chronicles of St. Mary's* 18 (May–June 1970).

———. "In Prison at Point Lookout," *Chronicles of St. Mary's* 11 (December 1963).

Bell, Whitfield J., Jr., ed. "Diary of George Bell: A Record of Captivity in a Federal Military Prison, 1862." *Georgia Historical Quarterly* 22 (1938).

Bennett, Pamela J., ed. "Curtis R. Burke's Civil War Journal." *Indiana Magazine of History* 65 (December 1969), 66 (June, December 1970), 67 (June 1971).

Benson, Susan, ed. *Berry Benson's Civil War Book: Memoirs of a Confederate Scout and Sharpshooter.* Athens: University of Georgia Press, 1992.

Bowman, Larry G., and Jack B. Scroggs, eds. "Diary of a Confederate Soldier." *Military Review* 62 (February 1982).

Buck, Martina, ed. "A Louisiana Prisoner-of-War on Johnson's Island, 1863–65." *Louisiana History* 4 (Summer 1963).

Cryder, George R., and Stanley R. Miller, eds. *A View from the Ranks: The Civil War Diaries of Corporal Charles E. Smith.* Delaware, OH: Delaware County Historical Society, 1999.

Curle, Mark, ed. "The Diary of Captain John Henry Guy, Goochland Light Artillery." *Goochland County Historical Society Magazine* 33 (2001).

Durham, Roger S., ed. *A Confederate Yankee: The Journal of Edward William Drummond, a Confederate Soldier from Maine.* Knoxville: University of Tennessee Press, 2004.

Durkin, Joseph T., ed. *John Dooley, Confederate Soldier: His War Journal.* Washington, DC: Georgetown University Press, 1945.

Garrett, Jill Knight, ed. *The Civil War Diary of Andrew Jackson Campbell.* Columbia, TN: Author, 1965.

Gregorie, Anna King, ed. "Diary of Captain Joseph Julius Wescoat." *South Carolina Historical Magazine* 59 (1958).

Griffith, Lucille, ed. "Fredericksburg's Hostages: The Old Capitol Journey of George Henry Clay Rowe." *Virginia Magazine of History and Biography* 72 (October 1964).

Hamilton, J. G. De Roulhac, ed. *The Papers of Randolph Shotwell.* 2 vols. Raleigh: North Carolina Historical Commission, 1931.

Hauberg, John H., ed. "A Confederate Prisoner at Rock Island: The Diary of Lafayette Rogan." *Journal of the Illinois State Historical Society* 34 (March 1934).

Keiley, Anthony. *In Vinculis; or, The Prisoner of War.* Petersburg, VA, Daily Index Office, 1866.

Meier, Walter F., ed. "A Confederate Private at Fort Donelson, 1862." *American Historical Review* 31 (April 1926).

Miller, Samuel H., ed. "Civil War Memoirs of the 1st Maryland Cavalry, C.S.A." *Maryland Historical Magazine* 58 (June 1963).

Minnigrode, Gordon, and Anna Meade Minnigrode, eds. *Journal of Prison Life by James T. Meade.* Birmingham, AL: Authors, 1987.

Moore, Robert H., ed. "Break Out!" *Civil War Times Illustrated* 30 (November–December, 1991).

Moss, James E., ed. "A Missouri Confederate in the Civil War: The Journal of Henry Martyn Cheavens, 1862–1863." *Missouri Historical Review* (October 1962).

Murphy, James B., ed. "A Confederate Soldier's View of Johnson's Island Prison." *Ohio History* 79 (Spring 1970).

Osborn, George C., ed. "A Confederate Prisoner at Camp Chase: Letters and Diary of James W. Anderson." *Ohio State Archaeological and Historical Quarterly* 59 (January 1950).

———. "Writings of a Confederate Prisoner of War." *Tennessee Historical Quarterly* 10 (March 1951).

Pierson, William Whatley, ed. *Whipt 'em Everytime: The Diary of Bartlett Yancey Malone.* Jackson, TN: McCowat-Mercer, 1960.

Runge, William H., ed. *Four Years in the Confederate Artillery: The Diary of Private Henry Robinson Berkeley.* Chapel Hill: University of North Carolina Press, 1961.

Schiller, Herbert M., ed. *A Captain's War: The Letters and Diaries of William H. S. Burgwyn.* Shippensburg, PA: White Mane, 1994.

Stamp, J. B. "Ten Months Experience in Northern Prisons." *Alabama Historical Quarterly* 18 (Winter 1956).

Stephenson, Wendell Holmes, and Edwin Adams Davis, eds. "The Civil War Diary of Willie Micajah Barrow, September 23, 1861–July 13, 1862." *Louisiana Historical Quarterly* 17 (October 1934).

Thornton, Mary Lindsay, ed. "The Prison Diary of Adjutant Francis Atherton Boyle, C.S.A." *North Carolina Historical Review* 39 (Winter 1962).

U.S. War Department. *The War of the Rebellion: A Compilation of the Official Records of the Union and Confederate Armies.* 128 vols. Washington, DC: Government Printing Office, 1880–1901.

Vandiver, Frank E., ed. "Extracts from the Diary of Richard H. Gayle, Confederate States Navy." *Tyler's Quarterly Magazine* 30 (1948).

Wall, Lillian T., and Robert M. McBride, eds. "'An Extraordinary Perseverance,' The Journal of Capt. Thomas J. Taylor, C.S.A." *Tennessee Historical Quarterly* 31 (1972).

Wallace, Lew. *Lew Wallace: An Autobiography.* 2 vols. New York, Harper & Brothers, 1906.

Whitely, Mrs. Wade Hampton, ed. "Civil War Journal of James E. Paton." *Kentucky Historical Society Register* 61 (1963).

Wilkeson, Frank. *Turned Inside Out: Recollections of a Private Soldier in the Army of the Potomac.* 1887. Reprint, Lincoln: University of Nebraska Press, 1997.

Wilson, W. Emerson, ed. *A Fort Delaware Journal: The Diary of a Yankee Private, A. J. Hamilton, 1862–65.* Wilmington, DE: Fort Delaware Society, 1981.

Secondary Sources

Adams, George Worthington. *Doctors in Blue: The Medical History of the Union Army in the Civil War.* 1952. Reprint, Baton Rouge: Louisiana State University Press, 1996.

Beitzell, Edwin W. *Point Lookout Prison Camp for Confederates.* Abell, MD: Author, 1972.

Bridges, Hal. *Lee's Maverick General: Daniel Harvey Hill.* New York, McGraw-Hill, 1961.

Cooling, Benjamin Franklin. *Benjamin Franklin Tracy: Father of the Modern American Fighting Navy.* Hamden, CN: Archon, 1973.

Downer, Edward T. "Johnson's Island." In William B. Hesseltine, ed., *Civil War Prisons.* Kent, OH: Kent State University Press, 1962.

Frohman, Charles E. *Rebels on Lake Erie.* Columbus: Ohio Historical Society, 1965.

Gray, Michael P. *The Business of Captivity: Elmira and Its Civil War Prison.* Kent, OH: Kent State University Press, 2001.

Hall, Sidney G. III. "Camp Morton: A Model Prison?" *Indiana Military History Journal* 6 (May 1981).

Hesseltine, William B. *Civil War Prisons: A Study in War Psychology.* 1930. Reprint, Columbus: Ohio State University Press, 1998.

———. "Military Prisons of St. Louis, 1861–1865." *Missouri Historical Review* 23 (April 1929).

Horigan, Michael. *Elmira: Death Camp of the North.* Mechanicsburg, PA, Stackpole, 2002.

Hunter, Leslie Gene. "Warden for the Union: General William Hoffman (1807–1884)." PhD diss., University of Arizona, 1971.

Hyman, Harold M. *A More Perfect Union: The Impact of the Civil War and Reconstruction on the Constitution.* Boston, Houghton Mifflin, 1975.

Keen, Nancy Travis. "Confederate Prisoners at Fort Delaware." *Delaware History* 13 (1968).

Klein, Maury. *Days of Defiance: Sumter, Secession, and the Coming of the Civil War.* New York, Alfred A. Knopf, 1997.

Layton, Larry Lawson. "Delaware's Forgotten Regiment, Ninth Delaware Volunteer Infantry Regiment," 1974. Copy available at Fort Delaware Society, Delaware City.

Levy, George. *To Die in Chicago: Confederate Prisoners at Camp Douglas, 1862–65.* Gretna, LA: Pelican, 1999.

McAdams, Benton. *Rebels at Rock Island: The Story of a Civil War Prison.* DeKalb: Northern Illinois University Press, 2000.

McLain, Minor H. "The Military Prison at Fort Warren." In William B. Hesseltine, ed., *Civil War Prisons.* Kent, OH: Kent State University Press, 1962.

McMurry, Richard M. *John Bell Hood and the War for Southern Independence.* Lincoln: University of Nebraska Press, 1992.

Miller, Robert Earnest. "War within Walls: Camp Chase and the Search for Administrative Reform." *Civil War History* 96 (Winter–Spring 1987).

Neely, Mark E., Jr. *The Fate of Liberty: Abraham Lincoln and Civil Liberties.* New York and Oxford: Oxford University Press, 1991.

Paludan, Philip Shaw. *"A People's Contest": The Union and the Civil War, 1861–1865.* New York: Harper & Row, 1988.

———. *The Presidency of Abraham Lincoln.* Lawrence: University Press of Kansas, 1994.

Peterson, William S. "A History of Camp Butler, 1861–1866." *Illinois Historical Journal* 82 (Summer 1989).

Pickenpaugh, Roger. *Camp Chase and the Evolution of Union Prison Policy.* Tuscaloosa, University of Alabama Press, 2007.

Powell, Morgan Allen. "Cotton for the Relief of Confederate Prisoners." *Civil War History* 9 (March 1963).

Quinn, Camilla A. Corlas. "Forgotten Soldiers: The Confederate Prisoners at Camp Butler, 1862–1863." *Illinois Historical Journal* 81 (Spring 1988).

Reid, Whitelaw. *Ohio in the War: Her Statesmen, Her Generals and Soldiers.* 2 vols. Cincinnati: Moore, Wilstach, & Baldwin, 1868.

Robertson, James I., Jr. "Old Capitol: Eminence to Infamy." *Maryland Historical Magazine* 65 (1970).

———. "The Scourge of Elmira," in William B. Hesseltine, ed., *Civil War Prisons.* Kent, OH: Kent State University Press, 1962.

Sanders, Charles W., Jr. *While in the Hands of the Enemy: Military Prisons of the Civil War.* Baton Rouge: Louisiana State University Press, 2005.

Speer, Lonnie R. *Portals to Hell: Military Prisons of the Civil War.* Mechanicsburg, PA: Stackpole, 1997.

Temple, Brian. *The Union Prison at Fort Delaware: A Perfect Hell on Earth.* Jefferson, NC: McFarland, 2003.

Thomas, Benjamin P., and Harold M. Hyman. *Stanton: The Life and Times of Lincoln's Secretary of War.* New York, Alfred A. Knopf, 1962.

Thomas, Eugene Marvin III. "Prisoner of War Exchange during the American Civil War." PhD diss., Auburn University, 1976.

Weigley, Russell F. *Quartermaster General of the Union Army: A Biography of M. C. Meigs.* New York: Columbia University Press, 1959.

Winslow, Hattie Lou, and Joseph R. H. Moore. *Camp Morton, 1861–1865: Indianapolis Prison Camp.* 1940. Reprint, Indianapolis: Indiana Historical Society, 1995.

Index

Abercrombie, John, 89
Adams, Richard Henry, 82, 197–198
Aiken's Landing, Virginia, 52
Alderson, J. Coleman, 122, 126, 192, 213
Alexander, Charles T., 78, 182, 207, 208, 217
Allen, Edward, 223
Allen, Robert, 82
Allison, Charles W. B., 40
Alton Prison, 40; commanders, 127, 128; conditions, 22–23; escapes from, 171; establishment of, 22; smallpox at, 212, 214
Ames, Edward, 46–47
Anderson, James W., 83, 84, 94–95, 110, 183, 186, 187–188, 192, 203, 212
Anderson, Robert, 43
Andrew, John, 50
Appomattox Court House, Virginia, 230
Archer, James, 185
Arkansas Post, 81
Aylett, P. H., 137

Baltimore, Maryland, 92
Barnes, James, 124, 210, 236
Barnes, Joseph K., 191, 216, 218
Barringer, Rufus, 231
Barrow, Willie Micajah, 26
Bartlett, Edward, 132, 135
baseball: played by prisoners, 34, 108–109
Beadles, Thomas R., 102, 103, 107, 137, 141, 194, 202–203, 213, 225, 228, 230, 234, 235
Beall, John Yates, 173
Beall, William N. R., 223–225
Beatie, James, 143
Bedford, A. M., 98
Bell, George, 34, 35
Belle Plain, Virginia, 88–89, 90, 91
Bellows, Henry W., 27
Benjamin, Judah P., 44, 47, 173
Benson, Berry, 113–114, 115, 116, 164–167
Benton Barracks, Missouri, 67, 69
Berkeley, Henry Robinson, 230, 231
Berryville, Virginia, 91
Biddle, James, 119
Big Black, Mississippi, 59
Bingham, Robert, 98–99, 108, 182, 185, 186, 187, 199, 204, 208, 216
Bisbee, George W., 133
Bishop, Frances, 134
Blagden, George, 210, 224
Borden, J. H., 140–141
Bowles, John, 168
Boyd, Belle, 7
Boyd, Samuel Beckett, 84, 85, 228, 230
Boyd, Thomas, 228
Boyle, Francis A., 98, 101, 112, 196, 199

Brady, Allen G., 124
Bragg, Braxton, 58, 60
Bristol, Tennessee, 84
Brown, George William, 14, 21
Brown, Ira, 133
Brown, John, Jr., 174
Brownlow, William G. "Parson," 49–50
Brunson, C. S., 202
Bruyn, J. C., 34, 35, 49, 56–57
Buchanan, James, 173
Buchanan, Robert, 121
Buckner, Simon B., 19, 21
Buell, Don Carlos, 67
Buford, Napoleon, 44
Bullitt, Henry Massie, 100
Burbank, Sidney, 22
Burgwyn, William H. S., 103, 110, 227, 229
Burke, Curtis, 95, 97, 104, 108, 112–113, 132, 135, 138–140, 163–164, 176, 178, 180–181, 203, 211, 215, 229
Burke, Martin, 9
Burnside, Ambrose, 33, 118, 125
Burrill, John H., 131
Burrows, Francis Asbury, 236
Burton, Henry, 121
Butler, Benjamin F., 9, 63, 225–226, 227
Butler, William, 23

Cairo, Illinois, 20, 28, 44, 52–54, 82
Cameron, Simon, 1–2, 5, 15, 126
Campbell, Andrew Jackson, 20–21, 31, 37, 51
Campbell, William B., 50
Campbell, William Lambert, 99
Camp Butler, 23–24, 39–40, 79
Camp Chase, 16, 29–30, 50, 57, 71, 79, 140, 184, 223, 237; activities of prisoners, 100, 101, 104, 107, 108, 116; allegations of leniency at, 36–37; commanders of, 30, 118, 121–122; conditions at, 31, 40–41, 94–95, 180, 192, 195, 206–208, 224, 230; escapes from, 167, 170–171, 172; establishment of, 15; guards at, 129, 132, 135, 138, 161–162, 172; as parole camp, 67, 68–69, 70; prisoners suffer from cold weather, 203; rats eaten by prisoners, 193–194; release of prisoners, 228, 235; shootings of prisoners at, 142–143, 171; smallpox at, 211–212
Camp Douglas, 32, 35, 49, 50, 52, 71, 112, 136, 137, 138–140, 144, 175, 182, 184, 222–223, 237; activities of prisoners, 107, 108, 113; commanders of, 25, 26–27, 119, 129, 160, 163–164; conditions at, 25–27, 95–96, 118, 180–181, 183, 204, 205, 216; escapes from, 162, 163–164, 168, 169–170, 171, 176, 179; establishment of, 24–25; guards at, 79, 132, 133, 135, 137, 140, 169, 172; oath takers abused, 200; as parole camp, 70–71; prisoners suffer from cold weather, 202–203; rats eaten by prisoners, 194; release of prisoners, 228, 229, 235; religious service prohibited, 111–112; shootings of prisoners at, 141, 142, 169, 172; smallpox at, 214, 215
Camp Lew Wallace, 68, 69
Camp Morton, 36, 50, 71, 180, 237; commanders of, 28, 52, 119, 122–123, 130; conditions at, 28–29, 95, 204–205, 209, 217; escapes from, 162–163, 170, 171; establishment of, 27–28; guards at, 127–128, 130, 133, 135, 140, 142; release of prisoners, 229; shootings of prisoners at, 67, 69–70, 188, 189–190
Camp Parole, 67, 69–70, 188, 189–190
Camp Randall, 41
Carter, John C., 174
Castle Williams, 10–11, 34, 141
Charleston, South Carolina, 1
Chase, Salmon P., 15
Chatham, Roland K., 55
Chattanooga, Tennessee, 74
Cheavens, Henry Martyn, 58–59
Chemung River, 78
Chesnut, Thomas, 29
Chicago Tribune, 70
Churchill, Thomas, 50
City Point, Virginia, 57
Clark, Augustus M., 83–84, 86, 128, 138, 208, 209, 210, 211, 213, 214
Cobb, Howell, 47
Cole, Charles H., 173–174
Colfax, Schuyler, 184
Collierville, Tennessee, 80

Colt, Henry V., 125–126, 131, 166
Columbia, Tennessee, 83
Columbus, Ohio, 67
Conrad, Charles M., 47
Cook, James Calvin, 20–21, 31
Copeland, Joseph, 127
cotton: sold to aid prisoners, 223–225
Cowgill, John, 130
Cox, E. L., 92, 102, 103–105, 107, 115, 135, 141, 182, 187, 196, 199, 203, 213–214, 231, 234, 236
Crawford, James W., 166, 167
Crescent, 196
Cressandra, 229
Cullum, George W., 19
Curry, William L., 69
Cutts, Richard, 22–23
Cuyler, John M., 87, 205

Darr, Joseph, 79
Davidson, J. H., 233
Davidson, W. T., 171
Davis, Creed Thomas, 233
Davis, Henry C., 59
Davis, Jefferson, 46, 62, 63, 64, 65, 173, 225
Davis, R. W., 211
Davis, Wilbur Fisk, 90
Davis, William H., 75–76, 84, 180, 200, 203, 204, 213
Davis, William Jonathan, 101, 107, 109, 186
De Land, Charles, 163–164, 172, 181, 202
Delaware Gazette, Ohio, 126
Demopolis, Alabama, 59–60
Dennison, William, 5, 15, 126
Dillon, William, 141, 161, 191, 194, 199, 201, 203, 204, 216, 228
Dimick, Justin, 12–13, 14, 22, 45, 56
Dix, John A., 48, 49
Dodson, W. C., 82, 138
Dooley, John, 87–88, 95, 101, 102, 106, 107–108, 115, 116, 229
Douglas, Adele, 214
Douglas, Stephen, 24
Draper, Alonzo, 124
Drummond, Edward William, 32–33, 34, 37, 49, 51, 53, 97, 100, 108, 109

Eastman, Seth, 76–77, 78, 124, 207
Edey, Arthur H., 104
Edwards, Ninian W., 184
Ekin, James, 29, 49
Election of 1864: prisoners' interest in, 102–103
Ellis, E. John, 100, 194, 231
Elmira Daily Advertiser, 77
Elmira Prison, 137–139, 178, 195, 200, 226, 237; activities of prisoners, 100, 104, 109, 111–116; commanders of, 76, 124–126; conditions at, 77–78, 97, 182, 209–210, 215, 224; establishment of, 76–77; guards, 127, 131, 134, 140–141, 142; health concerns at, 78, 207; prisoners suffer from cold weather, 203; release of prisoners, 227, 228–229; smallpox at, 212; tunnel escape at, 164–167
Enterprise, Alabama, 60
Ervin, James R., 99

Fanny Bullitt, 53
farmer's boilers, 181
Farris, J. K., 28, 50, 53, 55
Ferguson, J. K., 50, 57–58
Fish, Hamilton, 46–47
Fonda, John G., 24
Forrest, Nathan Bedford, 190
Fort Columbus (New York), 9, 10, 11–12, 34
Fort Delaware, 49, 51–21, 56, 71, 89, 199, 208, 226–227, 231, 237; activities of prisoners, 101, 104–107, 109, 112, 115; commanders at, 112, 121, 160; conditions at, 35, 88, 92, 96, 182, 187, 191–192, 205, 216, 224; escapes from, 178–179; establishment of, 34; guards at, 132–135, 137, 231; oath takers abused, 200; prisoners' mail at, 98; prisoners suffer from cold weather, 203; release of prisoners, 229, 236; shootings of prisoners at, 141
Fort Donelson, 19
Fort Henry, 21, 83
Fort Hindman, 81
Fort Lafayette, 8–9, 12, 174, 237
Fort McHenry, 8, 88
Fort Pillow, 89, 190

Fort Pulaski, 33, 197, 198
Fort Sumter, 1, 43
Fort Warren, 50, 56, 237; commanders at, 12–13; conditions at, 12–14, 21–22; establishment of and site history, 12
Forwood, Henry Hays, 229
Foster, John G., 195–196, 197, 198
Foster, William, 78
Foster's Pond, 78, 207
Franklin, Battle of, 84, 202
Fredericksburg, Virginia, 90
Freedley, Henry W., 39–40, 53, 86, 207–208
Fremont, John C., 6, 43
Fry, James, 75, 201
Fry, Speed S., 172–173
Fuller, Allen, 25, 35
Funkhouser, David, 217

Galloway, Samuel, 16
Gardner, William M., 60
Garfield, James, 15
Gayle, Richard H., 110
Geary, John W., 44
Gettysburg, Battle of, 71, 86–88
Gibbs, George C., 45
Gibson, Augustus, 121
Gibson, John Alexander, 96
Gilmore, Quincy A., 33, 198
Goldsborough, Louis M., 45
Governor's Island, New York, 9–12, 33–34, 100, 114, 141
Gramling, Wilbur Wightman, 78, 91, 97, 103, 104, 115, 138, 161, 186, 203, 212, 230, 234
Grant, Ulysses, 74, 88, 125, 223, 235; and Fort Donelson prisoners, 19; paroles Vicksburg prisoners, 59; and prisoner exchanges, 44, 225–226, 227–228, 234
Gratiot Street Prison, 16–17, 58, 176, 181
Gray, Michael P., 112, 114, 134
Gray, R. M., 116, 161–162
Gray, Richard L., 33, 53–54
Greenhow, Rose O'Neal, 7
Grenfell, George St. Leger, 175
Griffin, Thomas B., 45
Guthridge, Albert J., 119
Guy, John Henry, 32, 38, 55–56
Haigh, William H., 73, 114, 115, 117, 131, 185, 208
Hall, George Washington, 89–91, 96–97, 101, 111, 179, 187, 192, 205
Hall, Thomas W., 13, 21
Halleck, Henry W., 16–17, 59, 225, 228; and Fort Donelson prisoners, 19–20, 23, 25, 29, 37, 38; and Union retaliation policy, 191
Hamilton, A. J., 132–133, 134, 140, 178–179, 195, 196, 200
Hamilton, David W., 119
Hamlin, Theodore P., 175
Hammond, William, 205
Hammond General Hospital, 71, 124
Handy, Issac, 112
Hardee, William J., 60, 197
Hardie, James, 123, 128, 222
Harper's Ferry, West Virginia, 70
Harrison, Benjamin, 125
Hart's Island, New York, 139, 232
Hatteras Inlet, North Carolina, 9
Hawes, Samuel H., 197, 198
Hawkins, William, 224, 225
Hayes, Rutherford B., 15
Healey, Michael, 143
Hendrickson, Thomas, 212, 214
Heuston, Benjamin Franklin, 69
Hiawatha, 20
Hickey, John F., 122, 126
Hildebrand, Jesse, 40
Hill, Bennett, 173–174
Hill, Charles W., 123, 127, 137, 174, 176–177, 184, 235–236
Hill, Daniel Harvey, 48
Hilton Head, South Carolina, 198
Hinks, Edward W., 124
Hitchcock, Ethan Allen, 64, 189, 228
Hoffman, William, 6, 9, 17–18, 32, 79, 118, 120–121, 123, 143, 185, 199, 207; appointed commissary general of prisoners, 2; background of, 2–3; and Belle Plain facility, 88–89; complains of lack of authority, 38–39; demotion of, 200; desire for economy, 4, 181, 182, 207; and health of prisoners, 209–210, 211, 217–219; inspects prisons, 23–26, 28–29,

34–35, 41, 127; postwar life, 237; and prisoner exchanges, 52, 55, 66, 69–70, 227; and prison expansion, 72, 76–77, 232–233; and prison fund, 26, 39, 221–222; and release of prisoners, 235, 236, 237; selects Johnson's Island site, 3–4; and Union retaliation policy, 189–191, 221, 222
Hoffman Battalion, 5, 17
Holliday, B. T., 72–73, 131
Hood, John Bell, 222
House, Leroy B., 130–131, 132, 133–134
Huger, Benjamin, 44–45
Hupman, Henry, 142
Hutt, Charles Warren, 73, 74, 103, 137, 141, 178, 186, 205

Illinois State Journal, 23
Illinois State Register, 23
Illinois Troops: 13th Cavalry, 127; 17th Cavalry, 127
"Immortal 600," 196–199, 220
Indiana Troops: 51st Infantry, 128; 71st Infantry, 119; 73rd Infantry, 128
Invalid Corps. *See* Veteran Reserve Corps
Iowa Troops: 37th Infantry, 128–129, 134
Irvine, James Bennington, 231, 234
Island No. 10, 24, 62
Island Queen, 174

J. H. Dove, 53
Jackson, Gilmer G., 165
Jackson, Thomas J., 57, 70
Jeff Davis, 46
Jenner, Edward, 211
Johnson, Adolphus J., 124, 128, 129–130, 184, 201, 213, 217–218, 236; assumes command at Rock Island, 75; and escapes from, 162, 168–169, 171, 175–176
Johnson, Andrew, 50, 235
Johnson, Charles F., 133
Johnson, George K., 133, 182–183
Johnson, L. B., 186–187
Johnson, Lucius, 44
Johnson, Otis, 99
Johnson, Reverdy, 205
Johnson, W. Gart, 91–92
Johnson's Island Prison, 48–49, 51, 71, 137, 144, 167, 184, 192–193, 222, 226; activities of prisoners, 100–109, 111, 113–116, 123; commanders of, 5–6, 119–121; conditions at, 32–33, 95, 96, 97, 136, 138, 180, 182, 186–187, 191, 205, 209, 216; construction of, 4–5, 17; designated officers' prison, 31–32; escapes from, 168, 171, 176–177; guards at, 5, 17, 126–127, 132, 135–136, 141, 142, 161, 172; oath takers abused, 199–200; plot to liberate prisoners, 173–174; prisoners' mail at, 98–99, 100; prisoners suffer from cold weather, 203, 204; release of prisoners, 229, 235–236; shootings of prisoners at, 168; site selected, 4
Johnston, Joseph, 232, 234
Jones, C. W., 95, 104, 114, 124, 178, 194
Jones, Roger, 37
Jones, Sam, 67, 195
Jones, William M., 110, 114
Joyes, John, 97, 110, 174, 231

Kansas Troops: 10th Infantry, 127
Kean, A. C., 75, 85, 106, 138, 193
Keen, Nancy Travis, 34
Keiley, Anthony, 125–126, 132, 140, 215, 226, 227
Kelley's Island, 2, 4
Kentucky Troops: 20th Infantry, 85
Kern, Joseph, 73, 74, 104, 107, 113, 115, 132, 136, 180, 183, 203
Kidder, John S., 115
Kilbourn, E. G., 14
Kincaid, George, 128
Kipp, Charles J., 209
Kirkwood, Samuel J., 69, 128
Kitchin, Smith, 233

Lafayette, Indiana, 28, 29
Lamb, Robert, 129
Lazelle, Henry M., 39, 40–41, 52–53, 76, 184
Lee, Robert E., 48, 62, 71, 230
Levy, George, 175
Lewis, Bob, 34
Lincoln, Abraham, 15, 45–48, 64, 91, 102,

103, 184; assassination of, 231–232; and Union retaliation policy, 190
Lincoln, Mary Todd, 91, 184
Loomis, Gustavus, 9–10
Louisville, Kentucky, 85–86, 212–213, 223
Low, James A., 73
Ludlow, William H., 52, 64–66
Lurton, Horace Harmon, 107
Lynch, Bernard, 16

McAdams, Benton, 194
McClellan, George B., 8, 48, 102
McDowell, Irvin, 6
McDowell, Joseph, 16
McDowell Medical College, 16
McGavock, Randal W., 20, 21–22, 37, 50, 56
Macgill, Charles, 14
McKee, J. Cooper, 24
Mackey, James Taswell, 94, 132, 180
McKinley, William, 15
McLemore's Cove, 82
McMichael, James R., 196–197, 198
McMichael, Paul, 236–237
McNamara, Timothy, 50
McVickar, Brockholst, 27
Magruder, John Bankhead, 101
Malone, Bartlett Yancey, 74, 141
Malone, S. C., 165
Manassas, First Battle of, 6
Manassas, Second Battle of, 62
Marsh, Isaac, 81, 133
Marsh, John F., 123, 128
Marston, Gilman, 72, 123–124, 210
Maryland Troops: 5th Infantry, 127, 233
Mason, James, 14–15
Massachusetts Troops: 5th Cavalry, 132
Maull, John Fox, 165
Mayo, James, 96, 100, 105–106, 110, 111, 176, 204
Meade, George Gordon, 71, 123
Meade, James T., 231
Meigs, Montgomery, 1–2, 27, 32, 34, 38–39, 74, 206
Memphis, Tennessee, 80
Meredith, Sullivan, 66
Mettam, Henry, 161, 192, 194
Michigan, 120, 121, 173–174
Michigan Troops: 14th Infantry, 82–83
Middle Bass Island, 2, 3
Mills, Luther Rice, 115, 236
Milton, William A., 112, 139–140, 186, 194
Minnesota, 9
Mobile, Alabama, 224
Moffett, George H., 81, 132
Monitor, 56, 58
Moody, Granville, 30, 37
Moore, Josephus C., 48, 51
Moore, Lewis H., 169
Moore, Stephen, 126
Morey, James Marsh, 139, 232
Morgan, John Hunt, 97
Morgan, Thomas Gibbes, 97
Morris, William G. B., 237
Morris Island, 195
Morrison, Pitcairn, 24
Morton, Oliver P., 27, 119
Mosby, John S., 91
Mugler, Henri, 77–78, 92, 100, 102, 113, 131, 139, 178, 200, 210, 211, 212, 225, 230, 231; ridicules poorer prisoners, 188, 195
Mulligan, James A., 25, 26–27, 172
Mumford, William, 63
Murphey, Virgil S., 84–86, 95, 96, 100, 103, 116, 136, 183, 200, 203
Murray, Mungo, 15
Myers, Frederick, 30
Myrtle Street Prison, 16–17, 181

Nance, Washington Pickens, 225, 228
Nashville, Tennessee, 83–85, 222
Nelson, George Washington, 114, 196, 197, 198, 234
New Berne, North Carolina, 33
New Hampshire Troops: 5th Infantry, 136
New Orleans, Louisiana, 63, 179
Newport News, Virginia: establishment of prison at, 232–233; shootings of prisoners at, 233–234
New York & Erie Railroad, 77
New York Times, 47–48
Noble, Lazarus, 27–28, 36
Norfolk, Virginia, 92
Norman, T. J., 171

North Bass Island, 2, 3
Northern Central Railroad, 227, 229

oath of allegiance, 50–52, 199, 201, 234–235
Ohio Troops: 88th Infantry, 126; 128th Infantry, 126–127, 168; 173rd Infantry, 85–86
Old Capitol Prison, 72, 232; conditions at, 7–8; establishment and site history of, 6
Orme, William W., 163, 182
Ould, Robert, 52, 63, 64, 65–66, 223, 226
Owen, Richard, 28, 119

Paducah, Kentucky, 83
Page, T. M., 193, 202
Paine, Halbert E., 224
Parberry, Henry E., 99
Park, Robert, 124
Parsons, Henry, 168
Paton, James E., 20, 73
Patterson, Edmund DeWitt, 88, 96, 98, 107, 108–109, 110, 161, 167, 174, 177, 180, 191, 192
Pea Patch Island, 34, 205
Pearl, George W., 142, 232
Peel, William, 87, 100, 103, 105, 106, 107, 108, 111, 113, 114, 135, 137, 168, 174, 177, 185, 191, 193
Pemberton, John, 58, 60
Perkins, Delvan, 121
Petersburg, Virginia, 230
Peyton, George, 185
Phillips, John, 119
Philo Parsons, 174
Pickett, George, 87
Pierce, Charles, 177
Pierson, William S., 5–6, 32, 51, 99, 119–121
Pike, Albert, 66
Pillow, Gideon, 43
Pitchford, T. J., 98
Planet, 81–82
Point Lookout Prison, 89, 104, 136, 137, 185, 194, 231, 237; activities of prisoners, 104–105, 106, 107, 109, 114, 115, 116; commanders of, 72, 123–124; conditions at, 72–74, 95, 181–182, 205, 210, 216; escapes from, 168, 178; establishment of, 71–72; guards at, 131–132, 135, 232; prisoners rob prisoners at, 73; prisoners suffer from cold weather, 203; release of prisoners, 236; shootings of prisoners at, 141–142
Polk, Leonidas, 44, 60–61
Pope, John, 62
Porter, John M., 104, 183, 203
Port Hudson, Louisiana, 60, 81
Potter, Joseph A., 41
Price, Sterling, 58
Priest, B. E., 99
Printup, Daniel S., 97, 99, 203
prisoners: accompanied by slaves, 36–38; black, 64, 65–66; civilian, 6, 7, 14, 15–16, 112; mortality rate of, 202; paroled Union, 67–71
Purvis, Joseph E., 96, 97, 100
Putegnat, John P., 165
Put-in-Bay, Ohio, 174

Quinlan, L. G., 14

Raymond, Henry J., 125
Raymond, Mississippi, 59
Reynolds, Charles A., 74, 218
Richardson, William Pitt, 122, 126, 172, 181, 206–207, 211–212, 223, 228, 235
Richmond, Kentucky, 67
Richmond, Virginia, 230
Riddick, James A., 99
Robertson, James I., Jr., 6, 7
Rock Island Prison, 138, 184–185, 191, 199, 222, 237; activities of prisoners, 106, 109, 113; commanders of, 74–75, 124, 129–130; conditions at, 75–76, 96, 180; escapes from, 162, 168–169, 171, 175–176, 177–178; establishment of, 74–75; guards at, 128, 129–131, 132, 134, 142, 161; hospital at, 217–2128; prisoners suffer from cold weather, 203, 204; rats eaten by prisoners at, 194; release of prisoners, 236; smallpox at, 212–213; Union recruiting of prisoners at, 200–201
Rogan, Lafayette, 76, 96, 102, 113, 131, 186, 201

Root, Adrian R., 188
Rosamond, J. S., 140
Rose, David Garland, 52, 119
Rosecrans, William S., 15
Ross, David H., 177–178
Rowe, George Henry Clay, 7, 8
Royce, Abner, 69
Rucker, Daniel H., 71
Rumsey, Julian S., 25
Rush, Richard H., 74–75, 130
Ryan, M. A., 195

St. Louis, Missouri, 16–17
Salomon, Edward, 69
Sandusky, Ohio, 2, 173
Sandusky Register, 5, 126
Sanger, Eugene F., 209–210, 215–216
Sangster, George, 70
San Jacinto, 14
Sankey, Alexander, 126
Saurine, Frank E., 165
Savannah, 46
Schmidlin, Jeanne, 203
Schmidlin, Thomas, 203
Schoepf, Albin, 112, 121, 160–161, 206
Scott, Winfield, 121
Scovill, Edward, 182
Scruggs, J. P., 165
scurvy, 198, 209–210
Seddon, James A., 47, 60
Seward, William Henry, 14, 15, 38
Shanks, John T., 175
Sharpe, Thomas A., 94, 97, 101, 102, 172, 183, 192, 193, 211
Shelton, Glenn, 165
Sherman, John, 44
Sherman, William T., 102, 232, 234
Shotwell, Randolph, 187
Simpson, Josiah, 227
Simrall, Charles Barrington, 36
Slidell, John, 14, 15
Sloan, William J., 10–11, 210, 216
smallpox, 211–215
Smith, Charles E., 70–71
Smith, Edmund Kirby, 58, 67
Smith, G. B., 116
Smith, John, 15
Smith, R. S., 41
Sons of Liberty, 175
South Bass Island, 2, 3, 174
Sparrow, Thomas, 9, 10, 11–12, 13–14
Speer, William Henry Asbury, 33, 100
Sponable, Wells, 194
Spotsylvania Court House, Virginia, 89
Sprague, John W., 44
Stamp, J. B., 72, 89, 139, 178, 183, 213, 215
Stanton, Edwin M., 72, 89, 139, 178, 183, 213, 215; appointed secretary of war, 16; opposition to prisoner exchange, 46–48, 64, 65, 66; and Union retaliation policy, 189–191, 222
State of Maine, 12, 57
Steedman, Isaiah, 209, 211, 216, 232
Stevens, Ambrose, 122–123, 128, 130, 143, 162–163, 170
Stewart, T. H., 125, 131, 139, 210
Stringham, Silas H., 9
Strong, James, 129
Sweet, Benjamin, 129, 160, 169, 174–175

Taylor, Thomas Jones, 81–82, 103, 113, 187
Templin, William H., 165
Terrell, "Spot," 50, 55
Terry, Henry D., 123
Thomas, D. C., 80, 214
Thomas, George H., 74, 121
Thomas, James A., 135
Thomas, Lorenzo, 38, 52, 118, 220
Thompson, Adam D., 184–185
Thompson, Jacob, 173–174
Thompson, James H., 210
Thompson, John Philip, 103, 109, 114, 115, 192–193, 208
Thompson, Merriwether Jeff, 44, 98, 109
Tilghman, Lloyd, 21, 22
Tod, David, 5, 16, 29, 30–31, 36–37, 49, 67, 68, 118, 120, 206
Townsend, Edward D., 9, 76
Tracy, Benjamin F., 78, 125, 207, 210, 216, 224–225, 228–229
Traweek, Washington Brown, 164–167
Trent, 14
Trimble, Isaac, 223
Tucker, Joseph, 25, 26, 49
Tuttle, James M., 16

Twiggs, David, 3
Tyler, Daniel, 70
Tyree, Thomas M., 234

United States Colored Troops: 108th, 130–131, 134; 122nd, 233
Universe, 54

Vallandigham, Clement, 105
Vermont Troops: 125th Infantry, 70
Veteran Reserve Corps, 129–130, 134
Vicksburg, Mississippi, 52, 56, 58–59, 81

Wade, Benjamin Franklin, 190
Walker, Benjamin, 184
Wallace, Lew, 68–69
Wallace, W. H. L., 43–44
Wallace, William, 121–122, 143, 211, 222
Washington, D.C., 91
Watson, George, 134
Watts, N. G., 52
Wescoat, Joseph Julius, 115, 231
Wessells, Henry W., 210, 220–221, 224, 232
Westbrook, Joseph W., 50
Weston, George, 204, 208, 216
Wilderness, Battle of the, 89
Wilkes, Charles, 14
Wilkeson, Frank, 190
Willcox, Orlando B., 46
Williams, A. F., 35, 51, 178
Williams, Peter, 162
Wiseman, H. H., 102, 114, 171, 215
Withen, Henry, 171
Womack, J. K., 140
Wood, Fernando, 102
Woods, William G., 98
Wool, John E., 44–45, 47
Wren, George L. P., 8, 49, 56–57, 110

Yates, Richard, 23, 25, 40
Young, William H., 82, 84